The Collected Works of John Dewey, 1882–1953

John Dewey

The Later Works, 1925–1953

Volume 1: 1925

EDITED BY JO ANN BOYDSTON

ASSOCIATE TEXTUAL EDITORS,

PATRICIA BAYSINGER AND

BARBARA LEVINE

With an Introduction by Sidney Hook

With a New Introduction by John Dewey,
   edited by Joseph Ratner

Southern Illinois University Press
Carbondale

The Collected Works of John Dewey

COMMITTEE ON
SCHOLARLY EDITIONS

AN APPROVED EDITION

MODERN LANGUAGE
ASSOCIATION OF AMERICA

Editorial expenses for this edition have been met in part by grants
from the National Endowment for the Humanities. Publication
expenses have been met in part by grants from the John Dewey
Foundation and from Mr. Corliss Lamont.

ISBN-10: 0-8093-0986-6 (cloth: alk. paper)
ISBN-13: 978-0-8093-0986-3 (cloth: alk. paper)
ISBN-10: 0-8093-2811-9 (pbk.: alk. paper)
ISBN-13: 978-0-8093-2811-6 (pbk.: alk. paper)

Contents

Introduction
By Sidney Hook

In discussing the metaphysics of John Dewey, America's noted philosopher, it is tempting to relate him and his philosophy to both his time and his country. In these days of existential analysis, the natural assumption is that his metaphysics in some way reflected or influenced American national life, if not directly then through its bearings on other aspects of his philosophy that did. From the point of view of most traditional conceptions of metaphysics which regard it as a deductive discipline that gives us knowledge of the grammar of existence or necessary truths about anything that is or may be conceived, or of Being *qua* Being, any such reflections or influence would be sufficient to condemn it. For it would seem to be evidence of some apologetic intent very much like those metaphysical systems of the past, criticized by Dewey himself, that imposed some parochial scheme of values on the cosmos in order to justify the *status quo* or facilitate a consolatory reconciliation with it.

Although many things are unclear about Dewey's philosophy, no one can reasonably dispute the assertion that he did not hold this conception of the nature of metaphysics. If anything, the view of philosophy he proposed when he abandoned Hegelian idealism for naturalism made of it "the critical method of developing methods of criticism," and, because its subject matter involved an inescapable concern with values, the unremitting critic of the social order.

Dewey's *Experience and Nature* is both the most suggestive and most difficult of his writings, the source of the most widespread objections by hostile critics, and of the most diverse interpretations by sympathetic critics. I shall try to restate what I regard as its main position and relate it in passing not too arbitrarily to the life of the American nation. There is no evidence that Dewey himself was aware of any relation between American national life and his metaphysics or that it figured in his intent in the way in which it did when he wrote books on specific social or political questions, like *Individualism, Old and New,* and *Liberalism and Social Action.* Although Dewey believed that all his central views hung together, he had no system in the traditional sense. One could reject the views expressed in *Experience and Nature* and accept those in *Democracy and Education* or *Freedom and Culture.*

Nor am I saying that whatever the relation or connection between American life and Dewey's thought it is the most important aspect of his philosophy—indeed, in my view it is quite peripheral. Dewey himself would claim that to the extent that his philosophical positions were significant and relevant, they reflected the human condition in our time rather than the specific American condition. However, it might be argued with some plausibility that modern technological and cultural developments make the American condition and experience not unrepresentative of life in other Western industrialized nations, too.

Discussion today of Dewey's metaphysics in *Experience and Nature* must take note of the well-known fact that Dewey regarded the use of the terms "metaphysics" and "experience" as unfortunate. He was prepared to jettison both terms at the end of his long philosophical career in order to avoid misunderstanding. For "experience" he would have substituted "culture" in the anthropological sense. Culture is what characterizes man wherever he is found and differentiates *human* nature from animal nature. Human nature is cultural and historical rather than merely biological. Indeed, in a synoptic account of the history of philosophy in his unfinished new introduction to *Experience and Nature,* he contended that the relation between nature and human nature "was the standing if not always the outstanding problem" with which philosophy has perennially been concerned. He vowed on the eve of his 90th year "never to use the words [metaphysics and metaphysical] again in connection with any aspect of my own position" because, he complained, his use of the terms had been assimilated to the sense they bear "in the classic tradition based on Aristotle."

Regardless of what word he used instead of "metaphysics,"

Dewey would have had to concern himself with the matters to which it referred in his previous essays, viz., "the nature of the existential world in which we live,"[1] or, in many variations of the phrase, the study or "cognizance of the generic traits of existence" (p. 50). After all, Dewey has always argued and quite properly that the conduct of life, if it is to be intelligent, requires that we rely upon the relevant knowledge of the nature of nature. Otherwise all our plans and projects would be shipwrecked. Human nature is a part of nature, too, albeit a distinctive part, and must be studied in the same spirit and the same logic of inquiry, though not with the same techniques, as we study inanimate things and other animal behavior. The traits of nature and human nature function, as Dewey puts it, as "a ground map of the province of criticism." They are always relevant to what we do, and above all in the area in which the basic philosophic choices (that define wisdom) are made. The distinctive function of philosophy for Dewey, to the extent that it can be marked off for emphasis but not separation from other disciplines, is the *normative consideration of human values*—or, most simply put, the quest for a good life in a good society.

If knowledge of the nature of the physical, biological, and social world is necessary to develop a reasonable way of life, why do we need anything more than the knowledge of the special sciences and commonsense knowledge of ordinary affairs to guide us? After all, Dewey has affirmed on many occasions that empirical or experimental science is the paradigm of reliable knowledge, and he has dismissed the view that any claim to philosophical knowledge could serve as a rival to, or surrogate of, scientific knowledge. Dewey's answer is that certain misconceptions about the nature of knowledge, the nature of man, and especially the nature of human experience have prevented the fruitful application of such knowledge to human affairs; that certain traditional assumptions, drawn from philosophies of the past, and whose categories to some extent have entered our language, have generated insoluble problems, introducing unbridgeable dualisms between subject and object, the real and the

---

1. *Experience and Nature* (LaSalle, Illinois: Open Court Publishing Co.; 2d ed., New York: W. W. Norton and Co.), p. 45. This page reference is to the present edition, as are all subsequent page references in the Introduction.

apparent, the physical and the mental, man and nature, things of experience and things in themselves, the individual and society. This has resulted in consequence in making man a stranger in the world and the operation of human intelligence a mystery.

According to Dewey there are certain fundamental traits or features of natural existence (p. 67) which are studied by no specific scientific discipline, although implicitly recognized in some form by all of them as well as by commonsense reflections, that are to be found in some "proportional union" in all situations. The "doings and undergoings that constitute experience" are marked by a union of the precarious and the assured, the perilous and the safe, the novel and the familiar, or the irregular and the uniform. Dewey rings the changes on a long list of polarities.

> Structure and process, substance and accident, matter and energy, permanence and flux, one and many, continuity and discreteness, order and progress, law and liberty, uniformity and growth, tradition and innovation, rational will and impelling desires, proof and discovery, the actual and the possible, are names given to various phases of their conjunction, and the issue of living depends upon the art with which these things are adjusted to each other. [P. 67.]

There seems little difficulty in accepting this characterization as holding for the human condition and its predicaments anywhere and everywhere. It may even strike one as a set of truisms, important truisms when counterposed to absurdities which would reduce or expand the meaning of these traits to a point where they had no intelligible opposite. Even if one contests Dewey's reading of the history of philosophy which interprets most regnant philosophies of the past as attempts to glorify the certain, the fixed, and the eternal, and to degrade the probable, the contingent, and the temporal, the reading is intelligible. Nor is there much difficulty with Dewey's contention that the human condition and its predicaments fall entirely within nature. The difficulty begins with the further assertion that these traits and qualities that mark the human condition are the mark of nature, too. "The *world* is precarious and perilous," declares Dewey (p. 44). "In nature itself qualities and relations, individualities and uniformities, finalities and efficacies, contingencies and necessities are inextricably bound together" (p. 314). These generic traits "are manifested by existences of all kinds without regard to their differentiation into physical and mental" (p. 308). They are "traits discovered in every theme of discourse, since they are ineluctable traits of natural existence" (p. 308).

These traits or qualities are not "subjective" in the sense of having a private locus that cannot be shared by others. They characterize states of affairs, are functions of an environment; their presence is ascertainable in the same way as are other facts. For example, it is sometimes the case that a person feels anxiety or fear in a situation in which there really is no danger, in which there is nothing to be fearful about. In such a case his fear is real enough, manifested by his behavior in walking gingerly, as if he were picking his way in a minefield, on a sidewalk streaming with pedestrians on all sides of him. The persistence of this fear or anxiety in the situation would be evidence that he was suffering a neurosis. On the other hand, there may be an individual who even in an actual minefield feels no fear or danger as evidenced by the fact that his behavior is no different from what it is, say, on a picnic field. Now if it is a genuine minefield in which he finds himself, we may call him fearless but to call him such presupposes that *the situation itself* is fearful or dangerous. It is in these contexts that Dewey says, "the *world* is precarious and perilous."

This view has notoriously been a stone of stumbling to many of Dewey's contemporaries, notably Bertrand Russell and Morris R. Cohen. The difficulties for them reflect their differing view of the nature of experience. Fear for them is only a state of mind without any inherent connection with what exists or does not exist in nature. It has an exclusively private locus, like all tertiary and even secondary qualities, in the mind or nervous system of a specific person. Dewey regards this bifurcation between nature and experience as inherently untenable and as leading to conclusions that make our ordinary practical judgment incoherent. It does not account for the fact that in our judgments we can and do fruitfully distinguish between the experience of the person whose fear is justified in the situation and the experience of the person whose fear is unjustified. The fear is justified by what is truly fearful or dangerous *in the environment*. The fearfulness, the danger is objectively there, and we become aware of it; and if it isn't there, we don't create it by our neurotic fears. The dangerous possibility of a nuclear war is objectively rooted in the possession and proliferation of nuclear weapons by mutually hostile powers; would that it were only in our imagination.

It was in the hope of avoiding the misunderstanding that resulted from translating his views of experience into those of his critics that Dewey proposed to substitute the term culture. For although it is still possible, instead of asking "whose experience?" when the term appears in philosophical discourse, to ask "whose culture?" when that term is substituted, the qualities of culture in the anthropological sense cannot plausibly be considered as private and exclusive. The manifold dependences of cultures, especially primitive cultures, on the environing physical world is so intimate that the precarious and hazardous character of existence, the world of empirical things, is a pervasive and omnipresent fact of life. As early as the first edition of *Experience and Nature*, Dewey makes illustrative use of the anthropological notion of culture.

It is important to realize that in *his* use of the term "experience" and in his proposed substitution of the term "culture," Dewey is not differing with his critics merely on matters of lexicographical or linguistic policy, as one of his persistent critics asserts, but about an approach to the facts of personal and social life that will illumine phenomena like the facts of reflective behavior about which there is no dispute in the ordinary affairs of men. Morris Cohen once wrote:

> . . . what on earth could Dewey have had in mind in his answer to me[?] Not only does he beg the question in assuming that the word *experience must* be used in his all inclusive instead of my restricted sense (a question of linguistic policy) but he does not seem to realize that the continuity between thought and other natural events is factual to be established by empirical evidence and not to be violently asserted or stealthily smuggled in by a definition, by using words, so that real distinctions are blurred.[2]

Dewey's standing reply, so to speak, to criticisms of this sort is that first his conception of experience does recognize the distinc-

2. Morris R. Cohen to Sidney Hook, 21 August 1931. Private collection of Sidney Hook.

tion between experienc*ing* and the experienc*ed* (that is why he calls it a double-barrelled word), that far from *assuming* the continuity between thoughts and natural events, it is a view fortified by the cumulative results of the natural, biological-medical, and cultural disciplines. From the standpoint of scientific empiricism—which his critics profess to accept—thinking is a natural event or process, a form of behavior in which some natural events are used to direct and regulate other events. This approach explains why thinking makes a difference to the world, and accounts for the fact that thought can be practical, which according to Dewey is a complete mystery on his critics' traditional dualistic view.

Before developing this point, something should be said about the possible changes that the shift from experience to culture might make to Dewey's account of metaphysics. When we speak of culture rather than experience, it is not likely that culture in all its relativities will be identified only as a mode of knowing, for it is an affair of many types of doing and enjoying made possible by the nature of things. Man never faces nature as a solitary center of experience but as an acculturated organism, as part of a group or community. It is easier to locate the objective features of social life that determine the limits of normality. It is easier to see how the threatening and supporting features of associated life depend on the traits of the natural environment.

Nonetheless, although the traits that are observable in social life cannot be understood if we draw arbitrary lines between the natural and the cultural, it will not do to suggest that the traits of culture are no more than traits of nature as they appear in a social context or that every social trait is found in nature in the same way as in society. Granted that we do not have "to deny to nature the characters that make things loveable and contemptible, beautiful, adorable and awful," so we do not have to deny to nature the characters that make social life cooperative and competitive, peaceful and warring. But just as we must avoid the implication that the characters in nature which make or contribute to making things loveable and contemptible are themselves *eo ipso* loveable and contemptible, so we must avoid the implication that the characters in nature which make societies peaceful or in conflict are themselves intelligibly at peace or in conflict with each other. Certain existential traits in culture and/or experience are evidential of other existential traits in nature but they are not necessarily the same traits.

Dewey is not a pan-psychist for whom the conditions of sentience are themselves sentient. Nor is he a dialectical idealist or a dialectical materialist for whom there is an objective dialectic in nature. He is an evolutionary naturalist for whom all the qualities that emerge in human culture or experience require as conditions for their existence objective extraorganic natural traits. These traits are not given all together nor are they reducible to each other. Unless this much is made clear, it is a positive invitation to misunderstanding. Nature must be such "as to generate ignorance and inquiry," needs and wants, hunger and thirst, but it does not itself possess these traits in the same literal sense. It is one thing to say that there is an element of randomness or contingency, order or irregularity in nature, that situations are indeterminate. But to say that a situation is *problematic* already implies that it relates proleptically to a human or social predicament or at the very least to the presence of an element of sentience. Nature has no problems although the fact that *we* have problems tells us something about nature.

In revising *Experience and Nature*, Dewey would have done well in my view to modify his conception of metaphysics and to avoid the imputation that it is an independent discipline that gives us knowledge of the world that we cannot reach by any other study, and that what it gives us knowledge about are generic traits that are discoverable in any subject matter or every universe of discourse. I do not believe that there are any natural traits—physical, biological, personal, or social—that are generic in this sense. Nor does it seem to me that Dewey's view requires that he interpret traits in this way. What he is really interested in is cataloging and analyzing those features of the world that have an important bearing on the human condition, on human hopes and possibilities, that are often taken for granted without being clearly articulated, and yet sometimes ignored or even denied in the emphasis we give to other traits or in our failing to recognize the irreducibility of some feature of subject matter—and occasionally ending up by calling into question the very existence of the subject matter from which we have taken our point of departure. It is a world in which man learns that no matter how much power he acquires he cannot live or create like a God but that he need not therefore live like an animal or an automaton, that although he may not act wisely in what he does, he cannot act unnaturally—for even the unconventional is natural. To me this is what is conveyed by Dewey's metaphorical references to nature "supporting" or "frustrating" man or "withdrawing assistance" or "flouting its own creatures."

It may be objected that there are some generic traits that do turn up in all types or universes of discourse and which characterize all subject matters—for example individuality and continuity, unity and multiplicity, the novel and the familiar, the clear and the obscure, the distant and at hand, and a host of other polarities. These traits differ from those like the perilous and the safe, the aleatory and the certain, the contingent and the necessary which obviously are not applicable to all subject matters and universes of discourse. Nonetheless I believe it is demonstrable that with the first set of allegedly generic traits we are confronted with terms that stand for different meanings in the different fields in which they are in use. We are not dealing with an invariant meaning or trait but with a cluster of different meanings and traits. The trait—say individuality—that enables me to distinguish an individual number in a series of numbers is not the same as the trait that enables me to identify an individual shade of color or an individual atom or an individual person or an individual nation. As an abstraction the term "individual" like all others of its kind is systematically ambiguous until applied in a specific context.

Dewey himself is aware that the mere enumeration of generic traits of nature is not very helpful in understanding the world and guiding us to meet its problems and challenges. For, with respect to the specific issues with which we must cope, it is "the degree and ratio they [these traits] sustain to one another" that make the difference to the outcome. "Barely to note and register that contingency is a trait of natural events," Dewey tells us, "has nothing to do with wisdom. To note, however, contingency in connection with a concrete situation of life is that fear of the Lord which is at least the beginning of wisdom" (p. 309). We carry that wisdom forward when we allow for the contingent as we plan the affairs of life. How to do that properly requires much more knowledge than the knowledge of generic traits, as in planning for contingencies in building an atomic energy plant or a new school in an earthquake prone region. If we cannot be wise, we can at least avoid being invincibly foolish. To be foolish is cocksurely to ignore or deny the element of the contingent in all the affairs of man, society and nature, and therefore to run the needless risk of being overtaken by surprise if not disaster.

As I read Dewey, or if I am charged with misreading him, as I would revise him, what he calls metaphysics or metaphysical truths constitutes a philosophical anthropology, a selection of those gross features of the world that impinge upon the theatre of human life, the background against which, and in intersection with which human beings play out their roles.[3] The script for their roles is written neither in the stars nor in the patterns of DNA. Most of it is drawn from the culture in which human beings find themselves, but the lines are never final nor complete. Both the nature of man and of his culture is such that, although at the mercy of natural forces that may overwhelm and extinguish them, they can within modest limits, by virtue of intelligent behavior and luck, *reconstruct* some parts of the natural world, some of the institutions of their culture, and sublimate human passions so that they find expression in liberal and humane forms.

It is this reconstructive and redetermining role of man in culture and nature and therefore in modifying, however slowly, the nature of human nature that Dewey stresses most in his account of the interactions and transactions between the human organism and its environment. It explains his particular usage of the term "experience," and his rejection of the views of Russell, Cohen, and the philosophical tradition that identifies experience with the private, the mentalistic and subjective.

Dewey's analysis of the Cartesian tradition from which modern epistemological and psychophysical dualism stems is well known and need not be repeated here. His approach to the

3. Writing in the *Journal of Philosophy* 24 (1927): 59, after the publication of *Experience and Nature*, Dewey says:

This is the extent and method of my metaphysics: the large and constant features of human sufferings, enjoyments, trials, failures and successes together with the institutions of art, science, technology, politics and religion which mark them, communicate genuine features of the world within which man lives.

This does not mean that the features communicated are *identical* with the features of human suffering and enjoyment.

mind-body problem is biological—the material and the mental, the bodily and psychic, are not independent substances but "properties of particular fields of interacting events." The qualities of experience which on the traditional view are denied any existence outside mind, with the familiar incredible consequences of this root bifurcation—incredible because no one really acts on them—on Dewey's views are qualities of inclusive situations. The problems arising from dualism have led to blind alleys in whose mazes philosophers are still wandering.

We may briefly mention Dewey's treatment of the most celebrated of the epistemological problems that flow from the view that experience is narrowly restricted to what is given in sensation or perception. This generates the so-called problem of the existence of the external world: how can we infer from the immediately experienced objects of sense or sense data to the existence of anything outside or beyond that experience? How do we get from our visual, auditory, tactile, and kinaesthetic data to an external and public world? Dewey offers a cogent analysis to prove that the question is self-defeating, that it cannot be intelligibly put without already presupposing that something, outside of that allegedly immediate experience, already exists. The nub of his argument is that the very identification of data as visual or auditory implies reference to organs of the body whose function requires still further references to other bodies in space and time. That "color is visible or visual is a synthetic proposition." That I see with my eyes is just as much an empirical proposition as that I think with my brain, not with my heart. Further, the assignment of temporal quality to sense data at *this* given moment of time—when they are characterized as immediate or momentary, here rather than there—involves postulation of a series of things or events beyond the immediate experience in order to make reference to *other* times intelligible. Similarly, when we speak of "my or our own data" to identify the "I" or "our," it necessarily involves reference to a community and a system of language. Dewey concludes that we cannot significantly doubt the existence of the world but only the validity of some beliefs or assumptions about some things *within* it. There are echoes of Hegel and Peirce, to be sure, in this analysis but in no way does it entail their objective idealism.

More positive and less dialectical is Dewey's attempt to explain how thinking makes a difference to the world, something which is a mystery to all conceptions of experience that center it in consciousness as a substance or function isolated from the system of energies that constitute nature. If thinking merely mirrors or reflects the world as all traditional forms of the correspondence theory assume, how could we ever change the world by taking thought about it and its problems? Whatever one's philosophy, as human beings we are always urging the necessity of *reflective conduct* on our children, our students, our colleagues, and public officials. No one really questions the possibility of thoughtful behavior, even when doubtful in any specific situation of its presence. Yet it could be claimed for Dewey that no one before him came near to accounting for it without dissolving the whole world into a system of logical thought, and even then not being able to explain the specific failures and successes of thought. Here if anywhere it is plausible to believe that the transformation of the American wilderness into an industrial civilization in consequence of the applications of science and technology had some influence on Dewey's thinking about thinking. It is reflected in Dewey's conception of science and most suggestively expressed in his view, which has been scandalously caricatured, that from a liberal and humane point of view, science *in* application gives us knowledge in a preeminent degree. In a memorable passage he writes:

> Etymologically, "science" may signify tested and authentic instance of knowledge. But knowledge has also a meaning more liberal and more humane. It signifies events understood, events so discriminately penetrated by thought that mind is literally at home in them. . . . What is sometimes termed "applied" science, may then be more truly science than is what is conventionally called pure science. For it is directly concerned with not just instrumentalities, but instrumentalities at work in effecting modifications of existence in behalf of conclusions that are reflectively preferred. . . . Thus conceived, knowledge exists in engineering, medicine and the social arts more adequately than it does in mathematics, and physics. [P. 128.]

Application here means operational or practical embodiment, not for personal satisfaction or commercial gain. It means that in applied science we are making the world more rational and life more reasonable, if the purposes for which scientific knowledge is applied are worthy of moral approval. Regardless of whether one shares this assessment of the character of applied knowledge, its existence must be accounted for. It cannot be done by dualistic views which put the natural world and human thought in separate domains. For the mind on such an approach can only be an idle spectator. Indeed, what else can the mind not rooted in nature do but stare impotently at the world or dream about it. And even the substance of its dreams indicates that it is not unrelated to natural events.

On Dewey's view human beings make inferences as naturally as they do other things. In the course of interaction a mutual modification takes place, reflected in the product or outcome of the activity whether it is breathing or walking or getting to know. Different modes or manners of experiencing, considered as a series of activities, affect the status of the subject matter experienced. Knowing, then, like any other natural process is a form of behavior; but unlike other modes of experience, it operates through signs, symbols, and meanings to reconstruct problematic, indeterminate situations into determinate ones. But the meanings used in knowing or inquiry must at some point lead to overt acts, a laying on of hands, so to speak, on things, to reorder or reconstruct the material or subject matter of the situation being inquired into.

This view has given rise to some hilarity among Dewey's critics. If the object of knowledge is modified in the course of our knowing it, how can we ever know it? When we seek knowledge about the moon, surely the moon remains unchanged in the course of our inquiry. Of course it does, but to achieve confirmed knowledge about the moon something else is changed in the context and situation of inquiry—whether it be the position of an instrument or of the human body itself in the observations we make. The object of knowledge, the solution to the problem of inquiry, the objective, if one calls it that, cannot be changed in the course of inquiry without stultification, but when we are trying to find out or test a hypothesis about something doubtful, the situation at some point must be reconstructed to give us a warranted conclusion. Reflection on the role of experiment in inquiry should make this clear. All existential knowledge for

Dewey is experimental, which always involves an ordered change guided by some hypothesis. In passing we should note that what was once considered a *reductio ad absurdum* implication of Dewey's theory has recently lost its sting, since as a result of some experiments on the surface of the moon something about it, too, as well as the positions of the observers and the experimental apparatus, was changed.

If thought is practical, which means for Dewey not that it is personally useful or a crutch to the will to believe but that it involves practice or experiment, then as determined as nature may be, it is not a closed or finished system, not a block universe but an open one. If, as Justice Holmes graphically puts it, "The mode in which the inevitable comes to pass is through effort," then, at least to the extent that our effort has been spent, there is nothing altogether inevitable about the future or inevitable in all its respects and aspects. The world is open in the sense that there are some objective alternatives of development; that even when trends in nature or society are so overwhelmingly powerful that man cannot resist their cyclonic fury, the way one meets them or stands up to them is not foreclosed. We cannot as yet escape death, we can only postpone it. But the way we die may be more significant, if controllable, than the fact of death itself, not only in our own life but in the lives of others.

Whether the environing American society with its open frontier had a subconscious influence on Dewey's view of the open universe is hard to say. He himself recalls that during his early years "in imagination at least the country was still having an open frontier," that it was building a new society. Before he died he expressed the belief that the only open frontier left in America was the moral frontier—one in which all social problems must be considered moral problems too. Even more speculative is the presumption that Dewey's objective relativism expresses if not the actualities, then at least the promise of American democracy. For his objective relativism recognizes no superior realms of being, no hierarchy of realities, but acknowledges the equal existential status of all sorts of experience. "Illusions are illusions," he writes, "but the occurrence of illusions is not an illusion" (p. 27). Errors abound in the world but they consist not in unreal or inferior existence or appearances—things are as they are experienced *as*—but in mistaken *inferences* from what is truly there, to an assertion about its continued existence and behavior in a different spatial or temporal context. To be *truly* real, so to speak, is to be reliable in a specific context. And perhaps it is not altogether fanciful to see in Dewey's refusal to assign a superior reality to causes—despite the role causes play in control—the American tendency to give as much, perhaps more, weight to what a person becomes as to what and where he comes from.

It seems almost obvious that Dewey's social and political philosophy and his "faith in the possibilities of intelligence and education as a correlate of intelligence" reflect the culture of his time. He modestly says: "I did not invent this faith. I acquired it from my surroundings as far as these surroundings were animated by the democratic spirit." Since these surroundings contained much more than the democratic spirit, including ideas, attitudes, and institutional practices at variance with that spirit, it would be more accurate to say that the life of the nation was more truly reflected in what Dewey was critical of, in what he took issue with, as he developed his thoughts, than with his own positive teachings at the time. I am thinking of the exaltation of the individual and individualism in Dewey's lifetime, the absence, or rather the insufficiency, of social planning, and the failure to bring the resources of social intelligence to bear on the problems of social life. I want to say a few words about each.

As one would expect, Dewey rejected the standard and easy counterposition of the Individual and the Social as if they were fixed concepts or entities. Individuals are made not born—they are born only as particular organisms—and are made by the multiple associations of which society consists. And as those associations develop historically, different individuals are created. Concern then must be with specific social institutions, political, economic, educational, in their effects in releasing and organizing personal capacities to their fullest desirable growth. We must always ask, and judge a society by its answer, the question: What kind of person is being created?

Just as *the* individual is an abstraction for an immense variety of responses, dispositions, and susceptibilities developed in the relationships of persons to each other, so Society is an abstraction for all sorts of associations and institutions that regulate the joint experiences of human beings. The specific forms of these associations and institutions must be modified and planned whenever their functioning generates hardships that deprive any members of the community of the possibility of enjoying equal opportunities, and of sharing the goods and services on which the realization of these equal opportunities depend, that are necessary to develop as persons.

Planning today is a word in bad odor because of the failure of some recent ill-conceived and half-hearted social programs. In a complex and dangerous world where not only what we do but also what we fail to do has consequences, planning is necessary in order to survive, particularly if there are powerful forces and nations in the grip of an ideology that encompasses the destruction of the open societies of the West. The fact that planning always has unintended and unanticipated consequences does not militate against its wisdom until we compare it with the consequences of not planning. That unintended consequences flow from our plans and actions is a ground for more careful and better planning. Modern medicine in prolonging human life has unintentionally prolonged and intensified human suffering. Who would therefore draw the moral that we should not continue to plan to eliminate disease? We need not, we cannot, plan for everything. The question is always the specific one of what to plan, where and how? Dewey's slogan during the depression of the '30s "Regiment things, not persons," may have been too simplistic. But he lived long enough to believe it was possible to plan to expand human freedom—and, with an eye on the concentration camp economies of the world, to know what to avoid.

By the failure to bring the resources of organized intelligence to bear on social problems, Dewey means the failure to use scientific and rational methods of resolving social conflicts, of discovering the institutional changes required to extend the area of shared interests among the contestants, in the absence of which society is always in a state of incipient civil war. He undoubtedly oversimplified the difficulties of solving social problems even by extending "the methods of consultation, persuasion, negotiation and communication." Conflicting interests may count more heavily than shared interests. Until we discover ways of inducing man to rely on the values, attitudes, and habits of intelligence, can faith in intelligence be an intelligent faith? Dewey's best answer is that although the use of scientific method, as he describes it, may fail, no other method so far tried has succeeded.

Dewey denied he was a Utopian, denied that he believed all problems can be solved, or that intelligence will triumph in the strife of methods in resolving disputes or that it will save us from ruin or destruction. His most modest claim is that in a world where the only open frontier left to us is the moral frontier, in which, to repeat, all social problems must be considered moral and educational problems, the method of intelligence is worth trying. Certainly, it is worth trying but will it be tried? And, if it is tried, will it succeed in resolving problems that threaten the peace, the freedom and, some believe, the very existence of the habitable world?

The objective uncertainty illustrates the contingency of the world in which, according to Dewey, man lives and will always live if he survives. Human action cannot guarantee success—at its best, that is, at its most intelligent, it can only increase the odds. But that increase, however slight, might make all the difference in the world.

Experience and Nature

Preface

The publication of this new edition has made it possible to rewrite completely the first chapter as well as to make a few minor corrections throughout the volume. The first chapter was intended as an introduction. It failed of its purpose; it was upon the whole more technical and harder reading than the chapters which it was supposed to introduce. It was also rather confused in mode of presentation, and at one important point in thought as well. It is hoped that its new form is both simpler and possessed of greater continuity. If the original intent is now better fulfilled, it is largely due to the help of kindly critics. I wish to record my especial indebtedness to Professor M. C. Otto of the University of Wisconsin and Mr. Joseph Ratner of Columbia University.

In addition to the complete revision of the first chapter, the new edition affords an occasion for inserting in these prefatory remarks what is not to be found in the earlier text; namely, a summary of the thought of the book in the order of its development. The course of the ideas is determined by a desire to apply in the more general realm of philosophy the thought which is effective in dealing with any and every genuine question, from the elaborate problems of science to the practical deliberations of daily life, trivial or momentous. The constant task of such thought is to establish working connections between old and new subject-matters. We cannot lay hold of the new, we cannot even keep it before our minds, much less understand it, save by the use of ideas and knowledge we already possess. But just because the new *is* new it is not a mere repetition of something already had and mastered. The old takes on new color and meaning in being employed to grasp and interpret the new. The greater the gap, the disparity, between what has become a familiar possession and the traits presented in new subject-matter, the

greater is the burden imposed upon reflection; the distance between old and new is the measure of the range and depth of the
thought required.

Breaks and incompatibilities occur in collective culture as well
as in individual life. Modern science, modern industry and politics, have presented us with an immense amount of material
foreign to, often inconsistent with, the most prized intellectual
and moral heritage of the western world. This is the cause of our
modern intellectual perplexities and confusions. It sets the especial problem for philosophy to-day and for many days to come.
Every significant philosophy is an attempt to deal with it; those
theories to which this statement seems to apply least are attempts
to bridge the gulf by seeking an escape or refuge. I have not
striven in this volume for a reconciliation between the new and
the old. I think such endeavors are likely to give rise to casualties
to good faith and candor. But in employing, as one must do, a
body of old beliefs and ideas to apprehend and understand the
new, I have also kept in mind the modifications and transformations that are exacted of those old beliefs.

I believe that the method of empirical naturalism presented in
this volume provides the way, and the only way—although of
course no two thinkers will travel it in just the same fashion—by
which one can freely accept the standpoint and conclusions of
modern science: the way by which we can be genuinely naturalistic and yet maintain cherished values, provided they are critically
clarified and reinforced. The naturalistic method, when it is consistently followed, destroys many things once cherished; but it
destroys them by revealing their inconsistency with the nature of
things—a flaw that always attended them and deprived them of
efficacy for aught save emotional consolation. But its main purport is not destructive; empirical naturalism is rather a winnow-
ing fan. Only chaff goes, though perhaps the chaff had once been
treasured. An empirical method which remains true to nature
does not "save"; it is not an insurance device nor a mechanical
antiseptic. But it inspires the mind with courage and vitality to
create new ideals and values in the face of the perplexities of a
new world.

The new introductory chapter (Chapter 1) accordingly takes
up the question of method, especially with respect to the relation
that exists between experience and nature. It points to faith in

experience when intelligently used as a means of disclosing the realities of nature. It finds that nature and experience are not enemies or alien. Experience is not a veil that shuts man off from nature; it is a means of penetrating continually further into the heart of nature. There is in the character of human experience no index-hand pointing to agnostic conclusions, but rather a growing progressive self-disclosure of nature itself. The failures of philosophy have come from lack of confidence in the directive powers that inhere in experience, if men have but the wit and courage to follow them.

Chapter 2 explains our starting point: namely, that the things of ordinary experience contain within themselves a mixture of the perilous and uncertain with the settled and uniform. The need for security compels men to fasten upon the regular in order to minimize and to control the precarious and fluctuating. In actual experience this is a *practical* enterprise, made possible by knowledge of the recurrent and stable, of facts and laws. Philosophies have too often tried to forgo the actual work that is involved in penetrating the true nature of experience, by setting up a purely *theoretical* security and certainty. The influence of this attempt upon the traditional philosophic preference for unity, permanence, universals, over plurality, change and particulars is pointed out, as well as its effect in creating the traditional notion of substance, now undermined by physical science. The tendency of modern science to substitute qualitative events, marked by certain similar properties and by recurrences, for the older notion of fixed substances is shown to agree with the attitude of naïve experience, while both point to the idea of matter and mind as significant characters of events, presented in different contexts, rather than underlying and ultimate substances.

Chapters 3 and 4 discuss one of the outstanding problems in philosophy—namely, the question of laws, mechanical uniformities, on one hand and, on the other, ends, purposes, uses and enjoyments. It is pointed out that in actual experience the latter represent the consequences of series of changes in which the outcomes or ends have the value of consummation and fulfillment; and that because of this value there is a tendency to perpetuate them, render them stable, and repeat them. It is then shown that the foundation for value and the striving to realize it is found in nature, because when nature is viewed as consisting of events rather than substances, it is characterized by *histories*, that is, by continuity of change proceeding from beginnings to endings. Consequently, it is natural for genuine initiations and consummations to occur in experience. Owing to the presence of uncertain and precarious factors in these histories, attainment of ends, of goods, is unstable and evanescent. The only way to render them more secure is by ability to control the changes that intervene between the beginning and the end of a process. These intervening terms when brought under control are *means* in the literal and in the practical sense of the word. When mastered in actual experience they constitute tools, techniques, mechanisms, etc. Instead of being foes of purposes, they are means of execution; they are also tests for differentiating genuine aims from merely emotional and fantastic ideals.

The office of physical science is to discover those properties and relations of things in virtue of which they are capable of being used as instrumentalities; physical science makes claim to disclose not the inner nature of things but only those connections of things with one another that determine outcomes and hence can be used as means. The *intrinsic* nature of events is revealed in experience as the immediately felt qualities of things. The intimate coordination and even fusion of these qualities with the regularities that form the objects of knowledge, in the proper sense of the word "knowledge," characterizes intelligently directed experience, as distinct from mere casual and uncritical experience.

This conception of the instrumental nature of the objects of scientific knowing forms the pivot upon which further discussion turns (Chapter 5). That character of everyday experience which has been most systematically ignored by philosophy is the extent to which it is saturated with the results of social intercourse and communication. Because this factor has been denied, meanings have either been denied all objective validity, or have been treated as miraculous extra-natural intrusions. If, however, language, for example, is recognized as the instrument of social cooperation and mutual participation, continuity is established between natural events (animal sound, cries, etc.) and the origin and development of meanings. Mind is seen to be a function of social interactions, and to be a genuine character of natural events when these attain the stage of widest and most complex interaction with one another. Ability to respond to meanings and to employ them, instead of reacting merely to physical contacts, makes the difference between man and other animals; it is the agency for elevating man into the realm of what is usually called the ideal and spiritual. In other words, the social participation affected by communication, through language and other tools, is the naturalistic link which does away with the often alleged necessity of dividing the objects of experience into two worlds, one physical and one ideal.

Chapter 6 makes the transition from this realization that the social character of meanings forms the solid content of mind to considering mind as individual or "subjective." One of the most marked features of modern thought as distinct from ancient and medieval thought is its emphasis upon mind as personal or even private, its identification with selfhood. The connection of this underlying but misinterpreted fact with experience is made by showing that modern as distinct from ancient culture is characterized by the importance attached to initiation, invention and variation. Thus mind in its individual aspect is shown to be the method of change and progress in the significances and values attached to things. This trait is linked up to natural events by recurring to their particular and variable, their contingent, quality. In and of itself this factor is puzzling; it accounts for accidents and irrationalities. It was long treated as such in the history of mankind; the individual characteristics of mind were regarded as deviations from the normal, and as dangers against which society had to protect itself. Hence the long rule of custom, the rigid conservatism, and the still existing régime of conformity and intellectual standardization. The development of modern science began when there was recognized in certain technical fields a power to utilize variations as the starting points of new observations, hypotheses and experiments. The growth of the experimental as distinct from the dogmatic habit of mind is due to increased ability to utilize variations for constructive ends instead of suppressing them.

Life, as a trait of natural organisms, was incidentally treated in connection with the development of tools, of language and of individual variations. Its consideration as the link between physical nature and experience forms the topic of the mind-body problem (Chapter 7). The isolation of nature and experience from each other has rendered the undeniable connection of thought and effectiveness of knowledge and purposive action, with the body, an insoluble mystery. Restoration of continuity is shown to do away with the mind-body problem. It leaves us with an organism in which events have those qualities, usually called feelings, not realized in events that form inanimate things, and which, when living creatures communicate with one another so as to share in common, and hence universalized, objects, take on distinctively mental properties. The continuity of nature and experience is shown to resolve many problems that become only the more taxing when continuity is ignored.

The traits of living creatures are then considered (Chapter 8) in connection with the conscious aspect of behavior and experience, the quality of immediacy attaching to events when they are actualized in experience by means of organic and social interactions. The difference and the connection of mind and consciousness is set forth. The meanings that form mind become consciousness, or ideas, impressions, etc., when something within the meanings or in their application becomes dubious, and the meaning in question needs reconstruction. This principle explains the focal and rapidly shifting traits of the objects of consciousness as such. A sensitive and vital mental career thus depends upon being awake to questions and problems; consciousness stagnates and becomes restricted and dull when this interest wanes.

The highest because most complete incorporation of natural forces and operations in experience is found in art (Chapter 9). Art is a process of production in which natural materials are re-shaped in a projection toward consummatory fulfillment through regulation of trains of events that occur in a less regulated way on lower levels of nature. Art is "fine" in the degree in which ends, the final termini, of natural processes are dominant and conspicuously enjoyed. All art is instrumental in its use of techniques and tools. It is shown that normal artistic experience involves bringing to a better balance than is found elsewhere in either nature or experience the consummatory and instrumental phases of events. Art thus represents the culminating event of nature as well as the climax of experience. In this connection the usual sharp separation made between art and science is criticized; it is argued that science as method is more basic than science as subject-matter, and that scientific inquiry is an art, at once instrumental in control and final as a pure enjoyment of mind.

This recurrence to the topic of ends, or consummatory consequences, and of desire and striving for them, raises the question of the nature of values (Chapter 10). Values are naturalistically interpreted as intrinsic qualities of events in their consummatory reference. The question of the control of the course of events so that it may yield, as ends or termini, objects that are stable and that tend toward creation of other values, introduces the topic of value-judgments or valuations. These constitute what is generically termed *criticism*. A return is made to the theme of the first chapter by emphasizing the crucial significance of criticism in all phases of experience for its intelligent control. Philosophy, then, is a generalized theory of criticism. Its ultimate value for life-experience is that it continuously provides instruments for the criticism of those values—whether of beliefs, institutions, actions or products—that are found in all aspects of experience. The chief obstacle to a more effective criticism of current values lies in the traditional separation of nature and experience, which it is the purpose of this volume to replace by the idea of continuity.

January, 1929, New York City.

JOHN DEWEY.

1. Experience and Philosophic Method

The title of this volume, Experience and Nature, is intended to signify that the philosophy here presented may be termed either empirical naturalism or naturalistic empiricism, or, taking "experience" in its usual signification, naturalistic humanism.

To many the associating of the two words will seem like talking of a round square, so engrained is the notion of the separation of man and experience from nature. Experience, they say, is important for those beings who have it, but is too casual and sporadic in its occurrence to carry with it any important implications regarding the nature of Nature. Nature, on the other hand, is said to be complete apart from experience. Indeed, according to some thinkers the case is even in worse plight: Experience to them is not only something extraneous which is occasionally superimposed upon nature, but it forms a veil or screen which shuts us off from nature, unless in some way it can be "transcended." So something non-natural by way of reason or intuition is introduced, something supra-empirical. According to an opposite school experience fares as badly, nature being thought to signify something wholly material and mechanistic; to frame a theory of experience in naturalistic terms is, accordingly, to degrade and deny the noble and ideal values that characterize experience.

I know of no route by which dialectical argument can answer such objections. They arise from associations with words and cannot be dealt with argumentatively. One can only hope in the course of the whole discussion to disclose the meanings which are attached to "experience" and "nature," and thus insensibly produce, if one is fortunate, a change in the significations previously attached to them. This process of change may be hastened by calling attention to another context in which nature and experience get on harmoniously together—wherein experience presents itself as the method, and the only method, for getting at nature, penetrating its secrets, and wherein nature empirically disclosed (by the use of empirical method in natural science) deepens, enriches and directs the further development of experience.

In the natural sciences there is a union of experience and nature which is not greeted as a monstrosity; on the contrary, the inquirer must use empirical method if his findings are to be treated as genuinely scientific. The investigator assumes as a matter of course that experience, controlled in specifiable ways, is the avenue that leads to the facts and laws of nature. He uses reason and calculation freely; he could not get along without them. But he sees to it that ventures of this theoretical sort start from and terminate in directly experienced subject-matter. Theory may intervene in a long course of reasoning, many portions of which are remote from what is directly experienced. But the vine of pendant theory is attached at both ends to the pillars of observed subject-matter. And this experienced material is the same for the scientific man and the man in the street. The latter cannot follow the intervening reasoning without special preparation. But stars, rocks, trees, and creeping things are the same material of experience for both.

These commonplaces take on significance when the relation of experience to the formation of a philosophic theory of nature is in question. They indicate that experience, if scientific inquiry is justified, is no infinitesimally thin layer or foreground of nature, but that it penetrates into it, reaching down into its depths, and in such a way that its grasp is capable of expansion; it tunnels in all directions and in so doing brings to the surface things at first hidden—as miners pile high on the surface of the earth treasures brought from below. Unless we are prepared to deny all validity to scientific inquiry, these facts have a value that cannot be ignored for the general theory of the relation of nature and experience.

It is sometimes contended, for example, that since experience is a late comer in the history of our solar system and planet, and since these occupy a trivial place in the wide areas of celestial space, experience is at most a slight and insignificant incident in nature. No one with an honest respect for scientific conclusions can deny that experience as an existence is something that occurs only under highly specialized conditions, such as are found in a highly organized creature which in turn requires a specialized environment. There is no evidence that experience occurs everywhere and everywhen. But candid regard for scientific inquiry also compels the recognition that when experience does occur, no matter at what limited portion of time and space, it enters into possession of some portion of nature and in such a manner as to render other of its precincts accessible.

A geologist living in 1928 tells us about events that happened not only before he was born but millions of years before any human being came into existence on this earth. He does so by starting from things that are now the material of experience. Lyell revolutionized geology by perceiving that the sort of thing that can be experienced now in the operations of fire, water, pressure, is the sort of thing by which the earth took on its present structural forms. Visiting a natural history museum, one beholds a mass of rock and, reading a label, finds that it comes from a tree that grew, so it is affirmed, five million years ago. The geologist did not leap from the thing he can see and touch to some event in by-gone ages; he collated this observed thing with many others, of different kinds, found all over the globe; the results of his comparisons he then compared with data of other experiences, say, the astronomer's. He translates, that is, observed coexistences into non-observed, inferred sequences. Finally he dates his object, placing it in an order of events. By the same sort of method he predicts that at certain places some things not yet experienced will be observed, and then he takes pains to bring them within the scope of experience. The scientific conscience is, moreover, so sensitive with respect to the necessity of experience that when it reconstructs the past it is not fully satisfied with inferences drawn from even a large and cumulative mass of uncontradicted evidence; it sets to work to institute conditions of heat and pressure and moisture, etc., so as actually to reproduce in experiment that which he has inferred.

These commonplaces prove that experience is *of* as well as *in* nature. It is not experience which is experienced, but nature—stones, plants, animals, diseases, health, temperature, electricity, and so on. Things interacting in certain ways *are* experience; they are what is experienced. Linked in certain other ways with another natural object—the human organism—they are *how* things are experienced as well. Experience thus reaches down into nature; it has depth. It also has breadth and to an indefinitely elastic extent. It stretches. That stretch constitutes inference.

Dialectical difficulties, perplexities due to definitions given to the concepts that enter into the discussion, may be raised. It is said to be absurd that what is only a tiny part of nature should be competent to incorporate vast reaches of nature within itself. But even were it logically absurd one would be bound to cleave to it as a fact. Logic, however, is not put under a strain. The fact that something is an occurrence does not decide what kind of an occurrence it is; that can be found out only by examination. To argue from an experience "being an experience" to what it is of and about is warranted by no logic, even though modern thought has attempted it a thousand times. A bare event is no event at all; *something* happens. What that something is, is found out by actual study. This applies to seeing a flash of lightning and holds of the longer event called experience. The very existence of science is evidence that experience is such an occurrence that it penetrates into nature and expands without limit through it.

These remarks are not supposed to prove anything about experience and nature for philosophical doctrine; they are not supposed to settle anything about the worth of empirical naturalism. But they do show that in the case of natural science we habitually treat experience as starting point, and as method for dealing with nature, and as the goal in which nature is disclosed for what it is. To realize this fact is at least to weaken those verbal associations which stand in the way of apprehending the force of empirical method in philosophy.

The same considerations apply to the other objection that was suggested: namely, that to view experience naturalistically is to reduce it to something materialistic, depriving it of all ideal significance. If experience actually presents esthetic and moral traits, then these traits may also be supposed to reach down into nature, and to testify to something that belongs to nature as truly as does the mechanical structure attributed to it in physical science. To rule out that possibility by some general reasoning is to forget that the very meaning and purport of empirical method is that things are to be studied on their own account, so as to find out what is revealed when they are experienced. The traits possessed by the subject-matters of experience are as genuine as the characteristics of sun and electron. They are *found*, experienced, and are not to be shoved out of being by some trick of logic. When found, their ideal qualities are as relevant to the philosophic theory of nature as are the traits found by physical inquiry.

To discover some of these general features of experienced things and to interpret their significance for a philosophic theory of the universe in which we live is the aim of this volume. From the point of view adopted, the theory of empirical method in philosophy does for experienced subject-matter on a liberal scale what it does for special sciences on a technical scale. It is this aspect of method with which we are especially concerned in the present chapter.

If the empirical method were universally or even generally adopted in philosophizing, there would be no need of referring to experience. The scientific inquirer talks and writes about particular observed events and qualities, about specific calculations and reasonings. He makes no allusion to experience; one would probably have to search a long time through reports of special researches in order to find the word. The reason is that everything designated by the word "experience" is so adequately incorporated into scientific procedures and subject-matter that to mention experience would be only to duplicate in a general term what is already covered in definite terms.

Yet this was not always so. Before the technique of empirical method was developed and generally adopted, it was necessary to dwell explicitly upon the importance of "experience" as a starting point and terminal point, as setting problems and as testing proposed solutions. We need not be content with the conventional allusion to Roger Bacon and Francis Bacon. The followers of Newton and the followers of the Cartesian school carried on a definite controversy as to the place occupied by experience and experiment in science as compared with intuitive concepts and with reasoning from them. The Cartesian school relegated experience to a secondary and almost accidental place, and only when the Galilean-Newtonian method had wholly triumphed did it cease to be necessary to mention the importance of experience. We may, if sufficiently hopeful, anticipate a similar outcome in philosophy. But the date does not appear to be close at hand; we are nearer in philosophic theory to the time of Roger Bacon than to that of Newton.

In short, it is the contrast of empirical method with other methods employed in philosophizing, together with the striking dissimilarity of results yielded by an empirical method and professed non-empirical methods that make the discussion of the methodological import of "experience" for philosophy pertinent and indeed indispensable.

This consideration of method may suitably begin with the contrast between gross, macroscopic, crude subject-matters in primary experience and the refined, derived objects of reflection. The distinction is one between what is experienced as the result of a minimum of incidental reflection and what is experienced in consequence of continued and regulated reflective inquiry. For derived and refined products are experienced only because of the intervention of systematic thinking. The objects of both science and philosophy obviously belong chiefly to the secondary and refined system. But at this point we come to a marked divergence between science and philosophy. For the natural sciences not only draw their material from primary experience, but they refer it back again for test. Darwin began with the pigeons, cattle and plants of breeders and gardeners. Some of the conclusions he reached were so contrary to accepted beliefs that they were condemned as absurd, contrary to common sense, etc. But scientific men, whether they accepted his theories or not, employed his hypotheses as directive ideas for making new observations and experiments among the things of raw experience—just as the metallurgist who extracts refined metal from crude ore makes tools that are then set to work to control and use other crude materials. An Einstein working by highly elaborate methods of reflection, calculates theoretically certain results in the deflection of light by the presence of the sun. A technically equipped expedition is sent to South Africa so that by means of experiencing a thing—an eclipse—in crude, primary, experience, observations can be secured to compare with, and test the theory implied in, the calculated result.

The facts are familiar enough. They are cited in order to invite attention to the relationship between the objects of primary and of secondary or reflective experience. That the subject-matter of primary experience sets the problems and furnishes the first data of the reflection which constructs the secondary objects is evident; it is also obvious that test and verification of the latter is secured only by return to things of crude or macroscopic experience—the sun, earth, plants and animals of common, every-day life. But just what role do the objects attained in reflection play? Where do they come in? They *explain* the primary objects, they enable us to grasp them with *understanding*, instead of just having sense-contact with them. But how?

Well, they define or lay out a path by which return to experienced things is of such a sort that the meaning, the significant content, of what is experienced gains an enriched and expanded force because of the path or method by which it was reached. Directly, in immediate contact it may be just what it was before—hard, colored, odorous, etc. But when the secondary objects, the refined objects, are employed as a method or road for coming at them, these qualities cease to be isolated details; they get the meaning contained in a whole system of related objects; they are rendered continuous with the rest of nature and take on the import of the things they are now seen to be continuous with. The phenomena observed in the eclipse tested and, as far as they went, confirmed Einstein's theory of deflection of light by mass. But that is far from being the whole story. The phenomena themselves got a far-reaching significance they did not previously have. Perhaps they would not even have been noticed if the theory had not been employed as a guide or road to observation of them. But even if they had been noticed, they would have been dismissed as of no importance, just as we daily drop from attention hundreds of perceived details for which we have no intellectual use. But approached by means of theory these lines of slight deflection take on a significance as large as that of the revolutionary theory that led to their being experienced.

This empirical method I shall call the *denotative* method. That philosophy is a mode of reflection, often of a subtle and penetrating sort, goes without saying. The charge that is brought against the non-empirical method of philosophizing is not that it depends upon theorizing, but that it fails to use refined, secondary products as a path pointing and leading back to something in primary experience. The resulting failure is three-fold.

First, there is no verification, no effort even to test and check. What is even worse, secondly, is that the things of ordinary experience do not get enlargement and enrichment of meaning as they do when approached through the medium of scientific principles and reasonings. This lack of function reacts, in the third place, back upon the philosophic subject-matter in itself. Not tested by being employed to see what it leads to in ordinary experience and what new meanings it contributes, this subject-matter becomes arbitrary, aloof—what is called "abstract" when that word is used in a bad sense to designate something which exclusively occupies a realm of its own without contact with the things of ordinary experience.

As the net outcome of these three evils, we find that extraordinary phenomenon which accounts for the revulsion of many cultivated persons from any form of philosophy. The objects of reflection in philosophy, being reached by methods that seem to those who employ them rationally mandatory, are taken to be "real" in and of themselves—and supremely real. Then it becomes an insoluble problem why the things of gross, primary experience, should be what they are, or indeed why they should be at all. The refined objects of reflection in the natural sciences, however, never end by rendering the subject-matter from which they are derived a problem; rather, when used to describe a path by which some goal in primary experience is designated or denoted, they solve perplexities to which that crude material gives rise but which it cannot resolve of itself. They become means of control, of enlarged use and enjoyment of ordinary things. They may generate new problems, but these are problems of the same sort, to be dealt with by further use of the same methods of inquiry and experimentation. The problems to which empirical method gives rise afford, in a word, opportunities for more investigations yielding fruit in new and enriched experiences. But the problems to which non-empirical method gives rise in philosophy are blocks to inquiry, blind alleys; they are puzzles rather than problems, solved only by calling the original material of primary experience, "phenomenal," mere appearance, mere impressions, or by some other disparaging name.

Thus there is here supplied, I think, a first-rate test of the value of any philosophy which is offered us: Does it end in conclusions which, when they are referred back to ordinary life-experiences and their predicaments, render them more significant, more luminous to us, and make our dealings with them more fruitful? Or does it terminate in rendering the things of ordinary experience more opaque than they were before, and in depriving them of having in "reality" even the significance they had previously seemed to have? Does it yield the enrichment and increase of power of ordinary things which the results of physical science afford when applied in every-day affairs? Or does it become a mystery that these ordinary things should be what they are; and are philosophic concepts left to dwell in separation in some technical realm of their own? It is the fact, I repeat, that so many philosophies terminate in conclusions that make it necessary to disparage and condemn primary experience, leading those who hold them to measure the sublimity of their "realities" as philosophically defined by remoteness from the concerns of daily life, which leads cultivated common sense to look askance at philosophy.

These general statements must be made more definite. We must illustrate the meaning of empirical method by seeing some of its results in contrast with those to which non-empirical philosophies conduct us. We begin by noting that "experience" is what James called a double-barrelled word.[1] Like its congeners, life and history, it includes *what* men do and suffer, *what* they strive for, love, believe and endure, and also *how* men act and are acted upon, the ways in which they do and suffer, desire and enjoy, see, believe, imagine—in short, processes of *experiencing*. "Experience" denotes the planted field, the sowed seeds, the reaped harvests, the changes of night and day, spring and autumn, wet and dry, heat and cold, that are observed, feared, longed for; it also denotes the one who plants and reaps, who works and rejoices, hopes, fears, plans, invokes magic or chemistry to aid him, who is downcast or triumphant. It is "double-barrelled" in that it recognizes in its primary integrity no division between act and material, subject and object, but contains them both in an unanalyzed totality. "Thing" and "thought," as

1. *Essays in Radical Empiricism*, p. 10.

James says in the same connection, are single-barrelled; they refer to products discriminated by reflection out of primary experience.[2]

It is significant that "life" and "history" have the same fullness of undivided meaning. Life denotes a function, a comprehensive activity, in which organism and environment are included. Only upon reflective analysis does it break up into external conditions—air breathed, food taken, ground walked upon—and internal structures—lungs respiring, stomach digesting, legs walking. The scope of "history" is notorious: it is the deeds enacted, the tragedies undergone; and it is the human comment, record, and interpretation that inevitably follow. Objectively, history takes in rivers, mountains, fields and forests, laws and institutions; subjectively it includes the purposes and plans, the desires and emotions, through which these things are administered and transformed.

Now empirical method is the only method which can do justice to this inclusive integrity of "experience." It alone takes this integrated unity as the starting point for philosophic thought. Other methods begin with results of a reflection that has already torn in two the subject-matter experienced and the operations and states of experiencing. The problem is then to get together again what has been sundered—which is as if the king's men started with the fragments of the egg and tried to construct the whole egg out of them. For empirical method the problem is nothing so impossible of solution. Its problem is to note how and why the whole is distinguished into subject and object, nature and mental operations. Having done this, it is in a position to see *to what effect* the distinction is made: how the distinguished factors function in the further control and enrichment of the subject-matters of crude but total experience. Non-empirical method starts with a reflective product as if it were primary, as if it were the originally "given." To non-empirical method, therefore, object and subject, mind and matter (or whatever words and ideas are used) are separate and independent. Therefore it has upon its hands the problem of how it is possible to know at all; how an outer world can affect an inner mind; how the acts of

---

2. It is not intended, however, to attribute to James precisely the interpretation given in the text.

mind can reach out and lay hold of objects defined in antithesis to them. Naturally it is at a loss for an answer, since its premises make the fact of knowledge both unnatural and unempirical. One thinker turns metaphysical materialist and denies reality to the mental; another turns psychological idealist, and holds that matter and force are merely disguised psychical events. Solutions are given up as a hopeless task, or else different schools pile one intellectual complication on another only to arrive by a long and tortuous course at that which naïve experience already has in its own possession.

The first and perhaps the greatest difference made in philosophy by adoption respectively of empirical or non-empirical method is, thus, the difference made in what is selected as original material. To a truly naturalistic empiricism, the moot problem of the relation of subject and object is the problem of what consequences follow in and for primary experience from the distinction of the physical and the psychological or mental from each other. The answer is not far to seek. To distinguish in reflection the physical and to hold it in temporary detachment is to be set upon the road that conducts to tools and technologies, to construction of mechanisms, to the arts that ensue in the wake of the sciences. That these constructions make possible a better regulation of the affairs of primary experience is evident. Engineering and medicine, all the utilities that make for expansion of life, are the answer. There is better administration of old familiar things, and there is invention of new objects and satisfactions. Along with this added ability in regulation goes enriched meaning and value in things, clarification, increased depth and continuity—a result even more precious than is the added power of control.

The history of the development of the physical sciences is the story of the enlarging possession by mankind of more efficacious instrumentalities for dealing with the conditions of life and action. But when one neglects the connection of these scientific objects with the affairs of primary experience, the result is a picture of a world of things indifferent to human interests because it is wholly apart from experience. It is more than merely isolated, for it is set in opposition. Hence when it is viewed as fixed and final in itself it is a source of oppression to the heart and paralysis to imagination. Since this picture of the physical universe and philosophy of the character of physical objects is contradicted by every engineering project and every intelligent measure of public hygiene, it would seem to be time to examine the foundations upon which it rests, and find out how and why such conclusions are come to.

When objects are isolated from the experience through which they are reached and in which they function, experience itself becomes reduced to the mere process of experiencing, and experiencing is therefore treated as if it were also complete in itself. We get the absurdity of an experiencing which experiences only itself, states and processes of consciousness, instead of the things of nature. Since the seventeenth century this conception of experience as the equivalent of subjective private consciousness set over against nature, which consists wholly of physical objects, has wrought havoc in philosophy. It is responsible for the feeling mentioned at the outset that "nature" and "experience" are names for things which have nothing to do with each other.

Let us inquire how the matter stands when these mental and psychical objects are looked at in their connection with experience in its primary and vital modes. As has been suggested, these objects are not original, isolated and self-sufficient. They represent the discriminated analysis of the process of experiencing from subject-matter experienced. Although breathing is in fact a function that includes both air and the operations of the lungs, we may detach the latter for study, even though we cannot separate it in fact. So while we always know, love, act for and against *things*, instead of experiencing ideas, emotions and mental intents, the attitudes themselves may be made a special object of attention, and thus come to form a distinctive subject-matter of reflective, although not of primary, experience.

We primarily observe things, not observations. But the *act* of observation may be inquired into and form a subject of study and become thereby a refined object; so may the acts of thinking, desire, purposing, the state of affection, reverie, etc. Now just as long as these attitudes are not distinguished and abstracted, they are incorporated into subject-matter. It is a notorious fact that the one who hates finds the one hated an obnoxious and despicable character; to the lover his adored one is full of intrinsically delightful and wonderful qualities. The connection between such facts and the fact of animism is direct.

The natural and original bias of man is all toward the objective; whatever is experienced is taken to be there independent of the attitude and act of the self. Its "thereness," its independence of emotion and volition, render the properties of things, whatever they are, cosmic. Only when vanity, prestige, rights of possession are involved does an individual tend to separate off from the environment and the group in which he, quite literally, lives, some things as being peculiarly himself. It is obvious that a total, unanalyzed world does not lend itself to control; that, on the contrary it is equivalent to the subjection of man to whatever occurs, as if to fate. Until some acts and their consequences are discriminatingly referred to the human organism and other energies and effects are referred to other bodies, there is no leverage, no purchase, with which to regulate the course of experience. The abstraction of certain qualities of things as due to human acts and states is the *pou sto* of ability in control. There can be no doubt that the long period of human arrest at a low level of culture was largely the result of failure to select the human being and his acts as a special kind of object, having his own characteristic activities that condition specifiable consequences.

In this sense, the recognition of "subjects" as centres of experience together with the development of "subjectivism" marks a great advance. It is equivalent to the emergence of agencies equipped with special powers of observation and experiment, and with emotions and desires that are efficacious for production of chosen modifications of nature. For otherwise the agencies are submerged in nature and produce qualities of things which must be accepted and submitted to. It is no mere play on words to say that recognition of subjective minds having a special equipment of psychological abilities is a necessary factor in subjecting the energies of nature to use as instrumentalities for ends.

Out of the indefinite number of possible illustrations of the consequences of reflective analysis yielding personal or "subjective" minds we cite one case. It concerns the influence of habitual beliefs and expectations in their social generation upon *what* is experienced. The things of primary experience are so arresting and engrossing that we tend to accept them just as they are—the flat earth, the march of the sun from east to west and its sinking under the earth. Current beliefs in morals, religion and politics similarly reflect the social conditions which present themselves. Only analysis shows that the *ways* in which we believe and expect have a tremendous effect upon *what* we believe and expect. We have discovered at last that these ways are set, almost abjectly so, by social factors, by tradition and the influence of education. Thus we discover that we believe many things not because the things are so, but because we have become habituated through the weight of authority, by imitation, prestige, instruction, the unconscious effect of language, etc. We learn, in short, that qualities which we attribute to objects ought to be imputed to our own ways of experiencing them, and that these in turn are due to the force of intercourse and custom. This discovery marks an emancipation; it purifies and remakes the objects of our direct or primary experience. The power of custom and tradition in scientific as well as in moral beliefs never suffered a serious check until analysis revealed the effect of personal ways of believing upon things believed, and the extent to which these ways are unwittingly fixed by social custom and tradition. In spite of the acute and penetrating powers of observation among the Greeks, their "science" is a monument of the extent to which the effects of acquired social habits as well as of organic constitution were attributed directly to natural events. The depersonalizing and de-socializing of some objects, to be henceforth the objects of physical science, was a necessary precondition of ability to regulate experience by directing the attitudes and objects that enter into it.

This great emancipation was coincident with the rise of "individualism," which was in effect identical with the reflective discovery of the part played in experience by concrete selves, with their ways of acting, thinking and desiring. The results would have been all to the good if they had been interpreted by empirical method. For this would have kept the eye of thinkers constantly upon the origin of the "subjective" out of primary experience, and then directed it to the function of discriminating what is usable in the management of experienced objects. But for lack of such a method, because of isolation from empirical origin and instrumental use, the results of psychological inquiry were conceived to form a separate and isolated mental world in and of itself, self-sufficient and self-enclosed. Since the psychological movement necessarily coincided with that which set up physical objects as correspondingly complete and self-enclosed, there resulted that dualism of mind and matter, of a physical and a psychical world, which from the day of Descartes to the present dominates the formulation of philosophical problems.

With the dualism we are not here concerned, beyond pointing out that it is the inevitable result, logically, of the abandoning of acknowledgment of the primacy and ultimacy of gross experience—primary as it is given in an uncontrolled form, ultimate as it is given in a more regulated and significant form—a form made possible by the methods and results of reflective experience. But what we are directly concerned with at this stage of discussion is the result of the discovery of subjective objects upon philosophy in creation of wholesale subjectivism. The outcome was, that while in actual life the discovery of personal attitudes and their consequences was a great liberating instrument, psychology became for philosophy, as Santayana has well put it, "malicious." That is, mental attitudes, *ways* of experiencing, were treated as self-sufficient and complete in themselves, as that which is primarily *given*, the sole original and therefore indubitable data. Thus the traits of genuine primary experience, in which natural things are the determining factors in production of all change, were regarded either as not-given dubious things that could be reached only by endowing the only certain thing, the mental, with some miraculous power, or else were denied all existence save as complexes of mental states, of impressions, sensations, feelings.[3]

One illustration out of the multitude available follows. It is taken almost at random, because it is both simple and typical. To illustrate the nature of experience, what experience really is, an author writes: "When I look at a chair, I say I experience it. But what I actually experience is only a very few of the elements that go to make up a chair, namely the color that belongs to the chair under these particular conditions of light, the shape which the

3. Because of this identification of the mental as the sole "given" in a primary, original way, appeal to experience by a philosopher is treated by many as necessarily committing one to subjectivism. It accounts for the alleged antithesis between nature and experience mentioned in the opening paragraph. It has become so deeply engrained that the empirical method employed in this volume has been taken by critics to be simply a re-statement of a purely subjective philosophy, although in fact it is wholly contrary to such a philosophy.

chair displays when viewed from this angle, etc." Two points are involved in any such statement. One is that "experience" is reduced to the traits connected with the *act of experiencing*, in this case the act of seeing. Certain patches of color, for example, assume a certain shape or form in connection with qualities connected with the muscular strains and adjustments of seeing. These qualities, which define the act of seeing when it is made an object of reflective inquiry, *over against what is seen*, thus become the chair itself for immediate or direct experience. Logically, the chair disappears and is replaced by certain qualities of sense attending the act of vision. There is no longer any other object, much less the chair which was bought, that is placed in a room and that is used to sit in, etc. If we ever get back to this total chair, it will not be the chair of direct experience, of use and enjoyment, a thing with its own independent origin, history and career; it will be only a complex of directly "given" sense qualities as a core, plus a surrounding cluster of other qualities revived imaginatively as "ideas."

The other point is that, even in such a brief statement as that just quoted, there is compelled recognition of an *object* of experience which is infinitely other and more than what is asserted to be alone experienced. There is the *chair* which is looked at; the *chair displaying* certain colors, the *light* in which they are displayed; the angle of vision implying reference to an organism that possesses an optical apparatus. Reference to these *things* is compulsory, because otherwise there would be no meaning assignable to the sense qualities—which are, nevertheless, affirmed to be the sole data experienced. It would be hard to find a more complete recognition, although an unavowed one, of the fact that in reality the account given concerns only a selected portion of the actual experience, namely that part which defines the act of experiencing, to the deliberate omission, *for the purpose of the inquiry in hand*, of *what* is experienced.

The instance cited is typical of all "subjectivism" as a philosophic position. Reflective analysis of one element in actual experience is undertaken; its result is then taken to be primary; as a consequence the subject-matter of actual experience from which the analytic result was derived is rendered dubious and problematic, although it is assumed at every step of the analysis. Genuine empirical method sets out from the actual subject-matter of primary experience, recognizes that reflection discriminates a new factor in it, the *act* of seeing, makes an object of that, and then uses that new object, the organic response to light, to regulate, when needed, further experiences of the subject-matter already contained in primary experience.

The topics just dealt with, segregation of physical and mental objects, will receive extended attention in the body of this volume.[4] As respects *method*, however, it is pertinent at this point to summarize our results. Reference to the primacy and ultimacy of the material of ordinary experience protects us, in the first place, from creating artificial problems which deflect the energy and attention of philosophers from the real problems that arise out of actual subject-matter. In the second place, it provides a check or test for the conclusions of philosophic inquiry; it is a constant reminder that we must replace them, as secondary reflective products, in the experience out of which they arose, so that they may be confirmed or modified by the new order and clarity they introduce into it, and the new significantly experienced objects for which they furnish a method. In the third place, in seeing how they thus function in further experiences, the philosophical results themselves acquire empirical value; they are what they contribute to the common experience of man, instead of being curiosities to be deposited, with appropriate labels, in a metaphysical museum.

There is another important result for philosophy of the use of empirical method which, when it is developed, introduces our next topic. Philosophy, like all forms of reflective analysis, takes us away, for the time being, from the things had in primary experience as they directly act and are acted upon, used and enjoyed. Now the standing temptation of philosophy, as its course abundantly demonstrates, is to regard the results of reflection as having, in and of themselves, a reality superior to that of the material of any other mode of experience. The commonest assumption of philosophies, common even to philosophies very different from one another, is the assumption of the identity of objects of knowledge and ultimately real objects. The assumption is so deep that it is usually not expressed; it is taken for granted as something so fundamental that it does not need to be

4. Chapters 4 and 6.

stated. A technical example of the view is found in the contention of the Cartesian school—including Spinoza—that emotion
as well as sense is but confused thought which when it becomes
clear and definite or reaches its goal is *cognition*. That esthetic
and moral experience reveal traits of real things as truly as does
intellectual experience, that poetry may have a metaphysical import as well as science, is rarely affirmed, and when it is asserted,
the statement is likely to be meant in some mystical or esoteric
sense rather than in a straightforward everyday sense.

Suppose however that we start with no presuppositions save
that what is experienced, since it is a manifestation of nature,
may, and indeed, must be used as testimony of the characteristics
of natural events. Upon this basis, reverie and desire are pertinent for a philosophic theory of the true nature of things; the
possibilities present in imagination that are not found in observation, are something to be taken into account. The features of
objects reached by scientific or reflective experiencing are important, but so are all the phenomena of magic, myth, politics,
painting, and penitentiaries. The phenomena of social life are as
relevant to the problem of the relation of the individual and
universal as are those of logic; the existence in political organization of boundaries and barriers, of centralization, of interaction
across boundaries, of expansion and absorption, will be quite as
important for metaphysical theories of the discrete and the continuous as is anything derived from chemical analysis. The existence of ignorance as well as of wisdom, of error and even
insanity as well as of truth will be taken into account.

That is to say, nature is construed in such a way that all these
things, since they are actual, are naturally possible; they are not
explained away into mere "appearance" in contrast with reality.
Illusions are illusions, but the occurrence of illusions is not an
illusion, but a genuine reality. What is really "in" experience
extends much further than that which at any time is *known*.
From the standpoint of knowledge, objects must be distinct;
their traits must be explicit; the vague and unrevealed is a limitation. Hence whenever the habit of identifying reality with the
object of knowledge as such prevails, the obscure and vague are
explained away. It is important for philosophic theory to be
aware that the distinct and evident are prized and why they are.
But it is equally important to note that the dark and twilight

abound. For in any object of primary experience there are always potentialities which are not explicit; any object that is overt is charged with possible consequences that are hidden; the most overt act has factors which are not explicit. Strain thought as far as we may and not all consequences can be foreseen or made an express or known part of reflection and decision. In the face of such empirical facts, the assumption that nature in itself is all of the same kind, all distinct, explicit and evident, having no hidden possibilities, no novelties or obscurities, is possible only on the basis of a philosophy which at some point draws an arbitrary line between nature and experience.

In the assertion (implied here) that the great vice of philosophy is an arbitrary "intellectualism," there is no slight cast upon intelligence and reason. By "intellectualism" as an indictment is meant the theory that all experiencing is a mode of knowing, and that all subject-matter, all nature, is, in principle, to be reduced and transformed till it is defined in terms identical with the characteristics presented by refined objects of science as such. The assumption of "intellectualism" goes contrary to the facts of what is primarily experienced. For things are objects to be treated, used, acted upon and with, enjoyed and endured, even more than things to be known. They are things *had* before they are things cognized.

The isolation of traits characteristic of objects known, and then defined as the sole ultimate realities, accounts for the denial to nature of the characters which make things lovable and contemptible, beautiful and ugly, adorable and awful. It accounts for the belief that nature is an indifferent, dead mechanism; it explains why characteristics that are the valuable and valued traits of objects in actual experience are thought to create a fundamentally troublesome philosophical problem. Recognition of their genuine and primary reality does not signify that no thought and knowledge enter in when things are loved, desired and striven for; it signifies that the former are subordinate, so that the genuine problem is how and why, to what effect, things thus experienced are transformed into objects in which cognized traits are supreme and affectional and volitional traits incidental and subsidiary.

"Intellectualism" as a sovereign method of philosophy is so foreign to the facts of primary experience that it not only compels recourse to non-empirical method, but it ends in making knowledge, conceived as ubiquitous, itself inexplicable. If we start from primary experience, occurring as it does chiefly in modes of action and undergoing, it is easy to see what knowledge contributes—namely, the possibility of intelligent administration of the elements of doing and suffering. We are about something, and it is well to know what we are about, as the common phrase has it. To be intelligent in action and in suffering (enjoyment too) yields satisfaction even when conditions cannot be controlled. But when there is possibility of control, knowledge is the sole agency of its realization. Given this element of knowledge in primary experience, it is not difficult to understand how it may develop from a subdued and subsidiary factor into a dominant character. Doing and suffering, experimenting and putting ourselves in the way of having our sense and nervous system acted upon in ways that yield material for reflection, may reverse the original situation in which knowing and thinking were subservient to action-undergoing. And when we trace the genesis of knowing along this line, we also see that knowledge has a function and office in bettering and enriching the subject-matters of crude experience. We are prepared to understand what we are about on a grander scale, and to understand what happens even when we seem to be the hapless puppets of uncontrollable fate. But knowledge that is ubiquitous, all-inclusive and all-monopolizing, ceases to have meaning in losing all context; that it does not appear to do so when made supreme and self-sufficient is because it is literally impossible to exclude that context of non-cognitive but experienced subject-matter which gives what is *known* its import.

While this matter is dealt with at some length in further chapters of this volume, there is one point worth mentioning here. When intellectual experience and its material are taken to be primary, the cord that binds experience and nature is cut. That the physiological organism with its structures, whether in man or in the lower animals, is concerned with making adaptations and uses of material in the interest of maintenance of the life-process, cannot be denied. The brain and nervous system are primarily organs of action-undergoing; biologically, it can be asserted without contravention that primary experience is of a corresponding type. Hence, unless there is breach of historic and natural continuity, cognitive experience must originate within that of a non-cognitive sort. And unless we start from knowing as a factor in action and undergoing we are inevitably committed to the intrusion of an extra-natural, if not a supernatural, agency and principle. That professed non-supernaturalists so readily endow the organism with powers that have no basis in natural events is a fact so peculiar that it would be inexplicable were it not for the inertia of the traditional schools. Otherwise it would be evident that the only way to maintain the doctrine of natural continuity is to recognize the secondary and derived character aspects of experience of the intellectual or cognitive. But so deeply grounded is the opposite position in the entire philosophic tradition, that it is probably not surprising that philosophers are loath to admit a fact which when admitted compels an extensive reconstruction in form and content.

We have spoken of the difference which acceptance of empirical method in philosophy makes in the problem of subject-object and in that of the alleged all-inclusiveness of cognitive experience.[5] There is an intimate connection between these two problems. When real objects are identified, point for point, with knowledge-objects, all affectional and volitional objects are inevitably excluded from the "real" world, and are compelled to find refuge in the privacy of an experiencing subject or mind. Thus the notion of the ubiquity of all comprehensive cognitive experience results by a necessary logic in setting up a hard and fast wall between the experiencing subject and that nature which is experienced. The self becomes not merely a pilgrim but an unnaturalized and unnaturalizable alien in the world. The only way to avoid a sharp separation between the mind which is the centre of the processes of experiencing and the natural world which is experienced is to acknowledge that all modes of experi-

5. To avoid misapprehension, it may be well to add a statement on the latter point. It is not denied that any experienced subject-matter whatever may *become* an object of reflection and cognitive inspection. But the emphasis is upon "become"; the cognitive never *is* all-inclusive: that is, when the material of a prior non-cognitive experience is the object of knowledge, it and the act of knowing are themselves included within a new and wider non-cognitive experience—and *this* situation can never be transcended. It is only when the temporal character of experienced things is forgotten that the idea of the total "transcendence" of knowledge is asserted.

encing are ways in which some genuine traits of nature come to manifest realization.

The favoring of cognitive objects and their characteristics at the expense of traits that excite desire, command action and produce passion, is a special instance of a principle of selective emphasis which introduces partiality and partisanship into philosophy. Selective emphasis, with accompanying omission and rejection, is the heart-beat of mental life. To object to the operation is to discard all thinking. But in ordinary matters and in scientific inquiries, we always retain the sense that the material chosen is selected for a purpose; there is no idea of denying what is left out, for what is omitted is merely that which is not relevant to the particular problem and purpose in hand.

But in philosophies, this limiting condition is often wholly ignored. It is not noted and remembered that the favored subject-matter is chosen for a purpose and that what is left out is just as real and important in its own characteristic context. It tends to be assumed that because qualities that figure in poetical discourse and those that are central in friendship do not figure in scientific inquiry, they have no reality, at least not the kind of unquestionable reality attributed to the mathematical, mechanical or magneto-electric properties that constitute matter. It is natural to men to take that which is of chief value to them at the time as *the* real. Reality and superior value are equated. In ordinary experience this fact does no particular harm; it is at once compensated for by turning to other things which since they also present value are equally real. But philosophy often exhibits a cataleptic rigidity in attachment to that phase of the total objects of experience which has become especially dear to a philosopher. *It* is real at all hazards and only it; other things are real only in some secondary and Pickwickian sense.

For example, certainty, assurance, is immensely valuable in a world as full of uncertainty and peril as that in which we live. As a result whatever is capable of certainty is assumed to constitute ultimate Being, and everything else is said to be merely phenomenal, or, in extreme cases, illusory. The arbitrary character of the "reality" that emerges is seen in the fact that very different objects are selected by different philosophers. These may be mathematical entities, states of consciousness, or sense data. That is, whatever strikes a philosopher from the angle of the particular problem that presses on him as being self-evident and hence completely assured, is selected by him to constitute reality. The honorable and dignified have ranked with the mundanely certain in determining philosophic definitions of the real. Scholasticism considered that the True and the Good, along with Unity, were the marks of Being as such. In the face of a problem, thought always seeks to unify things otherwise fragmentary and discrepant. Deliberately action strives to attain the good; knowledge is reached when truth is grasped. Then the goals of our efforts, the things that afford satisfaction and peace under conditions of tension and unrest, are converted into that which alone is ultimate real Being. Ulterior functions are treated as original properties.

Another aspect of the same erection of objects of selective preference into exclusive realities is seen in the addiction of philosophers to what is simple, their love for "elements." Gross experience is loaded with the tangled and complex; hence philosophy hurries away from it to search out something so simple that the mind can rest trustfully in it, knowing that it has no surprises in store, that it will not spring anything to make trouble, that it will stay put, having no potentialities in reserve. There is again the predilection for mathematical objects; there is Spinoza with his assurance that a true idea carries truth intrinsic in its bosom; Locke with his "simple idea"; Hume with his "impression"; the English neo-realist with his ultimate atomic data; the American neo-realist with his ready-made essences.

Another striking example of the fallacy of selective emphasis is found in the hypnotic influence exercised by the conception of the eternal. The permanent enables us to rest, it gives peace; the variable, the changing, is a constant challenge. Where things change something is hanging over us. It is a threat of trouble. Even when change is marked by hope of better things to come, that hope tends to project its object as something to stay once for all when it arrives. Moreover we can deal with the variable and precarious only by means of the stable and constant; "invariants"—for the time being—are as much a necessity in practice for bringing something to pass as they are in mathematical functions. The permanent answers genuine emotional, practical and intellectual requirements. But the demand and the response which meets it are empirically always found in a special context; they arise because of a particular need and in order to effect specifiable consequences. Philosophy, thinking at large, allows itself to be diverted into absurd search for an intellectual philosopher's stone of absolutely wholesale generalizations, thus isolating that which is permanent in a function and for a purpose, and converting it into the intrinsically eternal, conceived either (as Aristotle conceived it) as that which is the same at all times, or as that which is indifferent to time, out of time.

This bias toward treating objects selected because of their value in some special context as the "real," in a superior and invidious sense, testifies to an empirical fact of importance. Philosophical simplifications are due to choice, and choice marks an interest *moral* in the broad sense of concern for what is good. Our constant and unescapable concern is with prosperity and adversity, success and failure, achievement and frustration, good and bad. Since we are creatures with lives to live, and find ourselves within an uncertain environment, we are constructed to note and judge in terms of bearing upon weal and woe—upon value. Acknowledgment of this fact is a very different thing, however, from the transformation effected by philosophers of the traits they find good (simplicity, certainty, nobility, permanence, etc.) into fixed traits of real Being. The former presents something *to be accomplished*, to be brought about by the *actions* in which choice is manifested and made genuine. The latter ignores the need of action to effect the better and to prove the honesty of choice; it converts what is desired into antecedent and final features of a reality which is supposed to need only logical warrant in order to be contemplatively enjoyed as true Being.

For reflection the eventual is always better or worse than the given. But since it would also be better if the eventual good were now given, the philosopher, belonging by status to a leisure class relieved from the urgent necessity of dealing with conditions, converts the eventual into some kind of Being, something which *is*, even if it does not *exist*. Permanence, real essence, totality, order, unity, rationality, the *unum, verum et bonum* of the classic tradition, are eulogistic predicates. When we find such terms used to describe the foundations and proper conclusions of a philosophic system, there is ground for suspecting that an artificial simplification of existence has been performed. Reflection determining preference for an eventual good has dialectically wrought a miracle of transubstantiation.

Selective emphasis, choice, is inevitable whenever reflection occurs. This is not an evil. Deception comes only when the presence and operation of choice is concealed, disguised, denied. Empirical method finds and points to the operation of choice as it does to any other event. Thus it protects us from conversion of eventual functions into antecedent existence: a conversion that may be said to be *the* philosophic fallacy, whether it be performed in behalf of mathematical subsistences, esthetic essences, the purely physical order of nature, or God. The present writer does not profess any greater candor of intent than animates fellow philosophers. But the pursuance of an empirical method, is, he submits, the only way to secure execution of candid intent. Whatever enters into choice, determining its need and giving it guidance, an empirical method frankly indicates what it is for; and the fact of choice, with its workings and consequences, an empirical method points out with equal openness.

The adoption of an empirical method is no guarantee that all the things relevant to any particular conclusion will actually be found, or that when found they will be correctly shown and communicated. But empirical method points out when and where and how things of a designated description have been arrived at. It places before others a map of the road that has been travelled; they may accordingly, if they will, re-travel the road to inspect the landscape for themselves. Thus the findings of one may be rectified and extended by the findings of others, with as much assurance as is humanly possible of confirmation, extension and rectification. The adoption of empirical method thus procures for philosophic reflection something of that cooperative tendency toward consensus which marks inquiry in the natural sciences. The scientific investigator convinces others not by the plausibility of his definitions and the cogency of his dialectic, but by placing before them the specified course of searchings, doings and arrivals, in consequence of which certain things have been found. His appeal is for others to traverse a similar course, so as to see how what they find corresponds with his report.

Honest empirical method will state when and where and why the act of selection took place, and thus enable others to repeat it and test its worth. Selective choice, denoted as an empirical event, reveals the basis and bearing of intellectual simplifications; they then cease to be of such a self-enclosed nature as to be affairs only of opinion and argument, admitting no alternatives save complete acceptance or rejection. Choice that is disguised or denied is the source of those astounding differences of philosophic belief that startle the beginner and that become the plaything of the expert. Choice that is avowed is an experiment to be tried on its merits and tested by its results. Under all the captions that are called immediate knowledge, or self-sufficient certitude of belief, whether logical, esthetic or epistemological, there is something selected for a purpose, and hence not simple, not self-evident and not intrinsically eulogizable. State the purpose so that it may be re-experienced, and its value and the pertinency of selection undertaken in its behalf may be tested. The purport of thinking, scientific and philosophic, is not to eliminate choice but to render it less arbitrary and more significant. It loses its arbitrary character when its quality and consequences are such as to commend themselves to the reflection of others after they have betaken themselves to the situations indicated; it becomes significant when reason for the choice is found to be weighty and its consequences momentous. When choice is avowed, others can repeat the course of the experience; it is an experiment to be tried, not an automatic safety device.

This particular affair is referred to here not so much as matter of doctrine as to afford an illustration of the nature of empirical method. Truth or falsity depends upon what men find when they warily perform the experiment of observing reflective events. An empirical finding is refuted not by denial that one finds things to be thus and so, but by giving directions for a course of experience that results in finding its opposite to be the case. To convince of error as well as to lead to truth is to assist another to see and find something which he hitherto has failed to find and recognize. All of the wit and subtlety of reflection and logic find scope in the elaboration and conveying of directions that intelligibly point out a course to be followed. Every system of philosophy presents the consequences of some such experiment. As experiments, each has contributed something of worth to our observation of the events and qualities of experienceable objects. Some harsh criticisms of traditional philosophy have already been suggested; others will doubtless follow. But the criticism is not directed at the experiments; it is aimed at the denial to them by the philosophic tradition of selective experimental quality, a denial which has isolated them from their actual context and function, and has thereby converted potential illuminations into arbitrary assertions.

This discussion of empirical method has had a double content. On one hand, it has tried to make clear, from the analogy of empirical method in scientific inquiry, what the method signifies (and does *not* signify) for philosophy. Such a discussion would, however, have little definite import unless the *difference* that is made in philosophy by the adoption of empirical method is pointed out. For that reason, we have considered some typical ways and important places in which traditional philosophies have gone astray through failure to connect their reflective results with the affairs of every-day primary experience. Three sources of large fallacies have been mentioned, each containing within itself many more sub-varieties than have been hinted at. The three are the complete separation of subject and object, (of *what* is experienced from *how* it is experienced); the exaggeration of the features of known objects at the expense of the qualities of objects of enjoyment and trouble, friendship and human association, art and industry; and the exclusive isolation of the results of various types of selective simplification which are undertaken for diverse unavowed purposes.

It does not follow that the products of these philosophies which have taken the wrong, because non-empirical, method are of no value or little worth for a philosophy that pursues a strictly empirical method. The contrary is the case, for no philosopher can get away from experience even if he wants to. The most fantastic views ever entertained by superstitious people had some basis in experienced fact; they can be explained by one who knows enough about them and about the conditions under which they were formed. And philosophers have been not more but less superstitious than their fellows; they have been, as a class, unusually reflective and inquiring. If some of their products have been fantasies, it was not because they did not, even unwittingly, start from empirical method; it was not wholly because they substituted unchecked imagination for thought. No, the trouble has been that they have failed to note the empirical needs that generate their problems, and have failed to return the refined products back to the context of actual experience, there to receive their check, inherit their full content of meaning, and give illumination and guidance in the immediate perplexities which originally occasioned reflection.

The chapters which follow make no pretence, accordingly, of starting to philosophize afresh as if there were no philosophies already in existence, or as if their conclusions were empirically worthless. Rather the subsequent discussions rely, perhaps excessively so, upon the main results of great philosophic systems, endeavoring to point out their elements of strength and of weakness when their conclusions are employed (as the refined objects of all reflection must be employed) as guides back to the subject-matter of crude, everyday experience.

Our primary experience as it comes is of little value for purposes of analysis and control, crammed as it is with things that need analysis and control. The very existence of reflection is proof of its deficiencies. Just as ancient astronomy and physics were of little scientific worth, because, owing to the lack of apparatus and techniques of experimental analysis, they had to take the things of primary observation at their face value, so "common-sense" philosophy usually repeats current conventionalities. What is averred to be implicit reliance upon what is given in common experience is likely to be merely an appeal to prejudice to gain support for some fanaticism or defence for some relic of conservative tradition which is beginning to be questioned.

The trouble, then, with the conclusions of philosophy is not in the least that they are results of reflection and theorizing. It is rather that philosophers have borrowed from various sources the conclusions of special analyses, particularly of some ruling science of the day, and imported them direct into philosophy, with no check by either the empirical objects from which they arose or those to which the conclusions in question point. Thus Plato trafficked with the Pythagoreans and imported mathematical concepts; Descartes and Spinoza took over the presuppositions of geometrical reasoning; Locke imported into the theory of mind the Newtonian physical corpuscles, converting them into given "simple ideas"; Hegel borrowed and generalized without limit the rising historical method of his day; contemporary English philosophy has imported from mathematics the notion of primitive indefinable propositions, and given them a content from Locke's simple ideas, which had in the meantime become part of the stock in trade of psychological science.

Well, why not, as long as what is borrowed has a sound scientific status? Because in scientific inquiry, refined methods justify themselves by opening up new fields of subject-matter for exploration; they create new techniques of observation and experimentation. Thus when the Michelson-Morley experiment disclosed, as a matter of gross experience, facts which did not agree with the results of accepted physical laws, physicists did not think for a moment of denying the validity of what was found in that experience, even though it rendered questionable an elaborate intellectual apparatus and system. The coincidence of the bands of the interferometer was accepted at its face value in spite of its incompatibility with Newtonian physics. Because scientific inquirers accepted it at its face value they at once set to work to reconstruct their theories; they questioned their reflective premises, not the full "reality" of what they saw. This task of re-adjustment compelled not only new reasonings and calculations in the development of a more comprehensive theory, but opened up new ways of inquiry into experienced subject-matter. Not for a moment did they think of explaining away the features of an object in gross experience because it was not in logical harmony with theory—as philosophers have so often done. Had they done so, they would have stultified science and shut themselves off from new problems and new findings in subject-matter. In short, the material of refined scientific method is continuous with that of the actual world as it is concretely experienced.

But when philosophers transfer into their theories bodily and as finalities the refined conclusions they borrow from the sciences, whether logic, mathematics or physics, these results are not employed to reveal new subject-matters and illuminate old ones of gross experience; they are employed to cast discredit on the latter and to generate new and artificial problems regarding the reality and validity of the things of gross experience. Thus the discoveries of psychologies taken out of their own empirical context are in philosophy employed to cast doubt upon the reality of things external to mind and to selves, things and properties that are perhaps the most salient characteristics of ordinary experience. Similarly, the discoveries and methods of physical science, the concepts of mass, space, motion, have been adopted wholesale in isolation by philosophers in such a way as to make dubious and even incredible the reality of the affections, purposes and enjoyments of concrete experience. The objects of mathematics, symbols of relations having no explicit reference to actual existence, efficacious in the territory to which mathematical technique applies, have been employed in philosophy to determine the priority of essences to existence, and to create the insoluble problem of why pure essence ever descends into the tangles and tortuosities of existence.

What empirical method exacts of philosophy is two things: First, that refined methods and products be traced back to their origin in primary experience, in all its heterogeneity and fullness; so that the needs and problems out of which they arise and which they have to satisfy be acknowledged. Secondly, that the secondary methods and conclusions be brought back to the things of ordinary experience, in all their coarseness and crudity, for verification. In this way, the methods of analytic reflection yield material which form the ingredients of a method of designation, denotation, in philosophy. A scientific work in physics or astronomy gives a record of calculations and deductions that were derived from past observations and experiments. But it is more than a record; it is also an indication, an assignment, of further observations and experiments to be performed. No scientific report would get a hearing if it did not describe the apparatus by means of which experiments were carried on and results obtained; not that apparatus is worshipped, but because this procedure tells other inquirers how they are to go to work to get results which will agree or disagree in their experience with those previously arrived at, and thus confirm, modify and rectify the latter. The recorded scientific result is in effect a *designation* of a method to be followed and a *prediction* of what will be found when specified observations are set on foot. That is all a philosophy can be or do. In the chapters that follow I have undertaken a revision and reconstruction of the conclusions, the reports, of a number of historic philosophic systems, in order that they may be usable methods by which one may go to his own experience, and, discerning what is found by use of the method, come to understand better what is already within the common experience of mankind.

There is a special service which the study of philosophy may render. Empirically pursued it will not be a study of philosophy but a study, by means of philosophy, of life-experience. But this experience is already overlaid and saturated with the products of the reflection of past generations and by-gone ages. It is filled with interpretations, classifications, due to sophisticated thought, which have become incorporated into what seems to be fresh naïve empirical material. It would take more wisdom than is possessed by the wisest historic scholar to track all of these absorbed borrowings to their original sources. If we may for the moment call these materials prejudices (even if they are true, as long as their source and authority is unknown), then philosophy is a critique of prejudices. These incorporated results of past reflection, welded into the genuine materials of first-hand experience, may become organs of enrichment if they are detected and reflected upon. If they are not detected, they often obfuscate and distort. Clarification and emancipation follow when they are detected and cast out; and one great object of philosophy is to accomplish this task.

An empirical philosophy is in any case a kind of intellectual disrobing. We cannot permanently divest ourselves of the intellectual habits we take on and wear when we assimilate the culture of our own time and place. But intelligent furthering of culture demands that we take some of them off, that we inspect them critically to see what they are made of and what wearing them does to us. We cannot achieve recovery of primitive naïveté. But there is attainable a cultivated naïveté of eye, ear and thought, one that can be acquired only through the discipline of severe thought. If the chapters which follow contribute to an artful innocence and simplicity they will have served their purpose.

I am loath to conclude without reference to the larger liberal humane value of philosophy when pursued with empirical method. The most serious indictment to be brought against non-empirical philosophies is that they have cast a cloud over the things of ordinary experience. They have not been content to rectify them. They have discredited them at large. In casting aspersion upon the things of everyday experience, the things of action and affection and social intercourse, they have done something worse than fail to give these affairs the intelligent direction they so much need. It would not matter much if philosophy had been reserved as a luxury of only a few thinkers. We endure many luxuries. The serious matter is that philosophies have denied that common experience is capable of developing from within itself methods which will secure direction for itself and will create inherent standards of judgment and value. No one knows how many of the evils and deficiencies that are pointed to as reasons for flight from experience are themselves due to the disregard of experience shown by those peculiarly reflective. To waste of time and energy, to disillusionment with life that attends every deviation from concrete experience must be added the tragic failure to realize the value that intelligent search could reveal and mature among the things of ordinary experience. I cannot calculate how much of current cynicism, indifference and pessimism is due to these causes in the deflection of intelligence they have brought about. It has even become in many circles a sign of lack of sophistication to imagine that life is or can be a fountain of cheer and happiness. Philosophies no more than religions can be acquitted of responsibility for bringing this result to pass. The transcendental philosopher has probably done more than the professed sensualist and materialist to obscure the potentialities of daily experience for joy and for self-regulation. If what is written in these pages has no other result than creating and promoting a respect for concrete human experience and its potentialities, I shall be content.

2. Existence as Precarious and as Stable

It was suggested in the last chapter that experience has its equivalents in such affairs as history, life, culture. Reference to these other affairs enables us to put to one side the reminiscences which so readily give the word experience a sectarian and provincial content. According to Tylor, culture is "that complex whole which includes knowledge, belief, art, morals, custom, and any other capabilities acquired by a man as a member of society." It is, in some sense, a whole, but it is a complex, a diversified whole. It is differentiated into religion, magic, law, fine and useful art, science, philosophy, language, domestic and political relations, etc. Consider the following words of an anthropologist and ask if they do not fairly define the problem of philosophy, although intended for another purpose. "Cultural reality is never wholly deterministic nor yet wholly accidental, never wholly psychological nor yet wholly objective, never wholly of yesterday nor yet wholly of today, but combines all of these in its existential reality. . . . A reconstructive synthesis reestablishes the synthetic unity necessarily lost in the process of analytic dismemberment."[1] I do not mean that philosophy is to be merged in an anthropological view of culture. But in a different context and by a different method, it has the task of analytic dismemberment and synthetic reconstruction of experience; the phenomena of culture as presented by the anthropologist provide, moreover, precious material to aid the performance of this office, material more pertinent to the task of philosophizing than that of psychology isolated from a theory of culture.

A feature of existence which is emphasized by cultural phenomena is the precarious and perilous. Sumner refers to Grimm as authority for the statement that the Germanic tribes

1. Goldenweiser, "History, Psychology and Culture," p. 604.

had over a thousand distinct sayings, proverbs and apothegms, concerning luck. Time is brief, and this statement must stand instead of the discourse which the subject deserves. Man finds himself living in an aleatory world; his existence involves, to put it baldly, a gamble. The world is a scene of risk; it is uncertain, unstable, uncannily unstable. Its dangers are irregular, inconstant, not to be counted upon as to their times and seasons. Although persistent, they are sporadic, episodic. It is darkest just before dawn; pride goes before a fall; the moment of greatest prosperity is the moment most charged with ill-omen, most opportune for the evil eye. Plague, famine, failure of crops, disease, death, defeat in battle, are always just around the corner, and so are abundance, strength, victory, festival and song. Luck is proverbially both good and bad in its distributions. The sacred and the accursed are potentialities of the same situation; and there is no category of things which has not embodied the sacred and accursed: persons, words, places, times, directions in space, stones, winds, animals, stars.

Anthropologists have shown incontrovertibly the part played by the precarious aspect of the world in generating religion with its ceremonies, rites, cults, myths, magic; and it has shown the pervasive penetration of these affairs into morals, law, art, and industry. Beliefs and dispositions connected with them are the background out of which philosophy and secular morals slowly developed, as well as more slowly those late inventions, art for art's sake, and business is business. Interesting and instructive as is this fact, it is not the ramifications which here concern us. We must not be diverted to consider the consequences for philosophy, even for doctrines reigning today, of facts concerning the origin of philosophies. We confine ourselves to one outstanding fact: the evidence that the world of empirical things includes the uncertain, unpredictable, uncontrollable, and hazardous.

It is an old saying that the gods were born of fear. The saying is only too likely to strengthen a misconception bred by confirmed subjective habits. We first endow man in isolation with an instinct of fear and then we imagine him irrationally ejecting that fear into the environment, scattering broadcast as it were, the fruits of his own purely personal limitations, and thereby creating superstition. But fear, whether an instinct or an acquisition, is a function of the environment. Man fears because he

exists in a fearful, an awful world. The *world* is precarious and
perilous. It is as easily accessible and striking evidence of this fact
that primitive experience is cited. The voice is that of early man;
but the hand is that of nature, the nature in which we still live. It
was not fear of gods that created the gods.

For if the life of early man is filled with expiations and propiti-
ations, if in his feasts and festivals what is enjoyed is gratefully
shared with his gods, it is not because a belief in supernatural
powers created a need for expiatory, propitiatory and communal
offerings. Everything that man achieves and possesses is got by
actions that may involve him in other and obnoxious consequences in addition to those wanted and enjoyed. His acts are
trespasses upon the domain of the unknown; and hence atone-
ment, if offered in season, may ward off direful consequences
that haunt even the moment of prosperity—or that most haunt
that moment. While unknown consequences flowing from the
past dog the present, the future is even more unknown and perilous; the present by that fact is ominous. If unknown forces that
decide future destiny can be placated, the man who will not
study the methods of securing their favor is incredibly flippant.
In enjoyment of present food and companionship, nature, tradition and social organization have cooperated, thereby supple-
menting our own endeavors so petty and so feeble without this
extraneous reinforcement. Goods are by grace not of ourselves.
He is a dangerous churl who will not gratefully acknowledge by
means of free-will offerings the help that sustains him.

These things are as true today as they were in the days of early
culture. It is not the facts which have changed, but the methods
of insurance, regulation and acknowledgment. Herbert Spencer
sometimes colored his devotion to symbolic experiences with a
fact of direct experience. When he says that every fact has two
opposite sides, "the one its near or visible side and the other its
remote or invisible side," he expresses a persistent trait of every
object in experience. The visible is set in the invisible; and in the
end what is unseen decides what happens in the seen; the tangible rests precariously upon the untouched and ungrasped. The
contrast and the potential maladjustment of the immediate, the
conspicuous and focal phase of things, with those indirect and
hidden factors which determine the origin and career of what is
present, are indestructible features of any and every experience.

We may term the way in which our ancestors dealt with the contrast superstitious, but the contrast is no superstition. It is a primary datum in any experience.

We have substituted sophistication for superstition, at least measurably so. But the sophistication is often as irrational and as much at the mercy of words as the superstition it replaces. Our magical safeguard against the uncertain character of the world is to deny the existence of chance, to mumble universal and necessary law, the ubiquity of cause and effect, the uniformity of nature, universal progress, and the inherent rationality of the universe. These magic formulae borrow their potency from conditions that are not magical. Through science we have secured a degree of power of prediction and of control; through tools, machinery and an accompanying technique we have made the world more conformable to our needs, a more secure abode. We have heaped up riches and means of comfort between ourselves and the risks of the world. We have professionalized amusement as an agency of escape and forgetfulness. But when all is said and done, the fundamentally hazardous character of the world is not seriously modified, much less eliminated. Such an incident as the last war and preparations for a future war remind us that it is easy to overlook the extent to which, after all, our attainments are only devices for blurring the disagreeable recognition of a fact, instead of means of altering the fact itself.

What has been said sounds pessimistic. But the concern is not with morals but with metaphysics, with, that is to say, the nature of the existential world in which we live. It would have been as easy and more comfortable to emphasize good luck, grace, unexpected and unwon joys, those unsought for happenings which we so significantly call happiness. We might have appealed to good fortune as evidence of this important trait of hazard in nature. Comedy is as genuine as tragedy. But it is traditional that comedy strikes a more superficial note than tragedy. And there is an even better reason for appealing to misfortunes and mistakes as evidence of the precarious nature of the world. The problem of evil is a well-recognized problem, while we rarely or never hear of a problem of good. Goods we take for granted; they are as they should be; they are natural and proper. The good is a recognition of our deserts. When we pull out a plum we treat it as evidence of the *real* order of cause and effect in the world. For this reason it is difficult for the goods of existence to furnish as convincing evidence of the uncertain character of nature as do evils. It is the latter we term accidents, not the former, even when their adventitious character is as certain.

What of it all, it may be asked? In the sense in which an assertion is true that uncontrolled distribution of good and evil is evidence of the precarious, uncertain nature of existence, it is a truism, and no problem is forwarded by its reiteration. But it is submitted that just this predicament of the inextricable mixture of stability and uncertainty gives rise to philosophy, and that it is reflected in all its recurrent problems and issues. If classic philosophy says so much about unity and so little about unreconciled diversity, so much about the eternal and permanent, and so little about change (save as something to be resolved into combinations of the permanent), so much about necessity and so little about contingency, so much about the comprehending universal and so little about the recalcitrant particular, it may well be because the ambiguousness and ambivalence of reality are actually so pervasive. Since these things form the problem, solution is more apparent (although not more actual), in the degree in which whatever of stability and assurance the world presents is fastened upon and asserted.

Upon their surface, the reports of the world which form our different philosophies are various to the point of stark contrariness. They range from spiritualism to materialism, from absolutism to relativistic phenomenalism, from transcendentalism to positivism, from rationalism to sensationalism, from idealism to realism, from subjectivism to bald objectivism, from Platonic realism to nominalism. The array of contradictions is so imposing as to suggest to sceptics that the mind of man has tackled an impossible job, or that philosophers have abandoned themselves to vagary. These radical oppositions in philosophers suggest however another consideration. They suggest that all their different philosophies have a common premise, and that their diversity is due to acceptance of a common premise. Variant philosophies may be looked at as different ways of supplying recipes for denying to the universe the character of contingency which it possesses so integrally that its denial leaves the reflecting mind without a clew, and puts subsequent philosophising at the mercy of temperament, interest and local surroundings.

Quarrels among conflicting types of philosophy are thus family quarrels. They go on within the limits of a too domestic circle, and can be settled only by venturing further afield, and out of doors. Concerned with imputing complete, finished and sure character to the world of real existence, even if things have to be broken into two disconnected pieces in order to accomplish the result, the character desiderated can plausibly be found in reason or in mechanism; in rational conceptions like those of mathematics, or brute things like sensory data; in atoms or in essences; in consciousness or in a physical externality which forces and overrides consciousness.

As against this common identification of reality with what is sure, regular and finished, experience in unsophisticated forms gives evidence of a different world and points to a different metaphysics. We live in a world which is an impressive and irresistible mixture of sufficiencies, tight completenesses, order, recurrences which make possible prediction and control, and singularities, ambiguities, uncertain possibilities, processes going on to consequences as yet indeterminate. They are mixed not mechanically but vitally like the wheat and tares of the parable. We may recognize them separately but we cannot divide them, for unlike wheat and tares they grow from the same root. Qualities have defects as necessary conditions of their excellencies; the instrumentalities of truth are the causes of error; change gives meaning to permanence and recurrence makes novelty possible. A world that was wholly risky would be a world in which adventure is impossible, and only a living world can include death. Such facts have been celebrated by thinkers like Heracleitus and Lao-tze; they have been greeted by theologians as furnishing occasions for exercise of divine grace; they have been elaborately formulated by various schools under a principle of relativity, so defined as to become itself final and absolute. They have rarely been frankly recognized as fundamentally significant for the formation of a naturalistic metaphysics.

Aristotle perhaps came the nearest to a start in that direction. But his thought did not go far on the road, though it may be used to suggest the road which he failed to take. Aristotle acknowledges contingency, but he never surrenders his bias in favor of the fixed, certain and finished. His whole theory of forms and ends is a theory of the superiority in Being of rounded-out fixities. His physics is a fixation of ranks or grades of necessity and contingency so sorted that necessity measures dignity and equals degree of reality, while contingency and change measure degrees of deficiency of Being. The empirical impact and sting of the mixture of universality and singularity and chance is evaded by parcelling out the regions of space so that they have their natural abode in different portions of nature. His logic is one of definition and classification, so that its task is completed when changing and contingent things are distinguished from the necessary, universal and fixed, by attribution to inferior species of things. Chance appears in thought not as a calculus of probabilities in predicting the observable occurrence of any and every event, but as marking an inferior type of syllogism. Things that move are intrinsically different from things that exhibit eternal regularity. Change is honestly recognized as a genuine feature of *some* things, but the point of the recognition is avoided by imputing alteration to inherent deficiency of Being over against complete Being which never changes. Changing things belong to a purgatorial realm, where they wander aimlessly until redeemed by love of finality of form, the acquisition of which lifts them to a paradise of self-sufficient Being. With slight exaggeration, it may be said that the thoroughgoing way in which Aristotle defined, distinguished and classified rest and movement, the finished and the incomplete, the actual and potential, did more to fix tradition, *the* genteel tradition one is tempted to add, which identifies the fixed and regular with reality of Being and the changing and hazardous with deficiency of Being than ever was accomplished by those who took the shorter path of asserting that change is illusory.

His philosophy was closer to empirical facts than most modern philosophies, in that it was neither monistic nor dualistic but openly pluralistic. His plurals fall however, within a grammatical system, to each portion of which a corresponding cosmic status is allotted. Thus his pluralism solved the problem of how to have your cake and eat it too, for a classified and hierarchically ordered set of pluralities, of variants, has none of the sting of the miscellaneous and uncoordinated plurals of our actual world. In this classificatory scheme of separation he has been followed, though perhaps unwittingly, by many philosophers of different import. Thus Kant assigns all that is manifold and chaotic to one realm, that of sense, and all that is uniform and regular to that of reason. A single and all-embracing dialectic problem of the combination of sense and thought is thereby substituted for the concrete problems that arise through the mixed and varied union in existence of the variable and the constant, the necessary and that which proceeds uncertainly.

The device is characteristic of a conversion such as has already been commented upon of a moral insight to be made good in action into an antecedent metaphysics of existence or a general theory of knowledge. The striving to make stability of meaning prevail over the instability of events is the main task of intelligent human effort. But when the function is dropped from the province of art and treated as a property of given things, whether cosmological or logical, effort is rendered useless, and a premium is put upon the accidental good-fortune of a class that happens to be furnished by the toil of another class with products that give to life its dignity and leisurely stability.

The argument is not forgetful that there are, from Heracleitus to Bergson, philosophies, metaphysics, of change. One is grateful to them for keeping alive a sense of what classic, orthodox philosophies have whisked out of sight. But the philosophies of flux also indicate the intensity of the craving for the sure and fixed. They have deified change by making it universal, regular, sure. To say this is not, I hope, verbal by-play. Consider the wholly eulogistic fashion in which Hegel and Bergson, and the professedly evolutionary philosophers of becoming, have taken change. With Hegel becoming is a rational process which defines logic, although a new and strange logic, and an absolute, although new and strange, God. With Spencer, evolution is but the transitional process of attaining a fixed and universal equilibrium of harmonious adjustment. With Bergson, change is the creative operation of God, or *is* God—one is not quite sure which. The change of change is not only cosmic pyrotechnics, but is a process of divine, spiritual, energy. We are here in the presence of prescription, not description. Romanticism is an evangel in the garb of metaphysics. It sidesteps the painful, toilsome labor of understanding and of control which change sets us, by glorifying it for its own sake. Flux is made something to revere, something profoundly akin to what is best within ourselves, will and creative energy. It is not, as it is in experience, a call to effort, a challenge to investigation, a potential doom of disaster and death.

If we follow classical terminology, philosophy is love of wisdom, while metaphysics is cognizance of the generic traits of existence. In this sense of metaphysics, incompleteness and precariousness is a trait that must be given footing of the same rank as the finished and fixed. Love of wisdom is concerned with finding its implications for the conduct of life, in devotion to what is good. On the cognitive side, the issue is largely that of measure, of the ratio one bears to others in the situations of life. On the practical side, it is a question of the use to be made of each, of turning each to best account. Man is naturally philosophic, rather than metaphysical or coldly scientific, noting and describing. Concerned with prudence if not with what is honorifically called wisdom, man naturally prizes knowledge only for the sake of its bearing upon success and failure in attaining goods and avoiding evils. This is a fact of our structure and nothing is gained by recommending it as an ideal truth, and equally nothing is gained by attributing to intellect an intrinsic relationship to pure truth for its own sake or bare fact on its own account. The first method encourages dogma, and the second expresses a myth. The love of knowledge for its own sake is an ideal of morals; it is an integral condition of the wisdom that rightly conceives and effectually pursues the good. For wisdom as to ends depends upon acquaintance with conditions and means, and unless the acquaintance is adequate and fair, wisdom becomes a sublimated folly of self-deception.

Denial of an inherent relation of mind to truth or fact for its own sake, apart from insight into what the fact or truth exacts of us in behavior and imposes upon us in joy and suffering; and simultaneous affirmation that devotion to fact, to truth, is a necessary moral demand, involve no inconsistency. Denial relates to natural events as independent of choice and endeavor; affirmation relates to choice and action. But choice and the reflective effort involved in it are themselves such contingent events and so bound up with the precarious uncertainty of other events, that philosophers have too readily assumed that metaphysics, and science of fact and truth, are themselves wisdom, thinking thus to avoid the necessity of either exercising or recognizing choice. The consequence is that conversion of unavowed morals or wisdom into cosmology, and into a metaphysics of nature, which was termed in the last chapter *the* philosophic fallacy. It supplies the formula of the technique by which thinkers have relegated the uncertain and unfinished to an invidious state of unreal being, while they have systematically exalted the assured and complete to the rank of true Being.

Upon the side of wisdom, as human beings interested in good and bad things in their connection with human conduct, thinkers are concerned to mitigate the instability of life, to introduce moderation, temper and economy, and when worst comes to worst to suggest consolations and compensations. They are concerned with rendering more stable good things, and more unstable bad things; they are interested in how changes may be turned to account in the consequences to which they contribute. The facts of the ongoing, unfinished and ambiguously potential world give point and poignancy to the search for absolutes and finalities. Then when philosophers have hit in reflection upon a thing which is stably good in quality and hence worthy of persistent and continued choice, they hesitate, and withdraw from the effort and struggle that choice demands:—namely, from the effort to give it some such stability in observed existence as it possesses in quality when thought of. Thus it becomes a refuge, an asylum for contemplation, or a theme for dialectical elaboration, instead of an ideal to inspire and guide conduct.

Since thinkers claim to be concerned with knowledge of existence, rather than with imagination, they have to make good the pretention to knowledge. Hence they transmute the imaginative perception of the stably good object into a definition and description of true reality in contrast with lower and specious existence, which, being precarious and incomplete, alone involves us in the necessity of choice and active struggle. Thus they remove from actual existence the very traits which generate philosophic reflection and which give point and bearing to its conclusions. In briefest formula, "reality" becomes what we wish existence to be, after we have analyzed its defects and decided upon what would remove them; "reality" is what existence would be if our reasonably justified preferences were so completely established in nature as to exhaust and define its entire being and thereby render search and struggle unnecessary. What is left over, (and since trouble, struggle, conflict, and error still empirically exist, something *is* left over) being excluded by definition from full reality is assigned to a grade or order of being which is asserted to be metaphysically inferior; an order variously called appearance, illusion, mortal mind, or the merely empirical, against what really and truly is. Then the problem of metaphysics alters: instead of being a detection and description of the generic traits of existence, it becomes an endeavor to adjust or reconcile to each other two separate realms of being. Empirically we have just what we started with: the mixture of the precarious and problematic with the assured and complete. But a classificatory device, based on desire and elaborated in reflective imagination, has been introduced by which the two traits are torn apart, one of them being labelled reality and the other appearance. The genuinely moral problem of mitigating and regulating the troublesome factor by active employment of the stable factor then drops out of sight. The dialectic problem of logical reconciliation of two notions has taken its place.

The most widespread of these classificatory devices, the one of greatest popular appeal, is that which divides existence into the supernatural and the natural. Men may fear the gods but it is axiomatic that the gods have nothing to fear. They lead a life of untroubled serenity, the life that pleases them. There is a long story between the primitive forms of this division of objects of experience and the dialectical imputation to the divine of omnipotence, omniscience, eternity and infinity, in contrast with the attribution to man and experienced nature of finitude, weakness, limitation, struggle and change. But in the make-up of human psychology the later history is implicit in the early crude division. One realm is the home of assured appropriation and possession; the other of striving, transiency and frustration. How many persons are there today who conceive that they have disposed of ignorance, struggle and disappointment by pointing to man's "finite" nature—as if finitude signifies anything else but an abstract classificatory naming of certain concrete and discriminable traits of nature itself—traits of nature which generate ignorance, arbitrary appearance and disappearance, failure and striving. It pleases man to substitute the dialectic exercise of showing how the "finite" can exist with or within the "infinite" for the problem of dealing with the contingent, thinking to solve the problem by distinguishing and naming its factors. Failure of the exercise is certain, but the failure can be flourished as one more proof of the finitude of man's intellect, and the needlessness because impotency of endeavor of "finite" creatures to attack ignorance and oppressive fatalities. Wisdom then consists in administration of the temporal, finite and human in its relation to the eternal and infinite, by means of dogma and cult, rather than in regulation of the events of life by understanding of actual conditions.

It does not demand great ingenuity to detect the inversion here. The starting point is precisely the existing mixture of the regular and dependable and the unsettled and uncertain. There are a multitude of recipes for obtaining a vicarious possession of the stable and final without getting involved in the labor and pain of intellectual effort attending regulation of the conditions upon which these fruits depend.

This situation is worthy of remark as an exemplification of how easy it is to arrive at a description of existence via a theory of wisdom, of reflective insight into goods. It has a direct bearing upon a metaphysical doctrine which is not popular, like the division into the supernatural, and natural, but which is learned and technical. The philosopher may have little esteem for the crude forms assumed by the popular metaphysics of earth and heaven, of God, nature, and man. But the philosopher has often proceeded in a manner analogous to that which resulted in this popular metaphysics; some of the most cherished metaphysical distinctions seem to be but learned counterparts, dependent upon an elaborate intellectual technique, for these rough, crude notions of supernatural and natural, divine and human, in popular belief. I refer to such things as the Platonic division into ideal archetypes and physical events; the Aristotelian division into form which is actuality and matter which is potential, when that is understood as a distinction of ranks of reality; the noumenal things, things-in-themselves of Kant in contrast with natural objects as phenomenal; the distinction, current among contemporary absolute idealists, of reality and appearance.

The division however is not confined to philosophers with leanings toward spiritualistic philosophies. There is some evidence that Plato got the term Idea, as a name for essential form, from Democritus. Whether this be the case or no, the Idea of Democritus, though having a radically diverse structure from the

Platonic Idea, had the same function of designating a finished, complete, stable, wholly unprecarious reality. Both philosophers craved solidity and both found it; corresponding to the Platonic phenomenal flux are the Democritean things as they are in custom or ordinary experience: corresponding to the ideal archetypes are substantial indivisible atoms. Corresponding, again, to the Platonic theory of Ideas is the modern theory of mathematical structures which are alone independently real, while the empirical impressions and suggestions to which they give rise is the counterpart of his realm of phenomena.

Apart from the materialistic and spiritualistic schools, there is the Spinozistic division into attributes and modes; the old division of essence and existence, and its modern counterpart subsistence and existence. It is impossible to force Mr. Bertrand Russell into any one of the pigeon-holes of the cabinet of conventional philosophic schools. But moral, or philosophical, motivation is obvious in his metaphysics when he says that mathematics takes us "into the region of absolute necessity, to which not only the actual world but every possible world must conform." Indeed with his usual lucidity, he says, mathematics "finds a habitation eternally standing, where our ideals are fully satisfied and our best hopes are not thwarted." When he adds that contemplation of such objects is the "chief means of overcoming the terrible sense of impotence, of weakness, of exile amid hostile powers, which is too apt to result from acknowledging the all-but omnipotence of alien forces," the presence of moral origin is explicit.

No modern thinker has pointed out so persuasively as Santayana that "every phase of the ideal world emanates from the natural," that "sense, art, religion, society express nature exuberantly." And yet unless one reads him wrong, he then confounds his would-be disciples and confuses his critics by holding that nature is *truly* presented only in an esthetic contemplation of essences reached by physical science, an envisagement reached through a dialectic which "is a transubstantiation of matter, a passage from existence to eternity." This passage moreover is so utter that there is no road back. The stable ideal meanings which are the fruit of nature are forbidden, in the degree in which they are its highest and truest fruits, from dropping seeds in nature to its further fructification.

The perception of genetic continuity between the dynamic flux of nature and an eternity of static ideal forms thus terminates in a sharp division, in reiteration of the old tradition. Perhaps it is a caricature to say that the ultimate of reason is held to be ability to behold nature as a complete mechanism which generates and sustains the beholding of the mechanism, but the caricature is not wilful. If the separation of contingency and necessity is abandoned, what is there to exclude a belief that science, while it is grasp of the regular and stable mechanism of nature, is also an organ of regulating and enriching, through its own expansion, the more exuberant and irregular expressions of nature in human intercourse, the arts, religion, industry, and politics?

To follow out the latter suggestion would take us to a theme reserved for later consideration. We are here concerned with the fact that it is the intricate mixture of the stable and the precarious, the fixed and the unpredictably novel, the assured and the uncertain, in existence which sets mankind upon that love of wisdom which forms philosophy. Yet too commonly, although in a great variety of technical modes, the result of the search is converted into a metaphysics which denies or conceals from acknowledgment the very characters of existence which initiated it, and which give significance to its conclusions. The form assumed by the denial is, most frequently, that striking division into a superior true realm of being and lower illusory, insignificant or phenomenal realm which characterizes metaphysical systems as unlike as those of Plato and Democritus, St. Thomas and Spinoza, Aristotle and Kant, Descartes and Comte, Haeckel and Mrs. Eddy.

The same jumble of acknowledgment and denial attends the conception of Absolute Experience: as if any experience could be more absolutely experience than that which marks the life of humanity. This conception constitutes the most recent device for first admitting and then denying the combinedly stable and unstable nature of the world. Its plaintive recognition of our experience as finite and temporal, as full of error, conflict and contradiction, is an acknowledgment of the precarious uncertainty of the objects and connections that constitute nature as it emerges in history. Human experience however has also the pathetic longing for truth, beauty and order. There is more than the longing: there are moments of achievement. Experience exhibits ability to possess harmonious objects. It evinces an ability, within limits, to safeguard the excellent objects and to deflect and reduce the obnoxious ones. The concept of an absolute experience which is only and always perfect and good, first explicates these desirable implications of things of actual experience, and then asserts that they alone are real. The experienced occurrences which give poignancy and pertinency to the longing for a better world, the experimental endeavors and plans which make possible actual betterments within the objects of actual experience, are thus swept out of real Being into a limbo of appearances.

The notion of Absolute Experience thus serves as a symbol of two facts. One is the ineradicable union in nature of the relatively stable and the relatively contingent. The division of the movement and leadings of things which are experienced into two parts, such that one set constitutes and defines absolute and eternal experience, while the other set constitutes and defines finite experience, tells us nothing about absolute experience. It tells us a good deal about experience as it exists: namely, that it is such as to involve permanent and general objects of reference as well as temporally changing events; the possibility of truth as well as error; conclusive objects and goods as well as things whose purport and nature is determinable only in an indeterminate future. Nothing is gained—except the delights of a dialectic problem—in labelling one assortment absolute experience and the other finite experience. Since the appeal of the adherents of the philosophy of absolute and phenomenal experience is to a logical criterion, namely, to the implication in every judgment, however erroneous, of a standard of consistency which excludes any possibility of contradictoriness, the inherent logical contradictions in the doctrine itself are worth noting.

In the first place, the contents as well as the form of ultimate Absolute Experience are derived from and based upon the features of actual experience, the very experience which is then relegated to unreality by the supreme reality derived from its unreality. It is "real" just long enough to afford a spring-board into ultimate reality and to afford a hint of the essential contents of the latter and then it obligingly dissolves into mere appearance. If we start from the standpoint of the Absolute Experience thus reached, the contradiction is repeated from its side. Although absolute, eternal, all-comprehensive, and pervasively integrated into a whole so logically perfect that no separate patterns, to say nothing of seams and holes, can exist in it, it proceeds to play a tragic joke upon itself—for there is nothing else to be fooled—by appearing in a queer combination of rags and glittering gew-gaws, in the garb of the temporal, partial and conflicting things, mental as well as physical, of ordinary experience. I do not cite these dialectic contradictions as having an inherent importance. But the fact that a doctrine which avowedly takes logical consistence for its method and criterion, whose adherents are noteworthy for dialectic acumen in specific issues, should terminate in such thoroughgoing contradictions may be cited as evidence that after all the doctrine is merely engaged in an arbitrary sorting out of characters of things which in nature are always present in conjunction and interpenetration.

The union of the hazardous and the stable, of the incomplete and the recurrent, is the condition of all experienced satisfaction as truly as of our predicaments and problems. While it is the source of ignorance, error and failure of expectation, it is the source of the delight which fulfillments bring. For if there were nothing in the way, if there were no deviations and resistances, fulfillment would be at once, and in so being would fulfill nothing, but merely be. It would not be in connection with desire or satisfaction. Moreover when a fulfillment comes and is pronounced good, it is *judged* good, distinguished and asserted, simply because it is in jeopardy, because it occurs amid indifferent and divergent things. Because of this mixture of the regular and that which cuts across stability, a good object once experienced acquires ideal quality and attracts demand and effort to itself. A particular ideal may be an illusion, but having ideals is no illusion. It embodies features of existence. Although imagination is often fantastic it is also an organ of nature; for it is the appropriate phase of indeterminate events moving toward eventualities that are now but possibilities. A purely stable world permits of no illusions, but neither is it clothed with ideals. It just exists. To be good is to be better than; and there can be no better except where there is shock and discord combined with enough assured order to make attainment of harmony possible. Better objects when brought into existence are existent not ideal; they retain ideal quality only retrospectively as commemorative of issue from prior conflict and prospectively, in contrast with forces which make for their destruction. Water that slakes thirst, or a conclusion that solves a problem have ideal character as long as thirst or problem persists in a way which qualifies the result. But water that is not a satisfaction of need has no more ideal quality than water running through pipes into a reservoir; a solution ceases to be a solution and becomes a bare incident of existence when its antecedent generating conditions of doubt, ambiguity and search are lost from its context. While the precarious nature of existence is indeed the source of all trouble, it is also an indispensable condition of ideality, becoming a sufficient condition when conjoined with the regular and assured.

We long, amid a troubled world, for perfect being. We forget that what gives meaning to the notion of perfection is the events that create longing, and that, apart from them, a "perfect" world would mean just an unchanging brute existential thing. The ideal significance of esthetic objects is no exception to this principle. Their satisfying quality, their power to compose while they arouse, is not dependent upon definite prior desire and effort as is the case with the ideally satisfying quality of practical and scientific objects. It is part of their peculiar satisfying quality to be gratuitous, not purchased by endeavor. The contrast to other things of this detachment from toil and labor in a world where most realizations have to be bought, as well as the contrast to trouble and uncertainty, give esthetic objects their peculiar traits. If all things came to us in the way our esthetic objects do, none of them would be a source of esthetic delight.

Some phases of recent philosophy have made much of need, desire and satisfaction. Critics have frequently held that the outcome is only recurrence to an older subjective empiricism, though with substitution of affections and volitional states for cognitive sensory states. But need and desire are exponents of natural being. They are, if we use Aristotelian phraseology, actualizations of its contingencies and incompletenesses; as such nature itself is wistful and pathetic, turbulent and passionate. Were it not, the existence of wants would be a miracle. In a world where everything is complete, nothing requires anything else for its completion. A world in which events can be carried to a finish only through the coinciding assistance of other transitory events, is already necessitous, a world of begging as well as of beggarly elements. If human experience is to express and reflect this world, it must be marked by needs; in becoming aware of the needful and needed quality of things it must project satisfactions or completions. For irrespective of whether a satisfaction is conscious, a satisfaction or non-satisfaction is an objective thing with objective conditions. It means fulfillment of the demands of objective factors. Happiness may *mark* an awareness of such satisfaction, and it may *be* its culminating form. But satisfaction is not subjective, private or personal: it is conditioned by objective partialities and defections and made real by objective situations and completions.

By the same logic, necessity implies the precarious and contingent. A world that was all necessity would not be a world of necessity; it would just be. For in its being, nothing would be necessary for anything else. But where some things are indigent, other things are necessary if demands are to be met. The common failure to note the fact that a world of complete being would be a world in which necessity is meaningless is due to a rapid shift from one universe of discourse to another. First we postulate a whole of Being; then we shift to a part; now since a "part" is logically dependent as such in its existence and its properties, it is necessitated by other parts. But we have unwittingly introduced contingency in the very fact of marking off something as just a part. If the logical implications of the original notion are held to firmly, a part is already a part-of-a-whole. Its being what it is, is not necessitated by the whole or by other parts: its being what it is, is just a name for the whole being what it is. Whole and parts alike are but names for existence there as just what it is. But wherever we can say *if* so-and-so, then something else, there is necessity, because partialities are implied which are not just parts-of-a-whole. A world of "ifs" is alone a world of "musts"—the "ifs" express real differences; the "musts" real connections. The stable and recurrent is needed for the fulfillment of the possible; the doubtful can be settled only through its adaptation to stable objects. The necessary is always necessary for, not necessary in and of itself; it is conditioned by the contingent, although itself a condition of the full determination of the latter.

One of the most striking phases of the history of philosophic thought is the recurrent grouping together of unity, permanence (or "the eternal"), completeness and rational thought, while upon another side fall multiplicity, change and the temporal, the partial, defective, sense and desire. This division is obviously but another case of violent separation of the precarious and unsettled from the regular and determinate. One aspect of it however, is worthy of particular attention: the connection of thought and unity. Empirically, all reflection sets out from the problematic and confused. Its aim is to clarify and ascertain. When thinking is successful, its career closes in transforming the disordered into the orderly, the mixed-up into the distinguished or placed, the unclear and ambiguous into the defined and unequivocal, the disconnected into the systematized. It is empirically assured that the goal of thinking does not remain a mere ideal, but is attained often enough so as to render reasonable additional efforts to achieve it.

In these facts we have, I think, the empirical basis of the philosophic doctrines which assert that reality is really and truly a rational system, a coherent whole of relations that cannot be conceived otherwise than in terms of intellect. Reflective inquiry moves in each particular case from differences toward unity; from indeterminate and ambiguous position to clear determination, from confusion and disorder to system. When thought in a given case has reached its goal of organized totality, of definite relations of distinctly placed elements, its object is the accepted starting point, the defined subject-matter, of further experiences; antecedent and outgrown conditions of darkness and of unreconciled differences are dismissed as a transitory state of ignorance and inadequate apprehensions. Retain connection of the goal with the thinking by which it is reached, and then identify it with true reality in contrast with the merely phenomenal, and the outline of the logic of rational and "objective" idealisms is before us. Thought like Being, has two forms; one real, the other phenomenal. It is compelled to take on *reflective* form, it involves doubt, inquiry and hypothesis, because it sets out from a subject-matter conditioned by sense, a fact which proves that thought, intellect, is not pure in man, but restricted by an animal organism that is but one part linked with other parts, of nature. But the conclusion of reflection affords us a pattern and guarantee of thought which is *constitutive*; one with the system of objective reality. Such in outline is the procedure of all ontological logics.

A philosophy which accepts the denotative or empirical method accepts at full value the fact that reflective thinking transforms confusion, ambiguity and discrepancy into illumination, definiteness and consistency. But it also points to the contextual situation in which thinking occurs. It notes that the starting point is the actually *problematic*, and that the problematic phase resides in some actual and specifiable situation.

It notes that the means of converting the dubious into the assured, and the incomplete into the determinate, is use of assured and established things, which are just as empirical and as indicative of the nature of experienced things as is the uncertain. It thus notes that thinking is no different in kind from the use of natural materials and energies, say fire and tools, to refine, reorder, and shape other natural materials, say ore. In both cases, there are matters which as they stand are unsatisfactory and there are also adequate agencies for dealing with them and connecting them. At no point or place is there any jump outside empirical, natural objects and their relations. Thought and reason are not specific powers. They consist of the procedures intentionally employed in the application to each other of the unsatisfactorily confused and indeterminate on one side and the regular and stable on the other. Generalizing from such observations, empirical philosophy perceives that thinking is a continuous process of temporal re-organization within one and the same world of experienced things, not a jump from the latter world into one of objects constituted once for all by thought. It discovers thereby the empirical basis of rational idealism, and the point at which it empirically goes astray. Idealism fails to take into account the specified or concrete character of the uncertain situation in which thought occurs; it fails to note the empirically concrete nature of the subject-matter, acts, and tools by which determination and consistency are reached; it fails to note that the conclusive eventual objects having the latter properties are themselves as many as the situations dealt with. The conversion of the logic of reflection into an ontology of rational being is thus due to arbitrary conversion of an eventual natural function of unification into a causal antecedent reality; this in turn is due to the tendency of the imagination working under the influence of emotion to carry unification from an actual, objective and experimental enterprise, limited to particular situations where it is needed, into an unrestricted, wholesale movement which ends in an all-absorbing dream.

The occurrence of reflection is crucial for dualistic metaphysics as well as for idealistic ontologies. Reflection occurs only in situations qualified by uncertainty, alternatives, questioning, search, hypotheses, tentative trials or experiments which test the worth of thinking. A naturalistic metaphysics is bound to consider reflection as itself a natural event occurring *within* nature because of traits of the latter. It is bound to inference from the empirical traits of thinking in precisely the same way as the sciences make inferences from the happening of suns, radioactivity, thunder-storms or any other natural event. Traits of reflection are as truly indicative or evidential of the traits of *other* things as are the traits of these events. A theory of the nature of the occurrence and career of a sun reached by denial of the obvious traits of the sun, or by denial that these traits are so connected with the traits of other natural events that they can be used as evidence concerning the nature of these other things, would hardly possess scientific standing. Yet philosophers, and strangely enough philosophers who call themselves realists, have constantly held that the traits which are characteristic of thinking, namely, uncertainty, ambiguity, alternatives, inquiring, search, selection, experimental reshaping of external conditions, do not possess the same existential character as do the objects of valid knowledge. They have denied that these traits are evidential of the character of the world within which thinking occurs. They have not, as realists, asserted that these traits are mere appearances; but they have often asserted and implied that such things are only personal or psychological in contrast with a world of objective nature. But the interests of empirical and denotative method and of naturalistic metaphysics wholly coincide. The world must actually be such as to generate ignorance and inquiry; doubt and hypothesis, trial and temporal conclusions; the latter being such that they develop out of existences which while wholly "real" are not as satisfactory, as good, or as significant, as those into which they are eventually re-organized. The ultimate evidence of genuine hazard, contingency, irregularity and indeterminateness in nature is thus found in the occurrence of thinking. The traits of natural existence which generate the fears and adorations of superstitious barbarians generate the scientific procedures of disciplined civilization. The superiority of the latter does not consist in the fact that they are based on "real" existence, while the former depend wholly upon a human nature different from nature in general. It consists in the fact that scientific inquiries reach *objects* which are better, because reached by method which controls them and which adds greater control to life itself, method which mitigates accident, turns contingency to account, and releases thought and other forms of endeavor.

The conjunction of problematic and determinate characters in nature renders every existence, as well as every idea and human act, an experiment in fact, even though not in design. To be intelligently experimental is but to be conscious of this intersection of natural conditions so as to profit by it instead of being at its mercy. The Christian idea of this world and this life as a probation is a kind of distorted recognition of the situation; distorted because it applied wholesale to one stretch of existence in contrast with another, regarded as original and final. But in truth anything which can exist at any place and at any time occurs subject to tests imposed upon it by surroundings, which are only in part compatible and reinforcing. These surroundings test its strength and measure its endurance. As we can discourse of change only in terms of velocity and acceleration which involve relations to other things, so assertion of the permanent and enduring is comparative. The stablest thing we can speak of is not free from conditions set to it by other things. That even the solid earth mountains, the emblems of constancy, appear and disappear like the clouds is an old theme of moralists and poets. The fixed and unchanged being of the Democritean atom is now reported by inquirers to possess some of the traits of his nonbeing, and to embody a temporary equilibrium in the economy of nature's compromises and adjustments. A thing may endure *secula seculorum* and yet not be everlasting; it will crumble before the gnawing tooth of time, as it exceeds a certain measure. Every existence is an event.

This fact is nothing at which to repine and nothing to gloat over. It is something to be noted and used. If it is discomfiting when applied to good things, to our friends, possessions and precious selves, it is consoling also to know that no evil endures forever; that the longest lane turns sometime, and that the memory of loss of nearest and dearest grows dim in time. The eventful character of all existences is no reason for consigning them to the realm of mere appearance any more than it is a reason for idealizing flux into a deity. The important thing is measure, relation, ratio, knowledge of the comparative tempos of change. In mathematics some variables are constants in some problems; so it is in nature and life. The rate of change of some things is so slow, or is so rhythmic, that these changes have all the advantages of stability in dealing with more transitory and irregular happenings—if we know enough. Indeed, if any one thing that concerns us is subject to change, it is fortunate that all other things change. A thing "absolutely" stable and unchangeable would be out of the range of the principle of action and reaction, of resistance and leverage as well as of friction. Here it would have no applicability, no potentiality of use as measure and control of other events. To designate the slower and the regular rhythmic events structure, and more rapid and irregular ones process, is sound practical sense. It expresses the function of one in respect to the other.

But spiritualistic idealism and materialism alike treat this relational and functional distinction as something fixed and absolute. One doctrine finds structure in a framework of ideal forms, the other finds it in matter. They agree in supposing that structure has some superlative reality. This supposition is another form taken by preference for the stable over the precarious and uncompleted. The fact is that all structure is structure *of* something; anything defined as structure is a character of *events*, not something intrinsic and *per se*. A set of traits is called structure, because of its limiting function in relation to other traits of events. A house has a structure; in comparison with the disintegration and collapse that would occur without its presence, this structure is fixed. Yet it is not something external to which the changes involved in building and using the house have to submit. It is rather an arrangement of changing events such that properties which change slowly, limit and direct a series of quick changes and give them an order which they do not otherwise possess. Structure is constancy of means, of things used for consequences, not of things taken by themselves or absolutely. Structure is what makes construction possible and cannot be discovered or defined except in some realized construction, construction being, of course, an evident order of changes. The isolation of structure from the changes whose stable ordering it is, renders it mysterious—something that is metaphysical in the popular sense of the word, a kind of ghostly queerness.

The "matter" of materialists and the "spirit" of idealists is a creature similar to the Constitution of the United States in the minds of unimaginative persons. Obviously the real constitution is certain basic relationships among the activities of the citizens of the country; it is a property or phase of these processes, so connected with them as to influence their rate and direction of change. But by literalists it is often conceived of as something external to them; in itself fixed, a rigid framework to which *all* changes must accommodate themselves. Similarly what we call matter is that character of natural events which is so tied up with changes that are sufficiently rapid to be perceptible as to give the latter a characteristic rhythmic order, the causal sequence. It is no cause or source of events or processes; no absolute monarch; no principle of explanation; no substance behind or underlying changes—save in that sense of substance in which a man well fortified with this world's goods, and hence able to maintain himself through vicissitudes of surroundings, is a man of substance. The name designates a character in operation, not an entity.

That structure, whether of the kind called material or of the kind summed up in the word mental, is stable or permanent relationally and in its office, may be shown in another way. There is no action without reaction; there is no exclusively one-way exercise of conditioning power, no mode of regulation that operates wholly from above to below or from within outwards or from without inwards. Whatever influences the changes of other things is itself changed. The idea of an activity proceeding only in one direction, of an unmoved mover, is a survival of Greek physics. It has been banished from science, but remains to haunt philosophy. The vague and mysterious properties assigned to mind and matter, the very conceptions of mind and matter in traditional thought, are ghosts walking underground. The notion of matter actually found in the practice of science has nothing in common with the matter of materialists—and almost everybody is still a materialist as to matter, to which he merely adds a second rigid structure which he calls mind. The matter of science is a character of natural events and changes as they change; their character of regular and stable order.

Natural events are so complex and varied that there is nothing surprising in their possession of different characterizations, characters so different that they can be easily treated as opposites.

Nothing but unfamiliarity stands in the way of thinking of both mind and matter as different characters of natural events, in which matter expresses their sequential order, and mind the order of their meanings in their logical connections and dependencies. Processes may be eventful for functions which taken in abstract separation are at opposite poles, just as physiological processes eventuate in both anabolic and katabolic functions. The idea that matter and mind are two sides or "aspects" of the same things, like the convex and the concave in a curve, is literally unthinkable.

A curve is an intelligible object and concave and convex are defined in terms of this object; they are indeed but names for properties involved in its meaning. We do not start with convexity and concavity as two independent things and then set up an unknown *tertium quid* to unite two disparate things. In spite of the literal absurdity of the comparison, it may be understood however in a way which conveys an inkling of the truth. That to which both mind and matter belong is the complex of events that constitute nature. This becomes a mysterious *tertium quid*, incapable of designation, only when mind and matter are taken to be static structures instead of functional characters. It is a plausible prediction that if there were an interdict placed for a generation upon the use of mind, matter, consciousness as nouns, and we were obliged to employ adjectives and adverbs, conscious and consciously, mental and mentally, material and physically, we should find many of our problems much simplified.

We have selected only a few of the variety of the illustrations that might be used in support of the idea that the significant problems and issues of life and philosophy concern the rate and mode of the conjunction of the precarious and the assured, the incomplete and the finished, the repetitious and the varying, the safe and sane and the hazardous. If we trust to the evidence of experienced things, these traits, and the modes and tempos of their interaction with each other, are fundamental features of natural existence. The experience of their various consequences, according as they are relatively isolated, unhappily or happily combined, is evidence that wisdom, and hence that love of wisdom which is philosophy, is concerned with choice and administration of their proportioned union. Structure and process, substance and accident, matter and energy, permanence and flux, one and many, continuity and discreteness, order and progress, law and liberty, uniformity and growth, tradition and innovation, rational will and impelling desires, proof and discovery, the actual and the possible, are names given to various phases of their conjunction, and the issue of living depends upon the art with which these things are adjusted to each other.

While metaphysics may stop short with noting and registering these traits, man is not contemplatively detached from them. They involve him in his perplexities and troubles, and are the source of his joys and achievements. The situation is not indifferent to man, because it forms man as a desiring, striving, thinking, feeling creature. It is not egotism that leads man from contemplative registration of these traits to interest in managing them, to intelligence and purposive art. Interest, thinking, planning, striving, consummation and frustration are a drama enacted by these forces and conditions. A particular choice may be arbitrary; this is only to say that it does not approve itself to reflection. But choice is not arbitrary, not in a universe like this one, a world which is not finished and which has not consistently made up its mind where it is going and what it is going to do. Or, if we call it arbitrary, the arbitrariness is not ours but that of existence itself. And to call existence arbitrary or by any moral name, whether disparaging or honorific, is to patronize nature. To assume an attitude of condescension toward existence is perhaps a natural human compensation for the straits of life. But it is an ultimate source of the covert, uncandid and cheap in philosophy. This compensatory disposition it is which forgets that reflection exists to guide choice and effort. Hence its love of wisdom is but an unlaborious transformation of existence by dialectic, instead of an opening and enlarging of the ways of nature in man. A true wisdom, devoted to the latter task, discovers in thoughtful observation and experiment the method of administering the unfinished processes of existence so that frail goods shall be substantiated, secure goods be extended, and the precarious promises of good that haunt experienced things be more liberally fulfilled.

3. Nature, Ends and Histories

Human experience in the large, in its coarse and conspicuous features, has for one of its most striking features preoccupation with direct enjoyment: feasting and festivities, ornamentation, dance, song, dramatic pantomime, telling yarns and enacting stories. In comparison with intellectual and moral endeavor, this trait of experience has hardly received the attention from philosophers that it demands. Even philosophers who have conceived that pleasure is the sole motive of man and the attainment of happiness his whole aim, have given a curiously sober, drab, account of the working of pleasure and the search for happiness. Consider the utilitarians how they toiled, spun and wove, but who never saw man arrayed in joy as the lilies of the field. Happiness was to them a matter of calculation and effort, of industry guided by mathematical book-keeping. The history of man shows however that man takes his enjoyment neat, and at as short range as possible.

Direct appropriations and satisfactions were prior to anything but the most elementary and exigent prudence, just as the useful arts preceded the sciences. The body is decked before it is clothed. While homes are still hovels, temples and palaces are embellished. Luxuries prevail over necessities except when necessities can be festally celebrated. Men make a game of their fishing and hunting, and turn to the periodic and disciplinary labor of agriculture only when inferiors, women and slaves, cannot be had to do the work. Useful labor is, whenever possible, transformed by ceremonial and ritual accompaniments, subordinated to art that yields immediate enjoyment; otherwise it is attended to under the compulsion of circumstance during abbreviated surrenders of leisure. For leisure permits of festivity, in revery, ceremonies and conversation. The pressure of necessity is, however, never wholly lost, and the sense of it led men, as if with uneasy conscience at their respite from work, to impute practical efficacy to play and rites, endowing them with power to coerce events and to purchase the favor of rulers of events.

But it is possible to magnify the place of magical exercise and superstitious legend. The primary interest lies in staging the show and enjoying the spectacle, in giving play to the ineradicable interest in stories which illustrate the contingencies of existence combined with happier endings for emergencies than surrounding conditions often permit. It was not conscience that kept men loyal to cults and rites, and faithful to tribal myths. So far as it was not routine, it was enjoyment of the drama of life without the latter's liabilities that kept piety from decay. Interest in rites as means of influencing the course of things, and the cognitive or explanation office of myths were hardly more than an embroidery, repeating in pleasant form the pattern which inexpugnable necessities imposed upon practice. When rite and myth are spontaneous rehearsal of the impact and career of practical needs and doings, they must also seem to have practical force. The political significance of July Fourth, 1776, is perhaps renewed by the juvenile celebrations of Independence Day, but this effect hardly accounts for the fervor of the celebration. Any excuse serves for a holiday and the more the holiday is decked out with things that contrast with the pressure of workaday life while re-enacting its form, the more a holiday it is. The more unrestrained the play of fancy the greater the contrast. The supernatural has more thrills than the natural, the customary; holidays and holy-days are indistinguishable. Death is an occasion for a wake, and mourning is acclaimed with a board of funeral meats.

Reflected upon, this phase of experience manifests objects which are final. The attitude involved in their appreciation is esthetic. The operations entering into their production is fine art, distinguished from useful art. It is dangerous however to give names, especially in discourse that is far aloof from the things named—direct enjoyment of the interplay of the contingent and the effective, purged of practical risks and penalties. Esthetic, fine art, appreciation, drama have an eulogistic flavor. We hesitate to call the penny-dreadful of fiction artistic, so we call it debased fiction or a travesty on art. Most sources of direct enjoyment for the masses are not art to the cultivated, but perverted art, an unworthy indulgence. Thus we miss the point. A passion of anger, a dream, relaxation of the limbs after effort, swapping of jokes, horse-play, beating of drums, blowing of tin whistles, explosion of firecrackers and walking on stilts, have the same quality of immediate and absorbing finality that is possessed by things and acts dignified by the title of esthetic. For man is more preoccupied with enhancing life than with bare living; so that a sense of living when it attends labor and utility is borrowed not intrinsic, having been generated in those periods of relief when activity was dramatic.

To say these things is only to say that man is naturally more interested in consummations than he is in preparations; and that consummations have first to be hit upon spontaneously and accidentally—as the baby gets food and all of us are warmed by the sun—before they can be objects of foresight, invention and industry. Consciousness so far as it is not dull ache and torpid comfort is a thing of the imagination. The extensions and transformations of existence generated in imagination may come at last to attend work so as to make it significant and agreeable. But when men are first at the height of business, they are too busy to engage either in fancy or reflective inquiry. At the outset the hunt was enjoyed in the feast, or in the calm moments of shaping spears, bows and arrows. Only later was the content of these experiences carried over into hunting itself, so that even its dangers might be savored. Labor, through its structure and order, lends play its pattern and plot; play then returns the loan with interest to work, in giving it a sense of beginning, sequence and climax. As long as imagined objects are satisfying, the logic of drama, of suspense, thrill and success, dominates the logic of objective events. Cosmogonies are mythological not because savages indulge in defective scientific explanations, but because objects of imagination are consummatory in the degree in which they exuberantly escape from the pressure of natural surroundings, even when they re-enact its crises. The congenial is first form of the consistent.

As Goldenweiser says, if supernaturalism prevails in early culture it is largely because, "the phantasmagoria of supernaturalism is aesthetically attractive, it has beauty of thought and form and of movement, it abounds in delightful samples of logical coherence, and is full of fascination for the creator, the systematizer and the beholder." And it is safe to add, that the esthetic character of logical coherence rather than its tested coherence with fact is that which yields the delight. Again speaking of the place of ceremonialism in early culture, Goldenweiser well characterizes it as a kind of "psychic incandescence"; because of its presence, there is "no cooling of the ever glowing mass [the conglomerate of customs], no flagging of the emotions, no sinking of the cultural associations to the more precarious level of purely ideational connections."

Modern psychiatry as well as anthropology have demonstrated the enormous role of symbolism in human experience. The word symbolism, however, is a product of reflection upon direct phenomena, not a description of what happens when so-called symbols are potent. For the feature which characterizes symbolism is precisely that the thing which later reflection calls a symbol is not a symbol, but a direct vehicle, a concrete embodiment, a vital incarnation. To find its counterpart we should betake ourselves not to signal flags which convey information, ideas and direction, but to a national flag in moments of intense emotional stir of a devout patriot. Symbolism in this sense dominates not only all early art and cult but social organization as well. Rites, designs, patterns are all charged with a significance which we may call mystic, but which is immediate and direct to those who have and celebrate them. Be the origin of the totem what it may, it is not a cold, intellectual sign of a social organization; it is that organization made present and visible, a centre of emotionally charged behavior. It is not otherwise with the symbolism uncovered in dreams and neurotic states by psychological analysis. Such symbols are not indicative or intellectual signs; they are condensed substitutes of actual things and events, which embody actual things with more direct and enhanced import than do the things themselves with their distractions, impositions, and irrelevances. Meanings are intellectually distorted and depressed, but immediately they are heightened and concentrated.

Jespersen speaks of the origin of language in similar terms. He says that many linguistic philosophers appear to "imagine our primitive ancestors after their own image as serious and well-meaning men, endowed with a large share of common-sense. . . . They leave you with the impression that these first framers of speech were sedate citizens with a strong interest in the purely business and matter-of-fact aspects of life." But Jespersen finds that the prosaic side of early culture was capable only "of calling forth short monosyllabic interjections; they are the most immutable portions of language, and remain now at essentially the same stand-point as thousands of years ago." He concludes that the "genesis of language is found . . . in the poetic side of life; the source of speech is not gloomy seriousness, but merry play and youthful hilarity." And no one would deny, I suppose, that literature rather than business and science has developed and fixed our present linguistic resources.

It would be difficult to find a fact more significant of the traits of nature, more instructive for a naturalistic metaphysics of existence, than this cleavage of the things of human experience into actual but hard objects, and enjoyed but imagined objects. One might think that philosophers in their search for some datum that possesses properties that put it beyond doubt, might have directed their attention to this direct phase of experience, in which objects are not a matter of sensations, ideas, beliefs or knowledge, but are something had and enjoyed. All that "self-evidence" can intelligibly mean is obviousness of presence; commonplaces like human interest in the things of sport and celebration are the most conspicuously obvious of all. In comparison, the "self-evident" things of philosophers are recondite and technical.

The other most self-evident thing in experience is useful labor and its coercive necessity. As direct appreciative enjoyment exhibits things in their consummatory phase, labor manifests things in their connections of things with one another, in efficiency, productivity, furthering, hindering, generating, destroying. From the standpoint of enjoyment a thing is what it directly does for us. From that of labor a thing is what it will do to other things—the only way in which a tool or an obstacle can be defined. Extraordinary and subtle reasons have been assigned for belief in the principle of causation. Labor and the use of tools seem, however, to be a sufficient empirical reason: indeed, to be the only empirical events that can be specifically pointed to in this connection They are more adequate grounds for acceptance of belief in causality than are the regular sequences of nature or than a category of reason, or the alleged fact of will. The first thinker who proclaimed that every event is effect of something and cause of something else, that every particular existence is both conditioned and condition, merely put into words the procedure of the workman, converting a mode of practice into a formula. External regularity is familiar, customary, taken for granted, not thought of, embodied in thoughtless routine. Regularity, orderly sequence, in productive labor presents itself to thought as a controlling principle. Industrial arts are the type-forms of experience that bring to light the sequential connections of things with one another.

In contrast, the enjoyment (with which suffering is to be classed) of things is a declaration that natural existences are not mere passage ways to another passage way, and so on *ad infinitum*. Thinkers interested in esthetic experience are wont to point out the absurdity of the idea that things are good or valuable only for something else; they dwell on the fact vouchsafed by esthetic appreciation that there are things that have their goodness or value in themselves, which are not cherished for the sake of anything else. These philosophers usually confine this observation however to human affairs isolated from nature, which they interpret exclusively in terms of labor, or causal connections. But in every event there is something obdurate, self-sufficient, wholly immediate, neither a relation nor an element in a relational whole, but terminal and exclusive. Here, as in so many other matters, materialists and idealists agree in an underlying metaphysics which ignores in behalf of relations and relational systems, those irreducible, infinitely plural, undefinable and indescribable qualities which a thing must *have* in order to be, and in order to be capable of becoming the subject of relations and a theme of discourse. Immediacy of existence is ineffable. But there is nothing mystical about such ineffability; it expresses the fact that of direct existence it is futile to say anything to one's self and impossible to say anything to another. Discourse can but intimate connections which if followed out may lead one to *have* an existence. Things in their immediacy are unknown and unknowable, not because they are remote or behind some impenetrable veil of sensation or ideas, but because knowledge has no concern with them. For knowledge is a memorandum of conditions of their appearance, concerned, that is, with sequences, coexistences, relations. Immediate things may be *pointed to* by words, but not described or defined. Description when it occurs is but a part of a circuitous method of pointing or denoting; index to a starting point and road which if taken may lead to a direct and ineffable presence. To the empirical thinker, immediate enjoyment and suffering are the conclusive exhibition and evidence that nature has its finalities as well as its relationships.

Many modern thinkers, influenced by the notion that knowledge is the only mode of experience that grasps things, assuming the ubiquity of cognition, and noting that immediacy or qualitative existence has no place in authentic science, have asserted that qualities are always and only states of consciousness. It is a reasonable belief that there would be no such thing as "consciousness" if events did not have a phase of brute and unconditioned "isness," of being just what they irreducibly are. Consciousness as sensation, image and emotion is thus a particular case of immediacy occurring under complicated conditions. And also without immediate qualities those relations with which science deals would have no footing in existence and thought would have nothing beyond itself to chew upon or dig into. Without a basis in qualitative events, the characteristic subject-matter of knowledge would be algebraic ghosts, relations that do not relate. To dispose of things in which relations terminate by calling them elements, is to discourse within a relational and logical scheme. Only if elements are more than just elements in a whole, only if they have something qualitatively their own, can a relational system be prevented from complete collapse.

The Greeks were more naïve than we are. Their thinkers were as much dominated by the esthetic characters of experienced objects as modern thinkers are by their scientific and economic (or relational) traits. Consequently they had no difficulty in recognizing the importance of qualities and of things inherently closed or final. They thought of mind as a realization of natural existence or a participation in it. Thus they were saved from the epistemological problem of how things and mind, defined antithetically, can have anything to do with each other. If existence in its immediacies could speak it would proclaim, "I may *have* relatives but *I* am not related." In esthetic objects, that is in all

immediately enjoyed and suffered things, in things directly possessed, they thus speak for themselves; Greek thinkers heard
their voice.

Unfortunately however, these thinkers were not content to
speak as artists, of whom they had a low opinion. Since they
were thinkers, aiming at truth or knowledge, they put art on a
lower plane than science; and the only enjoyment they found
worth serious attention was that of objects of thought. In consequence they formulated a doctrine in which the esthetic and the
rational are confused on principle, and they bequeathed the confusion as an intellectual tradition to their successors. Aristotle
spoke more truly than he was aware when he said that philosophy began in leisure "when almost all the necessaries and things
that make for comfort and recreation were present." For it was
philosophic, rather than scientific "knowledge" which thus began. Philosophy was a telling of the story of nature after the style
of all congenial stories, a story with a plot and climax, given such
coherent properties as would render it congenial to minds demanding that objects satisfy logical canons.

Objects are certainly none the worse for having wonder and
admiration for their inspiration and art for their medium. But
these objects are distorted when their affiliation with the epic,
temple and drama is denied, and there is claimed for them a
rational and cosmic status independent of piety, drama and
story. In the classic philosophy of Greece the picture of the world
that was constructed on an artistic model proffered itself as
being the result of intellectual study. A story composed in the
interests of a refined type of enjoyment, ordered by the needs of
consistency in discourse, or dialectic, became cosmology and
metaphysics. Its authors took toward art and rite much the same
sort of superior attitude that the modern esthete takes to vulgar
forms of esthetic satisfaction. A claim for superiority in
subject-matter and mode of artistic treatment was indeed legitimate; but a claim was made for difference in kind. Art was an
embellished imitation of the everyday or empirical affairs of life
in their natural setting; philosophy was science, an envisagement
of realities behind all copies, all phenomena; or a grasp of essences within them forming their valid substance. The delight
attending the insight was attributed to the final intrinsic dignity
of the cosmic objects perceived by reason, instead of being

frankly recognized to be due to a selection and arrangement of things with a view to enhancement of tranquil enjoyment.

Devotion to rites, stories and revery springs on its magical side from practical desire to control the contingent; but in larger measure it embodies the happiness that attends the sense of successful issue from the uncertainly hazardous. Imagination is primarily dramatic, rather than lyric, whether it takes the form of the play enacted on the stage, of the told story or silent soliloquy. The constant presence of instability and trouble gives depth and poignancy to the situations in which are pictured their subordination to final issues possessed of calm and certainty. To re-enact the vicissitudes, crises and tragedies of life under conditions that deprive them of their overt dangers, is the natural role of "consciousness," which is tamed to respect actualities only when circumstance enforces the adoption of the method of labor, a discipline that is fortunate if it retain some of the liberation from immediate exigencies which characterizes dramatic imagination.

Modern critics of esthetics have criticized the conception of Plato and Aristotle that art is imitation. But in its original statement, this conception was a description of the observed facts of drama, music and epic rather than theoretical interpretation. For these thinkers were not so stupid as to hold that art is an imitation of inert things; they held that it was a mimesis of the critical and climactic behavior of natural forces within human career and destiny. Such a reproduction is naturally in a new and liberal medium; it permits idealization, but the idealization is of natural events. It is self-sufficing, an end in itself, while the events seem to exist only to render the perfection of an idealized reproduction possible and pertinent. Resort to esthetic objects is the spontaneous human escape and consolation in a trying and difficult world. A world that consisted entirely of stable objects directly presented and possessed would have no esthetic qualities; it would just be, and would lack power to satisfy and to inspire. Objects are actually esthetic when they turn hazard and defeat to an issue which is above and beyond trouble and vicissitude. Festal celebration and consummatory delights belong only in a world that knows risk and hardship.

Greek philosophy as well as Greek art is a memorial of the joy in what is finished, when it is found amid a world of unrest, struggle, and uncertainty in what, since it is ended, does not commit us to the uncertain hazards of what is still going on. Without such experiences as those of Greek art it is hardly conceivable that the craving for the passage of change into rest, of the contingent, mixed and wandering into the composed and total, would have found a model after which to design a universe like the cosmos of Platonic and Aristotelian tradition. Form was the first and last word of philosophy because it had been that of art; form is change arrested in a prerogative object. It conveys a sense of the imperishable and timeless, although the material in which it is exemplified is subject to decay and contingency. It thus conveys an intimation of potentialities completely actualized in a happier realm, where events are not events, but are arrested and brought to a close in an eternal self-sustaining activity. Such a realm is intrinsically one of secure and self-possessed meaning. It consists of objects of immediate enjoyment hypostatized into transcendent reality. Such was the conversion of Greek esthetic contemplation effected by Greek reflection.

The technical structure of the resulting metaphysics is familiar. The cosmically real is one with the finished, the perfect, or wholly done. Even with Aristotle, a coldly defining theory, called metaphysics, of the traits of Being, becomes a theology, or science of ultimate and eternal reality to which only ecstatic predicates are attributable. It consists of pure forms, self-sufficient, self-enclosed and self-sustaining; self-movement or life at eternal full-tide. Forms are ideal, and the ideal is the rational apprehended by reason. The material for this point of view was found empirically in what is consummatory and final; and the dominion exercised by art in Greek culture fostered and enhanced attention to objects of this immediately enjoyed kind. To the spectator, artistic objects are given; they need only to be envisaged; Greek reflection, carried on by a leisure class in the interest of liberalizing leisure, was preeminently that of the spectator, not that of the participator in processes of production. Labor, production, did not seem to create form, it dealt with matter or changing things so as to furnish an occasion for incarnation of antecedent forms in matter. To artisans form is alien, unperceived and unenjoyed; absorbed in laboring with material, they live in a world of change and matter, even when their labors have an end in manifestation of form. Plato was so troubled by the consequences of this ignorance of form on the part of all who live in the world of practice, industrial and political, that he elaborated a plan by which their activities might be regulated by those who, above labor and entanglement in change and practice, provide in laws forms to shape the habits of those who work. Aristotle escaped the dilemma by putting nature above art, and endowing nature with skilled purpose that for the most part achieves ends or completions. Thus the role of the human artisan whether in industry or politics became relatively negligible, and the miscarriages of human art a matter of relative insignificance.

The Aristotelian conception of four-fold "causation" is openly borrowed from the arts, which for the artisan are utilitarian and menial, and are "fine" or liberal only for the cultivated spectator who is possessed of leisure—that is, is relieved from the necessity of partaking laboriously in change and matter. Nature is an artist that works from within instead of from without. Hence all change, or matter, is potentiality for finished objects. Like other artists, nature first possesses the forms which it afterwards embodies. When arts follow fixed models, whether in making shoes, houses, or dramas, and when the element of individual invention in design is condemned as caprice, forms and ends are necessarily external to the individual worker. They preceded any particular realization. Design and plan are anonymous and universal, and carry with them no suggestion of a designing, purposive mind. Models are objectively given and have only to be observed and followed. Thus there was no difficulty, such as one may feel to-day, in ascribing definite and regulative forms to the changes of nature, which are actualized in objects that are finalities, closures of change. The actualization in an organic body of the forms that are found in things constitutes mind as the end of nature. Their immediate possession and celebration constitutes consciousness, as far as the idea of consciousness is found in Greek thought.

This doctrine was not an arbitrary speculation; it flowed naturally from the fact that Greek thinkers were fortunate to find ready-made to hand and eye a realm of esthetic objects with traits of order and proportion, form and finality. The arts were pursued upon the basis of a fund of realized, objective and impersonal designs and plans, which were prior to individual devising and execution rather than products of individual purpose and invention. The philosophers did not create out of their own speculations, the idea of materials subdued to the acceptance and manifestation of objective forms. They found the fact in the art of their period, translating it into an intellectual formula. Philosophers were not the authors of an identification of objects informed with ideal order and proportion with a final and arresting outcome of processes of antecedent change. That identification was at least implicit in the operation of artisans. Nor were the philosophers the originators of the idea that mental appropriation of some objects is intrinsically a state of elevated satisfaction. That fact was given to them in the esthetic culture of their civilization. What the philosophers are responsible for is a peculiar one-sided interpretation of these empirical facts, an interpretation, however, which has its roots in features, although less admirable ones, of Greek culture.

For the Greek community was marked by a sharp separation of servile workers and free men of leisure, which meant a division between acquaintance with matters of fact and contemplative appreciation, between unintelligent practice and unpractical intelligence, between affairs of change and efficiency—or instrumentality—and of rest and enclosure—finality. Experience afforded therefore no model for a conception of experimental inquiry and of reflection efficacious in action. In consequence, the sole notability, intelligibility, of nature was conceived to reside in objects that were ends, since they set limits to change. Changing things were not capable of being known on the basis of relationship to one another, but only on the basis of their relationship to objects beyond change, because marking its limit, and immediately precious. The terminal objects lent changing objects the properties which made them knowable; such stability of character as they possessed was derived from the form of the end-objects toward which they moved. Hence an inherent appetition or nisus toward these terminal and static objects was attributed to them. The whole scheme of cosmic change was a vehicle for attaining ends possessed of properties which caused them to be objects of attraction of all lesser things, rendering the latter uneasy and restless until they attained the end-object which constitutes their real nature. Thus an immediate contemplative possession and enjoyment of objects, dialectically ordered, was interpreted as defining both true knowledge and the highest end and good of nature. A doctrine of morals, of what is better in reflective choice, was thus converted into a metaphysics and science of Being, the moral aspect being disguised to the modern mind by the fact that the highest good was conceived esthetically, instead of in the social terms which upon the whole dominate modern theories of morality.

The doctrine that objects as ends are the proper objects of science, because they are the ultimate forms of real being, met its doom in the scientific revolution of the seventeenth century. Essences and forms were attacked as occult; "final causes" were either wholly denied or relegated to a divine realm too high for human knowledge. The doctrine of natural ends was displaced by a doctrine of designs, ends-in-view, conscious aims constructed and entertained in individual minds independent of nature. Descartes, Spinoza and Kant are upon this matter at least in agreement with Bacon, Hume and Helvétius. The imputation to natural events of cosmic appetition towards ends, the notion that their changes were to be understood as efforts to reach a natural state of rest and perfection, were indicated as the chief source of sterility and fantasy in science; the syllogistic logic connected with the doctrine was discarded as verbal, polemical, and at its best irrelevant to the subtle operations of nature; purpose and contingency were alike relegated to the purely human and personal; nature was evacuated of qualities and became a homogeneous mass differentiated by differences of homogeneous motion in a homogeneous space. Mechanical relations, which Greek thought had rejected as equivalent to the chaotic reign of pure accident, became the head corner-stone of the conception of law, of uniformity and order. If ends were recognized at all, it was only under the caption of design, and design was defined as conscious aim rather than as objective order and architectonic form. Wherever the influence of modern physics penetrated, the classic theory became remote, faded, factitious, with its assertion that natural changes are inherent movements toward objects which are their fulfillments or perfections, so that the latter are true objects of knowledge, supplying the forms or characters under which alone changes may be known. With the decay of this doctrine, departed also belief in cosmic qualitative differences and kinds, so that of necessity quality and immediacy had no recourse, expelled from objective nature, save to take refuge in personal consciousness.

Is this reversal of classic theories of existence inevitable? Must belief in ends involved in nature itself be surrendered, or be asserted only by means of a roundabout examination of the nature of knowledge which starting from conscious intent to know, finally infers that the universe is a vast, non-natural fulfillment of a conscious intent? Or is there an ingredient of truth in ancient metaphysics which may be extracted and re-affirmed? Empirically, the existence of objects of direct grasp, possession, use and enjoyment cannot be denied. Empirically, things are poignant, tragic, beautiful, humorous, settled, disturbed, comfortable, annoying, barren, harsh, consoling, splendid, fearful; are such immediately and in their own right and behalf. If we take advantage of the word esthetic in a wider sense than that of application to the beautiful and ugly, esthetic quality, immediate, final or self-enclosed, indubitably characterizes natural situations as they empirically occur. These traits stand in themselves on precisely the same level as colors, sounds, qualities of contact, taste and smell. Any criterion that finds the latter to be ultimate and "hard" data will, impartially applied, come to the same conclusion about the former. *Any* quality as such is final; it is at once initial and terminal; just what it is as it exists. It may be referred to other things, it may be treated as an effect or as a sign. But this involves an extraneous extension and use. It takes us beyond quality in its immediate qualitativeness. If experienced things are valid evidence, then nature in having qualities within itself has what in the literal sense must be called ends, terminals, arrests, enclosures.

It is dangerous to venture at all upon the use of the word "ends" in connection with existential processes. Apologetic and theological controversies cluster about it and affect its signification. Barring this connotation, the word has an almost inexpugnable honorific flavor, so that to assert that nature is characterized by ends, the most conspicuous of which is the life of mind, seems like engaging in an eulogistic, rather than an empirical account of nature. Something much more neutral than any such implication is, however, meant. We constantly talk about things coming or drawing to a close; getting ended, finished, done with, over with. It is a commonplace that no *thing* lasts forever. We may be glad or we may be sorry but that is wholly a matter of the kind of history which is being ended. We may conceive the end, the close, as due to fulfillment, perfect attainment, to satiety, or to exhaustion, to dissolution, to something having run down or given out. Being an end may be indifferently an ecstatic culmination, a matter-of-fact consummation, or a deplorable tragedy. Which of these things a closing or terminal object is, has nothing to do with the property of being an end.

The genuine implications of natural ends may be brought out by considering beginnings instead of endings. To insist that nature is an affair of beginnings is to assert that there is no one single and all-at-once beginning of everything. It is but another way of saying that nature is an affair *of* affairs, wherein each one, no matter how linked up it may be with others, has its *own* quality. It does not imply that every beginning marks an advance or improvement; as we sadly know accidents, diseases, wars, lies and errors, begin. Clearly the fact and idea of beginning is neutral, not eulogistic; temporal, not absolute. And since wherever one thing begins something else ends, what is true of beginnings is true of endings. Popular fiction and drama show the bias of human nature in favor of happy endings, but by being fiction and drama they show with even greater assurance that unhappy endings are natural events.

To minds inured to the eulogistic connotation of ends, such a neutral interpretation of the meaning of ends as has just been set forth may seem to make the doctrine of ends a matter of indifference. If ends are only endings or closings of temporal episodes, why bother to call attention to ends at all, to say nothing of framing a theory of ends and dignifying it with the name of natural teleology? In the degree, however, in which the mind is weaned from partisan and ego-centric interest, acknowledgement of nature as a scene of incessant beginnings and endings, presents itself as the source of philosophic enlightenment. It enables thought to apprehend causal mechanisms and temporal finalities as phases of the same natural processes, instead of as competitors where the gain of one is the loss of the other. Mechanism is the order involved in an historic occurrence, capable of definition in terms of the order which various histories sustain to each other. Thus it is the instrumentality of control of any particular termination since a sequential order involves the last term. The traditional conception of natural ends was to the effect that nature does nothing in vain; the accepted meaning of this phrase was that every change is for the sake of something which does not change, occurring in its behalf. Thus the mind started with a ready-made list of good things or perfections which it was the business of nature to accomplish. Such a view may verbally distinguish between something called efficient causation and something else called final causation. But in effect the distinction is only between the causality of the master who contents himself with uttering an order and the efficacy of the servant who actually engages in the physical work of execution. It is only a way of attributing ultimate causality to what is ideal and mental—the directive order of the master—, while emancipating it from the supposed degradation of physical labor in carrying it out, as well as avoiding the difficulties of inserting an immaterial cause within the material realm. But in a legitimate account of ends as endings, all directional order resides in the sequential order. This no more occurs for the sake of the end than a mountain exists for the sake of the peak which is its end. A musical phrase has a certain close, but the earlier portion does not therefore exist for the sake of the close as if it were something which is done away with when the close is reached. And so a man is not an adult until after he has been a boy, but childhood does not exist for the sake of maturity.

By the nature of the case, causality, however it be defined, consists in the sequential order itself, and not in a last term which as such is irrelevant to causality, although it may, of course be, in addition, an initial term in another sequential order. The view held—or implied—by some "mechanists," which treats an initial term as if it had an inherent generative force which it somehow emits and bestows upon its successors, is all of a piece with the view held by teleologists which implies that an end brings about its own antecedents. Both isolate an event from the history in which it belongs and in which it has its character. Both make a factitiously isolated position in a temporal order a mark of true reality, one theory selecting initial place and the other final place. But in fact causality is another name for the sequential order itself; and since this is an order of a history having a beginning and end, there is nothing more absurd than setting causality over against either initiation or finality.

The same considerations permit a naturalistic interpretation of the ideas of dynamic and static. Every end is as such static; this statement is but a truism; changing into something else, a thing is obviously transitive, not final. Yet the thing which is a close of one history is always the beginning of another, and in this capacity the thing in question is transitive or dynamic. This statement also is tautology, for dynamic does not mean possessed of "force" or capable of emitting it so as to stir up other things and set them in motion; it means simply change in a connected series of events. The traditional view of force points necessarily to something transcendental, because outside of events, whether called God or Will or The Unknowable. So the traditional view of the static points to something fixed and rigid, incapable of change, and therefore also outside the course of things and consequently non-empirical. Empirically, however, there is a history which is a succession of histories, and in which any event is at once both beginning of one course and close of another; is both transitive and static. The phrase constantly in our mouths, "state of affairs," is accurately descriptive, although it makes sheer nonsense in both the traditional spiritual and mechanistic theories. There are no changes that do not enter into an affair, *Res*, and there is no affair that is not bounded and thereby marked off as a state or condition. When a state of affairs is perceived, the perceiving-of-a-state-of-affairs is a further state of affairs. Its subject-matter is a thing in the idiomatic sense of thing, *res*, whether a solar-system, a stellar constellation, or an atom, a diversified and more or less loose interconnection of events, falling within boundaries sufficiently definite to be capable of being approximately traced. Such is the unbiased evidence of experience in gross, and such in effect is the conclusion of recent physics as far as a layman can see. For this reason, and not because of any unique properties of a separate kind of existence, called psychic or mental, every situation or field of consciousness is marked by initiation, direction or intent, and consequence or import. What is unique is not these traits, but the property of awareness or perception. Because of this property, the initial stage is capable of being judged in the light of its probable course and consequence. There is anticipation. Each successive event being a stage in a serial process is both expectant and commemorative. What is more precisely pertinent to our present theme, the terminal outcome when anticipated (as it is when a moving cause of affairs is perceived) becomes an end-in-view, an aim, purpose, a prediction usable as a plan in shaping the course of events. In classic Greek thought, the perception of ends was simply an esthetic contemplation of the forms of objects in which natural processes were completed. In most modern thought, it is an arbitrary creation of private mental operations guided by personal desire, the theoretical alternative being that they are finite copies of the fulfilled intentions of an infinite mind. In empirical fact, they are projections of possible consequences; they are ends-in-view. The in-viewness of ends is as much conditioned by antecedent natural conditions as is perception of *contemporary* objects external to the organism, trees and stones, or whatever. That is, natural processes must have actually terminated in specifiable consequences, which give those processes definition and character, before ends can be mentally entertained and be the objects of striving desire. In so far, we must side with Greek thought. But empirical ends-in-view are distinguished in two important respects from ends as they are conceived in classic thought. They are not objects of contemplative possession and use, but are intellectual and regulative means, degenerating into reminiscences or dreams unless they are employed as plans within the state of affairs. And when they are attained, the objects which they inform are conclusions and fulfillments; *only* as these objects are the consequence of prior reflection, deliberate choice and directed effort are they fulfillments, conclusions, completions, perfections. A natural end which occurs without the intervention of human art is a terminus, a de facto boundary, but it is not entitled to any such honorific status of completions and realizations as classic metaphysics assigned them.

When we regard conscious experience, that is to say, the *object* and *qualities* characteristic of conscious life, as a natural end, we are bound to regard *all* objects impartially as distinctive ends in the Aristotelian sense. We cannot pick or choose; when we do pick and choose we are obviously dealing with practical ends—with objects and qualities that are deemed worthy of selection by reflective, deliberate choice. These "ends" are not the less natural, if we have an eye to the continuity of experienced objects with other natural occurrences, but they are not ends without the intervention of a special affair, reflective survey and choice. But popular thought, in accord with the Greek tradition, picks and chooses among all ends those which it likes and honors, at the same time ignoring and implicitly denying the act of choice. Like those who regard a happy escape from a catastrophe as a providential intervention, neglecting all who have not escaped, popular teleology regards *good* objects as natural ends, *bad* objects and qualities being regarded as mere accidents or incidents, regrettable mechanical excess or defect. Popular teleology like Greek metaphysics, has accordingly been apologetic, justificatory of the beneficence of nature; it has been optimistic in a complacent way.

Primitive man like naïve common sense imputes terminating qualities to nature—in which it follows a sound realistic metaphysics. But it also imputes to them the property of causal determination, an imputation rejected by science. Rejection by science does not prove these qualities to be mere "subjective" or "private" appearances; it only shows that they are termini, closings of serial events. Events that achieve and possess them are linked, mediatory, transitive, indicative, and the proper material of knowledge. From the standpoint of causal sequence, or the order with which science is concerned, qualities are superfluous, irrelevant and immaterial. We could never predict their occurrence from the fullest acquaintance with the properties that form the objects of knowledge as such.

From the standpoint of the latter, the relational orders, ends are abrupt and interruptive. Hence to a philosophy that takes the subject-matter of knowledge to be exclusive and exhaustive—as so much of modern philosophy has done—they form a most perplexing problem, a mystery. For with extrusive and superfluous status they combine the property of being permeating and absorbing. They alone, as we say, are of interest, and they are the cause of taking interest in other things. For living creatures they form the natural platform for regarding other things. They are the basis, directly and indirectly, of active response to things. As compared with them, other things are obstacles and means of procuring and avoiding the occurrence of situations having them. When the word "consciousness" is—as it often is—used for a short name for the sum total of such immediate qualities as actually present themselves, it is the end or terminus of natural events. As such it is also gratuitous, superfluous and inexplicable when reality is defined in terms of the relational objects of science.

By "ends" we also mean ends-in-view, aims, things viewed after deliberation as worthy of attainment and as evocative of effort. They are formed from objects taken in their immediate and terminal qualities; objects once having occurred as endings, but which are not now in existence and which are not likely to come into existence save by an action which modifies surroundings. Classic metaphysics is a confused union of these two senses of ends, the primarily natural and the secondarily natural, or practical, moral. Each meaning is intelligible, grounded, legitimate in itself. But their mixture is one of the Great Bads of philosophy. For it treats as natural ends apart from reflection just those objects that are worthy and excellent to reflective choice. Popular teleology has unknowingly followed the leadings that controlled Greek thought; spiritualistic quasi-theological metaphysics has consciously adopted the latter's point of view.

The features of this confused metaphysics are: First, elimination from the status of natural ends of all objects that are evil and troublesome; Secondly, the grading of objects selected to constitute natural ends into a fixed, unchangeable hierarchical order. Objects that possess and import qualities of struggle, suffering and defeat are regarded not as ends, but as frustrations of ends, as accidental and inexplicable deviations. Theology has resorted to an act of original sin to make their occurrence explicable, Greek metaphysics resorted to the presence in nature of a recalcitrant, obdurate, factor. To this provincially exclusive view of natural termini, popular teleology adds a ranking of objects according to which some are more completely ends than others, until there is reached an object which is only end, never eventful and temporal—*the* end. The hierarchy is explicit in Greek thought: first, and lowest are vegetative ends, normal growth and reproduction; second in rank, come animal ends, locomotion and sensibility; third in rank, are ideal and rational ends, of which the highest is blissful contemplative possession in thought of all the forms of nature. In this gradation, each lower rank while an *end* is also means or preformed condition of higher ends. Empirical things, things of useful arts, belonging to the second class but, affected by an adventitious mixture of thought, are ultimately instrumentalities potential for the life of pure rational possession of ideal objects. Modern teleologies are much less succinct and definite, they agree however in the notion of rows of inferior ends which prepare for and culminate in something which is *the* end.

Such a classificatory enterprise is naturally consoling to those who enjoy a privileged status, whether as philosophers, as saints or scholars, and who wish to justify their special status. But its consoling apologetics should not blind us to the fact that to think of objects as more or less ends is nonsense. They either have immediate and terminal quality; or they do not: quality as such is absolute not comparative. A thing may be of some shade of blue when compared with some quality that is wanted and striven for; but its blue is not itself more nor less blue than blueness, and so with the quality of being terminal and absorbing. Objects may be more or less absorptive and arresting and thus possess degrees of intensity with respect to finality. But this difference of intensity is not, save as subject to reflective choice, a distinction in rank or class of finality. It applies to different tooth-aches as well as to different objects of thought; but it does not apply, inherently, to the difference between a tooth-ache and an ideal object—save that a thing like a tooth-ache is often possessed of greater intensity of finality. If we follow the clew of the latter fact, we shall probably conclude that search for pure and unalloyed finality carries us to inarticulate sensation and overwhelming passion. For such affairs are the best instances of things that are complete in themselves with no outleadings.

If then rational essences or meanings are better objects of contemplation than are seizures by sensory and passionate objects, it is not because the former are fulfillments of higher or more "real" antecedent processes. They are not graded on the basis of being lesser or greater actualizations. It is because they present themselves to reflective appraisal as more worthy to be striven for. And this rational character implies that the *things* which have the better qualities possess also transitiveness, instrumentality, as well as immediacy and finality. They are potential and productive. They lead somewhere, perhaps to other affairs having qualities to be envisaged and deeply meditated. If dialectic were not so esthetically enjoyable to some, it would never have played the role it has played in liberating man from the dominion of sensation and impulse. This shows that the esthetic object may be useful and an useful one esthetic, or that immediacy and efficacy[1] though distinguishable qualities are not disjoined existentially. But it is no reason for making contemplative knowledge or any other particular affair the highest of all natural ends. Whether the given or the deliberately constructed is a better or higher end is not a question of intrinsic quality, but a matter of reflectively determined judgment. It is conceivable that just because certain objects are immediately good, that which secures and extends their occurrence may itself become for reflective choice a supreme immediate good.

History is full of ingratitude. All existences are something more than products; they have qualities of their own and assert independent life. There is something of King Lear's daughters in all offspring. This ingratitude is reproachable only when it turns to deny its ancestry. That Plato and Aristotle should have borrowed from the communal objects of the fine arts, from ceremonies, worship and the consummatory objects of Greek culture, and should have idealized their borrowings into new objects of art is something to be thankful for. That, after having enforced the loan, they spurned the things from which they derived their models and criteria is not so admirable. This lack of piety concealed from them the poetic and religious character of their own constructions, and established in the classic Western philosophic tradition the notions that immediate grasp and incorporation of objects is knowledge; that things are placed in graded reality in accordance with their capacity to afford a cultivated mind such a grasp or beholding; and that the order of reality in Being is coincident with a predetermined rank of Ends.

If we recognize that all qualities directly had in conscious experience apart from use made of them, testify to nature's

---

1. To avoid misapprehension it should perhaps be explicitly stated the term "efficacy" employed here and elsewhere, does not imply an interpretation in terms of the old theory of something engaged in emitting force. It is used purely denotatively; it designates empirical position in a course of affairs having a specifiable ending; its meaning is defined not by any theory, but by such affairs as that to get a fire, a match is applied and that it is applied not to a stone but to paper or shavings. The words agency, instrumentality, causal condition, which appear frequently in these pages are to be similarly translated.

characterization by immediacy and finality, there is ground for unsophisticated recognition of use and enjoyment of things as natural, as belonging to the things as well as to us. *Things* are beautiful and ugly, lovely and hateful, dull and illuminated, attractive and repulsive. Stir and thrill in us is as much theirs as is length, breadth, and thickness. Even the utility of things, their capacity to be employed as means and agencies, is first of all not a relation, but a quality possessed; immediately possessed, it is as esthetic as any other quality. If labor transforms an orderly sequence into a means of attaining ends, this not only converts a casual ending into a fulfillment, but it also gives labor an immediate quality of finality and consummation. Art, even fine art, is long, as well as a joy.

From the standpoint of control and utilization, the tendency to assign superior reality to causes is explicable. A "cause" is not merely an antecedent; it is that antecedent which if manipulated regulates the occurrence of the consequent. This is why the sun rather than night is the causal condition of day. Knowing that consequences will take care of themselves if conditions can be had and managed, an ineradicable natural pragmatism indulges in a cheap and short conversion, and conceives the cause as intrinsically more primary and necessary. This practical tendency is increased by the fact that time is a softener and dignifier; present troubles lose their acuteness when they are no longer present. Old times are proverbially the good old times, and history begins with a Garden of Paradise or a Golden Age. Good, being congenial, is held to be normal; and what is suffered is a deviation, creating the problem of evil. Thus the earlier gets moral dignity as well as practical superiority. But in existence, or metaphysically, cause and effect are on the same level; they are portions of one and the same historic process, each having immediate or esthetic quality and each having efficacy, or serial connection. Since existence is historic it can be known or understood only as each portion is distinguished and related. For knowledge "cause" and "effect" alike have a partial and truncated being. It is as much a part of the real being of atoms that they give rise in time, under increasing complication of relationships, to qualities of blue and sweet, pain and beauty, as that they have at a cross-section of time extension, mass, or weight.

The problem is neither psychological nor epistemological. It is metaphysical or existential. It is whether existence consists of events, or is possessed of temporal quality, characterized by beginning, process and ending. If so, the affair of later and earlier, however important it is for particular practical matters, is indifferent to a theory of valuation of existence. It is as arbitrary to assign complete reality to atoms at the expense of mind and conscious experience as it is to make a rigid separation between here and there in space. Distinction is genuine and for some purpose necessary. But it is not a distinction of kinds or degrees of reality. Space here is joined to space there, and events then are joined to events now; the reality is as much in the joining as in the distinction. In order to control the course of events it is indispensable to know their conditions. But to characterize the conditions, it is necessary to have followed them to some term, which is not fully followed till we arrive at something enjoyed or suffered, had and used, in conscious experience. Vital and conscious events exhibit actualization of properties that are not fully displayed in the simpler relationships that are by definition termed physical.

Temporal quality is however not to be confused with temporal order. Quality is quality, direct, immediate and undefinable. Order is a matter of relation, of definition, dating, placing and describing. It is discovered in reflection, not directly had and denoted as is temporal quality. Temporal order is a matter of science; temporal quality is an immediate trait of every occurrence whether in or out of consciousness. Every event as such is passing into other things, in such a way that a later occurrence is an integral part of the *character* or *nature* of present existence. An "affair," *Res*, is always at issue whether it concerns chemical change, the emergence of life, language, mind or the episodes that compose human history. Each comes from something else and each when it comes has its own initial, unpredictable, immediate qualities, and its own similar terminal qualities. The later is never just resolved into the earlier. What we call such resolution is merely a statement of the order by means of which we regulate the passage of an earlier into the later. We may explain the traits of maturity by better knowledge of childhood, but maturity is never just infancy plus.

It is not easy to distinguish between ends as *de facto* endings, and ends as fulfillments, and at the same time to bear in mind the connection of the latter with the former. We respond so directly to some objects in experience with intent to preserve and perpetuate them that it is difficult to keep the conception of a thing as terminus free from the element of deliberate choice and endeavor; when we think of it or discourse about it, we introduce connection. Since we turn away from trouble and suffering, since these things are not the objects of choice and effort save in avoidance, it seems forced to call them ends. To name them such appears an impropriety of language. I am quite willing to concede the linguistic point, provided its implications are acknowledged and adhered to. For in this case we are left, apart from a deliberately directed course of events, only with objects immediately used, enjoyed and suffered but having in themselves no claim to the title of ends. Health in this case is not in itself an end of any natural process; much less an end-in-itself. It is an enjoyed good when it happens just as disease is a suffered ill. Similarly, truth of belief and statement is an affair that has the quality of good; but it is not an end just because it is good; it becomes an end only when, because of its goodness, it is actively sought for and reached as a conclusion. On this basis, all ends are ends-in-view; they are no longer ideal as characters of Being, as they were when they were in Greek theory, but are the objects of conscious intent. When achieved in existence they are ends because they are then conclusions attained through antecedent endeavor, just as a post is not a goal in itself, but becomes a goal in relation to a runner and his race. Either we must consistently stick to the equivalence of ends with objectives of conscious endeavor, or admit that all things directly possessed of irreducible and self-sufficing quality, red and blue, pain, solidity, toughness, smoothness and so on through the list, are natural ends.

There is however nothing self-evident, or even clear, in the exclusive identification of ends with ends-in-view and of the latter with psychic states. The identification isolates conscious life from objective nature. It was a particular historic situation that effected the division. Modern science made it clear that nature has no preference for good things over bad things; its mills turn out any kind of grist indifferently. If Greek thought had contented itself with asserting that all immediacy of existence has a certain ultimacy and finality, a certain incommensurability and incommutability, if it had cited conscious experience as a striking instance of the indifference of natural processes to termini of good and evil, modern science would have had no destructive impact upon the doctrine of natural ends. It would rather have added resourcefulness to this doctrine. In explicit discovery of just the conditions antecedent to this good and that bad, it puts in our hands means of regulating the occurrence of things possessed of these qualities. But discovery of the indifference of natural energies to the production of good and bad endings, and the discovery of the overlapping and intermixture of processes leading to different outcomes, so completely overthrew the classic doctrine of ends, that it seemed to abolish any and every conception of natural ends. The logical result was to cut off "consciousness," as the collectivity of immediate qualities, from nature, and to create the dualism of physical nature and mind which is the source of modern epistemological problems.

A reconsideration of the theory of natural termini, is in historic sequel necessary to a correct envisagement of the connection of conscious life with nature. "Consciousness" in one of its many significations, is identical with direct apparition, obvious and vivid presence of qualities and of meanings. Take these apparitions as something else than emphatic characters of natural events and physical events, and objects become themselves remote and uncertain in existence arrived at only through the mediation of consciousness. Moreover, while quality is immediate and absolute, any particular quality is notoriously unstable and transitory. Immediate objects are the last word of evanescence. Consciousness, in the sense just indicated, is flux in which nothing abides. Persistence, "substance" is found only in some unapproachable things, which have to be invoked to supply this flux with a substratum and locus. Thus we are confronted with the perplexing riddles familiar in epistemological theory. It suffices at this time to note but one. The realm of immediate qualities contains everything of worth and significance. But it is uncertain, unstable and precarious. The first consideration induces us to prize consciousness supremely; the second leads us to deny reality to it as compared with alleged underlying things with their fixity and permanence. Since immediate qualities come and go without inherent rhyme and reason, since life is more unstable than inanimate things and conscious life is even more evanescent than life physiologically considered, since the coming and going of immediate qualities is susceptible of regulation only through the medium of things out of consciousness, "consciousness" becomes an anomaly. "Matter" as a complex of indirect, not immediately given, and in some sense unknowable, things becomes alone real and solid.

If we discount practical bias toward the regular and repeated, and hence toward "causes" as opposed to consequences, all that is indicated by the transiency of immediate qualitative affairs is that immediacy is immediacy. By the nature of the case the occurrence of the immediate is at the mercy of the sequential order. In the case of the things which appeal to common sense as substances, properties like mass and inertia, unchanged solidity and extension, count most. Rate of change is slow, and presents itself as a matter of attrition and accumulation; spatial qualities which are static chiefly figure. Time is of comparative indifference to the change of solid substances; a million years is a day. But whatever depends for its existence upon the interaction of a large number of independent variables is in unstable equilibrium; its rate of change is rapid; successive qualities have no obvious connection with one another; any shift of any part may alter the whole pattern. Thus, while light and water are "substances," a rainbow, depending upon a highly specialized conjunction of light and vapor, and being transient, is only a "phenomenon." Such immediate qualities as red and blue, sweet and sour, tone, the pleasant and unpleasant, depend upon an extraordinary variety and complexity of conditioning events; hence they are evanescent. They are never exactly reduplicated, because the exact combination of events of which they are termini does not precisely recur. Hence they are even more "phenomenal" than a rainbow; they must be hitched to substance as its "modes" to get standing in "reality."

Thus the things that are most precious, that are final, being just the things that are unstable and most easily changing, seem to be different in kind from good, solid, old-fashioned substance. Matter has turned out to be nothing like as lumpy and chunky as unimaginative prejudice conceived it to be. But as compared with the changes of immediate qualities it seems in any case solid and substantial; a fact which accounts, I suppose, for the insertion of an immaterial sort of substance, after the analogy of matter-substance, underneath mental affairs. But when it is recognized that the latter are eventual and consummatory to highly complicated interactions of natural events, their transiency becomes itself intelligible; it is no ground of argument for a radical difference from the physical, the latter being also resolvable into a character of the course of events. While "consciousness" as the conspicuous and vivid presence of immediate qualities and of meanings, is alone of direct worth, things not immediately present, whose intrinsic qualities are not directly had, are primary from the standpoint of control. For just because the things that are directly had are both precious and evanescent, the only thing that can be thought of is the conditions under which they are had. The common, pervasive and repeated *is* of superior rank from the standpoint of safeguarding and buttressing the having of terminal qualities. Directly we can do nothing with the latter save have, enjoy and suffer them. So reflection is concerned with the order which conditions, prevents and secures their occurrence. The irony of many historic systems of philosophy is that they have so inverted the actualities of the case. The general, recurrent and extensive has been treated as the worthy and superior kind of Being; the immediate, intensive, transitory, and qualitatively individualized taken to be of importance only when it is imputed to something ordinary, which is all the universal can denotatively mean. In truth, the universal and stable are important because they are the instrumentalities, the efficacious conditions, of the occurrence of the unique, unstable and passing.

The system which Aristotle bequeathed to the modern world through Latin Christianity expresses the consequences of taking the universal which is instrumental, as if it were final. Actually, consummatory objects instead of being a graded series of numerable and unalterable species or kinds of existence ranked under still fewer genera, are infinitely numerous, variable and individualized affairs. Poets who have sung of despair in the midst of prosperity, and of hope amid darkest gloom, have been the true metaphysicians of nature. The glory of the moment and its tragedy will surely pass. The contingent, uncertain and incomplete give depth and scope to consummatory objects while things not directly had, things approachable only through reflective imagination and rational constructions are the conditions of such regulation of their occurrence as is feasible.

The richer and fuller are the terminal qualities of an object the more precarious is the latter, because of its dependence upon a greater diversity of events. At the best, therefore, control is partial and experimental. All prediction is abstract and hypothetical. Given the stability of other events, and it follows that certain conditions, selected in thought, determine the predictability of the occurrence of say, red. But since the other conditions do not remain unalterably put, what actually occurs is never just what happens in thought; the thing of mere redness does not happen, but some thing with just this shade and tinge of red, in just this unduplicable content. Thus something unpredictable, spontaneous, unformulable and ineffable is found in any terminal object. Standardizations, formulae, generalizations, principles, universals, have their place, but the place is that of being instrumental to better approximation to what is unique and unrepeatable.

We owe to Romanticism the celebration of this fact; no fact apparently being fully discovered and communicated save as it is too much celebrated. Aversion to Romanticism as a system is quite justifiable; but even an obnoxious system may hit upon a truth unknown to soberer schemes. Call the facts romantic or by some sweeter sounding name, and it still remains true that immediate and terminal qualities (whether or not called consciousness) form an unpredictable and unformulable flow of immediate, shifting, impulsive, adventured finalities, with respect to which the universal and regular objects and principles celebrated in classic thought are instrumental.

Perhaps we may prudently close this chapter with a reminder. To point out something as a fact is not the same thing as to commend or eulogize the fact. I am not saying that it is a fine and noble thing that whatever is immediately consummatory and precious should be also evanescent and unique, never completely subject to principle and rule. A reporter is not necessarily to blame for the state of things that he reports. The fact hereby reported is so unescapable and so obvious to a candid empiricist that there is no occasion for either eulogy or condemnation. The only question is what is going to be done about the various instances of it which compose our lives, and give them humor and tragedy. The question is urgent for reflection; it is urgent for the most practical of acts in "getting a living," where the need to do something is constantly imperative. Materials used in reflection change even more rapidly than materials employed in meeting hunger and thirst. Their metabolism is at a quicker pace. Genuinely to think of a thing is to think of implications that are no sooner thought of than we are hurried on to *their* implications. There is no rest for the thinker, save in the *process* of thinking. Possibly it is for this reason that reflection upon the whole has been identified in human culture with onerous labor, with the sombre and melancholic. Reverie travels fast, but in reverie the labor of making connections taut and consistent is not involved. Only in circumstances as fortunate as those of ancient Greece does effort to understand become a rich and full delight, so that it may be conceived of not only as an end of nature, but as its end of ends, for the sake of which all else happens.

Participation in this consummatory activity has, however, been confined to a few. Since it was conceived of as an end given spontaneously or "naturally" to a few, not as a practical and reflective conclusion to be achieved, it was concluded that some men are servile by nature, having as sole function to supply the materials which made it possible for other men to indulge in pure theoretical activity, without distraction by the need of making a living. Thus the conception that thought is the final and complete end of nature became a "rationalization" of an existing division of classes in society. The division of men into the thoughtless and the inquiring was taken to be the intrinsic work of nature; in effect it was identical with the division between workers and those enjoying leisure. Philosophers and scientific inquirers became the utmost acme of nature's perfection, being the least dependent upon outward acts and connections.

In a sense, this occurrence of thought and leisurely insight was natural; it happened in the course of natural processes. It was "given." Like any finality it had to be hit upon, achieved without premeditation before it might become an object of reflective choice and endeavor. But when it came to be reflected upon, its terms were misconceived. The conception that contemplative thought is *the* end in itself was at once a compensation for inability to make reason effective in practice, and a means for perpetuating a division of social classes. A local and temporal polity of historical nature became a metaphysics of everlasting being. Thought when it achieves truth may, indeed, be said to fulfill the regularities and universalities of nature; to be their natural end. But its incarnation as an end in some, not others, does not partake of any universality. It is contingent, accidental; its achievement is a rational fulfillment only when it is the product of deliberate arts of politics and education.

Since nothing in nature is exclusively final, rationality is always means as well as end. The doctrine of the universality and necessity of rational ends can be validated only when those in whom the good is actualized employ it as a means to modify conditions so that others may also participate in it, and its universality exist in the course of affairs. The more it is asserted that thought and understanding are "ends in themselves," the more imperative is it that thought should discover why they are realized only in a small and exclusive class. The ulterior problem of thought is to make thought prevail in experience, not just the results of thought by imposing them upon others, but the active process of thinking. The ultimate contradiction in the classic and genteel tradition is that while it made thought universal and necessary and the culminating good of nature, it was content to leave its distribution among men a thing of accident, dependent upon birth, economic, and civil status. Consistent as well as humane thought will be aware of the hateful irony of a philosophy which is indifferent to the conditions that determine the occurrence of reason while it asserts the ultimacy and universality of reason. In as far as qualities of objects are found worthy of finality, the finding must eventuate in arts. Only thereby will thinking and knowing take their full place as events falling within natural processes, not only in their origin but also in their outcome.

4. Nature, Means and Knowledge

No mythology is more familiar than that which tells how labor is due to trespass of man upon divine prerogatives, an act that brought curse upon the earth and woe to man. Because of this primeval rebellion against God, men toil amid thorns to gain an uncertain livelihood, and women bring forth children in pain. The tale is touching evidence that man finds it natural that nature should support his activities, and unnatural that the burden of continued and hard endeavor should be placed upon him. Festivity is spontaneous; labor needs to be accounted for. There is a long distance between the birth of the old legend and the formulation of classic political economy; but the doctrine of the latter that labor which is the source of value signifies cost, onerous sacrifice of present consummation to attainment of later good, expresses the same human attitude.

Yet, in fact, it was not enjoyment of the apple but the enforced penalty of labor that made man as the gods, *knowing* good and evil instead of just having and enjoying them. The exacting conditions imposed by nature, that have to be observed in order that work be carried through to success, are the source of all noting and recording of nature's doings. They supply the discipline that chastens exuberant fancy into respect for the operation of events, and that effects subjection of thought to a pertinent order of space and time. While leisure is the mother of drama, sport and literary spell-binding, necessity is the mother of invention, discovery and consecutive reflection. While at happy junctures the course of extraordinary events may be bound or wheedled by enjoyed rite and ceremony, only work places a conclusive spell upon homely, everyday affairs. Spears, snares, gins, traps, utensils, baskets and webs may have their potency enhanced by adherence to ceremonial design, but the design is never a complete substitute for conformity to the efficacious resistances and adaptations of natural materials. Acumen, shrewdness, inventiveness, accumulation and transmission of information are products of the necessity under which man labors to turn away from absorption in direct having and enjoying, so as to consider things in their active connections as means and as signs. The same need converts immediate emotion irrelevant to everything save its own thrill into ordered interest in the movements and possibilities of natural events. Everything is done to bedeck utilities, instrumentalities, with reminders of consummatory events so as to lessen their burden, but useful arts in return supply ceremonial arts with their materials, appliances and patterns.

Tools, means, agencies are the characteristic thing in industry; such a statement is tautology. By its nature technology is concerned with things and acts in their instrumentalities, not in their immediacies. Objects and events figure in work not as fulfillments, realizations, but in behalf of other things of which they are means and predictive signs. A tool is a particular thing, but it is more than a particular thing, since it is a thing in which a connection, a sequential bond of nature is embodied. It possesses an objective relation as its own defining property. Its perception as well as its actual use takes the mind to other things. The spear suggests the feast not directly but through the medium of other external things, such as the game and the hunt, to which the sight of the weapon transports imagination. Man's bias towards himself easily leads him to think of a tool solely in relation to himself, to his hand and eyes, but its primary relationship is toward other external things, as the hammer to the nail, and the plow to the soil. Only through this objective bond does it sustain relation to man himself and his activities. A tool denotes a perception and acknowledgment of sequential bonds in nature.

Classic philosophy was conceived in wonder, born in leisure and bred in consummatory contemplation. Hence it noted the distinction between objects consummatory or final in the fine arts and instrumental and operative in the industrial. It then employed the distinction to interpret nature in terms of a dialectical physics. Useful arts are *possible* because things have observable efficiencies; but they are *necessary* because of lack, privation, imperfection, Non-being. This deficiency is manifest in sensation and appetite; the very transitiveness of materials which renders them capable of transformation into serviceable forms is evidence that they too lack fullness of Being. Things have potentialities or are instrumental because they are not Being, but rather Being in process of becoming. They lend themselves to operative connections that fulfill them because they are not themselves Real in an adequate sense. This point of view protected Greek thought from that modern onesidedness which conceives tools as mere subjective conveniences. But the safeguard was at the expense of the introduction into nature of a split in Being itself, its division into some things which are inherently defective, changing, relational, and other things which are inherently perfect, permanent, self-possessed. Other dualisms such as that between sensuous appetite and rational thought, between the particular and universal, between the mechanical and the telic, between experience and science, between matter and mind, are but the reflections of this primary metaphysical dualism.

The counterpart of the conversion of esthetic objects into objects of science, into the one, true and good, was the conversion of operative and transitive objects into things which betray absence of full Being. This absence causes their changing instability which is, none the less, after the model of materials of the useful arts, potentially useful for ends beyond themselves. The social division into a laboring class and a leisure class, between industry and esthetic contemplation, became a metaphysical division into things which are mere means and things which are ends. Means are menial, subservient, slavish; and ends liberal and final; things as means testify to inherent defect, to dependence, while ends testify to independent and intrinsically self-sufficing being. Hence the former can never be *known* in themselves but only in their subordination to objects that are final, while the latter can be known in and through themselves by self-enclosed reason. Thus the identification of knowledge with esthetic contemplation and the exclusion from science of trial, work, manipulation and administration of things, comes full circle.

The ingratitude displayed by thinkers to artists who by creation of harmoniously composed objects supplied idealistic philosophy with empirical models of their ultimately real objects, was shown in even greater measure to artisans. The accumulated results of the observations and procedures of farmers, navigators, builders furnished matter-of-fact information about natural events, and also supplied the pattern of logical and metaphysical subordination of change to directly possessed and enjoyed fulfillments. While thinkers condemned the industrial class and despised labor, they borrowed from them the facts and the conceptions that gave form and substance to their own theories. For apart from processes of art there was no basis for introducing the idea of fulfillment, realization, into the notion of end nor for interpreting antecedent operations as potentialities.

Yet we should not in turn exhibit ingratitude. For if Greek thinkers did not achieve science, they achieved the idea of science. This accomplishment was beyond the reach of artist and artisan. For no matter how solid the content of their own observations and beliefs about natural events, that content was bound down to occasions of origin and use. The relations they recognized were of local areas in time and place. Subject-matter underwent a certain distortion when it was lifted out of this context, and placed in a realm of eternal forms. But the idea of knowledge was thereby liberated, and the scheme of logical relationships among existences held up as an ideal of inquiry. Thinking was uncovered as an enterprise having its own objects and procedures; and the discovery of thought as method of methods in all arts added a new dimension to all subsequent experience. It would be an academic matter to try to balance the credit items due to the discovery of thought and of logic as a free enterprise, against the debit consequences resulting from the hard and fast separation of the instrumental and final.

A great change took place in Greek experience between the time of Homer and Hesiod and the fifth century before Christ. The earlier period evinces a gloomy temper of life. The sense of the sovereignty of fortune, largely ill-fortune, is prevalent. The temper is shown by such quotations as the following: "Thus the gods have decided for unhappy mortals that men should live in misery while they themselves live free from suffering." "A thousand woes traverse the abode of man; the earth is gorged with them and the sea filled; day and night bring grief. They come in silence for prudent Zeus has taken away their voice." "Men favored by Hecate have no need for knowledge, memory or effort to achieve success; she acts alone without the assistance of her favorites." Divination of the intent of unseen powers and pious sacrifice are man's only resource, but this is of no avail. Reckon no man happy till after his death. The gods have indeed bestowed arts on man to ameliorate his hard lot, but their issue is uncertain. The end rests with the gods and with fate who rules even the gods, a fate to be neither bribed with offerings nor yet compelled by knowledge and art.

By the days of the Sophists and their great Athenian successors there is marked change in mood. The conditions then existed that have occasioned the myth of Greek serenity. The Sophists taught that man could largely control the fortunes of life by mastery of the arts. No one has exceeded Plato in awareness of present ills. But since they are due to ignorance and opinion, they are remediable, he holds, by adequate knowledge. Philosophy should terminate in an art of social control. The great rival of Plato taught that fortune "is a fantom which men have invented to excuse their own imprudence. Fortune does not easily resist thought and for the most part an instructed and far-seeing soul will attain its goal." In short, arts based on knowledge cooperate with nature and render it amenable to human happiness. The gods recede into twilight. Divination has a powerful competitor. Worship becomes moral. Medicine, war, and the crafts desert the temple and the altar of the patron-god of the guild, as inventions, tools, techniques of action and works multiply.

This period of confident expansion did not endure. It soon gave way; it was succeeded by what Gilbert Murray has so well named the failure of nerve, and a return to the supernatural, philosophy changing from a supreme art into a way of access to the supernatural. Yet the episode even if brief is more than historically significant. It manifests another way open to man in the midst of an uncertain, incomplete and precarious universe; another way, that is, in addition to that of celebrating such moments of respite and festal joy as occur in the troubled life of man. Through instrumental arts, arts of control based on study of nature, objects which are fulfilling and good, may be multiplied and rendered secure. This road after almost two millennia of obscuration and desertion was refound and retaken; its rediscovery marks what we call the modern era. Consideration of the significance of science as a resource in a world of mixed uncertainty, peril, and of uniformity, stability, furnishes us with the theme of this chapter of experience.

That the sciences were born of the arts, the physical sciences of the crafts and technologies of healing, navigation, war and the working of wood, metals, leather, flax and wool; the mental sciences of the arts of political management, is I suppose, an admitted fact. The distinctively intellectual attitude which marks scientific inquiry was generated in efforts at controlling persons and things so that consequences, issues, outcomes would be more stable and assured. The first step away from oppression by immediate things and events was taken when man employed tools and appliances, for manipulating things so as to render them contributory to desired objects. In responding to things not in their immediate qualities but for the sake of ulterior results, immediate qualities are dimmed, while those features which are signs, indices of something else, are distinguished. A thing is more significantly what it makes possible than what it immediately is. The very conception of cognitive meaning, intellectual significance, is that things in their immediacy are subordinated to what they portend and give evidence of. An intellectual sign denotes that a thing is not taken immediately but is referred to something that may come in consequence of it. Intellectual meanings may themselves be appropriated, enjoyed and appreciated; but the character of intellectual meaning is instrumental. Fortunate for us is it that tools and their using can be directly enjoyed; otherwise all work would be drudgery. But this additive fact does not alter the definition of a tool; it remains a thing used as an agency for some concluding event.

The first groping steps in defining spatial and temporal qualities, in transforming purely immediate qualities of local things into generic relationships, were taken through the arts. The finger, the foot, the unit of walking were used to measure space; measurements of weight originated in the arts of commercial exchange and manufacture. Geometry, beginning as agricultural art, further emancipated space from being a localized quality of immediate extensity. But the radically different ways of conceiving geometry found in ancient and in modern science is evidence of the slowness of the process of emancipation of even geometrical forms from direct or esthetic traits. In Greek astronomy the intrinsic qualities of figures always dominated their instrumental significance in inquiry; they were forms to which phenomena had to conform instead of means of indirect measurements. Hardly till our own day did spatial relations get emancipated from esthetic and moral qualities, and become wholly intellectual and relational, abstracted from immediate qualifications, and thereby generalized to their limit.

Anything approaching a history of the growth of recognition of things in their intellectual or instrumental phase is far beyond our present scope. We can only point out some of its net results. In principle the step is taken whenever objects are so reduced from their status of complete objects as to be treated as signs or indications of other objects. Enter upon this road and the time is sure to come when the appropriate object-of-knowledge is stripped of all that is immediate and qualitative, of all that is final, self-sufficient. Then it becomes an anatomized epitome of just and only those traits which are of indicative or instrumental import. Abstraction is not a psychological incident; it is a following to its logical conclusion of interest in those phases of natural existence which are dependable and fruitful signs of other things; which are means of prediction by formulation in terms implying other terms. Self-evidence ceases to be a characteristic trait of the fundamental objects of either sensory or noetic objects. Primary propositions are statements of objects in terms which procure the simplest and completest forming and checking of other propositions. Many systems of axioms and postulates are possible, the more the merrier, since new propositions as consequences are thus brought to light. Genuine science is impossible as long as the object esteemed for its own intrinsic qualities is taken as the object of knowledge. Its completeness, its immanent meaning, defeats its use as indicating and implying.

Said William James, "Many were the ideal prototypes of rational order: teleological and aesthetic ties between things . . . as well as logical and mathematical relations. The most promising of these things at first were of course the richer ones, the more sentimental ones. The baldest and least promising were mathematical ones; but the history of the latter's application is a history of steadily advancing successes, whilst that of the sentimentally richer ones is one of relative sterility and failure. Take those aspects of phenomena which interest you as a human being most . . . and barren are all your results. Call the things of nature as much as you like by sentimental, moral, and aesthetic names, no natural consequences follow from the naming. . . . But when you give the things mathematical and mechanical names and call them just so many solids in just such positions, describing just such paths with just such velocities, all is changed. . . . Your 'things' realize the consequences of the names by which you classed them."[1]

A fair interpretation of these pregnant sentences is that as long as objects are viewed telically, as long as the objects of the truest knowledge, the most real forms of being, are thought of as ends, science does not advance. Objects are possessed and appreciated, but they are not *known*. To know, means that men have become willing to turn away from precious possessions; willing to let drop what they own, however precious, in behalf of a grasp of objects which they do not as yet own. Multiplied and secure ends depend upon letting go existent ends, reducing them to indicative and implying means. The great historic obstacle to science was unwillingness to make the surrender, lest moral, esthetic and religious objects suffer. To large groups of persons, the bald and dry objects of natural science are still objects of fear. The mechanical or mathematical-logical object presents itself as a rival of the ideal and final object. Then philosophy becomes a device for conserving "the spiritual values of the universe" by devices of interpretation which converts the material and mechanical into mind. By means of a dialectic of the implications of the possibility of knowledge, the physical is transformed into something mental, psychic—as if psychic existence were sure to be inherently more ideal than the physical.

The net result of the new scientific method was conception of nature as a mathematical-mechanical object. If modern philosophy, reflecting the tendencies of the new science, abolished final causes from nature, it was because concern with qualitative ends, already existing objects of possession and enjoyment, blocked inquiry, discovery and control, and ended in barren dialectical disputes about definitions and classifications. A candid mind can hardly deny that sensory qualities, colors, moist and dry, hard and soft, light and heavy are genuine natural ends. In them the potentialities of the body are brought into functioning, while the activity of the body thus achieved brings in turn to completion potentialities in nature outside of the body. Nevertheless the

1. James, *Principles of Psychology*, Vol. II, pp. 665–66.

theory that final objects are the appropriate objects of knowledge, in assimilating knowledge to esthetic contemplation had
fatal consequences for science. All natural phenomena had to be
known in terms of qualities. Hot and cold, wet and dry, up and
down, light and heavy were things to know with and by. They
were essential forms, active principles of nature. But Galileo and
his scientific and philosophical followers (like Descartes and
Hobbes) reversed the method by asserting that these sensory
forms are things to be known, challenges to inquiry, problems,
not solutions nor terms of solution. The assertion was a general
one; it necessitated *search* for objects of knowledge. Dependable
material with which to know was found in a different realm of
being; in spatial relations, positions, masses, mathematically defined, and in motion as change of space having direction and
velocity. Qualities were no longer things to do with; they were
things already done, effects, requiring to be known by statement
and description in mathematical and mechanical relations. The
only world which defines and describes and explains was a
world of masses in motion, arranged in a system of Cartesian
coordinates.

When we view experientially this change, what occurs is the
kind of thing that happens in the useful arts when natural
objects, like crude ores, are treated as materials for getting something else. Their character ceases to lie in their immediate qualities, in just what they are and as directly enjoyed. Their character is now representative; some pure metal, iron, copper, etc. is
their essence, which may be extracted as their "true" nature,
their "reality." To get at this reality many existent constituents
have to be got rid of. From the standpoint of the *object*, pure
metal, these things to be eliminated are "false," irrelevant and
obstructive. They stand in the way, and in the existent thing
those qualities are alone significant which indicate the ulterior
objective and which offer means for attaining it.

Modern science represents a generalized recognition and
adoption of the point of view of the useful arts, for it proceeds by
employment of a similar operative technique of manipulation
and reduction. Physical science would be impossible without the
appliances and procedures of separation and combinations of the
industrial arts. In useful arts, the consequence is increase of
power, multiplication of ends appropriated and enjoyed, and an

enlarged and varied flexibility and economy in means used to achieve ends. Metal can be put to thousands of uses, while the crude ore can only be beheld for whatever esthetic qualities it happens to present, or be hurled bodily at game or an enemy. Reduction of natural existences to the status of means thus presents nothing inherently adverse to possessed and appreciated ends, but rather renders the latter a more secure and extensive affair.

Why then has it been so often assumed in modern philosophy that the advance of physical science has created a serious metaphysical problem; namely, that of the relation of a mechanical world as the object of knowledge to ends; the reconciliation of antithetical worlds of description and appreciation? In empirical fact, the advance of mechanistic science has multiplied and diversified ends; has increased wants and satisfactions, and has multiplied and diversified the means of attaining them. Why the problem? There are two historical empirical reasons to be given in answer. In the first place, the Aristotelian metaphysics of potentiality and actuality, of objects consummatory of natural processes, was intricately entangled with an astronomy and physics which had become incredible. It was also entangled with doctrines and institutions in politics and economics which were fast getting out of relationship to current social needs. The simplest recourse was to treat the classic tradition as the Jonah of science and throw it bodily overboard. The method was imperious and impatient, but it served a need. By a single act it relieved scientific inquiries of notions that were hampering, even paralyzing investigation into nature and that were limiting new practices by outworn sanctions.

By itself alone, however, this cause would hardly have created more than a passing historic episode. The reason that rendered the abandonment of any theory of natural ends something more than a gesture of impatient haste lies in the persistence of the classic theory of knowledge. Greek thought regarded possession, contemplation, as the essence of science, and thought of the latter as such a complete possession of reality as incorporates it with mind. The notion of knowledge as immediate possession of Being was retained when knowing as an actual affair radically altered. Even when science had come to include a method of experimental search and finding, it was still defined as insight

into, grasp of, real being as such, in comparison with which
other modes of experience are imperfect, confused and perverted. Hence a serious problem. If the proper object of science is
a mathematico-mechanical world (as the achievements of science
have proved to be the case) and if the object of science defines the
true and perfect reality (as the perpetuation of the classic tradition asserted), then how can the objects of love, appreciation—
whether sensory or ideal—and devotion be included within true
reality?

Efforts to answer this question constitute a large part of the
technical content of modern metaphysical thought. Given the
premises, its import covers almost every thing from the problem
of freedom, ideals and ideas to the relation of the physical and
the mental. With respect to the latter, there is the causal problem
of their existential relation; and there is the cognitive problem of
how one order of existence can refer to the other in such a way as
to know it. We are not concerned here with the voluminous
literature and various (controversial and controverted) points of
view that have emerged. It is pertinent, however, to recall the
source of the problems; and to register the statement that without the underlying dubious assumption, we are not called upon
to find solutions; they cease to be perplexities as soon as certain
premises are surrendered. The premise which concerns us here is
that science is grasp of reality in its final self-sufficing form. If the
proper object of knowledge has the character appropriate to the
subject-matter of the useful arts, the problem in question evapo-
rates. The objects of science, like the direct objects of the arts, are
an order of relations which serve as tools to effect immediate
havings and beings. Goods, objects with qualities of fulfillment
are the natural fruition of the discovery and employment of
means, when the connection of ends with a sequential order is
determined. Immediate empirical things are just what they always were: endings of natural histories. Physical science does not
set up another and rival realm of antithetical existence; it reveals
the state or order upon which the occurrence of immediate and
final qualities depends. It adds to casual having of ends an ability
to regulate the date, place and manner of their emergence.
Fundamentally, the assertion that this condition of ordered relationships is mathematic, mechanical, is tautology; that is, the
meaning of anything which is such that perception and use of it

enables us to regulate consequences or attain terminal qualities is a mathematical, mechanical—or if you please—logical order. If we did not discover those which we have found, we should have to find another, if deliberate planning and execution are to occur.

If science be perfect grasp, or envisagement of being, and if science terminate with a mathematico-mechanical world, then, in the second place, we have upon our hands the problems of reality and appearance. In ancient thought, the problem occurred in a simple form. There were higher and lower forms of knowledge; but all stages of knowledge were alike realizations of some level of Being, so that appearance in contrast with reality meant only a lower degree of Being, being imperfect or not fully actualized. In modern science, with its homogenous natural world, this contrast of perfect and defective Being is meaningless. It is a question of knowledge or error, not of differences of cognitive grasp in one to one correspondence with different levels of Being. In the ancient view, sensation and opinion are good forms of knowledge in their place; *what* they know, their place, is just an inferior grade of Being. To the modern mind, they are not knowledge of anything unless they are brought to agree with the deliverances of science. Is matter an appearance of mind as true reality? Or is the mental only an appearance of the physical as the final reality? Or are both of them appearances of some still more ultimate reality?

Such questions are as necessary as they are unanswerable, given the premise which defines knowledge as direct grasp and envisagement. They vanish if the proper objects of science are nature in its instrumental characters. Any immediate object then *becomes* for inquiry, as something *to be* known, an appearance. To call it "appearance" denotes a functional status, not a kind of existence. Any quality in its immediacy is doubly an appearance. In the first place it appears; it is evident, conspicuous, outstanding; it is, to recur to language already used, *had*. A thing appears in the sense in which a bright object appears in a dark room, while other things remain obscure, hidden. The affair is one of physical and physiological limits of vision and audition, etc. We see islands floating as it were upon the sea; we call them islands because of their apparent lack of continuity with the medium that immediately surrounds them. But they are projections of the very earth upon which we walk; the connecting links do not ordinarily appear; they are there, but are not had. The difference between the appearing and the unappearing is of immense practical and theoretical import, imposing upon us need for inference, which would not exist if things appeared to us in their full connections, instead of with sharply demarcated outlines due to limits of perceptibility. But the ground of the difference is as physical as that between solid, liquid and gas. The endings of organic events, seeing, hearing, etc. are for the time being, or immediately, endings of the history of all natural events. To re-establish a connection of histories within a longer course of events and a more inclusive state of affairs, requires delving, probing, and extension by artifice beyond the apparent. To link the things which are immediately and apparitionally had with one another by means of what is not immediately apparent and thus to create new historic successions with new initiations and new endings depends in turn upon the system of mathematical-mechanical systems which form the proper objects of science as such.

The empirical basis of the distinction between the apparent and the non-apparent thus lies in the need for inference. When we take the outstandingly evident as evidence, its status is subordinate to that of unperceived things. For the nonce, it is a way of establishing something more fundamental than it is itself with respect to the object of inquiry. If we conceive of the world of immediately apparent things as an emergence of peaks of mountains which are submerged except as to their peaks or endings, and as a world of initial climbings whose subsequent career emerges above the surface only here and there and by fits and starts; and if we give attention to the fact that any ability of control whatever depends upon ability to unite these disparate appearances into a serial history, and then give due attention to the fact that connection into a consecutive history can be effected only by means of a scheme of constant relationships (a condition met by the mathematical-logical-mechanical objects of physics), we shall have no difficulty in seeing why it is that the immediate things from which we start lend themselves to interpretation as signs or appearances of the objects of physics; while we also recognize that it is only with respect to the function of instituting connection that the objects of physics can be said to be more "real." In the total situation in which they function, they are means to weaving together otherwise disconnected beginnings and endings into a consecutive history. Underlying "reality" and surface "appearance" in this connection have a meaning fixed by the function of inquiry, not an intrinsic metaphysical meaning.

To treat therefore the object of science—which in effect is the object of physics—as a complete and self-sufficient object, the end of knowing, is to burden ourselves with an unnecessary and insoluble problem. It commits us on one side to a realm of immediately apparent things, the so-called perceptual order which is an order only by courtesy, and on the other to a realm of inferred and logically constructed real objects. These two realms are rivals of each other. If knowledge is possession or grasp, then there are two incompatible kinds of knowledge, one sensible, the other rational. Which is the genuine article and which the counterfeit? If we say sensible knowledge is the genuine, then we are committed to phenomenalism of a somewhat chaotic kind, unless we follow Berkeley and invoke deity to hold the immediate things together.

If we say rational knowledge is the genuine article, then true reality becomes the reality of materialism or of logical realism or of objective idealism, according to training and temperament. To follow the clues of experience is to see that the so-called sensible world is a world of immediate beginnings and endings; not at all an affair of cases of knowledge but a succession of qualitative events; while the so-called conceptual order is recognized to be the proper object of science, since it constitutes the scheme of constant relationships by means of which spare, scattered and casual events are bound together into a connected history. These emergent immediate events remain the beginning and the end of knowledge; but since their *occurrence* is one with their being sensibly, affectionally and appreciatively *had*, they are not themselves things known. That the qualities and characters of these immediate apparitions are tremendously modified when they are linked together by "physical objects"—that is, by means of the mathematical-mechanical objects of physics—is a fact of the same nature as that a steel watch-spring is a modification of crude iron ore. The objects of physics subsist precisely in order to bring about this transformation—to change, that is, casual endings into fulfillments and conclusions of an ordered series, with the development of meaning therein involved.

Practically all epistemological discussion depends upon a sud-

den and unavowed shift to and fro from the universe of having to
the universe of discourse. At the outset, ordinary empirical affairs, chairs, tables, stones, sticks, etc., are called physical
objects—which is obviously a term of theoretical interpretation
when it is so applied, carrying within itself a complete metaphysical commitment. Then physical objects are defined as the objects of physics, which is, I suppose, the only correct mode of
designation. But such objects are clearly very different things
from the plants, lamps, chairs, thunder and lightning, rocks etc.
that were first called physical objects. So another transformation
phantasmagoria in the tableau is staged. The original "physical
things," ordinary empirical objects, not being the objects of
physics, are not physical at all but mental. Then comes the grand
dissolving climax in which objects of physics are shown as themselves hanging from empirical objects now dressed up as mental,
and hence as themselves mental.

Everything now being mental, and the term having lost its
original contrasting or differential meaning, a new and different
series of transformation scenes is exhibited. Immediate empirical
things are resolved into hard sensory data, which are called the
genuine physical things, while the objects of physical science are
treated as are logical constructions; all that remains to constitute
mental existence is images and feelings. It is not necessary to
mention other permutations and combinations, familiar to the
student of theories of the possibility of knowledge. The samples
mentioned are illustrations of the sort of thing which happens
when the having of immediate objects, whether sensible, affectional or appreciatoral, is treated as a mode of knowledge.

If objects which are colored, sonorous, tactile, gustatory,
loved, hated, enjoyed, admired, which are attractive and repulsive, exciting, indifferent and depressive, in all their infinitely
numerous modes, are beginnings and endings of complex natural
affairs, and if physical objects (defined as objects of physical
science) are constituted by a mathematical-mechanical order,
then physical objects instead of involving us in the predicament
of having to choose between opposing claimants to reality, have
precisely the characters which they should have in order to serve
effectively as means for securing and avoiding immediate objects. Four of these characters may be noted. First, immediate
things come and go; events in the way of direct seeing, hearing,

touching, liking, enjoying, and the rest of them are in rapid change; the subject-matter of each has a certain uniqueness, unrepeatedness. Spatial-temporal orders, capable of mathematical formulation are, by contrast, constant. They present stability, recurrence at its maximum, raised to the highest degree. Qualitative affairs like red and blue, although in themselves unlike, are subject to comparison in terms of objects of physics; on the basis of connection with orders of sequence, a qualitative spectrum or scale becomes a scheme of numerable variations of a common unit.

The second character of objects of science follows from this feature. The possibility of regulating the occurrence of any event depends upon the possibility of instituting substitutions. By means of the latter, a thing which is within grasp is used to stand for another thing which is not immediately had, or which is beyond control. The technique of equations and other functions characteristic of modern science is, taken generically, a method of thoroughgoing substitutions. It is a system of exchange and mutual conversion carried to its limit.[2] The cognitive result is the homogeneous natural world of modern science, in its contrast with the qualitatively heterogeneous world of ancient science; the latter being made up of things different in inherent kinds and in qualities of movement, such as up and down, lateral and circular, and heterogeneous according to periods of time, such as earlier and later. These become amenable to transformations in virtue of reciprocal substitutions.

In the third place, objects of knowledge as means explain the importance attached to elements, or numerically discrete units. Control of beginnings and ends by means is possible only when the individual, the unique, is treated as a composite of parts, made by sequential differentiations and integrations.[3] In its own integrity an immediate thing just exists as it exists; it stays or it

2. The modern mathematical conception of infinity as correspondence of part and whole appears to represent this function in its generalized form.
3. Leibniz, whose monadism is the first philosophical manifestation of this notion, and the prototype of analytic realism, or theory of external relations, asserted the existence of monads on the ground that every composite implies elements. Surely. But he omitted to note that metaphysically the case was begged as soon as an affair, no matter how elaborate in structure, is regarded as *being* composite. To *be* a composite is one thing; to be capable of reduction to a composite by certain measures, is another thing.

passes; it is enjoyed or suffered. That is all that can be said. But when it is treated as the outcome of a complex convergence or coincidence of a large number of elementary independent variables, points, moments, numerical units, particles of mass and energy or more elementary space-times, (which in spite of their independence are capable of one to one correspondence with one another) the situation changes. The simples or elements are in effect the last pivots upon which regulation of conditions turns; last, that is to say, as far as present appliances permit.

Preoccupation with elementary units is as marked in logic, biology, and psychology, as in physics and chemistry. Sometimes it seems to have resulted in taking merely dialectical entities for actual unitary elements; but that is not logically necessary. Such an outcome signifies only that the right units were not found. Serious objection holds when the instrumental character of the elements is forgotten; and they are treated as independent, ultimate; when they are treated as metaphysical finalities, insoluble epistemological problems result. Whatever are designated as elements, whether logical, mathematical, physical or mental, depend especially upon the existence of immediate, qualitatively integral objects. Search for elements starts with such empirical objects already possessed. Sensory data, whether they are designated psychic or physical, are thus not starting points; they are the products of analysis. Denial of the primary reality of immediate empirical objects logically terminates in an abrogation of the reality of elements; for sensory data, or sensa and *sensibilia*, are the residua of analysis of these primary things. Moreover every step of analysis depends upon continual reference to these empirical objects. Drop them from mental view for a moment and any clew in search for elements is lost. Unless macroscopic things are recognized, cells, electrons, logical elements become meaningless. The latter have meaning only as elements *of*. Since, for example, only propositions have implications, a proposition cannot be a mere conjunction of terms; terms having no implications, a proposition so formed would have no significance. Terms must have a significance and since that they have only in a proposition, they depend upon some prior unity. In similar fashion, a purely unitary physical element would have no efficacy; it could not act or be acted upon.

We quote from a psychiatric writer speaking of his own field, in dealing with a particular matter on its own merits. With reference to one stage in the development of the theory of mental disorders, Dr. Adolf Meyer said that "there was a quest for elements of mind and their immediate correlation with the latest discoveries in the structure of the brain. The centre theory and the cell and neuronic theory seemed obligatory standpoints. Today we have become shy of such a one-sided not sufficiently functional materialism. . . . There is always a place for elements, but there is certainly also a place for the large momentous facts of human life just as we find it. . . . The psychopathologist had to learn to do more than the so-called 'elementalist,' who always goes back to the elements and smallest units and then is apt to shirk the responsibility of making an attempt to solve the concrete problems of greater complexity. The psychiatrist has to study individuals and groups as wholes, as complex units, as the 'you' or 'he' or 'she' or 'they' we have to work with. We recognize that throughout nature we have to face the general principle of unit-formation, and the fact that new units need not be a mere sum of the component parts, but can be an actually new entity not wholly predictable from the component parts and known only through actual experience with the specific product."[4]

Lastly, the instrumental nature of objects of knowledge accounts for the central position of laws, relations. These are the formulations of the regularities upon which intellectual and other regulation of things as immediate apparitions depends. Variability of elements in mathematical science is specious; elements vary independently of one another, but not independently of a *relation* to others, the relation or law being the constancy among variations. It is a truism that mathematics is the method by which elements can be stated as terms in constant relations, and be subjected to equations and other functions of transformation and substitution. An element is appropriately represented by a mathematical variable; for since any variable falls within some equation, it is treated as a constant function of other variables. The shift from variability to constancy is repeated as often as is needed. It is thus only *pro forma* that the variable is variable. It is not variable in the sense in which unique individualized existences are variable. The inevitable consequence is the subjection of individuals or unique modes of variation to external relations, to laws of uniformity; that is to say, the elimination of individu-

4. Adolf Meyer, *A Psychiatric Milestone*, pp. 32, 38.

ality. Bear in mind the instrumental nature of the relation of elements, and this abrogation of individuality merely means a temporary neglect—an abstracted gaze—in behalf of attending to conditions under which individualities present themselves. Convert the objects of knowledge into real things by themselves, and individuals become anomalous or unreal; they are not individualized for science but are instances, cases, specimens, of some generical relation or law.

The difficulty under which morals labor in this case is evident. They can be "saved" only by the supposition of another kind of Being from that with which natural sciences are concerned. History and anthropology are implicated in a similar predicament. The former has for subject-matter not only individual persons but unduplicated situations and events. The attempt to escape the dilemma by recourse to uniform and unilinear laws of sequence or "evolution" is inept; it contradicts the premises assumed, and is not borne out by facts. Contemporary anthropologists have made clear the historical nature of the phenomena with which they deal. Cultures are in many respects individual or unique, and their manifestations are "explained" by correlations with one another and by borrowings due to chance contacts. The chief, even if not sole, law of their changes is that of transmission from other individualized cultures.

It is no wonder that *Historismus* has become the preoccupying problem of a whole school of thinkers, many of whom now hold that the only attitude which can be taken toward historic situations and characters is non-intellectual, being esthetic appreciation, or sympathetic artistic rehabilitation. The theory which identifies knowledge with the beholding or grasp of self-sufficient objects reaches an impasse where it comes to deal with historical science in contrast with physics. Windelband justly draws the conclusion that Being and knowledge compel "antinomianism," certain problems inevitably force themselves upon us, but all efforts at solution are hopeless.[5]

5. "It remains an unsolved problem why timeless reality needs realisation in the temporal course of the event or why it tolerates in itself an event in the temporal course of which there is something that differs from its own nature. We do not understand why that which is also has nevertheless to happen; and still less why something different happens from that which is in itself without time." *Introduction to Philosophy*, English translation, p. 299.

Empirically, individualized objects, unique affairs, exist. But they are evanescent, unstable. They tremble on the verge of disappearance as soon as they appear. Useful arts prove that, within limits, neglect of their uniqueness and attention to what is common, recurrent, irrelevant to time, procures and perpetuates the happening of some of these unique things. Timeless laws, *taken by themselves*, like all universals, express dialectic intent, not any matter-of-fact existence. But their ultimate implication is application; they are methods, and when applied as methods they regulate the precarious flow of unique situations. Objects of natural science are not metaphysical rivals of historical events; they are means of directing the latter. Events change; one individual gives place to another. But individually qualified things have some qualities which are pervasive, common, stable. They are out of time in the sense that a particular temporal quality is irrelevant to them. If anybody feels relieved by calling them eternal, let them be called eternal. But let not "eternal" be then conceived as a kind of absolute perduring existence or Being. It denotes just what it denotes: irrelevance to existence in its temporal quality. These non-temporal, mathematical or logical qualities are capable of abstraction, and of conversion into relations, into temporal, numerical and spatial *order*.[6] As such they are dialectical, non-existential. But also as such they are tools, instrumentalities applicable to historic events to help regulate their course.

This entire discussion has but a single point. It aims to show that the problems which constitute modern epistemology with its rival materialistic, spiritualistic, dualistic doctrines; and rival realistic, idealistic, representational theories; and rival doctrines of relation of mind and matter, occasionalism, pre-established

6. For a convincing discussion see Brown's essay, "Intelligence and Mathematics," in the volume, *Creative Intelligence,* especially the section entitled "Things, Relations, and Quantities." "Instead of reducing qualities to relations, it seems to me a much more intelligible view to conceive relations as abstract ways of taking qualities in general, as qualities thought of in their function of bridging a gap or making a transition between two bits of reality that have previously been taken as separate things." P. 159. Thus terms (elements) and relations are both (p. 160) abstract replacements of qualitatively heterogeneous realities of such a sort as "to symbolize their *effective* nature in particular respects." The word "effective" brings out the agreement of the text with this point of view, for which I am much indebted to Dr. Brown.

harmony, parallelism, panpsychism, etc., have a single origin in the dogma which denies temporal quality to reality as such. Such a theory is bound to regard things which are causally explanatory as superior to results and outcomes; for the temporal dependence of the latter cannot be disguised, while "causes" can be plausibly converted into independent beings, or laws, or other non-temporal forms. As has been pointed out, this denial of change to true Being had its source in bias in favor of objects of contemplative enjoyment, together with a theory that such objects are the adequate subject-matter of science.

The bias is spontaneous and legitimate. The accompanying theory of knowledge and reality is a distortion. The legitimate implication of the preference for worthy objects of appreciation is the necessity of art, or control of the sequential order upon which they depend; a necessity which carries with it the further implication that this order, which is to be discovered by inquiry and confirmed by experimental action, is the proper object of knowledge. Such a recognition would, however, have conceded the dependence of the contemplative functions of the leisure class upon the appliances and technique of artisans—among whom all artists were included. And since in olden time the practice of the arts was largely routine, fixed by custom and ready-made patterns, such a recognition would have carried with it the need of transforming the arts themselves, if the occurrence of ends was to be a real fulfillment, a realization, and not a contingent accident. The introduction of inventive thought into the arts and the civil emancipation of the industrial class at last made the transformation possible.

When the appliances of a technology that had grown more deliberate were adopted in inquiry, and the lens, pendulum, magnetic needle, lever were used as tools of knowing, and their functions were treated as models to follow in interpreting physical phenomena, science ceased to be identified with appreciative contemplation of noble and ideal objects, was freed from subjection to esthetic perfections, and became an affair of time and history intelligently managed. Ends were in consequence no longer determined by physical accident and social traditions. Anything whatsoever for which means could be found was an end to be averted or to be secured. Liberation from a fixed scheme of ends made modern science possible. In large affairs, practice precedes the possibility of observation and formulation; the results of practice must accumulate before mind has anything to observe. There is little cause for wonder therefore that long after the objects of science had become instrumentalities rather than things in their own rights, the old theory persisted, and philosophy spent much of its effort in the effort to reconcile the traditional theory of knowledge as immediate possession with the terms and conclusions of the new method of practice.

It is characteristic of the inevitable moral pre-possession of philosophy, together with the subjective turn of modern thought, that many critics take an "instrumental" theory of knowledge to signify that the value of knowing is instrumental to the knower. This is a matter which is as it may be in particular cases; but certainly in many cases the pursuit of science is sport, carried on, like other sports, for its own satisfaction. But "instrumentalism" is a theory not about personal disposition and satisfaction in knowing, but about the proper objects of science, what is "proper" being defined in terms of physics.

The distinction between tools (or things in their objectivities) and fulfilled products of the use of tools accounts for the distinction between known objects on one side and objects of appreciation and affection on the other. But the distinction primarily concerns objects themselves; only secondarily does it apply to attitudes, dispositions, motivations. Making and using tools may be intrinsically delightful. Prior to the introduction of machinery for quantitative production and sale of commodities for profit, utensils were themselves usually works of art, esthetically satisfying. This fact does not however define them *as* utensils; it does not confer upon them their characteristic property. In like manner, the pursuit of knowledge is often an immediately delightful event; its attained products possess esthetic qualities of proportion, order, and symmetry. But these qualities do not mark off or define the characteristic and appropriate *objects* of science. The character of the object is like that of a tool, say a lever; it is an order of determination of sequential changes terminating in a foreseen consequence.

We are brought to the question of method. In ancient science the essence of science was demonstration; the life blood of modern science is discovery. In the former, reflective inquiry existed for the sake of attaining a stable subject-matter; in the latter systematized knowledge exists in practice for the sake of stimulating, guiding and checking further inquiries. In ancient science, "learning" belonged in the realm of inferior being, of becoming, change; it was transitive, and ceased in the actualization of final and fixed objects. It was thought of after the analogy of master and disciple; the former was already in possession of the truth, and the learner merely appropriated what already is there in the store house of the master. In modern science, learning is finding out what nobody has previously known. It is a transaction in which nature is teacher, and in which the teacher comes to knowledge and truth only through the learning of the inquiring student.

Characteristic differences in logic thus accompany the change from "knowledge" whose subject-matter is final affairs to knowledge dealing with instrumental objects. Where the objects of knowledge are taken to be final, perfect, complete, metaphysical fulfillments of nature, proper method consists in definition and classification; learning closes with demonstration of the rational necessity of definitions and classifications. Demonstration is an exhibition of the everlasting, universal, final and fixed nature of objects. Investigation denoted merely the accumulation of material with which to fill in gaps in an antecedent ready-made hierarchy of species. Discovery was merely the perception that some particular material hitherto unclassified by the learner came under a universal form already known. The universal is already known because given to thought; and the particular is already known, because given to perception; learning merely brings these two given forms into connection, so that what is "discovered" is the subsumption of particular under its universal.

Apart from their theories, or in spite of them, the Greeks were possessed by a lively curiosity, and their practice was better than their logic. In the medieval Christian period, the logic was taken literally. Revelation, scriptures, church fathers and other authentic sources, increased the number of given universal truths, and also of given particular facts and events. The master-teacher was God, who taught not through the dim instrumentality of rational thought alone, but directly through official representatives. The form of apprehension of truth remained the demonstrative syllogism; the store of universal truths was supplemented by the

gracious gift of revelation, and the resources of the minor premise extended by divinely established historic facts. Truth was
given to reason and faith; and the part of the human mind was to
humble itself to hearken, accept and obey.

The scheme was logically complete; it carried out under new
circumstances the old idea that the highest end and good of man
is knowledge of true Being, and that such knowledge in the
degree of its possession effects an assimilation of the mind to the
reality known. It added to old theoretical premises such institutions and practices as were practically required to give them
effect, so that the humblest of human creatures might at least
start on the road to that knowledge the possession of which is
salvation and bliss. In comparison, most modern theories are an
inconsistent mixture; dialectically the modernist is easy prey to
the traditionalist; he carries so many of the conceptions of the
latter in his intellectual outfit that he is readily confuted. It is his
practice not his theory that gets him ahead. His professed logic is
still largely that of antecedent truths, demonstration and certitude; his practice is doubting, forming hypotheses, conducting
experiments. When he surrenders antecedent truths of reason it
is usually only to accept antecedent truths of sensation. Thus
John Stuart Mill conceives of an inductive logic in which certain
canons shall bear exactly the same relation to inquiry into fact
that the rules of the syllogism bore to classic "deductive" proof
or dialectic. He recognizes that science is a matter of inference,
but he is as certain as was Aristotle that inference rests upon
certain truths which are immediately possessed, differing only
about the organ through which they come into our possession.

But in the practice of science, knowledge is an affair of *making*
sure, not of grasping antecedently given sureties. What is already
known, what is accepted as truth, is of immense importance;
inquiry could not proceed a step without it. But it is held subject
to use, and is at the mercy of the discoveries which it makes
possible. It has to be adjusted to the latter and not the latter to it.
When things are defined as instruments, their value and validity
reside in what proceeds from them; consequences not antecedents supply meaning and verity. Truths already possessed may
have practical or moral certainty, but logically they never lose a
hypothetic quality. They are true *if*: if certain other things eventually present themselves; and when these latter things occur

they in turn suggest further possibilities; the operation of doubt-inquiry-finding recurs. Although science is concerned in practice with the contingent and its method is that of making hypotheses which are then tried out in actual experimental change of physical conditions, its traditional formulation persists in terms of necessary and fixed objects. Hence all kinds of incoherences occur. The more stubbornly the traditional formulation is clung to, the more serious become these inconsistencies.

Leonardo virtually announced the birth of the method of modern science when he said that true knowledge begins with opinion. The saying involves a revolution; no other statement could be so shocking to the traditional logic. Not that opinion as such is anything more than opinion or an unconfirmed and unwarranted surmise; but that such surmises may be used; when employed as hypotheses they induce experimentation. They then become fore-runners of truth, and mind is released from captivity to antecedent beliefs. Opinion, in the classic conception, was concerned with what was inherently contingent and variable as to possibility and probability, in contrast with knowledge concerned with the inherently necessary and everlasting. It therefore was as ultimate and unquestionable *in its proper sphere* as science was in its place. But opinion as a venture, as an "it seems to me probable," is an occasion of new observations, an instigator of research, an indispensable organ in deliberate discovery. Taken in this fashion, opinion was the source of new histories, the beginning of operations that terminated in new conclusions. Its worth lay neither in itself nor in a peculiar realm of objects to which it was applied, but in the direction of inquiries which it set agoing. It was a starting point, and like any beginning of any history was altered and displaced in the history of which it was the initiation.

Sometimes discovery is treated as a proof of the opposite of what it actually shows. It is viewed as evidence that the object of knowledge is already there in full-fledged being and that we just run across it; we uncover it as treasure-hunters find a chest of buried gold. That there is existence antecedent to search and discovery is of course admitted; but it is denied that as such, as other than the conclusion of the historical event of inquiry in its connection with other histories, it is already the object of knowledge. The Norsemen are said to have discovered America. But in what sense? They landed on its shores after a stormy voyage; there was discovery in the sense of hitting upon a land hitherto untrod by Europeans. But unless the newly found and seen object was used to modify old beliefs, to change the sense of the old map of the earth, there was no discovery in any pregnant intellectual sense, any more than mere stumbling over a chair in the dark is discovery till used as basis of inference which connects the stumbling with a body of meanings. Discovery of America involved insertion of the newly touched land in a map of the globe. This insertion, moreover, was not merely additive, but transformative of a prior picture of the world as to its surfaces and their arrangements. It may be replied that it was not the world which was changed but only the map. To which there is the obvious retort that after all the map is part of the world, not something outside it, and that its meaning and bearings are so important that a change in the map involves other and still more important objective changes.

It was not simply states of consciousness or ideas inside the heads of men that were altered when America was actually discovered; the modification was one in the public meaning of the world in which men publicly act. To cut off this meaning from the world is to leave us in a situation where it makes no difference what change takes place in the world; one wave more or less in a puddle is of no account. Changing the meaning of the world effected an existential change. The map of the world is something more than a piece of linen hung on a wall. A new world does not appear without profound transformations in the old one; a discovered America was a factor interacting with Europe and Asia to produce consequences previously impossible. A potential object of further exploration and discoveries now existed in Europe itself; a source of gold; an opportunity for adventure; an outlet for crowded and depressed populations, an abode for exiles and the discounted, an appeal to energy and invention: in short, an agency of new events and fruitions, at home as well as abroad. In some degree, every genuine discovery creates some such transformation of both the meanings and the existences of nature.

Modern idealistic theories of knowledge have displayed some sense of the method and objective of science. They have apprehended the fact that the object of knowledge implies that the found rather than the given is the proper subject-matter of science. Recognizing the part played by intelligence in this finding, they have framed a theory of the constitutive operation of mind in the determination of real objects. But idealism, while it has had an intimation of the constructively instrumental office of intelligence, has mistranslated the discovery. Following the old tradition, in its exclusive identification of the object of knowledge with reality, equating truth and Being, it was forced to take the work of thought absolutely and wholesale, instead of relatively and in detail. That is, it took re-constitution to be constitution; re-construction to be construction. Accepting the premise of the equivalence of Reality with the attained object of knowledge, idealism had no way of noting that thought is intermediary between some empirical objects and others. Hence an office of transformation was converted into an act of original and final creation. A conversion of actual immediate objects into *better*, into more secure and significant, objects was treated as a movement from merely apparent and phenomenal Being to the truly Real. In short, idealism is guilty of neglect that thought and knowledge are histories.

To call action of thought in constituting objects direct is the same as to say that it is miraculous. For it is not thought as idealism defines thought which exercises the reconstructive function. Only action, interaction, can change or remake objects. The analogy of the skilled artist still holds. His intelligence is a factor in forming new objects which mark a fulfillment. But this is because intelligence is incarnate in overt action, using things as means to affect other things. "Thought," reason, intelligence, whatever word we choose to use, is existentially an adjective (or better an adverb), not a noun. It is disposition of activity, a quality of that conduct which foresees consequences of existing events, and which uses what is foreseen as a plan and method of administering affairs.

This theory, explicitly about thought as a condition of science, is actually a theory about nature. It involves attribution to nature of three defining characteristics. In the first place, it is implied that some natural events are endings whether enjoyed or obnoxious, which occur, apart from reflective choice and art, only casually, without control. In the second place, it implies that events, being events and not rigid and lumpy substances, are ongoing and hence as such unfinished, incomplete, indeterminate. Consequently they possess a possibility of being so managed and steered that ends may become fulfillments not just termini, conclusions not just closings. Suspense, doubt, hypotheses, experiment with alternatives are exponents of this phase of nature. In the third place, regulation of ongoing and incomplete processes in behalf of selected consequences, implies that there are orders of sequence and coexistence involved; these orders or relations when ascertained are intellectual means which enable us to use events as concrete means of directing the course of affairs to forecast conclusions. The belief that these orders of relation, which are the appropriate object of science, are therefore the sole ultimately "real" objects is the source of that assertion of a symmetrical, dovetailed and completed universe made by both traditional materialism and idealism. The belief is due to neglect of the fact that such relations are always relations of ongoing affairs characterized by beginnings and endings which mark them off into unstable individuals. Yet this neglected factor is empirically so pervasive and conspicuous that it has to be acknowledged in some form; it is usually acknowledged in a backhanded way—and one which confuses subsequent reflection—by attributing all qualities inconsistent with nature thus defined to "finite" mind, in order to account for ignorance, doubt, error and the need of inference and inquiry.

If nature is as finished as these schools have defined it to be, there is no room or occasion in it for such a mind; it and the traits it is said to possess are literally supernatural or at least extra-natural.

A realist may deny this particular hypothesis that, existentially, mind designates an instrumental method of directing natural changes. But he cannot do so in virtue of his realism; the question at issue is what the real is. If natural existence is qualitatively individualized or genuinely plural, as well as repetitious, and if things have both temporal quality and recurrence or uniformity, then the more realistic knowledge is, the more fully it will reflect and exemplify these traits. Science seizes upon whatever is so uniform as to make the changes of nature rhythmic, and hence predictable. But the contingencies of nature make discovery of these uniformities with a view to prediction needed and possible. Without the uniformities, science would be impossible. But if they alone existed, thought and knowledge would be impossible and meaningless. The incomplete and uncertain gives point and application to ascertainment of regular relations and orders. These relations in themselves are hypothetical, and when isolated from application are subject-matter of mathematics (in a non-existential sense). Hence the *ultimate* objects of science are *guided* processes of change.

Sometimes the use of the word "truth" is confined to designating a logical property of propositions; but if we extend its significance to designate character of existential reference, this is the meaning of truth: processes of change so directed that they achieve an intended consummation. Instrumentalities are actually such only in operation; when they operate, an end-in-view is in process of actualization. The means is fully a means only *in* its end. The instrumental objects of science are completely themselves only as they direct the changes of nature toward a fulfilling object. Thus it may be said intelligibly and not as mere tautology that the end of science is knowledge, implying that knowledge is more than science, being its fruit.

Knowledge is a word of various meanings. Etymologically, "science" may signify tested and authentic instance of knowledge. But knowledge has also a meaning more liberal and more humane. It signifies events understood, events so discriminately penetrated by thought that mind is literally at home in them. It means comprehension, or inclusive reasonable agreement. What is sometimes termed "applied" science, may then be more truly science than is what is conventionally called pure science. For it is directly concerned with not just instrumentalities, but instrumentalities at work in effecting modifications of existence in behalf of conclusions that are reflectively preferred. Thus conceived the characteristic subject-matter of knowledge consists of fulfilling objects, which as fulfillments are connected with a history to which they give character. Thus conceived, knowledge exists in engineering, medicine and the social arts more adequately than it does in mathematics, and physics. Thus conceived, history and anthropology are scientific in a sense in which bodies of information that stop short with general formulae are not.

"Application" is a hard word for many to accept. It suggests some extraneous tool ready-made and complete, which is then put to uses that are external to its nature. To call the arts applications of science is then to introduce something foreign to the sciences which the latter irrelevantly and accidentally serve. Since the application is in human use, convenience, enjoyment and improvement, this view of application as something external and arbitrary reflects and strengthens the theories which detach man from nature, which, in the language of philosophy, oppose subject and object. But if we free ourselves from preconceptions, application of "science" means application *in*, not application *to*. Application *in* something signifies a more extensive interaction of natural events with one another, an elimination of distance and obstacles; provision of opportunities for interactions that reveal potentialities previously hidden and that bring into existence new histories with new initiations and endings. Engineering, medicine, social arts realize relationships that were unrealized in actual existences. Surely in their new context the latter are understood or known as they are not in isolation. Prejudice against the abstract, as something remote and technical, is often irrational; but there is sense in the conviction that in the abstract there is something lacking which should be recovered. The serious objection to "applied" science lies in limitation of the application, as to private profit and class advantage.

"Pure" science is of necessity relational and abstract: it fulfills its meaning and gains full truth when included within a course of concrete events. The proposition that "pure" science is non-existential is a tacit admission that only "applied" science is existential. Something else than history and anthropology loses all scientific standing when standards of "purity" are set up as ultimate; namely, all science of existential events. There is superstitious awe reflected in the current estimate of science. If we could free ourselves from a somewhat abject emotion, it would be clear enough that what makes any proposition scientific is its power to yield understanding, insight, intellectual at-homeness, in connection with any existential state of affairs, by filling events with coherent and tested meanings. The case of history is typical and basic. Upon the current view, it is a waste of time to discuss whether there can be such a thing as a science of history. History and science are by definition at opposite poles. And yet if all natural existences *are* histories, divorce between history and the logical mathematical schemes which are the appropriate objects of pure science, terminates in the conclusion that of existences there is no science, no adequate knowledge. Aside from mathematics, all knowledge is historic; chemistry, geology, physiology, as well as anthropology and those human events to which, arrogantly, we usually restrict the title of history. Only as science is seen to be fulfilled and brought to itself in intelligent management of historical processes in their continuity can man be envisaged as within nature, and not as a supernatural extrapolation. Just because nature is what it is, history is capable of being more truly known—understood, intellectually realized—than are mathematical and physical objects. Do what we can, there always remains something recondite and remote in the latter, until they are restored in the course of affairs from which they have been sequestrated. While the humanizing of science contributes to the life of humanity, it is even more required in behalf of science, in order that it may be intelligible, simple and clear; in order that it may have that correspondence with reality which true knowledge claims for itself.

One can understand the sentiment that animates the bias of scientific inquirers against the idea that all science is ultimately applied. It is justified in the sense in which it is intended; for it is directed against two conceptions which are harmful, but which, also, are irrelevant to the position here taken. One of these conceptions is that the concern or personal motive of the inquirer should be in each particular inquiry some specific practical application. This is just as it happens to be. Doubtless many important scientific discoveries have been thus instigated, but that is an incident of human history rather than of scientific inquiry as such. And upon the whole, or if this animating interest were to become general, the undoubted effect is limitation of inquiry and thereby in the end of the field of application. It marks a recurrence to the dogma of fixed predetermined ends, while emancipation from the influence of this dogma has been the chief service rendered modern scientific methods.

The evil thus effected is increased by the second notion, namely, that application is identical with "commercialized" use. It is an incident of human history, and a rather appalling incident, that applied science has been so largely made an equivalent of use for private and economic class purposes and privileges. When inquiry is narrowed by such motivation or interest, the consequence is in so far disastrous both to science and to human life. But this limitation does not spring from nor attach to the conception of "application" which has been just presented. It springs from defects and perversions of morality as that is embodied in institutions and their effects upon personal disposition. It may be questioned whether the notion that science is pure in the sense of being concerned exclusively with a realm of objects detached from human concerns has not conspired to reinforce this moral deficiency. For in effect it has established another class-interest, that of intellectualists and aloof specialists. And it is of the nature of any class-interest to generate and confirm other class-interests, since division and isolation in a world of continuities are always reciprocal. The institution of an interest labelled ideal and idealistic in isolation tends of necessity to evoke and strengthen other interests lacking ideal quality. The genuine interests of "pure" science are served only by broadening the idea of application to include all phases of liberation and enrichment of human experience.

5. Nature, Communication and Meaning

Of all affairs, communication is the most wonderful. That things should be able to pass from the plane of external pushing and pulling to that of revealing themselves to man, and thereby to themselves; and that the fruit of communication should be participation, sharing, is a wonder by the side of which transubstantiation pales. When communication occurs, all natural events are subject to reconsideration and revision; they are re-adapted to meet the requirements of conversation, whether it be public discourse or that preliminary discourse termed thinking. Events turn into objects, things with a meaning. They may be referred to when they do not exist, and thus be operative among things distant in space and time, through vicarious presence in a new medium. Brute efficiencies and inarticulate consummations as soon as they can be spoken of are liberated from local and accidental contexts, and are eager for naturalization in any non-insulated, communicating, part of the world. Events when once they are named lead an independent and double life. In addition to their original existence, they are subject to ideal experimentation: their meanings may be infinitely combined and re-arranged in imagination, and the outcome of this inner experimentation—which is thought—may issue forth in interaction with crude or raw events. Meanings having been deflected from the rapid and roaring stream of events into a calm and traversable canal, rejoin the main stream, and color, temper and compose its course. Where communication exists, things in acquiring meaning, thereby acquire representatives, surrogates, signs and implicates, which are infinitely more amenable to management, more permanent and more accommodating, than events in their first estate.

By this fashion, qualitative immediacies cease to be dumbly rapturous, a possession that is obsessive and an incorporation that involves submergence: conditions found in sensations and passions. They become capable of survey, contemplation, and ideal or logical elaboration; when something can be said of qualities they are purveyors of instruction. Learning and teaching come into being, and there is no event which may not yield information. A directly enjoyed thing adds to itself meaning, and enjoyment is thereby idealized. Even the dumb pang of an ache achieves a significant existence when it can be designated and descanted upon; it ceases to be merely oppressive and becomes important; it gains importance, because it becomes representative; it has the dignity of an office.

In view of these increments and transformations, it is not surprising that meanings, under the name of forms and essences, have often been hailed as modes of Being beyond and above spatial and temporal existence, invulnerable to vicissitude; nor that thought as their possession has been treated as a non-natural spiritual energy, disjoined from all that is empirical. Yet there is a natural bridge that joins the gap between existence and essence; namely communication, language, discourse. Failure to acknowledge the presence and operation of natural interaction in the form of communication creates the gulf between existence and essence, and that gulf is factitious and gratuitous.

The slight respect paid to larger and more pervasive kinds of empirical objects by philosophers, even by professed empiricists, is apparent in the fact that while they have discoursed so fluently about many topics they have discoursed little about discourse itself. Anthropologists, philologists and psychologists have said most that has been said about saying. Nevertheless it is a fact of such distinction that its occurrence changed dumb creatures—as we so significantly call them—into thinking and knowing animals and created the realm of meanings. Speaking from the standpoint of anthropology Franz Boas says: "The two outer traits in which the distinction between the minds of animals and man finds expression are the existence of organized articulate speech in man and the use of utensils of varied application."[1] It is antecedently probable that sole external marks of difference are more than external; that they have intimate connection with such intrinsic differences as religion, art and science, industry

1. *The Mind of Primitive Man*, p. 96.

and politics. "Utensils" were discussed in the last chapter, in connection with the useful arts and knowledge, and their indispensable relation with science pointed out. But at every point appliances and application, utensils and uses, are bound up with directions, suggestions and records made possible by speech; what has been said about the role of tools is subject to a condition supplied by language, the tool of tools.

Upon the whole, professed transcendentalists have been more aware than have professed empiricists of the fact that language makes the difference between brute and man. The trouble is that they have lacked naturalistic conception of its origin and status. Logos has been correctly identified with mind; but logos and hence mind was conceived supernaturally. Logic was thereby supposed to have its basis in what is beyond human conduct and relationships, and in consequence the separation of the physical and the rational, the actual and the ideal, received its traditional formulation.

In protest against this view empirical thinkers have rarely ventured in discussion of language beyond reference to some peculiarity of brain structure, or to some psychic peculiarity, such as tendency to "outer expression" of "inner" states. Social interaction and institutions have been treated as products of a ready-made *specific* physical or mental endowment of a self-sufficing individual, wherein language acts as a mechanical go-between to convey observations and ideas that have prior and independent existence. Speech is thus regarded as a practical convenience but not of fundamental intellectual significance. It consists of "mere words," sounds, that happen to be associated with perceptions, sentiments and thoughts which are complete prior to language. Language thus "expresses" thought as a pipe conducts water, and with even less transforming function than is exhibited when a wine-press "expresses" the juice of grapes. The office of signs in creating reflection, foresight and recollection is passed by. In consequence, the occurrence of ideas becomes a mysterious parallel addition to physical occurrences, with no community and no bridge from one to the other.

It is safe to say that psychic events, such as are anything more than reactions of a creature susceptible to pain and diffuse comfort, have language for one of their conditions. It is altogether likely that the "ideas" which Hume found in constant flux whenever he looked within himself were a succession of words silently uttered. Primary to these events there was, of course, a substratum of organic psycho-physical actions. But what made the latter identifiable objects, events with a perceptible character, was their concretion in discourse. When the introspectionist thinks he has withdrawn into a wholly private realm of events disparate in kind from other events, made out of mental stuff, he is only turning his attention to his own soliloquy. And soliloquy is the product and reflex of converse with others; social communication not an effect of soliloquy. If we had not talked with others and they with us, we should never talk to and with ourselves. Because of converse, social give and take, various organic attitudes become an assemblage of persons engaged in converse, conferring with one another, exchanging distinctive experiences, listening to one another, over-hearing unwelcome remarks, accusing and excusing. Through speech a person dramatically identifies himself with potential acts and deeds; he plays many roles, not in successive stages of life but in a contemporaneously enacted drama. Thus mind emerges.

It is significant of the differences between Greek and modern experience, that when their respective philosophers discovered discourse, they gave such different accounts of it. The moderns made of it a world separate from spatial and material existences, a separate and private world made of sensations, images, sentiments. The Greeks were more nearly aware that it was *discourse* they had discovered. But they took the structure of discourse for the structure of things, instead of for the forms which things assume under the pressure and opportunity of social cooperation and exchange. They overlooked the fact that meanings as objects of thought are entitled to be called complete and ultimate only because they are not original but are a happy outcome of a complex history. They made them primitive and independent forms of things, intrinsically regulative of processes of becoming. They took a work of social art to be nature independent of man. They overlooked the fact that the import of logical and rational essences is the consequence of social interactions, of companionship, mutual assistance, direction and concerted action in fighting, festivity, and work. Hence they conceived of ideal meanings as the ultimate framework of events, in which a system of substances and properties corresponded to subjects and predicates of the uttered proposition. Things conformed naturally and exactly to parts of speech, some being inherently subject-matter of nouns, proper and common; others of verbs, of which some expressed self-activity, while others designated adjectival and adverbial changes to which things are exposed on account of their own defects; some being external relations in which substances stand to one another, and subject-matter of prepositions.

The resulting theory of substances, essential properties, accidental qualities and relations, and the identification of Being, (by means of the copula "is") with the tenses of the verb, (so that the highest Being was, is now, and ever shall be, in contrast to existence now and then, occasional, wholly past, merely just now, or possibly at some passing time in the future) controlled the whole scheme of physics and metaphysics, which formed the philosophic tradition of Europe. It was a natural consequence of the insight that things, meanings, and words correspond.

The insight was perverted by the notion that the correspondence of things and meanings is prior to discourse and social intercourse. Hence, every true affirmation was an assertion of the fixed belonging to one another of two objects in nature; while every true denial was an assertion of intrinsic exclusion of one object by another. The consequence was belief in ideal essences, individually complete, and yet connected in a system of necessary subordinations and dependencies. Dialectic of their relationships, definition, classification, division in arranging essences, constituted scientific truth about the inmost constituents of nature. Thus a discovery which is the greatest single discovery of man, putting man in potential possession of liberation and of order, became the source of an artificial physics of nature, the basis of a science, philosophy and theology in which the universe was an incarnate grammatical order constructed after the model of discourse.

The modern discovery of inner experience, of a realm of purely personal events that are always at the individual's command, and that are his exclusively as well as inexpensively for refuge, consolation and thrill is also a great and liberating discovery. It implies a new worth and sense of dignity in human individuality, a sense that an individual is not a mere property of nature, set in place according to a scheme independent of him, as an article is put in its place in a cabinet, but that he adds something, that he makes a contribution. It is the counterpart of what distinguishes modern science, experimental, hypothetical; a logic of discovery having therefore opportunity for individual temperament, ingenuity, invention. It is the counterpart of modern politics, art, religion and industry where individuality is given room and movement, in contrast to the ancient scheme of experience, which held individuals tightly within a given order subordinated to its structure and patterns. But here also distortion entered in. Failure to recognize that this world of inner experience is dependent upon an extension of language which is a social product and operation led to the subjectivistic, solipsistic and egotistic strain in modern thought. If the classic thinkers created a cosmos after the model of dialectic, giving rational distinctions power to constitute and regulate, modern thinkers composed nature after the model of personal soliloquizing.

Language considered as an experienced event enables us to interpret what really happened when rational discourse and logic were discovered by the ancients, and when "inner" experience and its interest were discovered by moderns. Language is a natural function of human association; and its consequences react upon other events, physical and human, giving them meaning or significance. Events that are objects or significant exist in a context where they acquire new ways of operation and new properties. Words are spoken of as coins and money. Now gold, silver, and instrumentalities of credit are first of all, prior to being money, physical things with their own immediate and final qualities. But as money they are substitutes, representations, and surrogates, which embody relationships. As a substitute, money not merely facilitates exchange of such commodities as existed prior to its use, but it revolutionizes as well production and consumption of all commodities, because it brings into being new transactions, forming new histories and affairs. Exchange is not an event that can be isolated. It marks the emergence of production and consumption into a new medium and context wherein they acquire new properties.

Language is similarly not a mere agency for economizing energy in the interaction of human beings. It is a release and amplification of energies that enter into it, conferring upon them the added quality of meaning. The quality of meaning thus introduced is extended and transferred, actually and potentially, from sounds, gestures and marks, to all other things in nature. Natural events become messages to be enjoyed and administered, precisely as are song, fiction, oratory, the giving of advice and instruction. Thus events come to possess characters; they are demarcated, and noted. For character is general and distinguished.

When events have communicable meaning, they have marks, notations, and are capable of con-notation and de-notation. They are more than mere occurrences; they have implications. Hence inference and reasoning are possible; these operations are reading the message of things, which things utter because they are involved in human associations. When Aristotle drew a distinction between sensible things that are more noted—known—to us and rational things that are more noted—known—in themselves, he was actually drawing a distinction between things that operate in a local, restricted universe of discourse, and things whose marks are such that they readily enter into indefinitely extensive and varied discourse.

The interaction of human beings, namely, association, is not different in origin from other modes of interaction. There is a peculiar absurdity in the question of how individuals become social, if the question is taken literally. Human beings illustrate the same traits of both immediate uniqueness and connection, relationship, as do other things. No more in their case than in that of atoms and physical masses is immediacy the whole of existence and therefore an obstacle to being acted upon by and affecting other things. Everything that exists in as far as it is known and knowable is in interaction with other things. It is associated, as well as solitary, single. The catching up of human individuals into association is thus no new and unprecedented fact; it is a manifestation of a commonplace of existence. Significance resides not in the bare fact of association, therefore, but in the consequences that flow from the distinctive patterns of human association. There is, again, nothing new or unprecedented in the fact that assemblage of things confers upon the assembly and its constituents, new properties by means of unlocking energies hitherto pent in. The significant consideration is that assemblage of organic human beings transforms sequence and coexistence into participation.

Gestures and cries are not primarily expressive and communicative. They are modes of organic behavior as much as are locomotion, seizing and crunching. Language, signs and significance, come into existence not by intent and mind but by overflow, by-products, in gestures and sound. The story of language is the story of the *use* made of these occurrences; a use that is eventual, as well as eventful. Those rival accounts of the origin of language that go by the nicknames of bow-wow, pooh-pooh, and ding-dong theories are not in fact theories of the origin of *language*. They are accounts, of some plausibility, of how and why certain sounds rather than others were selected to signify objects, acts and situations. If the mere existence of sounds of these kinds constituted language, lower animals might well converse more subtly and fluently than man. But they became language only when used within a context of mutual assistance and direction. The latter are alone of prime importance in considering the transformation of organic gestures and cries into names, things with significance, or the origin of language.

Observable facts of animal experience furnish us with our starting point. "Animals respond to certain stimuli . . . by the contraction of certain muscles whose functioning is of no direct consequence to the animal itself, but affects other animals by stimulating them to act. . . . Let us call this class the signaling reflexes. A few, but very diversified examples of the signaling reflexes, are the lighting of a fire fly, the squeezing out of a black liquid from the ink bladder of a cuttle-fish, the crowing of a rooster . . . the spreading of its tail by a pea-cock. These reflex activities affect other animals by stimulating them. . . . If no other animals are present, or these other animals fail to respond by their own reflexes, the former reflex actions are completely wasted."[2]

Sub-human animals thus behave in ways which have no *direct* consequences of utility to the behaving animal, but which call out certain characteristic responses, sexual, protective, food-finding (as with the cluck of a hen to her chicks), in other animals. In some cases, the act evoked in other animals has in turn an important consequence for the first agent. A sexual act or a combined protective act against danger is furthered. In other

<hr>

2. Max Meyer, *Psychology of the Other-One*, 1922, p. 195; a statement of behavioristic psychology that has hardly received the attention it intrinsically deserves.

cases, the consequences turn out useful to the species, to a numerically indeterminate group including individuals not yet born. Signaling acts evidently form the basic *material* of language. Similar activities occur without intent in man; thus a babe's scream attracts the attention of an adult and evokes a response useful to the infant, although the cry itself is an organic overflow having no intent. So too a man's posture and facial changes may indicate to another things which the man himself would like to conceal, so that he "gives himself away." "Expression," or signs, communication of meaning, exists in such cases for the observer, not for the agent.

While signaling acts are a material condition of language they are not language nor yet are they its *sufficient* condition. Only from an external standpoint, is the original action even a signal; the response of other animals to it is not to a sign, but, by some preformed mechanism, to a direct stimulus. By habit, by conditioned reflex, hens run to the farmer when he makes a clucking noise, or when they hear the rattle of grain in a pan. When the farmer raises his arms to throw the grain they scatter and fly, to return only when the movement ceases. They act as if alarmed; his movement is thus not a sign of food; it is a stimulus that evokes flight. But a human infant learns to discount such movements; to become interested in them as events preparatory to a desired consummation; he learns to treat them as signs of an ulterior event so that his response is to their meaning. He treats them as means to consequences. The hen's activity is ego-centric; that of the human being is participative. The latter puts himself at the standpoint of a situation in which two parties share. This is the essential peculiarity of language, or signs.

A requests B to bring him something, to which A points, say a flower. There is an original mechanism by which B may react to A's movement in pointing. But natively such a reaction is to the movement, not to the *pointing*, not to the object pointed out. But B learns that the movement *is* a pointing; he responds to it not in itself, but as an index of something else. His response is transferred from A's direct movement to the *object* to which A points. Thus he does not merely execute the natural acts of looking or grasping which the movement might instigate on its own account. The motion of A attracts his gaze to the thing pointed to; then, instead of just transferring his response from A's movement to the native reaction he might make to the thing as stimulus, he responds in a way which is a function of A's *relationship*, actual and potential, to the thing. The characteristic thing about B's understanding of A's movement and sounds is that he responds to the thing from the standpoint of A. He perceives the thing as it may function in A's experience, instead of just ego-centrically. Similarly, A in making the request conceives the thing not only in its direct relationship to himself, but as a thing capable of being grasped and handled by B. He sees the thing as it may function in B's experience. Such is the essence and import of communication, signs and meaning. Something is literally made common in at least two different centres of behavior. To understand is to anticipate together, it is to make a cross-reference which, when acted upon, brings about a partaking in a common, inclusive, undertaking.

Stated in greater detail; B upon hearing A, makes a preparatory reaction of his eyes, hands and legs in view of the consummatory act of A's possession; he engages in the act of grasping, carrying and tendering the flower to A. At the same time, A makes a preparatory response to B's consummatory act, that of carrying and proffering the flower. Thus neither the sounds uttered by A, his gesture of pointing, nor the sight of the thing pointed to, is the occasion and stimulus of B's act; the stimulus is B's anticipatory share in the consummation of a transaction in which both participate. The heart of language is not "expression" of something antecedent, much less expression of antecedent thought. It is communication; the establishment of cooperation in an activity in which there are partners, and in which the activity of each is modified and regulated by partnership. To fail to understand is to fail to come into agreement in action; to misunderstand is to set up action at cross purposes. Take speech as behavioristically as you will, including the elimination of all private mental states, and it remains true that it is markedly distinguished from the signaling acts of animals. Meaning is not indeed a psychic existence; it is primarily a property of behavior, and secondarily a property of objects. But the behavior of which it is a quality is a distinctive behavior; cooperative, in that response to another's act involves contemporaneous response to a thing as entering into the other's behavior, and this upon both sides. It is difficult to state the exact physiological mechanism which is involved. But about the fact there is no doubt. It constitutes the intelligibility of acts and things. Possession of the capacity to engage in such activity is intelligence. Intelligence and meaning are natural consequences of the peculiar form which interaction sometimes assumes in the case of human beings.

Primarily meaning is intent and intent is not personal in a private and exclusive sense. A proposes the consummatory possession of the flower through the medium or means of B's action; B proposes to cooperate—or act adversely—in the fulfillment of A's proposal. Secondarily, meaning is the acquisition of significance by things in their status in making possible and fulfilling shared cooperation. In the first place, it is the *motion and sounds* of A which have meaning, or are signs. Similarly the movements of B, while they are immediate to him, are signs to A of B's cooperation or refusal. But secondarily the *thing* pointed out by A to B gains meaning. It ceases to be just what it brutely is at the moment, and is responded to in its potentiality, as a means to remoter consequences. The flower pointed to for example, *is* portable; but apart from language portability is a brute contingency waiting for its actualization upon circumstance. But when A counts upon the understanding and cooperation of B, and B responds to the intent of A, the flower *is* contemporaneously portable though not now actually in movement. Its potentiality, or conditioning of consequences, is an immediately recognized and possessed trait; the flower *means* portability instead of simply *being* portable. Animism, the attribution of desire and intent to inanimate things, is no mysterious projection of psychical traits; it is a misinterpretation of a natural fact, namely, that significant things are things actually implicated in situations of shared or social purpose and execution.

The logic of animism is simple. Since words act upon things indirectly, or as signs, and since words express the significant consequences of things, (the traits for the sake of which they are used), why should not words act also directly upon things to release their latent powers? Since we "call" things by their names, why should they not answer? And if they assist us as our friends do when appealed to, is not this proof they are animated by friendly intent; or if they frustrate us, proof that they are filled with the same traits which inspirit our enemies? "Animism" is thus the consequence of a direct transfer of properties of a social situation to an immediate relationship of natural things to a person. Its legitimate and constant form is poetry, in which things and events are given voice and directly communicate with us.

If we consider the *form* or scheme of the situation in which meaning and understanding occur, we find an involved simultaneous presence and cross-reference of immediacy and efficiency, overt actuality and potentiality, the consummatory and the instrumental. *A* in making the request of *B*, at the same time makes the incipient and preparatory response of receiving the thing at the hands of *B*; he performs in readiness the consummatory act. *B*'s understanding of the meaning of what *A* says, instead of being a mere reaction to sound, is an anticipation of a consequence, while it is also an immediate activity of eyes, legs, and hands in getting and giving the flower to *A*. The flower is the thing which it immediately is, and it also is means of a conclusion. All of this is directly involved in the existence of intelligible speech. No such simultaneous presence of finality and agency, is possible in things as *purely* physical—in abstraction, that is, of potential presence in a situation of communication. Since we have discovered that all things have a phase of potential communicability, that is, that any conceivable thing may enter into discourse, the retrospective imputation of meanings and logical relationships to bare things is natural; it does no harm, save when the imputation is dogmatic and literal. What a physical event immediately is, and what it *can* do or its relationship are distinct and incommensurable. But when an event has meaning, its potential consequences become its integral and funded feature. When the potential consequences are important and repeated, they form the very nature and essence of a thing, its defining, identifying, and distinguishing form. To recognize the thing is to grasp its definition. Thus we become capable of perceiving things instead of merely feeling and having them. To *perceive* is to acknowledge unattained possibilities; it is to refer the present to consequences, apparition to issue, and thereby to behave in deference to the *connections* of events. As an attitude, perception or awareness is predictive expectancy, wariness. Since potential consequences also *mark* the thing itself, and form its nature, the event thus marked becomes an object of contemplation; as meaning, future consequences already belong to the thing. The act of striving to bring them existentially into the world may be commuted into esthetic enjoyed possession of form.

Essence, as has been intimated, is but a pronounced instance of meaning; to be partial, and to assign *a* meaning to a thing as *the* meaning is but to evince human subjection to bias. Since consequences differ also in their consequence and hence importance, practical good sense may attach to this one-sided partiality, for the meaning seized upon as essence may designate extensive and recurrent consequences. Thus is explained the seeming paradox of the distinction and connection of essence and existence. Essence is never existence, and yet it is the essence, the distilled import, of existence; the significant thing about it, its intellectual voucher, the means of inference and extensive transfer, and object of esthetic intuition. In it, feeling and understanding are one; the meaning of a thing is the sense it makes.

Since the consequences which are liked have an emphatic quality, it is not surprising that many consequences, even though recognized to be inevitable, are regarded as if they were accidental and alien. Thus the very essence of a thing is identified with those consummatory consequences which the thing has when conditions are felicitous. Thus *the* essence, one, immutable and constitutive, which *makes* the thing *what* it is, emerges from the various meanings which vary with varying conditions and transitory intents. When essence is then thought to contain existence as the perfect includes the imperfect, it is because a legitimate, practical measure of reality in terms of importance is illegitimately altered into a theoretical measure.

Discourse itself is both instrumental and consummatory. Communication is an exchange which procures something wanted; it involves a claim, appeal, order, direction or request, which realizes want at less cost than personal labor exacts, since it procures the cooperative assistance of others. Communication is also an immediate enhancement of life, enjoyed for its own sake. The dance is accompanied by song and becomes the drama; scenes of danger and victory are most fully savored when they are told. Greeting becomes a ceremonial with its prescribed rites. Language is always a form of action and in its instrumental use is always a means of concerted action for an end, while at the

same time it finds in itself all the goods of its possible consequences. For there is no mode of action as fulfilling and as rewarding as is concerted consensus of action. It brings with it the
sense of sharing and merging in a whole. Forms of language are
unrivalled in ability to create this sense, at first with direct participation on the part of an audience; and then, as literary forms
develop, through imaginative identification. Greek thinkers had
distinguished patterns in Greek literary art of consummatory
uses of speech, and the meanings that were discovered to be
indispensable to communication were treated as final and ultimate in nature itself. Essences were hypostatized into original
and constitutive forms of all existence.

The idea put forth about the connection of meaning with language is not to be confused with traditional nominalism. It does
not imply that meaning and essence are adventitious and arbitrary. The defect of nominalism lies in its virtual denial of interaction and association. It regarded the word not as a mode of
social action with which to realize the ends of association, but as
an expression of a ready-made, exclusively individual, mental
state; sensation, image or feeling, which, being an existence, is
necessarily particular. For the sound, gesture, or written mark
which is involved in language is a particular existence. But as
such it is not a *word*, and it does not become a word by declaring
a mental existence; it becomes a word by gaining meaning; and it
gains meaning when its use establishes a genuine community of
action. Interaction, operative relationship, is as much a fact
about events as are particularity and immediacy. Language and
its consequences are characters taken on by natural interaction
and natural conjunction in specified conditions of organization.
Nominalism ignores organization, and thus makes nonsense of
meanings.

Language is specifically a mode of interaction of at least two
beings, a speaker and a hearer; it presupposes an organized
group to which these creatures belong, and from whom they
have acquired their habits of speech. It is therefore a relationship, not a particularity. This consideration alone condemns traditional nominalism. The meaning of signs moreover always
includes something common as between persons and an object.
When we attribute meaning to the speaker as *his* intent, we take
for granted another person who is to share in the execution of

the intent, and also something, independent of the persons concerned, through which the intent is to be realized. Persons and thing must alike serve as means in a common, shared consequence. This community of partaking is meaning.

The invention and use of tools have played a large part in consolidating meanings, because a tool is a thing used as means to consequences, instead of being taken directly and physically. It is intrinsically relational, anticipatory, predictive. Without reference to the absent, or "transcendence," nothing is a tool. The most convincing evidence that animals do not "think" is found in the fact that they have no tools, but depend upon their own relatively-fixed bodily structures to effect results. Because of such dependence they have no way of distinguishing the immediate existence of anything from its potential efficiencies; no way of projecting its consequences to define a nature or essence. Anything whatever used as a tool exhibits distinction and identification. Fire existentially burns; while fire which is employed in order to cook and keep warm, especially after other things, like rubbing sticks together, are used as means to generate it, is an existence having meaning and potential essence. The presence of inflammation and terror or discomfort is no longer the whole story; an occurrence is now an object; and while it is absurd to hold (as idealism virtually does) that the meaning of an existence is the real substance of the existence, it is equally absurd not to recognize the full transformative import of what has happened.

As to be a tool, or to be used as means for consequences, is to have and to endow with meaning, language, being the tool of tools, is the cherishing mother of all significance. For other instrumentalities and agencies, the things usually thought of as appliances, agencies and furnishings, can originate and develop only in social groups made possible by language. Things become tools ceremonially and institutionally. The notoriously conventionalized and traditional character of primitive utensils and their attendant symbolizations demonstrate this fact. Moreover, tools and artifices of agency are always found in connection with some division of labor which depends upon some device of communication. The statement can be proved in a more theoretical way. Immediacy as such is transient to the point of evanescence, and its flux has to be fixed by some easily recoverable and recurrent act within control of the organism, like gesture and spoken sounds, before things can be intentionally utilized. A creature might accidentally warm itself by a fire or use a stick to stir the ground in a way which furthered the growth of food-plants. But the effect of comfort ceases with the fire, existentially; a stick even though once used as a lever would revert to the status of being just a stick, unless the *relationship* between it and its consequence were distinguished and retained. Only language, or some form of artificial signs, serves to register the relationship and make it fruitful in other contexts of particular existence. Spears, urns, baskets, snares may have originated accidentally in some consummatory consequence of natural events. But only repetition through concerted action accounts for their becoming institutionalized as tools, and this concert of action depends upon the use of memoranda and communication. To make another aware of the possibility of a use or objective relationship is to perpetuate what is otherwise an incident as an agency; communication is a condition of consciousness.

Thus every meaning is generic or universal. It is something common between speaker, hearer and the thing to which speech refers. It is universal also as a means of generalization. For a meaning is a method of action, a way of using things as means to a shared consummation, and method is general, though the things to which it is applied are particular. The meaning, for example, of portability is something in which two persons and an object share. But portability after it is once apprehended becomes a way of treating other things; it is extended widely. Whenever there is a chance, it is applied; application ceases only when a thing refuses to be treated in this way. And even then refusal may be only a challenge to develop the meaning of portability until the thing can be transported. Meanings are rules for using and interpreting things; interpretation being always an imputation of potentiality for some consequence.

It would be difficult to imagine any doctrine more absurd than the theory that general ideas or meanings arise by the comparison of a number of particulars, eventuating in the recognition of something common to them all. Such a comparison may be employed to check a suggested widened application of a rule. But generalization is carried spontaneously as far as it will plausibly go; usually much further than it will actually go. A newly acquired meaning is forced upon everything that does not obviously resist its application, as a child uses a new word whenever he gets a chance or as he plays with a new toy. Meanings are self-moving to new cases. In the end, conditions force a chastening of this spontaneous tendency. The scope and limits of application are ascertained experimentally in the process of application. The history of science, to say nothing of popular beliefs, is sufficient indication of the difficulty found in submitting this irrational generalizing tendency to the discipline of experience. To call it *a priori* is to express a fact; but to impute the *a priori* character of the generalizing force of meanings to *reason* is to invert the facts. Rationality is acquired when the tendency becomes circumspect, based upon observation and tested by deliberate experiment.

Meaning is objective as well as universal. Originating as a concerted or combined method of using or enjoying things, it indicates a possible interaction, not a thing in separate singleness. A meaning may not of course have the particular objectivity which is imputed to it, as whistling does not actually portend wind, nor the ceremonial sprinkling of water indicate rain. But such magical imputations of external reference testify to the objectivity of meaning as such. Meanings are naturally the meaning of something or other; difficulty lies in discriminating the right thing. It requires the discipline of ordered and deliberate experimentation to teach us that some meanings delightful or horrendous as they are, are meanings communally developed in the process of communal festivity and control, and do not represent the polities, and ways and means of nature apart from social arts. Scientific meanings were superadded to esthetic and affectional meanings when objects instead of being defined in terms of their consequences in social interactions and discussion were defined in terms of their consequences with respect to one another. This discrimination permitted esthetic and affective objects to be freed from magical imputations, which were due to attributing to them *in rerum natura* the consequences they had in the transmitted culture of the group.

Yet the truth of classic philosophy in assigning objectivity to meanings, essences, ideas remains unassailable. It is heresy to conceive meanings to be private, a property of ghostly psychic existences. Berkeley with all his nominalism, saw that "ideas," though particular in existence, are general in function and office.

His attribution of the ideas which are efficacious in conduct to an order established by God, while evincing lack of perception of their naturalistic origin in communication or communal interaction, manifests a sounder sense of the objectivity of meanings than has been shown by those who eliminated his theology while retaining his psychology. The inconsistency of the sensationalists who, stopping short of extreme scepticism, postulate that some associations of ideas correspond to conjunctions among things is also reluctantly extorted evidence of how intimation of the objectivity of ideas haunts the mind in spite of theory to the contrary.

Meanings are objective because they are modes of natural interaction; such an interaction, although primarily between organic beings, as includes things and energies external to living creatures. The regulative force of legal meanings affords a convenient illustration. A traffic policeman holds up his hand or blows a whistle. His act operates as a signal to direct movements. But it is more than an episodic stimulus. It embodies a rule of social action. Its proximate meaning is its near-by consequences in coordination of movements of persons and vehicles; its ulterior and permanent meaning—essence—is its consequence in the way of security of social movements. Failure to observe the signal subjects a person to arrest, fine or imprisonment. The essence embodied in the policeman's whistle is not an occult reality superimposed upon a sensuous or physical flux and imparting form to it; a mysterious subsistence somehow housed within a psychical event. Its essence is the rule, comprehensive and persisting, the standardized habit, of social interaction, and for the sake of which the whistle is used. The pattern, archetype, that forms the essence of the whistle as a particular noise is an orderly arrangement of the movements of persons and vehicles established by social agreement as its consequence. This meaning is independent of the psychical landscape, the sensations and imagery, of the policeman and others concerned. But it is not on that account a timeless spiritual ghost nor pale logical subsistence divorced from events.

The case is the same with the essence of any non-human event, like gravity, or virtue, or vertebrate. Some consequences of the interaction of things concern us; the consequences are not *merely* physical; they enter finally into human action and destiny. Fire burns and the burning is of moment. It enters experience; it is fascinating to watch swirling flames; it is important to avoid its dangers and to utilize its beneficial potencies. When we name an event, calling it fire, we speak proleptically; we do not name an immediate event; that is impossible. We employ a term of discourse; we invoke a meaning, namely, the potential consequences of the existence. The ultimate meaning of the noise made by the traffic officer is the total consequent system of social behavior, in which individuals are subjected, by means of noise, to social coordination; its proximate meaning is a coordination of the movements of persons and vehicles in the neighborhood and directly affected. Similarly the ultimate meaning, or essence, denominated fire, is the consequences of certain natural events within the scheme of human activities, in the experience of social intercourse, the hearth and domestic altar, shared comfort, working of metals, rapid transit, and other such affairs. "Scientifically," we ignore these ulterior meanings. And quite properly; for when a sequential order of changes is determined, the final meaning in immediate enjoyments and appreciations is capable of control.

While classic thought, and its survival in later idealisms, assumed that the ulterior human meanings, meanings of direct association in discourse, are forms of nature apart from their place in discourse, modern thought is given to marking a sharp separation between meanings determined in terms of the causal relationship of things and meanings in terms of human association. Consequently, it treats the latter as negligible or as purely private, not the meanings of natural events at all. It identifies the proximate meanings with the only valid meanings, and abstract relations become an idol. To pass over in science the human meanings of the consequences of natural interactions is legitimate; indeed it is indispensable. To ascertain and state meanings in abstraction from social or shared situations is the only way in which the latter can be intelligently modified, extended and varied. Mathematical symbols have least connection with distinctively human situations and consequences; and the finding of such terms, free from esthetic and moral significance, is a necessary part of the technique. Indeed, such elimination of ulterior meanings supplies perhaps the best possible empirical definition of mathematical relations. They are meanings without direct reference to human behavior. Thus an essence becomes wholly "intellectual" or scientific, devoid of consummatory implication; it expresses the purely instrumental without reference to the objects to which the events in question are instrumental. It then becomes the starting point of reflection that may terminate in ends or consequences in human suffering and enjoyment not previously experienced. Abstraction from any particular consequence (which is the same thing as taking instrumentality generally), opens the way to new uses and consequences.

This is what happens when the meaning of the traffic officer's signal is detached from its own context, and taken up into, say, written and published language, a topic of independent consideration by experts or by civic administrators. In being placed in a context of other meanings, (theoretically and scientifically discussed), it is liberated from the contingencies of its prior use. The outcome may be the invention of a new and improved system of semaphores which exercise regulation of human interaction more effectively. Deliberate abstraction, however, from all ulterior human use and consequence is hardly likely to occur in the case of discourse about a signal system. In physical science, the abstraction or liberation is complete. Things are defined by means of symbols that convey only their consequences with respect to one another. "Water" in ordinary experience designates an essence of something which has familiar bearings and uses in human life, drink and cleansing and the extinguishing of fire. But H_2O gets away from these connections, and embodies in its essence only instrumental efficiency in respect to things independent of human affairs.

The counterpart of classic thought which took ends, enjoyments, uses, not simply as genuine termini of natural events (which they are), but as the essence and form of things independent of human experience, is a modern philosophy which makes reality purely mechanical and which regards the consequences of things in human experience as accidental or phenomenal by-products. In truth, abstraction from human experience is but a liberation from familiar and specific enjoyments, it provides means for detecting hitherto untried consequences, for invention, for the creation of new wants, and new modes of good and evil. In any sense in which the conception of essence is legitimate, these human consequences are the essence of natural events.

Water still has the meanings of water of everyday experience when it becomes the essence H_2O, or else H_2O would be totally meaningless, a mere sound, not an intelligible name.

Meaning, fixed as essence in a term of discourse, may be imaginatively administered and manipulated, experimented with. Just as we overtly manipulate things, making new separations and combinations, thereby introducing things into new contexts and environments, so we bring together logical universals in discourse, where they copulate and breed new meanings. There is nothing surprising in the fact that dialectic (or deduction, as it is termed by moderns) generates new objects; that, in Kantian language, it is "synthetic," instead of merely explicating what is already had. All discourse, oral or written, which is more than a routine unrolling of vocal habits, says things that surprise the one that says them, often indeed more than they surprise any one else. Systematic logical discourse, or ratiocination, is the same sort of thing conducted according to stricter rules. Even under the condition of rigid rules the emergence of new meanings is much more similar to what happens in general conversation than is conventionally supposed. Rules of logical order and consistency appertain to economy and efficiency of combination and separation in generating new meanings; not to meanings as such. They are rules of a certain kind of experimentation. In trying new combinations of meanings, satisfactory consequences of new meanings are hit upon; then they may be arranged in a system. The expert in thought is one who has skill in making experiments to introduce an old meaning into different situations and who has a sensitive ear for detecting resultant harmonies and discords. The most "deductive" thought in actual occurrence is a series of trials, observations and selections. In one sense of the ambiguous word intuition, it is a "series of intuitions," and logic is *ex post facto*, expressing a wit that formulates economically the congruities and incongruities that have manifested themselves. Any "syllogism" which is such *ab initio* is performed better by a machine that manipulates symbols automatically than by any "thinker."

This capacity of essences to enter readily into any number of new combinations, and thereby generate further meanings more profound and far reaching than those from which they sprang, gives them a semblance of independent life and career, a semblance which is responsible for their elevation by some thinkers into a realm separate from that of existence and superior to it. Consider the interpretations that have been based upon such essences as four, plus, the square root of minus one. These are at once so manipulable and so fertile in consequences when conjoined with others that thinkers who are primarily interested in their performances treat them not as significant terms of discourse, but as an order of entities independent of human invention and use. The fact that we can watch them and register what happens when they come together, and that the things that happen are as independent of our volition and expectation as are the discoveries of a geographic exploration, is taken as evidence that they constitute entities having subsistent Being independently not only of us but of all natural events whatever.

Alternatives are too narrowly conceived. Because meanings and essences are not states of mind, because they are as independent of immediate sensation and imagery as are physical things, and because nevertheless they are not physical things, it is assumed that they are a peculiar kind of thing, termed metaphysical, or "logical" in a style which separates logic from nature. But there are many other things which are neither physical nor psychical existences, and which are demonstrably dependent upon human association and interaction. Such things function moreover in liberating and regulating subsequent human intercourse; their essence is their contribution to making that intercourse more significant and more immediately rewarding. Take the sort of thing exemplified in the regulation of traffic. The sound of a whistle is a particular existential event numerically separate, with its own peculiar spatial temporal position. This may not be said of the rule or method of social cooperative interaction which it manifests and makes effective. A continuous way of organized action is not a particular, and hence is not a physical or psychical existence. Yet the consequences of using the method of adjusting movements, so that they do not interfere with one another, have both a physical and a mental phase. Physically, there is modification of the changes in space which would otherwise occur. Mentally, there are enjoyments and annoyances which would not otherwise happen. But no one of these incidents nor all of them put together form the essence or ulterior meaning of the sound of the whistle; they are qualifications of a more secure concert of human activity which, as a consequence of a legal order incarnate in the whistling, forms its significance.

Discussion of meaning and essence has reached such an impasse and is barbed with such entanglements, that it is further worth while to suggest consideration of legal entities as indicative of escape from the disjunction of essence from existence. What is a Corporation, a Franchise? A corporation is neither a mental state nor a particular physical event in space and time. Yet it is an objective reality, not an ideal Realm of Being. It is an objective reality which has multitudinous physical and mental consequences. It is something to be studied as we study electrons; it exhibits as does the latter unexpected properties, and when introduced into new situations behaves with new reactions. It is something which may be conducted, facilitated and obstructed, precisely as may be a river. Nevertheless it would not exist nor have any meaning and potency apart from an interaction of human beings with one another, an interaction in which external things are implicated. As legal essence, or concerted method of regulated interaction, corporation has its own and its developing career.

Again juridical rule implies jurisdiction; a particular body of persons within a certain territory to whom it applies. The legal significance of an act depends upon *where* it takes place. Yet an act is an interaction, a transaction, not isolated, self-sufficient. The initial stage of an act and the terminating consequences which, between them, determine its meaning, may be far apart in place as well as in time. Where then is the act? What is its locus? The readiest reply is in terms of the beginning of the act. The act was performed where the agent bodily was at the time of its occurrence. Suppose, however, that before discovery, the agent in a criminal transaction changes his abode and resides within another jurisdiction. The need of security leads to the generation, in its union with the conception of jurisdiction, of a new conception or essence, that of extradition, of comity of jurisdictions. New procedures with corresponding new technical concepts or meanings then develop by means of which a person charged with crime may be requisitioned and removed. The concept of jurisdiction in combination with that of security, justice, etc., deductively generates other concepts.

The process does not stop here. An agent implies a patient. Suppose a person in New York State shoots a bullet across the New Jersey line, and kills some one in that State; or sends poisoned candy by mail to some one in California who dies from eating it. *Where* is the crime committed? The guilty person is not within the jurisdiction of the State where the death resulted; hence, his crime, by definition, was not committed in that State. But since the death did not occur where he was bodily present at the time, no crime occurred in that jurisdiction, locus being defined in terms of the abode of the agent. The essence, extradition, does not apply because there is no crime for which to extradite him. In short, because of the accepted meaning of jurisdiction, no crime has been committed anywhere. Such an outcome is evidently prejudicial to the integrity and security of human association and intercourse. Thus the element of *transaction* in an act is noted; an act initiated within a given jurisdiction becomes a crime when its obnoxious consequences occur outside. The locus of the act now extends all the way from New York to California. Thus two independent particular events capable of direct observation, together with a connection between them which is inferred, not directly observable, are now included in so simple a meaning as that of the locus of an act. In the traditional language of philosophy, the essence is now ideal or rational, non-sensible. Furthermore a system of legal meanings is developed by modifying different ones with a view to consistency or logical order. Thus the meanings get more independent of the events that led up to them; they may be taught and expounded as a logical system, whose portions are deductively connected with one another.

In civil cases, however, the concept of locus even as thus extended fails to take care of all the consequences which are found to require regulation, by attachment of rights and liabilities to certain classes of acts. A transaction may concern goods or funds which operate in a jurisdiction different to that of either of the parties directly concerned in it. Its consequences include persons living in a third jurisdiction. The ultimate result is a tendency in some cases to reverse the earlier and more immediately physical (or spatially limited) concept of jurisdiction with respect to place. Jurisdiction comes to mean "power to deal legally" with a certain specific affair, rather than an "area within which action has occurred": that is, area is defined by power to act, which in turn is determined with respect to consequences found desirable, while originally a concept of fixed area had been employed to fix power of legal action. If it be asked, "where" a transaction is located, the only possible answer, on the basis of legal procedure, appears in many cases to be that it is located wherever it has consequences which it is deemed socially important to regulate.[3]

Juridical institutions everywhere embody essences which are as objective and coercive with respect to opinions, emotions and sensations of individuals as are physical objects; essences which are general, capable of independent examination; of fruitful connection with one another; and of extension to concrete phenomena not previously related to them. At the same time the origin and nature of such meanings can be empirically described by reference to social interactions and their consequences. They are means of regulating consequences, through establishing a present cross-reference to one another of the diverse acts of interacting agents. If we bear in mind the capacity to transfer such a regulative method to new and previously unconnected universes of discourse, there is nothing astonishing in the fact that a stain may mean an anatomical structure, a change in the size of a mercury column changes in atmospheric pressure and thus probable rain. There is nothing astonishing therefore in the fact that meanings expressed in symbols are capable of yielding a vast and growing system of mathematics. An essence which is a method of procedure can be linked to other methods of procedure so as to yield new methods; to bring about a revision of old methods, and form a systematic and ordered whole—all without reference to any application of any method to any particular set of concrete existences, and in complete abstraction from any particular consequences which the methods or logical universals are to regulate. For mathematics, they are as much independent objects

3. In this respect the actual tendency of law (though not always its doctrinal formulations) is further advanced than are views current among philosophers. Compare the discussions as to "where" an illusion is; or what is the locus of past experience, and "where" unrealized possibilities exist. Some writers find satisfaction in locating them "in" the mind, although they also deny that mind is spatial. Then, realizing that the psychical existence "in" which these affairs are located is itself a present particular existence, they find it necessary to place an "essence" or meaning within the skin of the psychical state.

as is the material with which a zoologist deals. Comparison with machines like a self-binding reaper or a telephone system is useful. Machines are evolved in human experience, not prior to it or independently of it. But they are objective and compelling with respect to present particular physical and psychical processes; they are general methods of reaching consequences; they are interactions of previously existing physical existences. Moreover, they depend for their efficacy upon other and independent natural existences; they produce consequences only when used in connection with other existences which limit and test their operation. When machines have attained a certain stage of development, engineers may devote themselves to the construction of new machines and to improvements in old machines without specific reference to concrete uses and applications. That is, inventors are guided by the inherent logic of existing machines, by observation of the consistency of relationships which parts of the machine bear to one another and to the pattern of the entire machine. An invention may thus result from purely mathematical calculations. Nevertheless the machine is still a machine, an instrumental device for regulating interactions with reference to consequences.

When the "concept" of a machine, its meaning or essence embodied in a symbol, deductively generates plans of new machines, essence is fruitful because it was first devised for a purpose. Its subsequent success or failure in fulfilling its purpose, in delivering the desired consequences, together with reflection upon the reason therefore, supply a basis for revising, extending, and modifying the essence in question; thus it has a career and consequence of its own. If we follow the lead of empirically verifiable cases, it would then appear that mathematical and moral essences may be dialectically fruitful, because like other machines they have been constructed for the purpose of securing certain consequences with the minimum of waste and the maximum of economy and efficiency.

Communication is consummatory as well as instrumental. It is a means of establishing cooperation, domination and order. Shared experience is the greatest of human goods. In communication, such conjunction and contact as is characteristic of animals become endearments capable of infinite idealization; they become symbols of the very culmination of nature. That God is love is a more worthy idealization than that the divine is power. Since love at its best brings illumination and wisdom, this meaning is as worthy as that the divine is truth. Various phases of participation by one in another's joy, sorrows, sentiments and purposes, are distinguished by the scope and depth of the objects that are held in common, from a momentary caress to continued insight and loyalty. When a psychologist like Bain reduced the "tender emotions" to sensations of contact he indicated a natural organic basis. But he failed to connect even organic contact with its vital function, assimilation and fruitful union; while (what is of greater import) he failed to note the transformation that this biological function undergoes when its consequences, being noted, become an objective meaning incorporated as its essence in a natural physiological occurrence.

If scientific discourse is instrumental in function, it also is capable of becoming an enjoyed object to those concerned in it. Upon the whole, human history shows that thinking in being abstract, remote and technical has been laborious; or at least that the process of attaining such thinking has been rendered painful to most by social circumstances. In view of the importance of such activity and its objects, it is a priceless gain when it becomes an intrinsic delight. Few would philosophize if philosophic discourse did not have its own inhering fascination. Yet it is not the satisfactoriness of the activity which defines science or philosophy; the definition comes from the structure and function of subject-matter. To say that knowledge as the fruit of intellectual discourse is an end in itself is to say what is esthetically and morally true for some persons, but it conveys nothing about the structure of knowledge; and it does not even hint that its objects are not instrumental. These are questions that can be decided only by an examination of the things in question. Impartial and disinterested thinking, discourse in terms of scrutinized, tested, and related meanings, is a fine art. But it is an art as yet open to comparatively few. Letters, poetry, song, the drama, fiction, history, biography, engaging in rites and ceremonies hallowed by time and rich with the sense of the countless multitudes that share in them, are also modes of discourse that, detached from immediate instrumental consequences of assistance and cooperative action, are ends for most persons. In them discourse is both instrumental and final. No person remains unchanged and has the same future efficiencies, who shares in situations made possible by communication. Subsequent consequences may be good or bad, but they are there. The part of wisdom is not to deny the causal fact because of the intrinsic value of the immediate experience. It is to make the immediately satisfactory object the object which will also be most fertile.

The saying of Matthew Arnold that poetry is a criticism of life sounds harsh to the ears of some persons of strong esthetic bent; it seems to give poetry a moral and instrumental function. But while poetry is not a criticism of life in intent, it is in effect, and so is all art. For art fixes those standards of enjoyment and appreciation with which other things are compared; it selects the objects of future desires; it stimulates effort. This is true of the objects in which a particular person finds his immediate or esthetic values, and it is true of collective man. The level and style of the arts of literature, poetry, ceremony, amusement, and recreation which obtain in a community, furnishing the staple objects of enjoyment in that community, do more than all else to determine the current direction of ideas and endeavors in the community. They supply the meanings in terms of which life is judged, esteemed, and criticized. For an outside spectator, they supply material for a critical evaluation of the life led by that community.

Communication is uniquely instrumental and uniquely final. It is instrumental as liberating us from the otherwise overwhelming pressure of events and enabling us to live in a world of things that have meaning. It is final as a sharing in the objects and arts precious to a community, a sharing whereby meanings are enhanced, deepened and solidified in the sense of communion. Because of its characteristic agency and finality, communication and its congenial objects are objects ultimately worthy of awe, admiration, and loyal appreciation. They are worthy as means, because they are the only means that make life rich and varied in meanings. They are worthy as ends, because in such ends man is lifted from his immediate isolation and shares in a communion of meanings. Here, as in so many other things, the great evil lies in separating instrumental and final functions. Intelligence is partial and specialized, because communication and participation are limited, sectarian, provincial, confined to class, party, professional group. By the same token, our enjoyment of ends is luxurious and corrupting for some; brutal, trivial, harsh for others; exclusion from the life of free and full communication excluding both alike from full possession of meanings of the things that enter experience. When the instrumental and final functions of communication live together in experience, there exists an intelligence which is the method and reward of the common life, and a society worthy to command affection, admiration, and loyalty.[4]

4. Since the above was originally written I have found the following by Dr. Malinowski in Ogden and Richards, *The Meaning of Meaning*: "A word, signifying an important utensil, is used in action, not to comment on its nature or reflect on its properties, but to make it appear, be handed over to the speaker, or to direct another man to its proper use. The meaning of the thing is made up of experiences of its active uses and not of intellectual contemplation. . . . A word *means* to a native the proper use of the thing for which it stands, exactly as an implement *means* something when it can be handled and means nothing when no active experience is at hand. Similarly a verb, a word for an action, receives its meaning through active participation in this action. A word is used when it can produce an action, and not to describe one, still less to translate thoughts" (pp. 488–89). I know of no statement about language that brings out with the same clearness and appreciation of the force of the fact that language is primarily a mode of action used for the sake of influencing the conduct of others in connection with the speaker. As he says, "The manner in which I am using language now, in writing these words, the manner in which the author of a book or a papyrus or hewn inscription has to use it, is a very far-fetched and derivative function of language. In its primitive uses, language functions as a link in concerted human activity, as a piece of human behaviour" (p. 474). He shows that to understand the meaning of savage language, we have to be able to re-instate the whole social context which alone supplies the meaning. While he lists narrative and ceremonial speech as well as active, he shows that the same principle permeates them. "When incidents are told or discussed among a group of listeners, there is, first, the situation of that moment made up of the respective social, intellectual and emotional attitudes of those present. Within this situation, the narrative creates new bonds and sentiments by the emotional appeal of the words. In every case, narrative speech is primarily a mode of social action rather than a mere reflection of thought" (p. 475). Then there is the use of language "in free, aimless, social intercourse." "In discussing the function of speech in mere sociabilities, we come to one of the bedrock aspects of human nature in society. There is in all human beings the well-known tendency to congregate, to be together, to enjoy each other's company. . . . Taciturnity means not only unfriendliness but directly a bad character. The breaking of silence, the communion of words, is the first act to establish links of fellowship" (pp. 476–77). Here speech has both the instrumental use of re-assurance and the consummatory good of enhanced sense of membership in a congenial whole. Thus communication is not only a means to common ends but is the sense of community, communion actualized. Nothing more important for philosophers to hearken to has been written than Dr. Malinowski's conclusion: "Language is little influenced by thought, but Thought on the contrary having

to borrow from action its tool—that is, language—is largely influenced thereby. To sum up we can say that the fundamental grammatical categories, universal to all human languages, can be understood only with reference to the pragmatic *Weltanschauung* of primitive man and that, through the use of language, the barbarous primitive categories must have deeply influenced the later philosophies of man" (p. 498). He goes on to show its influence in framing categories of (nouns) substance, of action centering around (verbs) objects, and spatial relations—prepositions. And he closes with an express warning against "the old realist fallacy that a word vouches for, or contains, the reality of its meaning. The migration of roots into improper places has given to the imaginary reality of hypostatised meaning a special solidity of its own. For since early experience warrants the substantival existence of anything found within the category of Crude Substance or *Protousia*, and subsequent linguistic shifts introduce there such roots as 'going,' 'rest,' 'motion,' etc., the obvious inference is that such abstract entities or ideas live in a world of their own" (p. 509). Here we have the source of the classic hypostatizing of essence which is described in the text as due to isolating important meanings of things from their context in human interaction.

6.   Nature, Mind and the Subject

Personality, selfhood, subjectivity are eventual functions that emerge with complexly organized interactions, organic and social. Personal individuality has its basis and conditions in simpler events. Plants and non-human animals act *as if* they were concerned that their activity, their characteristic receptivity and response, should maintain itself. Even atoms and molecules show a selective bias in their indifferencies, affinities and repulsions when exposed to other events. With respect to some things they are hungry to the point of greediness; in the presence of others they are sluggish and cold. It is not surprising that naïve science imputed appetition to their own consummatory outcome to all natural processes, and that Spinoza identified inertia and momentum with inherent tendency on the part of things to conserve themselves in being, and achieve such perfection as belongs to them. In a genuine although not psychic sense, natural beings exhibit preference and centeredness.

In regard to the nature of the individual, as in so many other respects, classic and modern philosophies have pursued opposite paths. In Greek reflection, love of perfection, or self-completion, was attributed to Being. The state of self-sufficiency excluding deficiency constituted the individual, significant change being thought of as the coming into being of such a whole. In consequence, in view of the obvious instability of particular existences such as moderns usually term individuals, a species immutable in time and having form was the true individual. What moderns call individuals were particulars, transient, partial, and imperfect specimens of the true individual. Mankind as species is more truly an individual than was this or that man. Although Aristotle criticized his master for giving Being to the genus or universal separate from particulars, he never doubted that the species was a real entity, a metaphysical or existential whole including and

characterizing all particulars. A type-form had no separate being; but, being embodied in particulars, it made them an
intrinsically unified and marked out class, which as a class was
ungenerated and indestructible, perfect and complete.

Modern science has made the conception strange. Yet it was a
natural interpretation of things found in ordinary experience.
The immediate qualitative differences of things cannot be recognized without noting that things possessed of these qualitative
traits fall into kinds, or families. That the family is more lasting,
important, and real than any of its members; that the family
confers upon its constituents their standing and character, so
that those who have no family are outcasts and wanderers, represents a notable situation in most forms of human culture. In
such a cultural scheme, those peculiar differences that constitute
for us personal individuality are only accidental variations from
the family type, the form which marks a kind enables a particular person to be placed, known, identified. The modern habit of
using self, "I," mind, and spirit interchangeably is inconceivable
when family and commune are solid realities. To the Greeks, a
mind was an organized system in which an ideal form unites
varying particulars into a genuine whole, and gives to them distinctive and recognizable character. The presence in things of the
generic form renders them knowable. Mind is but the ordered
system of all the characters which constitute kinds, differing
among men, differing according to differences of organic con-
stitutions. Upon such a view, subjectivity, individuality of mind
marks an anomaly; a failure of realization of objective forms on
the part of the indwelling family to impress itself adequately,
owing to stubborn resisting material constitution. What is prized
and exalted by moderns as individual was just the defect which is
the source of ignorance, opinion, and error.

Such a marked difference in the estimate of the status of individuality is proof of difference in the empirical content of ancient
and modern culture. In primitive cultures, experience is dominated by what a contemporary French school has called categories of participation and incorporation. Life and being belong
in a significant sense to the tribe and family; particular creatures
are only members of a consolidated whole. This state of social
affairs formed the pattern in accord with which all natural events
were construed. One need not endorse all the details of the

theories of this French school or even accept its general principles, in order to recognize a predominantly collectivistic character in early culture, and to perceive its influence upon early beliefs and modes of thought. An individual was a member of a
group-whole; in this membership were almost exhausted his accomplishments and possibilities. From birth, he was a subject for
assimilation and incorporation of group traditions and customs;
his personal measure was the extent in which he became their
vehicle. Private belief and invention were a deviation, a dangerous eccentricity, signs of disloyal disposition. The private was an
equivalent of the illicit; and all innovations and departures from
custom are illicit:—witness the fact that children have to be
educated and inducted into tradition and custom. This need of
education, moreover, and of maintenance of tradition against
deviation serve to bring otherwise unconscious customs to mind,
and to render consciousness of them acute and emotional.[1]
Thereby, customs are more than mere overt ways of action;
tradition is more than external imitation and reproduction of
what obtains in outward behavior. Custom is Nomos, lord and
king of all, of emotions, beliefs, opinions, thoughts as well as
deeds.

Yet mind in an individualized mode has occasionally some
constructive operation. Every invention, every improvement in
art, technological, military and political, has its genesis in the
observation and ingenuity of a particular innovator. All utensils,
traps, tools, weapons, stories, prove that some one exercised at
sometime initiative in deviating from customary models and
standards. Accident played its part; but *some one* had to observe
and utilize the accidental change before a new tool and custom
emerged. Men were not wholly and merely subdued to the demands of custom, even when innovations were looked upon as
threats to the welfare of the group, defiances of its gods.

As Goldenweiser has said: "Whether it is a pot, basket or
blanket that is being manufactured, or the soil that is being tilled,
or an animal that is being hunted or fought—in all of these
situations man faces an individual, technical task. In all of these

---

1. See Boas, *The Mind of Primitive Man.* Ch. VIII of this book seems to me to
supply what is sound in the view of the French school alluded to, free from its
exaggerations.

directions there is room for the development and exhibition of skill. In industry and the chase, in a seafaring expedition and a war raid, things can be done well and less well. . . . There is opportunity for comparison of individual efforts, there is rivalry."[2] As a fruit of this rivalry of individuals, pace-making occurs; those who excel set a standard for others to come up to; they furnish models of technique to be adopted by others, till gradually or suddenly they initiate a new custom. Even in cultures most committed to reproduction, there is always occurring some creative production, through specific variations, that is, through individuals. Thus, while negatively individuality means something to be subdued, positively it denotes the source of change in institutions and customs. While the negative side is most conscious and most asserted, the positive phase is there and is taken advantage of, even though by stealth and under cover. Upon the whole the imagination and effort of individual technicians and artists were submerged; in idea, the doctrine of fixed wholes with their fixed patterns prevailed. We may well follow the further statements of Dr. Goldenweiser. "When tradition is a matter of the spoken word, the advantage is all on the side of age. The elder is in the saddle"; because he is the most experienced man and the one who best embodies the net experience of the group. The group is small enough to be homogeneous; innovations are conspicuous and focus resentment; customary activities are moreover enmeshed in ceremonialism and have supernatural sanctions; variations when once they are adopted become automatic group habits; they endure not as ideas or because of insight into principles, but as "motor habits which represent nothing but knowledge and technical experience rendered mechanical through habituation"; individual "consciousness and ratiocination quickly are incorporated in objective results which are handed down while the thinking perishes; inventions become part of the technical equipment of behavior, not of thought and understanding." Under such circumstances, individual variations of thought remain private reveries or are soon translated into objective established institutions through gradual accumulation of imperceptible variations. The exceptional

2. *Early Civilization*, pp. 407–8.

character of creative individuality is reflected in attribution of the origin of the arts, industrial and political, to gods and semi-divine heroes. Thus the artist and artisan merely observe, as has been noted in another connection, ready-made models and patterns, and unquestioningly follow procedures antecedently established. Patterns and methods are accepted as belonging to the objective nature of things; there is next to no sense of any connection between them and personal desire and thought; to introduce such a connection would evince a dangerously subversive spirit. The point of view therein displayed is so far from that which animates modern psychology and philosophy that it is not easily recoverable; yet we do not have even today to go far to find a like notion regulative of action and belief. The mechanic who follows blueprints and a procedure dictated by his machine in the production of standardized commodities would, if he were both articulate and uncognizant of inventions by others, say the same thing. Legal formalities consciously adopt similar realistic conceptions in politics and morals, and find the exhibition of the spirit which they take for granted in science and industry to be anarchistic and destructive in less technical fields. Standards and patterns seem to them to be given in the nature of things; the intervention of initiative and invention, of individuality, are counted contrary to reason as well as to sincerity and loyalty.

When experience is of this sort, an individual worker or demi-urge has only to observe and conform. He is but a case to be subsumed in a fixed whole as far as may be; what is left over is merely quantitative and accidental. Plato found in the arts exemplifications of fixed archetypes governing particular processes of change through imparting to them measure and proportion; hence changes as far as knowable were subject in advance to the dialectic of geometry. As in the *Philebus,* measure comes first; then comes the measured, the symmetrical and beautiful; conscious mind and wisdom are in the third rank as observation of measure and the measured antecedently established. In similar fashion, Aristotle could draw his account of the four fundamental affairs of nature from analysis of the procedure of artisan, with no suspicion that he was thereby subjecting his metaphysics to an anthropomorphic rendering of nature; setting up the cumulative deposit of individual variations of insight and skill as the measure of nature. It is inept to charge these thinkers with hypostatizing psychical states and processes. Since their own experience exhibited subordination of individualized mind to objects, operations, patterns and ends that were pre-established and presented ready-made and complete, their metaphysic and logic were in so far a faithful report of what they found. Greek philosophy converted not psychological conditions but positive institutional affairs into cosmic realities. The idea that generalization, purposes, etc., are individual mental processes did not originate until experience had registered such a change that the functions of individualized mind were productive of objective achievements and hence capable of external observation.

When this happened, an extraordinary revolution occurred. The conception of the individual changed completely. No longer was the individual something complete, perfect, finished, an organized whole of parts united by the impress of a comprehensive form. What was prized as individuality was now something moving, changing, discrete, and above all initiating instead of final. As long as deviation of particulars from established order meant disorder, the metaphysics and logic of subordination of parts to the form of a pre-formed whole was reasonable. Mind as individualized could be recognized in other than a pejorative sense only when its variations were social, utilized in generating greater social security and fullness of life. This was possible only when social relationships were heterogeneous and expansive, when demand for initiative, invention and variation exceeded that for adherence and conformity. It is noteworthy that even Plato with all his zeal for a fixed organized whole could not imagine its coming into being save through the effort of some happily constituted and fortunately placed individual. Social heterogeneity alone does not promote a functioning of variations for socially desirable consequences, and thereby constitute individuality as something objective and socially acknowledged. It may signify only a break up of pious adherence to a cumulative and conserved outcome of prior history. But let there be a situation in which the tradition of order and unity is still vital while the actual state of affairs is one of variation and conflict, and there is a situation in which dependence must perforce be placed on individuality. Even though its office be conceived at first as merely restorative, a return to an earlier and better state of affairs, as Italian thinkers would return to Greco-Roman culture and the early Protestant to primitive Christianity, yet the operation of individuals rather than that of collective tradition is the hope and reliance. Under such circumstances, particularized centres of initiation and energy are prized because being emancipated from the net work of current forces, they are free to direct change to new objective consequences.

Individualism in modern life has been understood in diverse ways. To those retaining the classic tradition, it is a revolt of undisciplined barbarians, reverting to the spontaneous petulant egotism of childhood; in another version of this underlying idea, it is rebellion of unregenerate human nature against divine authority, established among men for their salvation. To still others, it is emancipation, the achieving of voluntary maturity; courageous independence in throwing off all external yokes and bondages, in asserting that every human being is an end in himself; in effect a transfer to each conscious unit of honorific predicates previously reserved for the class, species, universal. In any case, an individual is no longer just a particular, a part without meaning save in an inclusive whole, but is a subject, self, a distinctive centre of desire, thinking and aspiration.

An adherent of empirical denotative method can hardly accept either the view which regards subjective mind as an aberration or that which makes it an independent creative source. Empirically, it is an agency of novel reconstruction of a pre-existing order. Criticism of the history of political theory during the formation of modern European states may bring out the difference between such a view and that of both classic universalism and extreme modern subjectivism. The older theory had asserted that the state exists by nature. The modern declared that it existed by means of agreements between individuals who willed the institution of civil order. We may imagine reformers of the seventeenth century saying that the states they found about them did indeed exist by nature—that was precisely what was the matter with them. Because they were natural products, they were products of force, chance, fraud, tyranny. Hence they were naturally the scene of war, foreign and domestic, of servitudes and inequities, of intrigue and harsh coercion—one huge historical accident. A just and good state would be one brought into existence by voluntary convention; by promises exchanged and obligations mutually undertaken. A good state exists not by nature but by the contriving activities of individual selves in behalf of the satisfaction of their needs. It implies art, not nature; a clear perception by individuals of what they want and of the conditions through which their wants can be satisfied. In detail, thinkers divided into opposite schools. Some held that by nature individuals are non-social, becoming social when subjected to discipline by artificial and instituted law to which they are naturally adverse. Others attributed to the natural individual some degree of friendly and genial inclination. Both schools agreed that just political order, legitimate authority and subordination, is a product of voluntary conjunction of individuals naturally exempt from the universal of civil law.

The truth of which the social compact was a symbol is that social institutions as they exist can be bettered only through the deliberate interventions of those who free their minds from the standards of the order which obtains. The underlying fact was the perception of the possibility of a change, a change for the better, in social organization. The fact that the intent of the perception was veiled and distorted by the myth of an aboriginal single and one-for-all decisive meeting of wills is instructive as an aberration, but the myth should not disguise the intent and consequence. Social conditions were altered so that there were both need and opportunity for inventive and planning activities, initiated by innovating thought, and carried to conclusion only as the initiating mind secured the sympathetic assent of other individuals.

I say individual minds, not just individuals with minds. The difference between the two ideas is radical. There is an easy way by which thinkers avoid the necessity of facing a genuine problem. It starts with a self, whether bodily or spiritual being immaterial for present purposes, and then endows or identifies that self with mind, a formal capacity of apprehension, devising and belief. On the basis of this assumption, any mind is open to entertain any thought or belief whatever. There is here no problem involved of breaking loose from the weight of tradition and custom, of initiating observations and reflections, forming designs and plans, undertaking experiments on the basis of hypotheses, diverging from accepted doctrines and traditions. Or when it is observed that this departure occurs infrequently and is not easy, some vague reference to genius and originality disposes of the question. But the whole history of science, art and morals proves that the mind that appears *in* individuals is not as such individual mind. The former is in itself a system of belief, recognitions, and ignorances, of acceptances and rejections, of expectancies and appraisals of meanings which have been instituted under the influence of custom and tradition.

It is not easy to break away from current and established classifications and interpretations of the world. The difficulty in this respect, however, is eased by the notion that after all it is only error that the mind needs to cut loose from, and that it can do this by direct appeal to nature, by applying pure observation and reflection to pure objects. This notion of course is fiction; objects of knowledge are not given to us defined, classified, and labeled, ready for labels and pigeon-holes. We bring to the simplest observation a complex apparatus of habits, of accepted meanings and techniques. Otherwise observation is the blankest of stares, and the natural object is a tale told by an idiot, full only of sound and fury. In the case of social objects and patterns, institutions and arrangements, we have not the benefit of the mitigating fiction of direct correction by appeal of transparent mind to the court of nature. There *is* a contrast between physical objects and objects as they are believed to be, even though what they are believed to be is an unescapable medium in observing what they are. Where is such a contrast to be found in the case of existing social institutions and standards? The contrast is not, as it seems to be in the case of knowledge of physical existence, between a belief which is defective or false and an existence which is real; it is between an existence which is actual, and a belief, desire and aspiration for something which is better but non-existent.

Such facts exemplify the difference between a bodily or a psychic self *with* a mind and mind *as* individual. Either the better social object is sheer illusion, or else individual thought and desire denote a distinctive and unique mode of existence, an object held in solution, undergoing transformation, to emerge finally as an established and public object. Reference to imagination is pertinent. But the reference is too frequently used to disguise and avoid recognition of the essential fact and the problems involved in it. Imagination as mere reverie is one thing, a natural and additive event, complete in itself, a terminal object rich and consoling, or trivial and silly, as may be. Imagination which terminates in a modification of the objective order, in the institution of a new object is other than a merely added occurrence. It involves a dissolution of old objects and a forming of new ones in a medium which, since it is beyond the old object and not yet in a new one, can properly be termed subjective.

The point in placing emphasis upon the role of individual desire and thought in social life has in part been indicated. It shows the genuinely intermediate position of subjective mind: it proves it to be a mode of natural existence in which objects undergo directed reconstitution. Reference to the place of individual thought in political theory and practice has another value. Unless subjective intents and thoughts are to terminate in picturesque utopias or dogmas irrelevant to constructive action, they are subject to objective requirements and tests. Even in the crudest form of the contract theory, men had to *do* something. They had at least to meet together, come to agreement, give guarantees, and govern their subsequent conduct by agreements reached, or else suffer a tangible penalty. Thinking and desiring, no matter how subjective, are a preliminary, tentative and inchoate mode of action. They are "overt" behavior of a communicated and public form in process of construction, and behavior involves change of objects which tests the meanings animating behavior.

There is a peculiar intrinsic privacy and incommunicability attending the preparatory intermediate stage. When an old essence or meaning is in process of dissolution and a new one has not taken shape even as a hypothetical scheme, the intervening existence is too fluid and formless for publication, even to one's self. Its very existence is ceaseless transformation. Limits from which and to which are objective, generic, stateable; not so that which occurs between these limits. This process of flux and ineffability is intrinsic to any thought which is subjective and private. It marks "consciousness" as bare event. It is absurd to call a recognition or a conception subjective or mental because it takes place through a physically or socially numerically distinct existence; by this logic a house disappears from the spatial and material world when it becomes *my* house; even a physical movement would then be subjective when referred to particles.

Recognition of an object, conception of a meaning may be mine rather than yours; yours rather than his, at a particular moment; but this fact is about me or you, not about the object and essence perceived and conceived. Acknowledgment of this fact is compatible however with the conviction that after all there would be no *objects* to be perceived, no meanings to be conceived, if at some period of time uniquely individualized events had not intervened. There is a difference in kind between the thought which manipulates received objects and essences to derive new ones from their relations and implications, and the thought which generates a new method of observing and classifying them. It is like the difference between readjusting the parts of a wagon to make it more efficient, and the invention of the steam locomotive. One is formal and additive; the other is qualitative and transformative. He knows little who supposes that freedom of thought is ensured by relaxation of conventions, censorships and intolerant dogmas. The relaxation supplies opportunity. But while it is a necessary it is not a sufficient condition. *Freedom* of thought denotes freedom of *thinking*; specific doubting, inquiring, suspense, creating and cultivating of tentative hypotheses, trials or experimentings that are unguaranteed and that involve risks of waste, loss, and error. Let us admit the case of the conservative; if we once start thinking no one can guarantee where we shall come out, except that many objects, ends and institutions are surely doomed. Every thinker puts some portion of an apparently stable world in peril and no one can wholly predict what will emerge in its place.

In approaching the exaggerations of individual mind found in modern philosophy which go by the name of subjectivism and a large part of what is termed idealism, we may profitably recur to ancient thought. The question of the relation of the objective and subjective did not present itself under that name. The problem of the relation of the "natural" and the "positive" covered at least part of the same ground, and in a way closer to experience than does the course taken by much modern philosophy. The "positive" was a term used to cover everything of distinctively human institution, in languages, customs, manners, codes, laws, governments. The issue was whether nature was a norm for these arrangements or whether they were something to which nature should submit. The classic answer was in the former sense. But there were those who regarded nature as raw, crude, wild, and who thought of man and his doings as the standard and measure of nature.

The former conception, under theological sanctions and interpretations, was adopted into the medieval conception of natural law, and made absolutely controlling in morals and politics, wherever not supplemented by revelation, which after all was revelation of a higher nature. To put the problem in terms of the connection between nature and institutions has an advantage over the isolation of the ego by modern philosophy. It acknowledged the social factor. Even when the origin of the positive was sought in the will, in the decrees and enactments of particular persons, the latter were thought of as possessing a socially representative office, as heroes, lawgivers, not as isolated individual minds.

The complete subordination of the positive to natural law in the medieval version of the classic theory involved modern thought in a peculiar embarrassment when interest in humanity as distinct from divinity revived. The institutions which men wished to modify, for which they wished to substitute others or to which they wished to add others of a secular sort, were bound up with divinity, with authoritative natural and revealed law. It was not possible to put institutions as such in contrast to nature, for by accepted theory existing institutions were in the main expressions of the law of nature. The resource which offered itself was to place the mind of the individual as such in contrast to both nature and institutions. This historic fact, reinforced with the conspicuous assertion of medievalism that the individual soul is the ultimate end and ultimate subject of salvation or damnation, affords, it seems to me, the background and source of the isolation of the ego, the thinking self, in all philosophy influenced by either the new science or Protestantism. Descartes as well as Berkeley uses "self" as an equivalent of "mind," and does so spontaneously, as a matter of course, without attempt at argument and justification. If the given science of nature and given positive institutions expressed arbitrary prejudice, unintelligent custom and chance episodes, where could or should mind be found except in the independent and self-initiated activities of individuals? Wholesale revolt against tradition led to the illusion of equally wholesale isolation of mind as something wholly individual. Revolting and reforming thinkers like Descartes little noted how much of tradition they repeated and perpetuated in their very protests and reforms.

An adequate recognition of the empirical historical causes of the exaggeration of the ego in modern philosophy, due to its isolation from social customs, and these from the physical world, makes, it seems to me, criticism of the forms which it has assumed almost unnecessary. Thinkers may start out with a naïve assumption of minds connected with separate individuals. But developments soon show the inadequacy of such "minds" to carry the burden of science and objective institutions, like the family and state. The consequence was revealed to be sceptical, disintegrative, malicious. A transcendental supra-empirical self, making human, or "finite," selves its medium of manifestation, was the logical recourse. Such a conception is an inevitable conclusion, when the value of liberation and utilization of individual capacity in science, art, industry, and politics is a demonstrated empirical fact; and when at the same time, individuality instead of being conceived as historic, intermediate, temporally relative and instrumental, is conceived of as original, eternal and absolute. When concrete reconstructions of natural and social objects are thought of as a single and constitutive act, they inevitably become supernatural or transcendental. When the movement terminates, as in the later philosophy of Josiah Royce, with a "community of selves," the circle has returned to the empirical fact with which it might properly have started out; but the intervening insertion of a transcendent ego remains as a plague. It isolates the community of selves from natural existence and in order to get nature again in connection with mind, is compelled to reduce it to a system of volitions, feelings and thoughts.

It remains to mention another historic factor which helps account for the vogue of subjectivism in art and literature, through which it found its way more or less into common belief. Comte several times recurs to the idea that idiocy represents an excess of objectivism, a subordination of feelings and impressions to objects as given, while madness marks an excess of subjectivism. Still more significant is his added remark, that madness has to be construed historically and sociologically. Under primitive conditions all the larger ideas about nature are reveries constructed in the interest of emotions. Myths were fancies, but they were not insanities because they were the only reply to the challenge of nature which existing instrumentalities permitted. Assertion of similar ideas today is insanity, because available intellectual resources and agencies make possible and require radically different adjustments. To entertain and believe fancies which once were spontaneous and general is today a sign of failure, of mental disequilibration. Inability to employ the methods of forming and checking beliefs which are available at a given time, whatever be the source of that inability, constitutes a disorientation. These considerations are not introduced to make the offensive insinuation that philosophic subjectivism is a mode of insanity, and philosophic realism a mode of idiocy. The purpose is to suggest that while the tendency to revery, to intellectual somnambulism, is universal, the use made of revery—which may roughly stand for the subjective element in mind—depends upon contemporary conditions. In one situation fancy generates stories which are consistent with desire and are attractive. These are connected with ceremonies to which, in addition to their immediate good, external efficiency is imputed. They become nuclei about which observations and ideas continually gather; they are centres of mental as well as emotional systematizations. It is no wonder that myths long prevail. When the development of industry and tested inquiry makes it evident that the actual world will not accept them nor stand for them, their actuating springs remain in full force and the river of revery still flows. It may find public or communicated form in fiction recognized as such, in novel, drama and poetry which are enjoyed, although their objects are not believed in. Or they may remain private, and, with the play of desires and affections that produce them, constitute a new world enjoyed for its own sake—the "inner life."

The popular factor in subjectivism, that which renders philosophic subjectivism intelligible enough to prevent its being regarded as mere vagary, seems to be a confused union of two considerations. On the one hand there is the recognition, enforced by the course of events, of the constructive power of mind as individual, its re-creative function in objects of industry, art, and politics. On the other hand there is the discovery and exploitation of the inner life, a new, readily accessible and cheaply enjoyed esthetic field. The tales that will not be believed when they are told and that cannot be told in forms sufficiently artistic to command the attention of others, may still be told to one's self and afford relief, consolation and thrill. Products of fancy that cannot, because of the advance of knowledge, secure credence as reports of objective events, are castles in the air, but these castles are impregnable inner refuges.

The person who knows nothing of sensations or sensa, as the psychologist and epistemologist talk about them, is nevertheless aware that objects are other than bare things to which beliefs must subject themselves. He is aware that when things escape his power of control, they still generate "impressions" which he can entertain in all sorts of enjoyable and annoying ways. If he is devoid of ability to regulate conduct in actual employment of objects, this world of impressions will be one in which he loves to dwell. Its materials are pliable and exact no responsibility. He may be utterly innocent of the reduction of objects by theorists into conjoined sensations and images; the notion that his table consists largely of images would be to him a wild vagary, contradictory of common sense. But he knows very well that the incidents of life may produce fancies in him that are more exciting or more soothing than the incidents themselves. When there is neither the power to renounce revery nor to use it in any objective embodiment, we have a condition in which soil and atmosphere are prepared to find the spirit of subjective idealism congenial, even if the technical facts adduced and the dialectic employed in its behalf are beyond reach.

Our statements, however, are one-sided, as far as the full scope of the "inner life" is concerned. It is the home of aspirations and ideals that are noble and that may in time receive fulfillment as well as of figments and airy nothings. It may be charged with infinite humor and tragedy. It affords a realm in which king and court fool, prince and pauper, meet as equals. It is subject-matter for the philosopher as well as for the rebuffed and wistful. Recall the contrast which Royce had drawn between the dominant externalism of the seventeenth century and the spirit of the eighteenth. "It is no matter whether you are a philosopher and write essays on 'The Principles of Human Knowledge' or whether you are a heroine in an eighteenth-century novel, and write sentimental letters to a friend; you are part of the same movement. The spirit is dissatisfied with the mathematical order, and feels unfriendliness among the eternities of seventeenth-century thought. The spirit wants to be at home with itself, well-friended in the comprehension of its inner processes. It loves to be confidential in its heart outpourings, keen in its analysis, humane in its attitude toward life."

We are given to referring the beginnings of subjectivism to Descartes, with his *pensée* as the indubitable certainty, or to Locke with his simple idea as immediate object. Technically or with respect to later dialectical developments, this reference is correct enough. But historically it is wrong. Descartes' thought is the *nous* of classic tradition forced inwards because physical science had extruded it from its object. Its internality is a logical necessity of the attempt to reconcile the new science with the old tradition, not a thing intrinsically important. Similarly Locke's simple idea is the classic Idea, Form or Species dislodged from nature and compelled to take refuge in mind. For Locke, it is coerced by external existence and remains coercive for all subsequent intellectual operations. The subjective as such is alien to Locke's way of thinking; his whole bias is against it, and in favor of what is grounded in nature being a matter of relations already established. The "simple idea" is merely man's available point of contact with the objective order; and in this contact resides its whole import.

From the standpoint of "inner life" the simple idea became however, a sensation, that is, a feeling, a state of mind, an intrinsically interesting event having its own significant career. If this were true of such a rudimentary thing as blue or soft, how much more significantly it holds of imagination and emotion. Inner reveries and enjoyments constitute freedom to the natural man. Everywhere else is constraint, whether it be of study, of science, family life, industry, or government. The road to freedom by escape into the inner life is no modern discovery; it was taken by savages, by the oppressed, by children, long before it was formulated in philosophical romanticism. The generalized awareness of the fact is new however, and it added a new dimension to characteristically modern experience. It created new forms of art and new theories of esthetics, often promulgated by literary artists who have nothing but contempt for philosophical theories as such. Mr. Santayana is a thinker whose intent and basis are at one with classic thought. But if we note the importance assumed in his thinking by the "inward landscape," there is before us a measure of the pervasive influence of the kind of experience that was seized upon by Romanticism as the exclusive truth of experience.

The function of individualized mind in furthering experiment and invention and the directed reconstruction of events, together with the discovery that objects of sentiment and fancy, although rejected by the order of events in space and time, may form the contents of an inner and private realm, finds its legitimate outcome in the conception of experiencing, and in the discrimination of experiencing into a diversity of states and processes. To the Greeks, experience was the outcome of accumulation of practical acts, sufferings and perception gradually built up into the skill of the carpenter, shoemaker, pilot, farmer, general, and politician. There was nothing merely personal or subjective about it; it was a consolidation, effected by nature, of particular natural occurrences into actualization of the forms of such things as are thus and so usually, now and then, upon the whole, but not necessarily and always. Experience was adequate and final for this kind of thing because it was as much their culminating actualization as rational thought was the actualization of the forms of things that are what they are necessarily. To Aristotle, the copula was a true verb, always affected by tense. Things which fully and completely are, have been, will be, and now are, are exactly the same; their matter is completely mastered by form. Concerning them we can say "is" with demonstrative certainty: such things are few, though supremely good, and are the objects of science. Of other things we can only say that they have been and are not at the present time, or that though not existing at the present moment they may exist at some unspecified future time. Of them we can say "is" only with a perhaps or a probably, since they are subject to chance. In them matter is not wholly subdued to form. Experience is the actualization through an organic body of just these affairs. Experience was not some person's; it was nature's, localized in a body as that body happened to exist by nature.

As was remarked in the introductory chapter one can hardly use the term "experience" in philosophical discourse, but a critic rises to inquire "Whose experience?" The question is asked in adverse criticism. Its implication is that experience by its very nature is owned by some one; and that the ownership is such in kind that everything about experience is affected by a private and exclusive quality. The implication is as absurd as it would be to infer from the fact that houses are usually owned, are mine and yours and his, that possessive reference so permeates the properties of being a house that nothing intelligible can be said about the latter. It is obvious, however, that a house can be owned only when it has existence and properties independent of being owned. The quality of belonging to some one is not an all-absorbing maw in which independent properties and relations disappear to be digested into egohood. It is additive; it marks the assumption of a new relationship, in consequence of which the house, the common, ordinary, house, acquires new properties. It is subject to taxes; the owner has the right to exclude others from entering it; he enjoys certain privileges and immunities with respect to it and is also exposed to certain burdens and liabilities.

Substitute "experience" for "house," and no other word need be changed. Experience when it happens has the same dependence upon objective natural events, physical and social, as has the occurrence of a house. It has its own objective and definitive traits; these can be described without reference to a self, precisely as a house is of brick, has eight rooms, etc., irrespective of whom it belongs to. Nevertheless, just as for some purposes and with respect to some consequences, it is all important to note the added qualification of personal ownership of real property, so with "experience." In first instance and intent, it is not exact nor relevant to say "I experience" or "I think." "It" experiences or is experienced, "it" thinks or is thought, is a juster phrase. Experience, a serial course of affairs with their own characteristic properties and relationships, occurs, happens, and is what it is. Among and within these occurrences, not outside of them nor underlying them, are those events which are denominated selves. In some specifiable respects and for some specifiable consequences, these selves, capable of objective denotation just as are sticks, stones, and stars, assume the care and administration of certain objects and acts in experience. Just as in the case of the house, this assumption of ownership brings with it further liabilities and assets, burdens and enjoyments.

To say in a significant way, "*I* think, believe, desire," instead of barely "*it* is thought, believed, desired," is to accept and affirm a responsibility and to put forth a claim. It does not mean that the self is the source or author of the thought and affection nor its exclusive seat. It signifies that the self as a centred organization of energies identifies itself (in the sense of accepting their consequences) with a belief or sentiment of independent and external origination. The absurdity of any other conception appears upon examination of such affairs as are designated by "I do not believe" or "I do not like"; in them it is obvious that a relationship of incompatibility between two distinct and denoted objects is contained.

Authorship and liability look in two different ways, one to the past, the other to the future. Natural events—including social habits—originate thoughts and feelings. To say "*I* think, hope and love" is to say in effect that genesis is not the last word; instead of throwing the blame or the credit for the belief, affection and expectation upon nature, one's family, church, or state, one declares one's self to be henceforth a partner. An adoptive act is proclaimed in virtue of which one claims the benefit of future goods and admits liability for future ills flowing from the affair in question. Even in the most "individualistic" society some properties remain communal; and many things, like the bowels of the earth and the depths of the seas, are unowned by either group or person. The cogent line of defense of the institution of private property is that it promotes prudence, accountability, ingenuity and security, in the production and administration of commodities and resources which exist independently of the relationship of property. In like fashion, not all thoughts and emotions are owned either socially or personally; and either mode of appropriation has to be justified on the basis of distinctive consequences.

Analytic reflection shows that the ordinary conception of causation as a trait belonging to some one thing is the idea of responsibility read backward. The idea that some one thing, or any two or three things, are *the* cause of an occurrence is in effect an application of the idea of credit or blame—as in the Greek αἰτία. There is nothing in nature that *belongs* absolutely and exclusively to anything else; belonging is always a matter of reference and distributive assignment, justified in any particular case as far as it works out well. Greek metaphysics and logic are dominated

NATURE, MIND AND THE SUBJECT   181

by the idea of inherent belonging and exclusion; another instance of naïvely reading the story of nature in language appropriate to human association. Modern science has liberated
physical events from the domination of the notions of intrinsic
belonging and exclusion, but it has retained the idea with
exacerbated vigor in the case of psychological events. The elimination of the category from physics and its retention in psychology has provided a seeming scientific basis for the division between psychology and physics, and thereby for the egotism of
modern philosophy. Much subjectivism is only a statement of
the logical consequences of the doctrine sponsored by psychological "science" of the monopolistic possession of mental
phenomena by a self; or, after the idea of an underlying spiritual
substance became shaky, of the doctrine that mental events as
such constitute all there is to selfhood. For the philosophical
implications of the latter idea, as far as privacy, monopoly and
exclusiveness of causation and belonging are concerned, are
similar to those of the older dogma when it was applied to
cosmic nature.

Enough, however, of negation. The positive consequence is an
understanding of the shift of emphasis from the experienced, the
objective subject-matter, the *what*, to the experiencing, the
method of its course, the *how* of its changes. Such a shift occurs
whenever the problem of control of production of consequences
arises. As long as men are content to enjoy and suffer fire when it
happens, fire is just an objective entity which is what it is. That it
may be taken as a deity to be adored or propitiated, is evidence
that its "whatness" is all there is to it. But when men come to the
point of *making* fire, fire is not an essence, but a mode of natural
phenomena, an order in change, a "how" of a historic sequence.
The change from immediate use in enjoyment and suffering is
equivalent to recognition of a method of procedure, and of the
alliance of insight into method with possibility of control.

The development of the conception of experiencing as a distinctive operation is akin to the growth of the idea of fire-making
out of direct experiences with fire. Fire is fire, inherently just
what it is; but making fire is relational. It takes thought away
from fire to the other things that help and prevent its occurrence.
So with experience in the sense of things that are experienced;
they are *what* they are. But their occurrence as experienced

things is ascertained to be dependent upon attitudes and dispositions; the manner of their happening is found to be affected by
the habits of an organic individual. Since myth and science concern the same objects in the same natural world, sun, moon, and
stars, the difference between them cannot be determined exclusively on the basis of these natural objects. A differential has to
found in distinctive *ways* of experiencing natural objects; it is
perceived that man is an emotional and imaginative as well as an
observing and reasoning creature, and that different manners of
experiencing affect the status of subject-matter experienced. Capacity to distinguish between the sun and moon of science and
these same things as they figure in myth and cult depends upon
capacity to distinguish different attitudes and dispositions of the
subject; the heroes of legend and poetry are discriminated from
historic characters when memory, imagination and idealizing
emotion are taken into the reckoning. Again, it is discovered that
the good of some objects is connected with one way of experiencing, namely appetite, while the acquisition of goodness by other
objects is dependent upon the operation of reflection. In consequence, the experienced objects are differentiated as to their
goodness, although good as an essence is unchanged.

The importance of modes of experiencing for control of experienced objects may be illustrated from economic theory. A study
of various economic essences or concepts is possible:—definition, classification and dialectical reference to one another of
such meanings as value, utility, rent, exchange, profit, wages,
etc. There is also possible a positivistic study of existential economic régimes, resulting in description of their structures and
operations. If the presence and operation of dispositions and
attitudes be neglected, these alternatives exhaust the field of inquiry. Neither the study of objective essences nor of objective
existences is available, however, in problems of polity, in management of economic events. When the "psychological" factor is
introduced, say, a study of the effects of certain ways of experiencing, such as incentives, desires, fatigue, monotony, habit,
waste-motions, insecurity, prestige, team work, fashion, *esprit
de corps*, and a multitude of like factors, the situation changes.
Factors that are within control are specified, and a fuller degree
of deliberate administration of events is made possible. The ob-

jectivity of events remains what it was, but the discovery of the role of personal dispositions in conditioning their occurrence, enables us to interpret and connect them in new ways, ways which are susceptible of greater regulation than were the other ways. Banks, stores, factories do not become psychical when we ascertain the part played in their genesis and operation by psychological factors; they remain as external to the organism and to a particular mind as ever they were, things experienced as are winds and stars. But we get a new leverage, intellectual and practical, upon them when we can convert description of ready-made events and dialectical relation of ready-made notions into an account of a way of occurrence. For a perceived mode of becoming is always ready to be translated into a *method* of production and direction.

Since modern natural science has been concerned with discovery of conditions of production, to be employed as means for consequences, the development of interest in attitudes of individual subjects—the psychological interest—is but an extension of its regular business. Knowledge of conditions of the occurrence of experienced objects is not complete until we have included organic conditions as well as extra-organic conditions. Knowledge of the latter may account for a happening in the abstract but not for the concrete or experienced happening. A general knowledge of dispositions and attitudes renders us exactly the same sort of intellectual and practical service as possession of physical constants. The trouble lies in the inadequacy of our present psychological knowledge. And it is probably this deficiency, which renders such psychological knowledge as we possess unavailable for technological control, which, joined to spontaneous interest in "inner" life, has set off psychological subject-matter as a separate world of existence, instead of a discovery of attitudes and dispositions involved in the world of common experience. In truth, attitudes, dispositions and their kin, while capable of being distinguished and made concrete intellectual objects, are never separate existences. They are always *of, from, toward*, situations and things. They may be studied with a minimum of attention to the things at and away from which they are directed. The things with which they are concerned may for purposes of inquiry be represented by a blank, a symbol to be specifically filled in as occasion demands. But except as ways of seeking, turning from, appropriating, treating things, they have no existence nor significance.

Every type of culture has experienced resistance and frustration. These events are interpreted according to the bias dominating a particular type of culture. To the modern European mind they have been interpreted as results of the opposed existence of subject and object as independent forms of Being. The notion is now so established in tradition that to many thinkers it appears to be a datum, not an interpretative classification. But the East Indian has envisaged the same phenomena as evidence of the contrast of an illusory world to which corresponds domination by desires and a real world due to emancipation from desires, attained through ascetic discipline and meditation. The Greeks interpreted the same experience on the basis of the cosmic discrepancy of being and becoming, form and matter, as the reluctance of existence to become a complete and transparent medium of meaning. Taken absolutely, the interpretation on the basis of opposition of subject and object has no advantage over the other doctrines; it is a local and provincial interpretation. Taken inherently or absolutely, it has an absurdity from which they are free; for subject and object antithetically defined can have logically no transactions with each other. Taken as a factor in the enterprise of overcoming resistance and reducing the prospects of frustration, statement in terms of distinction of subject and object is intelligible, and is more valuable than the other modes of statement. Object is, as Basil Gildersleeve said, that which objects, that to which frustration is due. But it is also the objective; the final and eventual consummation, an integrated secure independent state of affairs. The subject is that which suffers, is subjected and which endures resistance and frustration; it is also that which attempts subjection of hostile conditions; that which takes the immediate initiative in remaking the situation as it stands. Subjective and objective distinguished as factors in a regulated effort at modification of the environing world have an intelligible meaning. Subjectivism as an "ism" converts this historic, relative and instrumental status and function into something absolute and fixed; while pure "objectivism" is a doctrine of fatalism.

To-day there is marked revival of objectivism, even of externalism. The world of physical science is no longer new and strange; to many it is now familiar; while many of those to whom it is personally unfamiliar take it for granted on authority. To a considerable extent its subject-matter is taking the place of the subject-matter of older creeds as something given ready-made, demanding unhesitating credence and passive acceptance. The doctrine of the opposition of subject and object in knowledge is fading, becoming reminiscent; that sense of strain which is lacking accompanied transition from one set of beliefs to another very different set. Only in politics and economics is the opposition of subject and institutional object poignant. And even in these fields radical and conservative increasingly appeal to objects which are collective, non-individual. The conservative recurs to the objectivism of established institutions, idealized into intrinsic stability; the radical looks forward to the completed outcome of an objective and necessary economic evolution. In spite of the appeal to the catchwords of individualism, private initiative, voluntary abstinence, personal industry and effort, there is more danger at present that the genuinely creative effort of the individual will be lost than there is of any return to earlier individualism. Everything makes for the mass. When private property is talked about, the product of individual labor is no longer meant; but a legally buttressed institution. Capital is no longer the outcome of deliberate personal sacrifice, but is an institution of corporations and finance with massive political and social ramifications. Appeals to secure action of a certain sort may use the old words; but the fears and hopes which are now aroused are not really connected with freedom of individual thought and effort, but with the objective foundations of society, established "law and order."

This resort to an objectivism which ignores initiating and reorganizing desire and imagination will in the end only strengthen that other phase of subjectivism which consists in escape to the enjoyment of inward landscape. Men who are balked of a legitimate realization of their subjectivity, men who are forced to confine innovating need and projection of ideas to technical modes of industrial and political life, and to specialized or "scientific" fields of intellectual activity, will compensate by finding release within their inner consciousness. There will be one philosophy, a realistic one, for mathematics, physical science and the established social order; another, and opposed, philosophy for the affairs of personal life. The objection to dualism is not just that it is a dualism, but that it forces upon us antithetical, non-convertible principles of formulation and interpretation. If there is complete split in nature and experience then of course no ingenuity can explain it away; it must be accepted. But in case no such sharp division actually exists, the evils of supposing there is one are not confined to philosophical theory. Consequences within philosophy as such are of no great import. But philosophical dualism is but a formulated recognition of an impasse in life; an impotence in interaction, inability to make effective transition, limitation of power to regulate and thereby to understand. Capricious pragmatism based on exaltation of personal desire; consolatory estheticism based on capacity for wringing contemplative enjoyment from even the tragedies of the outward spectacle; refugee idealism based on rendering thought omnipotent in the degree in which it is ineffective in concrete affairs;— these forms of subjectivism register an acceptance of whatever obstacles at the time prevent the active participation of the self in the ongoing course of events. Only when obstacles are treated as challenges to remaking of personal desire and thought, so that the latter integrate with the movement of nature and by participation direct its consequences, are opposition and duality rightly understood.

Existentially speaking, a human individual is distinctive opacity of bias and preference conjoined with plasticity and permeability of needs and likings. One trait tends to isolation, discreteness; the other trait to connection, continuity. This ambivalent character is rooted in nature, whose events have their own distinctive indifferencies, resistances, arbitrary closures and intolerances, and also their peculiar openness, warm responsiveness, greedy seekings and transforming unions. The conjunction in nature of whimsical contingency and lawful uniformity is the result of these two characters of events. They persist upon the human plane, and as ultimate characters are ineradicable. Boundaries, demarcations, abrupt and expansive over-reachings of boundaries impartially and conjunctively mark every phase of human life.

The human individual in his opacity of bias is in so far doomed to a blind solitariness. He hugs himself in his isolation and fights against disclosure, the give and take of communication, as for the very integrity of existence. Even communicable meanings are tinged with color of the uncommunicated; there is a quality of reserve in every publicity. Everything may be done with this irreducible uniqueness except to get rid of it. The sense of it may add a bitter loneliness to experience. It may lead to restless insatiable throwing of the self into every opportunity of external business and dissipation in order to escape from it. It may be cherished, nurtured, developed into a cultivated consolatory detachment from the affairs of life, ending in the delusion of the superiority of the private inner life to all else, or in the illusion that one can really succeed in emancipating himself in his pure inwardness from connection with the world and society. It may express itself in elaborated schemes of self-pity and in bursts of defiant exclamation: Here I stand and cannot otherwise. It may lead to unreasoned loyalty to seemingly lost causes and forlorn hopes—and events may sometimes justify the faith.

Romanticism has made the best and the worst of the discovery of the private and incommunicable. It has converted a pervasive and inevitable color and temper of experience into its substance. In conceiving that this inexpugnable uniqueness, this ultimate singularity, exhausts the self, it has created a vast and somnambulic egotism out of the fact of subjectivity. For every existence in addition to its qualitative and intrinsic boundaries has affinities and active outreachings for connection and intimate union. It is an energy of attraction, expansion and supplementation. The ties and bonds of associated life are spontaneous uncalculated manifestations of this phase of human selfhood, as the union of hydrogen and oxygen is natural and unpremeditated. Sociability, communication are just as immediate traits of the concrete individual as is the privacy of the closet of consciousness. To define one's self within closed limits, and then to try out the self in expansive acts that inevitably result in an eventual breaking down of the walled-in self, are equally natural and inevitable acts. Here is the ultimate "dialectic" of the universal and individual. One no sooner establishes his private and subjective self than he demands it be recognized and acknowledged by others, even if he has to invent an imaginary audience or an Absolute Self to satisfy the demand. And no person taught by experience ever escapes the reflection that no matter how much

188 EXPERIENCE AND NATURE

he does for himself, what endures is only what is done for others: an observation however which is most comforting when it takes the form of attributing desire to serve others to acts which indulge the exclusive self.

In some form or other, the dualism erected between the ego and the world of things and persons represents failure to attain solution of the problem set by this ambiguous nature of the self. It is a formulated acceptance of oscillation between surrender to the external and assertion of the inner. In science and in art, especially in the art of intercourse, real solutions occur. Private bias manages in them to manifest itself in innovations and deviations, which reshape the world of objects and institutions, and which eventually facilitate communication and understanding. Thereby the final and efficient, the limiting and the expansive, attain a harmony which they do not possess in other natural events.

Thus an individual existence has a double status and import. There is the individual that belongs in a continuous system of connected events which reinforce its activities and which form a world in which it is at home, consistently at one with its own preferences, satisfying its requirements. Such an individual is in its world as a member, extending as far as the moving equilibrium of which it is a part lends support. It is a natural end, not as an abrupt and immediate termination but as a fulfillment. Then there is the individual that finds a gap between its distinctive bias and the operations of the things through which alone its need can be satisfied; it is broken off, discrete, because it is at odds with its surroundings. It either surrenders, conforms, and for the sake of peace becomes a parasitical subordinate, indulges in egotistical solitude; or its activities set out to remake conditions in accord with desire. In the latter process, intelligence is born—not mind which appropriates and enjoys the whole of which it is a part, but mind as individualized, initiating, adventuring, experimenting, dissolving. Its possessed powers, its accomplished unions with the world, are now reduced to uncertain agencies to be forged into efficient instrumentalities in the stress and strain of trial.

The individual, the self, centred in a settled world which owns and sponsors it, and which in turn it owns and enjoys, is finished, closed. Surrender of what is possessed, disowning of what supports one in secure ease, is involved in all inquiry and discovery; the latter implicate an individual still to make, with all the risks implied therein. For to arrive at new truth and vision is to alter. The old self is put off and the new self is only forming, and the form it finally takes will depend upon the unforeseeable result of an adventure. No one discovers a new world without forsaking an old one; and no one discovers a new world who exacts guarantee in advance for what it shall be, or who puts the act of discovery under bonds with respect to what the new world shall do to him when it comes into vision. This is the truth in the exaggeration of subjectivism. Only by identification with remaking the objects that now obtain are we saved from complacent objectivism. Those who do not fare forth and take the risks attendant upon the formation of new objects and the growth of a new self, are subjected perforce to inevitable change of the settled and close world they have made their own. Identification of the bias and preference of selfhood with the process of intelligent remaking achieves an indestructible union of the instrumental and the final. For *this* bias can be satisfied no matter what the frustration of other desires and endeavors.

That an individual, possessed of some mode and degree of organized unity, participates in the genesis of every experienced situation, whether it be an object or an activity, is evident. That the way in which it is engaged affects the quality of the situation experienced is evident. That the way in which it is engaged has consequences that modify not merely the environment but which react to modify the active agent; that every form of life in the higher organisms constantly conserves some consequences of its prior experiences, is also evident. The constancy and pervasiveness of the operative presence of the self as a determining factor in all situations is the chief reason why we give so little heed to it; it is more intimate and omnipresent in experience than the air we breathe. Only in pathological cases, in delusions and insanities and social eccentricities, do we readily become aware of it; even in such cases it required long discipline to force attentive observation back upon the self. It is easier to attribute such things to invasion and possession from without, as by demons and devils. Yet till we understand operations of the self as the tool of tools, *the* means in all use of means, specifying its differential activities in their distinctive consequences in varying qualities of what is experienced, science is incomplete and the use made of it is at the mercy of an unknown factor, so that the ultimate and important consequence is in so far a matter of accident. Intentions and efforts bring forth the opposite of what was intended and striven for, and the result is confusion and catastrophe. Thus we are brought to a consideration of the psycho-physical mechanism and functioning of individual centres of action.

7.   Nature, Life and Body-Mind

A series of cultural experiences exhibits a series of diverging conceptions of the relation of mind to nature in general and to the organic body in particular. Greek experience included affairs that rewarded without want and struggle the contemplation of free men; they enjoyed a civic life full and rich with an equable adaptation to natural surroundings. Such a life seemed to be upon the whole for those in its full possession a gracious culmination of nature; the organic body was the medium through which the culmination took place. Since any created thing is subject to natural contingency, death was not a problem; a being who is generated shares while he may in mind and eternal forms, and then piously merges with the forces which generated him. But life does not always exist in this happy equilibrium: it is onerous and devastating, civil life corrupt and harsh. Under such circumstances, a spirit which believes that it was created in the image of a divine eternal spirit, in whose everlastingness it properly shares, finds itself an alien and pilgrim in a strange and fallen world. Its presence in that world and its residence in a material body which is a part of that world are an enigma. Again the scene shifts. Nature is conceived to be wholly mechanical. The existence within nature and as part of it of a body possessed of life, manifesting thought and enjoying consciousness is a mystery.

This series of experiences with their corresponding philosophies display characteristic factors in the problem of life and mind in relation to body. To the Greeks, all life was psyche, for it was self-movement and only soul moves itself. That there should be self-movement in a world in which movement was also up-and-down, to-and-fro, circular, was indeed interesting but not strange or untoward. Evidence of the fact of self-movement is directly had in perception; even plants exhibit it in a degree and hence have soul, which although only vegetative is a natural condition of animal soul and rational mind. Organic body occupies a distinctive position in the hierarchy of being; it is the highest actuality of nature's physical potentialities, and it is in turn the potentiality of mind. Greek thought, as well as Greek religion, Greek sculpture and recreation, is piously attentive to the human body.

In Pauline Christianity and its successors, the body is earthly, fleshly, lustful and passionate; spirit is Godlike, everlasting; flesh is corruptible; spirit incorruptible. The body was conceived in terms of a moral disparagement colored by supernatural religion. Since the body is material, the dyslogy extends to all that is material; the metaphysical discount put upon matter by Plato and Aristotle becomes in ascetic thought a moral and essential discount. Sin roots in the will; but occasions for sin come from the lusts of the body; appetites and desires spring from the body, distract attention from spiritual things; concupiscence, anger, pride, love of money and luxury, worldly ambition, result. Technically, the framework of Aristotelian thought is retained by the scholastics; St. Thomas Aquinas repeats his formulae concerning life and the body almost word for word. But actually and substantially this formal relationship has been distorted and corrupted through the seduction of spirit by flesh manifest in the fall of man and nature by Adam's sin. Add to moral fear of the flesh, interest in resurrection into the next world for eternal bliss or woe, and there is present a fullfledged antithesis of spirit and matter. In spite of this antithesis, however, they are conjoined in the body of man. Spirit is simple, one, permanent and indissoluble; matter is multiple, subject to change and dissolution. The possibility of the conjunction of two such opposite things formed a problem. But it would have been a remote, technical problem of no interest save to a few speculative thinkers, were it not given concreteness by the notion of an immortality to be spent in bliss or in woe unutterable, and the dependence of this ultimate destiny upon a life in which lust of the flesh along with the world of ambition and the devil of pride, was a standing temptation to sin and thereby an occasion of eternal damnation.

As long as the Aristotelian metaphysical doctrine persisted that nature is an ordered series from lower to higher of potentialities and actualizations, it was possible to conceive of the organic body as normally the highest term in a physical series and the lowest term in a psychical series. It occupied just that intermediate position where, in being the actualization of the potentialities of physical qualities, body was also potentiality for manifestation of their ideal actualities. Aside from moral and religious questions, there was in medieval thought no special problem attaching to the relation of mind and body. It was just one case of the universal principle of potentiality as the substrate of ideal actuality. But when the time came when the moral and religious associations of spirit, soul, and body persisted in full vigor, while the classic metaphysics of the potential and actual fell into disrepute, the full burden of the question of the relation of body, nature and man, of mind, spirit, and matter, was concentrated in the particular problem of the relation of the body and soul. When men ceased to interpret and explain facts in terms of potentiality and actuality, and resorted to that of causality, mind and matter stood over against one another in stark unlikeness; there were no intermediates to shade gradually the black of body into the white of spirit.

Moreover, both classic and medieval thought supplied influential empirical impetus to the new conception in spite of their theoretically divergent foundation. The old distinction between vegetative, animal and rational souls was, when applied to men, a formulation and justification of class divisions in Greek society. Slaves and mechanical artisans living on the nutritional, appetitive level were for practical purposes symbolized by the body—as obstructions to ideal ends and as solicitations to acts contrary to reason. The good citizen in peace and war was symbolized by the soul proper, amenable to reason, employing thought, but confining its operations after all to mundane matters, infected with matter. Scientific inquirers and philosophers alone exemplified pure reason, operating with ideal forms for the sake of the latter. The claim of this class for inherent superiority was symbolized by *nous*, pure immaterial mind. In Hellenistic thought, the three-fold distinction became that of body, mind or soul and spirit; spirit being elevated above all world affairs and acts, even moral concerns, having purely "spiritual" (immaterial) and religious objects. This doctrine fell in with the sharp separation made in Christianity for practical moral purposes, between flesh and spirit, sin and salvation, rebellion and obedience. Thus the abstract and technical Cartesian dualism found prepared for it a rich empirical field with which to blend, and one which afforded its otherwise empty formalism concrete meaning and substance.

The formalism and unreality of the problem remains, however, in the theories which have been offered as its "solutions." They range from the materialism of Hobbes, the apparatus of soul, pineal glands, animal spirits of Descartes, to interactionism, pre-established harmony, occasionalism, parallelism, pan-psychic idealism, epiphenomenalism, and the *élan vital*—a portentous array. The diversity of solutions together with the dialectical character of each doctrine which renders it impregnable to empirical attack, suggest that the trouble lies not so much in the solutions, as in the factors which determine statement of the problem. If this be so, the way out of the snarl is a reconsideration of the conceptions in virtue of which the problem exists. And these conceptions have primarily nothing to do with mind-body; they have to do with underlying metaphysical issues:—the denial of quality in general to natural events; the ignoring in particular of temporal quality and the dogma of the superior reality of "causes."

Empirically speaking, the most obvious difference between living and non-living things is that the activities of the former are characterized by needs, by efforts which are active demands to satisfy needs, and by satisfactions. In making this statement, the terms need, effort and satisfaction are primarily employed in a biological sense. By need is meant a condition of tensional distribution of energies such that the body is in a condition of uneasy or unstable equilibrium. By demand or effort is meant the fact that this state is manifested in movements which modify environing bodies in ways which react upon the body, so that its characteristic pattern of active equilibrium is restored. By satisfaction is meant this recovery of equilibrium pattern, consequent upon the changes of environment due to interactions with the active demands of the organism.

A plant needs water, carbon dioxide; upon occasion it needs to bear seeds. The need is neither an immaterial psychic force superimposed upon matter, nor is it merely a notional or conceptual distinction, introduced by thought after comparison of two different states of the organism, one of emptiness and one of repletion. It denotes a concrete state of events: a condition of tension in the distribution of energies such as involves pressure from points of high potential to those of low potential, which in turn effects distinctive changes such that the connection with the environment is altered, so that it acts differently upon the environment and is exposed to different influences from it. In this fact, taken by itself, there is nothing which marks off the plant from the physico-chemical activity of inanimate bodies. The latter also are subject to conditions of disturbed inner equilibrium, which lead to activity in relation to surrounding things, and which terminate after a cycle of changes—a terminus termed saturation, corresponding to satisfaction in organic bodies.

The difference between the animate plant and the inanimate iron molecule is not that the former has something in addition to physico-chemical energy; it lies in the *way* in which physico-chemical energies are interconnected and operate, whence different *consequences* mark inanimate and animate activity respectively. For with animate bodies, recovery or restoration of the equilibrium pattern applies to the complex integrated course or history. In inanimate bodies as such, "saturation" occurs indifferently, not in such a way as to tend to maintain a temporal pattern of activity. The interactions of the various constituent parts of a plant take place in such ways as to tend to continue a characteristically organized activity; they tend to utilize conserved consequences of past activities so as to adapt subsequent changes to the needs of the integral system to which they belong. Organization is a fact, though it is not an original organizing force. Iron as such exhibits characteristics of bias or selective reactions, but it shows no bias in favor of remaining simple iron; it had just as soon, so to speak, become iron-oxide. It shows no tendency in its interaction with water to modify the interaction so that consequences will perpetuate the characteristics of pure iron. If it did, it would have the marks of a living body, and would be called an organism. Iron as a genuine constituent of an *organized* body acts so as to tend to maintain the type of activity of the organism to which it belongs.

If we identify, as common speech does, the physical as such with the inanimate we need another word to denote the activity of organisms as such. Psycho-physical is an appropriate term. Thus employed, "psycho-physical" denotes the conjunctive presence in activity of need-demand-satisfaction, in the sense in which these terms have been defined. In the compound word, the prefix "psycho" denotes that physical activity has acquired additional properties, those of ability to procure a peculiar kind of interactive support of needs from surrounding media. Psychophysical does not denote an abrogation of the physico-chemical; nor a peculiar mixture of something physical and something psychical (as a centaur is half man and half horse); it denotes the possession of certain qualities and efficacies not displayed by the inanimate.

Thus conceived there is no problem of the relation of physical *and* psychic. There are specifiable empirical events marked by distinctive qualities and efficacies. There is first of all, *organization* with all which is implied thereby. The problem involved is one of definite factual inquiry. Under exactly what conditions does organization occur, and just what are its various modes and their consequences? We may not be able to answer these questions satisfactorily; but the difficulties are not those of a philosophical mystery, but such as attend any inquiry into highly complex affairs. Organization is an empirical trait of some events, no matter how speculative and dubious theories about it may be; especially no matter how false are certain doctrines about it which have had great vogue—namely, those doctrines which have construed it as evidence of a special force or entity called life or soul. Organization is so characteristic of the nature of some events in their sequential linkages that no theory about it can be as speculative or absurd as those which ignore or deny its genuine existence. Denial is never based on empirical evidence, but is a dialectical conclusion from a preconception that whatever appears later in time must be metaphysically unreal as compared with what is found earlier, or from a preconception that since the complex is controlled by means of the simpler, the latter is more "real."

Whenever the activities of the constituent parts of an organized pattern of activity are of such a nature as to conduce to the perpetuation of the patterned activity, there exists the basis of sensitivity. Each "part" of an organism is itself organized, and so of the "parts" of the part. Hence its selective bias in interactions with environing things is exercised so as to maintain *itself*, while also maintaining the whole of which it is a member. The root-tips of a plant interact with chemical properties of the soil in such ways as to serve organized life activity; and in such ways as to exact from the rest of the organism their own share of requisite nutrition. This pervasive operative presence of the whole in the part and of the part in the whole constitutes susceptibility—the capacity of feeling—whether or no this potentiality be actualized in plant-life. Responses are not merely selective, but are discriminatory, in behalf of some results rather than others. This discrimination is the essence of sensitivity. Thus with organization, bias becomes interest, and satisfaction a good or value and not a mere satiation of wants or repletion of deficiencies.

However it may be with plants and lower animals, in animals in which locomotion and distance-receptors exist, sensitivity and interest are realized as feeling, even though only as vague and massive uneasiness, comfort, vigor and exhaustion. A sessile organism requires no premonitions of what is to occur, nor cumulative embodiments of what has occurred. An organism with locomotion is vitally connected with the remote as well as with the nearby; when locomotor organs are accompanied by distance-receptors, response to the distant in space becomes increasingly prepotent and equivalent in effect to response to the future in time. A response toward what is distant is in effect an expectation or prediction of a later contact. Activities are differentiated into the preparatory, or anticipatory, and the fulfilling or consummatory. The resultant is a peculiar tension in which each immediate preparatory response is suffused with the consummatory tone of sex or food or security to which it contributes. Sensitivity, the capacity, is then actualized as feeling; susceptibility to the useful and harmful in surroundings becomes premonitory, an occasion of eventual consequences within life.

On the other hand, a consummation or satisfaction carries with it the continuation, in allied and reinforcing form, of preparatory or anticipatory activities. It is not only a culmination out of them, but is an integrated cumulation, a funded conservation *of* them. Comfort or discomfort, fatigue or exhilaration, implicitly sum up a history, and thereby unwittingly provide a means whereby, (when other conditions become present) the past can be unravelled and made explicit. For it is characteristic of feeling that while it may exist in a formless condition, or without configured distinctions, it is capable of receiving and bearing distinctions without end. With the multiplication of sensitive discriminatory reactions to different energies of the environment (the differentiation of sense-organs, extero-ceptors and proprio-ceptors) and with the increase in scope and delicacy of movements (the development of motor-organs, to which internal glandular organs for effecting a requisite redistribution of energy correspond), feelings vary more and more in quality and intensity.

Complex and active animals *have*, therefore, feelings which vary abundantly in quality, corresponding to distinctive directions and phases—initiating, mediating, fulfilling or frustrating—of activities, bound up in distinctive connections with environmental affairs. They *have* them, but they do not know they have them. Activity is psycho-physical, but not "mental," that is, not aware of meanings. As life is a character of events in a peculiar condition of organization, and "feeling" is a quality of life-forms marked by complexly mobile and discriminating responses, so "mind" is an added property assumed by a feeling creature, when it reaches that organized interaction with other living creatures which is language, communication. Then the qualities of feeling become significant of objective differences in external things and of episodes past and to come. This state of things in which qualitatively different feelings are not just had but are significant of objective differences, is mind. Feelings are no longer just felt. They have and they make *sense*; record and prophesy.

That is to say, differences in qualities (feelings) of acts when employed as indications of acts performed and to be performed and as signs of their consequences, *mean* something. And they mean it directly; the meaning is had as their own character. Feelings make sense; as immediate meanings of events and objects, they are sensations, or, more properly, sensa. Without language, the qualities of organic action that are feelings are pains, pleasures, odors, colors, noises, tones, only potentially and proleptically. With language they are discriminated and identified. They are then "objectified"; they are immediate traits of things. This "objectification" is not a miraculous ejection from the organism or soul into external things, nor an illusory attribution of psychical entities to physical things. The qualities never were "in" the organism; they always were qualities of interactions in which both extra-organic things and organisms partake. When named, they enable identification and discrimination of things to take place as means in a further course of inclusive interaction. Hence they are as much qualities of the things engaged as of the organism. For purposes of control they may be referred specifically to either the thing or to the organism or to a specified structure of the organism. Thus color which turns out not to be a reliable sign of external events becomes a sign of, say, a defect in visual apparatus. The notion that sensory affections discriminate and identify themselves, apart from discourse, as being colors and sounds, etc., and thus *ipso facto* constitute certain elementary modes of knowledge, even though it be only knowledge of their own existence, is inherently so absurd that it would never have occurred to any one to entertain it, were it not for certain preconceptions about mind and knowledge. Sentiency in itself is anoetic; it exists as any immediate quality exists, but nevertheless it is an indispensable means of any noetic function.

For when, through language, sentience is taken up into a system of signs, when for example a certain quality of the active relationship of organism and environment is named hunger, it is seen as an organic demand for an extra-organic object. To term a quality "hunger," to name it, is to refer to an object, to food, to that which will satisfy it, towards which the active situation moves. Similarly, to name another quality "red," is to direct an interaction between an organism and a thing to some object which fulfills the demand or need of the situation. It requires but slight observation of mental growth of a child to note that organically conditioned qualities, including those special sense-organs, are discriminated only as they are employed to designate objects; red, for instance, as the property of a dress or toy. The difficulty in the way of identifying the qualities of acts conditioned by proprio-ceptor organs is notoriously enormous. They just merge in the general situation. If they entered into communication as shared means to social consequences they would acquire the same objective distinctiveness as do qualities conditioned by the extero-ceptor organs. On the other hand, the qualities of the latter are just shades of the general tone of situations until they are used, in language, as common or shared means to common ends. Then they are identified as traits of objects. The child has to learn through social intercourse that certain qualities of action mean greediness or anger or fear or rudeness; the case is not otherwise with those qualities which are identified as red, musical tone, a foul odor. The latter may have instigated nausea, and "red" may have excited uneasiness (as blood makes some persons faint); but discrimination of the nauseating object *as* foul odor, and of the excitation *as* red occurs only when they are designated as signs.

The qualities of situations in which organisms and surrounding conditions interact, when discriminated, make sense. Sense is distinct from feeling, for it has a recognized reference; it is the qualitative characteristic of something, not just a submerged unidentified quality or tone. Sense is also different from signification. The latter involves use of a quality as a sign or index of something else, as when the red of a light signifies danger, and the need of bringing a moving locomotive to a stop. The sense of a thing, on the other hand, is an immediate and immanent meaning; it is meaning which is itself felt or directly had. When we are baffled by perplexing conditions, and finally hit upon a clew, and everything falls into place, the whole thing suddenly, as we say, "makes sense." In such a situation, the clew has signification in virtue of being an indication, a guide to interpretation. But the meaning of the *whole* situation as apprehended is sense. This idiomatic usage of the word sense is much nearer the empirical facts than is the ordinary restriction of the word in psychological literature to a single simple recognized quality, like sweet or red: the latter simply designates a case of *minimum* sense, deliberately limited for purposes of intellectual safety-first. Whenever a situation has this double function of meaning, namely signification and sense, mind, intellect is definitely present.

The distinction between physical, psycho-physical, and mental is thus one of levels of increasing complexity and intimacy of interaction among natural events. The idea that matter, life and mind represent separate kinds of Being is a doctrine that springs, as so many philosophic errors have sprung, from a substantiation of eventual functions. The fallacy converts consequences of interaction of events into causes of the occurrence of these consequences—a reduplication which is significant as to the *importance* of the functions, but which hopelessly confuses understanding of them. "Matter," or the physical, is a character of events when they occur at a certain level of interaction. It is not itself an event or existence; the notion that while "mind" denotes essence, "matter" denotes existence is superstition. It is more than a bare essence; for it is a property of a particular field of interacting events. But as it figures in *science* it is as much an essence as is acceleration, or the square root of minus one; which meanings also express derivative characters of events in interaction. Consequently, while the theory that life, feeling and thought are never independent of physical events may be deemed materialism, it may also be considered just the opposite. For it is reasonable to believe that the most adequate definition of the basic traits of natural existence can be had only when its properties are most fully displayed—a condition which is met in the degree of the scope and intimacy of interactions realized.

In any case, genuine objection to metaphysical materialism is neither moral nor esthetic. Historically speaking, materialism and mechanistic metaphysics—as distinct from mechanistic science—designate the doctrine that matter is the efficient cause of life and mind, and that "cause" occupies a position superior in reality to that of "effect." Both parts of this statement are contrary to fact. As far as the conception of causation is to be introduced at all, not matter but the natural events having matter as a character, "cause" life and mind. "Effects," since they mark the release of potentialities, are more adequate indications of the nature of nature than are just "causes." Control of the occurrence of the complex depends upon its analysis into the more elementary; the dependence of life, sentiency and mind upon "matter" is thus practical or instrumental. Lesser, more external fields of interaction are more manageable than are wider and more intimate ones, and only through managing the former can we direct the occurrence of the latter. Thus it is in virtue of the character of events which is termed matter that psycho-physical and intellectual affairs can be differentially determined. Every discovery of concrete dependence of life and mind upon physical events is therefore an addition to our resources. If life and mind had no mechanism, education, deliberate modification, rectification, prevention and constructive control would be impossible. To damn "matter" because of honorific interest in spirit is but another edition of the old habit of eulogizing ends and disparaging the means on which they depend.

This, then, is the significance of our introductory statement that the "solution" of the problem of mind-body is to be found in a revision of the preliminary assumptions about existence which generate the problem. As we have already noted, fruitful science of nature began when inquirers neglected immediate qualities, the "sense" of events, wet and dry, hot and cold, light and heavy, up and down, in behalf of "primary," namely, signifying, qualities, and when they treated the latter, although called qualities, not as such but as relations. This device made possible a totally different dialectical treatment. Classic science operated in terms of properties already attached to qualitative phenomena of sense and custom. Hence it could only repeat these phenomena in a changed vocabulary;—the vocabulary of sensory forms and forces which were, after all nothing but the already given meanings of things reduplicated. But the new dialectic was that of mathematical equations and functions. It started from meanings which ignored obvious characters or meanings of phenomena; hence it could lead to radically new relationships and generalizations—new in kind, and not merely in detail. No longer was the connection or classification of one color simply with other colors, but with all events involving rhythmic rates of change. Thus events hitherto disjoined were brought together under principles of inclusive formulation and prediction. Temporal qualities were stated as spatial velocities; thereby mathematical functions directly applicable to spatial positions, directions and distances, made it possible to reduce sequence of events into calculable terms. Neglect of temporal qualities as such centered thought upon *order* of succession, an order convertible into one of coexistence.

All this in effect is equivalent to seizing upon relations of events as the proper objects of knowledge. The surrender of immediate qualities, sensory and significant, as objects of science, and as proper forms of classification and understanding, left in reality these immediate qualities just as they were; since they are *had* there is no need to *know* them. But, as we have had frequent occasion to notice, the traditional view that the object of knowledge is reality *par excellence* led to the conclusion that the proper object of science was preeminently metaphysically real. Hence immediate qualities, being extruded from the object of science, were left thereby hanging loose from the "real" object. Since their *existence* could not be denied, they were gathered together into a psychic realm of being, set over against the object of physics. Given this premise, all the problems regarding the relation of mind and matter, the psychic and the bodily, necessarily follow. Change the metaphysical premise; restore, that is to say, immediate qualities to their rightful position as qualities of inclusive situations, and the problems in question cease to be epistemological problems. They become specifiable scientific problems: questions, that is to say, of how such and such an event having such and such qualities actually occurs.

Greek science imputed efficacy to qualities like wet and dry, hot and cold, heavy and light and to such qualitative differences in movement as up and down, to and fro, around and around. The world was formulated and explained on the basis of the causal efficacy of these qualities. The scientific revolution of the seventeenth century took its departure from a denial of causal status (and hence of significance for science) of these and all other direct qualities. On account, however, of the conversion of this fact about scientific procedure into a denial of the existence of qualities outside of mind and consciousness, psycho-physical and mental functions became inexplicable anomalies, supernatural in the literal sense of the word. The error of Greek science lay not in assigning qualities to natural existence, but in misconceiving the locus of their efficacy. It attributed to qualities apart from organic action efficiencies which qualities possess only through the medium of an organized activity of life and mind. When life and mind are recognized to be characters of the highly complex and extensive interaction of events, it is possible to give natural existential status to qualities, without falling into the mistake of Greek science. Psycho-physical phenomena and higher mental phenomena may be admitted in their full empirical reality, without recourse to dualistic breach in historic, existential continuity.

When knowing inanimate things, qualities as such may be safely disregarded. They present themselves as intensities and vector directions of movement capable of statement in mathematical terms. Thus their immediate individuality is got around; it is impertinent for science, concerned as the latter is with relationships. The most that can be said about qualities in the inanimate field is that they mark the limit of the contact of historical affairs, being abrupt ends or termini, boundaries of beginning and closing where a particular interaction ceases. They are like a line of foam marking the impact of waves of different directions of movement. They have to be noted and accepted in order to delimit a field of inquiry, but they do not enter into the inquiry as factors or terms.

In life and mind they play an active role. The delimitation or individualization they constitute on this level is not external to events. It is all one with the organization which permeates them, and which in permeating them, converts prior limitations of intensity and direction of energy into actual and intrinsic qualities, or sentient differences. For in feeling a quality exists as quality, and not merely as an abrupt, discrete, unique delimitation of interaction. Red differs from green for purposes of physical science as that which gives specific meaning to two sets of numbers applied to vibrations, or to two different placements of lines in a spectrum. The difference is proleptically qualitative; it refers to a unique difference of potentiality in the affairs under consideration. But as far as calculation and prediction are concerned these differences remain designable by non-qualitative indices of number and form. But in an organic creature sensitive to light, these differences of potentiality may be realized as differences in immediate sentiency. To say that they are *felt*, is to say that they come to independent and intrinsic existence on their own account. The proposition does not mean that feeling has been extraneously superadded to something else, or that a mode of extrinsic cognitive access to a purely physical thing has entered intrusively into a world of psychical things. "Feeling" is in general a name for the newly actualized quality acquired by events previously occurring upon a physical level, when these events come into more extensive and delicate relationships of interaction. More specifically, it is a name for the coming to existence of those ultimate differences in affairs which mark them off from one another and give them discreteness; differences which upon the physical plane can be spoken of only in anticipation of subsequent realization, or in terms of different numerical formulae, and different space-time positions and contiguities.

Thus qualities characteristic of sentiency are qualities *of* cosmic events. Only because they are such, is it possible to establish the one to one correspondence which natural science does establish between series of numbers and spatial positions on one hand

and the series and spectra of sensory qualities on the other. The notion that the universe is split into two separate and disconnected realms of existence, one psychical and the other physical, and then that these two realms of being, in spite of their total disjunction, specifically and minutely correspond to each other—as a serial order of numbered vibrations corresponds to the immediately felt qualities of vision of the prismatic spectrum—presents the acme of incredibility. The one-to-one agreement is intelligible only as a correspondence of properties and relations in one and the same world which is first taken upon a narrower and more external level of interaction, and then upon a more inclusive and intimate level. When we recall that by taking natural events on these two levels and instituting point to point correspondence (or "parallelism") between them, the richer and more complex display of characters is rendered amenable to prediction and deliberate guidance, the intelligibility of the procedure becomes concretely sensible.

Thus while modern science is correct in denying direct efficacy and position in the described sequence of events to say, red, or dry; yet Greek science was correct in its underlying naïve assumption that qualities count for something highly important. Apart from sentiency and life, the career of an event can indeed be fully described without any reference to its having red as a quality,—though even in this case, since description is an event which happens only through mental events, dependence upon an overt or actualized quality of red is required in order to delimit the phenomenon of which a mathematical-mechanical statement is made. Qualities actually become specifically effective however, in psycho-physical situations. Where animal susceptibility exists, a red or an odor or sound may instigate a determinate mode of action; it has selective power in maintenance of a certain pattern of energy-organization. So striking is this fact that we might even define the difference between an inanimate body and a vital and psycho-physical one, by saying that the latter responds to qualities while the former does not. In this response, qualities become productive of results, and hence potentially significant. That is, in achieving effects, they become connected with consequences, and hence capable of meaning, knowable if not known. This explains the fact that while we are forced to ascribe qualities to events on the physical level, we cannot *know* them on this level;

they have when assigned strictly to that level no consequences. But through the medium of living things, they generate effects, which, when qualities are used as means to produce them, are consequences. Thus qualities become intelligible, knowable.

In the higher organisms, those with distance-receptors of ear and eye and, in lesser degree, of smelling, qualities further achieve a difference which is the material basis or substratum of a distinction into activities having preparatory and having consummatory status. "Ends" are not necessarily fulfillments or consummations. They may be mere closures, abrupt cessations, as a railway line may by force of external conditions come to an end, although the end does not fulfill antecedent activities. So there are starts, beginnings which are in no sense preparatory, being rather disturbances and interferences. Events of the physical type have such ends and beginnings which mark them off qualitatively and individually. But as such they are not in any true sense possessed of instrumental nor fulfilling character. They neither initiate nor complete. But when these qualities are realized through organic action, giving rise to acts of utilization, of adaptation (response to quality), they are converted into a series, in which some acts are preparatory and others consummatory. An original contact-activity (including intra-organic disturbances or needs) renders distance receptors open to stimulation; the responses which take place in consequence tend to occur in such a way as to terminate in a further contact-activity in which original need is satisfied.

This series forms the immediate material of thought when social communication and discourse supervene. The beginning not only *is* the initial term in a *series* (as distinct from a *succession*), but it gains the *meaning* of subsequent activity moving toward a consequence of which it is the first member. The concluding term conserves within itself the meaning of the entire preparatory process. Thereby the original status of contact and distance activities is reversed. When activity is directed by distant things, contact activities must be inhibited or held in. They become instrumental; they function only as far as is needed to direct the distance-conditioned activities. The result is nothing less than revolutionary. Organic activity is liberated from subjection to what is closest at hand in space and time. Man is led or drawn rather than pushed. The immediate is significant in respect to what has occurred and will occur; the organic basis of memory and expectation is supplied. The subordination of contact-activity to distance-activity is equivalent to possibility of release from submergence in the merely given, namely, to abstraction, generalization, inference. It institutes both a difference and a connection between matters that prepare the way for other events and the affairs finally appropriated; it furnishes the material for the relation of thing signifying and thing signified—a relation that is actualized when discourse occurs. When this juncture of events is reached, there comes about the distinction mentioned between sense and signification. The latter denotes the possibility of a later fulfilling sense of things in immediate appropriations and enjoyments. But meanwhile there is a sentience that has to be transformed by subordination to the distance-conditioned activity; which till it is thus transformed is vacant, confused, demanding but lacking meaning. Meanwhile also the distance-conditioned activities acquire as an integral part of their own quality the consequences of their prior fulfillments. They have *significance* with respect to their consequences; but they have perspicuous and coherent *sense* of their own. Thus they become final, and the qualities of contact-activity instrumental. In short, hearing and vision are notoriously the intellectual *and* esthetic senses—an undeniable fact which throws much light on the doctrine of those theorists about value who attempt to divide thought and enjoyable liking from each other in their definitions of value, and who also—quite logically on this premise—sharply separate values into contributory and intrinsic.

The foregoing discussion is both too technical and not elaborately technical enough for adequate comprehension. It may be conceived as an attempt to contribute to what has come to be called an "emergent" theory of mind. But every word that we can use, organism, feeling, psycho-physical, sensation and sense, "emergence" itself, is infected by the associations of old theories, whose import is opposite to that here stated. We may, however attempt a recapitulation by premising that while there is no isolated occurrence in nature, yet interaction and connection are not wholesale and homogenous. Interacting events have tighter and looser ties, which qualify them with certain beginnings and endings, and which mark them off from other fields of interaction. Such relatively closed fields come into conjunction at times so as to interact with each other, and a critical alteration is effected. A new larger field is formed, in which new energies are released, and to which new qualities appertain. Regulation, conscious direction and science imply ability to smooth over the rough junctures, and to form by translation and substitution a homogenous medium. Yet these functions do not abrogate or deny qualitative differences and unlike fields or ranges of operation, from atoms to solar systems. They do just what they are meant to do: give facility and security in utilizing the simpler manageable field to predict and modify the course of the more complete and highly organized.

In general, three plateaus of such fields may be discriminated. The first, the scene of narrower and more external interactions, while qualitatively diversified in itself, is physical; its distinctive properties are those of the mathematical-mechanical system discovered by physics and which define matter as a general character. The second level is that of life. Qualitative differences, like those of plant and animal, lower and higher animal forms, are here even more conspicuous; but in spite of their variety they have qualities in common which define the psycho-physical. The third plateau is that of association, communication, participation. This is still further internally diversified, consisting of individualities. It is marked throughout its diversities, however, by common properties, which define mind as intellect; possession of and response to meanings.

Each one of these levels having its own characteristic empirical traits has its own categories. They are however categories of description, conceptions required to state the fact in question. They are not "explanatory" categories, as explanation is sometimes understood; they do not designate, that is, the operation of forces as "causes." They stick to empirical facts noting and denoting characteristic qualities and consequences peculiar to various levels of interaction. Viewed from this standpoint, the traditional "mechanical" and "teleological" theories both suffer from a common fallacy, which may be suggested by saying that they both purport to be explanatory in the old, non-historical sense of causality. One theory makes matter account for the existence of mind; the other regards happenings that precede the appearance of mind as preparations made for the sake of mind in a sense of preparation that is alleged to explain the occurrence of these antecedents.

Mechanistic metaphysics calls attention to the fact that the latter occurrence could not have taken place without the earlier; that given the earlier, the latter was bound to follow. Spiritualistic metaphysics calls attention to the fact that the earlier, material affairs, prepare the way for vital and ideal affairs, lead up to them; promote them. Both statements are equally true descriptively; neither statement is true in the explanatory and metaphysical meaning imputed to it.

The notion of causal explanation involved in both conceptions implies a breach in the continuity of historic process; the gulf created has then to be bridged by an emission or transfer of force. If one starts with the assumption that mind and matter are two separate things, while the evidence forces one to see that they are connected, one has no option save to attribute the power to make the connection, to carry from one to the other, to one or the other of the two things involved. The one selected is then "cause"; it accounts for the existence of the other. One person is struck by such affairs as that when a match is struck and paper is near-by the paper catches fire, whether any one wished or intended it to do so or not. He is struck by a compulsory power exercised by the earlier over the later; given the lighted match and contiguous paper and the latter *must* burst into flame. Another person is struck by the fact that matches and paper exist only because somebody has use for them; that the intent and purpose of use preceded the coming into being of match and paper. So he concludes that thought, purpose, starts an emission and transfer of force which brought things into existence in order to accomplish the object of thought. Or, if a little less devoted to human analogies, one notes the cunning continuity of nature, how neatly one thing leads up to another, and how elegantly the later registers and takes advantage of what has gone before, and, beholding that the later is the more complex and the more significant, decides that what goes before occurs for the sake of the later, in its behalf, on its account. The eventual has somehow been there from the start, "implicitly," "potentially," but efficaciously enough to attend to its own realization by using material conditions at every stage.

The gratuitous nature of both assumptions is seen if we set out with any acknowledged historic process,—say—the growth from infancy to maturity, or the development of a melodic theme. There are those who regard childhood as merely getting ready for the supreme dignity of adulthood, and there are those who seem quite sure that adult life is merely an unrolling by way of mechanical effects of the "causal" forces found in childhood. One of the theories makes youth a preliminary and intrinsically insignificant journey toward a goal; the other makes adulthood a projection, on a supernumerary screen, of a plate and pattern previously inserted in the projecting apparatus of childhood or of prenatal condition, or of heredity, or wherever the fixed and separated antecedent be located. Nevertheless the notion of growth makes it easy, I think, to detect the fallacy residing in both views: namely, the breaking up of a continuity of historical change into two separate parts, together with the necessity which follows from the breaking-in-two for some device by which to bring them together again.

The reality *is* the growth-process itself; childhood and adulthood are phases of a continuity, in which just because it is a history, the later cannot exist until the earlier exists ("mechanistic materialism" in germ); and in which the later makes use of the registered and cumulative outcome of the earlier—or, more strictly, *is* its utilization ("spiritualistic teleology" in germ). The real existence is the history in its entirety, the history as just what it is. The operations of splitting it up into two parts and then having to unite them again by appeal to causative power are equally arbitrary and gratuitous. Childhood is the childhood *of* and *in* a certain serial process of changes which is just what it is, and so is maturity. To give the traits of either phase a kind of independent existence, and then to use the form selected to account for or explain the rest of the process is a silly reduplication; reduplication, because we have after all only parts of one and the same original history; silly because we fancy that we have accounted for the history on the basis of an arbitrary selection of part of itself.

Substitute for such growth a more extensive history of nature and call it the evolution of mind from matter, and the conclusion is not different. In the old dispute as to whether a stag runs because he has long and slender legs, or has the legs in order that he may run, both parties overlook the natural descriptive statement; namely, that it is of the nature of what goes on in the world that the stag has long legs and that having them he runs. When mind is said to be implicit, involved, latent, or potential in matter, and subsequent change is asserted to be an affair of making it explicit, evolved, manifest, actual, what happens is that a natural history is first cut arbitrarily and unconsciously in two, and then the severance is consciously and arbitrarily cancelled. It is simpler not to start by engaging in such manoeuvers.

The discussion gives an understanding of the adaptation of nature and life and mind to one another. A mystery has not seldom been made of the fact that objective nature lends itself to man's sense of fitness, order and beauty; or, in another region of discourse, that objective nature submits to mental operations sufficiently to be known. Or, the mystery is conceived from the other end: it seems wonderful that man should be possessed of a sense of order, beauty and rightness; that he should have a capacity of thinking and knowing, so that man is elevated far above nature and seated with angels. But the wonder and mystery do not seem to be other than the wonder and mystery that there should be such a thing as nature, as existential events, at all, and that in being they should be what they are. The wonder should be transferred to the whole course of things. Only because an arbitrary breach has previously been introduced by which the world is first conceived as something quite different from what it demonstrably is, does it then appear passing strange that after all it should be just what it is. The world is subject-matter for knowledge, because mind has developed *in* that world; a body-mind, whose structures have developed according to the structures of the world in which it exists, will naturally find some of its structures to be concordant and congenial with nature, and some phases of nature with itself. The latter are beautiful and fit, and others ugly and unfit. Since mind cannot evolve except where there is an organized process in which the fulfillments of the past are conserved and employed, it is not surprising that mind when it evolves should be mindful of the past and future, and that it should use the structures which are biological adaptations of organism and environment as its own and its only organs. In ultimate analysis the mystery that mind should use a body, or that a body should have a mind, is like the mystery that a man cultivating plants should use the soil; or that the soil which grows plants at all should grow those adapted to its own physico-chemical properties and relations.

The account which has been given will be repeated from a more analytic point of view, starting with evident empirical consideration. Every "mind" that we are empirically acquainted with is found in connection with some organized body. Every such body exists in a natural medium to which it sustains some adaptive connection: plants to air, water, sun, and animals to these things and also to plants. Without such connections, animals die; the "purest" mind would not continue without them. An animal can live only as long as it draws nutriment from its medium, finds their means of defence, and ejects into it waste and superfluous products of its own making. Since no particular organism lasts forever, life in general goes on only as an organism reproduces itself; and the only place where it can reproduce itself is in the environment. In all higher forms reproduction is sexual; that is, it involves the meeting of two forms. The medium is thus one which contains similar and conjunctive forms. At every point and stage, accordingly, a living organism and its life processes involve a world or nature temporally and spatially "external" to itself but "internal" to its functions.

The only excuse for reciting such commonplaces is that traditional theories have separated life from nature, mind from organic life, and thereby created mysteries. Restore the connection, and the problem of how a mind can know an external world or even know that there is such a thing, is like the problem of how an animal eats things external to itself; it is the kind of problem that arises only if one assumes that a hibernating bear living off its own stored substance defines the normal procedure, ignoring moreover the question where the bear got its stored material. The problem of how one person knows the existence of other persons, is, when the relation of mind and life is genuinely perceived, like the problem of how one animal can associate with other animals, since other is other. A creature generated in a conjunctive union, dependent upon others (as are at least all higher forms) for perpetuation of its being, and carrying in its own structure the organs and marks of its intimate connection with others will know other creatures if it knows itself. Since both the inanimate and the human environment are involved in the functions of life, it is inevitable, if these functions evolve to the point of thinking and if thinking is naturally serial with biological functions, that it will have as the material of thought, even of its erratic imaginings, the events and connections of this environment. And if the animal succeeds in putting to use any of its thinkings as means of sustaining its functions, those thoughts will have the characters that define knowledge.

In contrast with lower organisms, the more complex forms have distance receptors and a structure in which activators and effectors are allied to distance even more extensively than to contact receptors. What is done in response to things near-by is so tied to what is done in response to what is far away, that a higher organism acts with reference to a spread-out environment as a single situation. We find also in all these higher organisms that what is done is conditioned by consequences of prior activities; we find the fact of learning or habit-formation. In consequence, an organism acts with reference to a time-spread, a serial order of events, as a unit, just as it does in reference to a unified spatial variety. Thus an environment both extensive and enduring is immediately implicated in present behavior. Operatively speaking, the remote and the past are "in" behavior making it what it is. The action called "organic" is not just that of internal structures; it is an integration of organic-environmental connections. It may be a mystery that there should be thinking but it is no mystery that if there is thinking it should contain in a "present" phase, affairs remote in space and in time, even to geologic ages, future eclipses and far away stellar systems. It is only a question of how far what is "in" its actual experience is extricated and becomes focal.

It is also an obvious empirical fact that animals are connected with each other in inclusive schemes of behavior by means of signaling acts, in consequence of which certain acts and consequences are deferred until a joint action made possible by the signaling occurs. In the human being, this function becomes language, communication, discourse, in virtue of which the consequences of the experience of one form of life are integrated in the behavior of others. With the development of recorded speech, the possibilities of this integration are indefinitely widened—in principle the cycle of objective integration within the behavior of a particular organism is completed. Not merely its own distant world of space-time is involved in its conduct but the world of its fellows. When consequences which are unexperienced and future to one agent are experienced and past to another creature with which it is in communication, organic prudence becomes conscious expectation, and future affairs living present realities. Human learning and habit-forming present thereby an integration of organic-environmental connections so vastly superior to those of animals without language that its experience appears to be super-organic.

Another empirical fact follows. Strict repetition and recurrence decrease relatively to the novel. Apart from communication, habit-forming wears grooves; behavior is confined to channels established by prior behavior. In so far the tendency is toward monotonous regularity. The very operation of learning sets a limit to itself, and makes subsequent learning more difficult. But this holds only of a habit, a habit in isolation, a non-communicating habit. Communication not only increases the number and variety of habits, but tends to link them subtly together, and eventually to subject habit-forming in a particular case to the habit of recognizing that new modes of association will exact a new use of it. Thus habit is formed in view of possible future changes and does not harden so readily. As soon as a child secretes from others the manifestation of a habit there is proof that he is practically aware that he forms a habit subject to the requirements of others as to his further habit formations.

Now an animal given to forming habits, is one with an increasing number of needs, and of new relationships with the world about it. Each habit demands appropriate conditions for its exercise and when habits are numerous and complex, as with the human organism, to find these conditions involves search and experimentation; the organism is compelled to make variations, and exposed to error and disappointment. By a seeming paradox, increased power of forming habits means increased susceptibility, sensitiveness, responsiveness. Thus even if we think of habits as so many grooves, the power to acquire many and varied grooves denotes high sensitivity, explosiveness. Thereby an old habit, a fixed groove if one wishes to exaggerate, gets in the way of the process of forming a new habit while the tendency to form a new one cuts across some old habit. Hence instability, novelty, emergence of unexpected and unpredictable combinations. The more an organism learns—the more that is, the former terms of a historic process are retained and integrated in this present phase—the more it has to learn, in order to keep itself going; otherwise death and catastrophe. If mind is a further process in life, a further process of registration, conservation and use of what is conserved, then it must have the traits it does empirically have: being a moving stream, a constant change which nevertheless has axis and direction, linkages, associations as well as initiations, hesitations and conclusions.

The thing essential to bear in mind is that living as an empirical affair is not something which goes on below the skin-surface of an organism: it is always an inclusive affair involving connection, interaction of what is within the organic body and what lies outside in space and time, and with higher organisms far outside. For this reason, organic acts are a kind of fore-action of mind; they look as if they were deliberate and consciously intelligent, because, of necessity, intelligent action in utilizing the mechanisms they supply, reproduces their patterns. The evidence usually adduced in support of the proposition that lower animals, animals without language, think, turns out, when examined, to be evidence that when men, organisms with power of social discourse, think, they do so with the organs of adaptation used by lower animals, and thus largely repeat in imagination schemes of overt animal action. But to argue from this fact to the conclusion that animals think is like concluding that because every tool, say a plow, originated from some pre-existing natural production, say a crooked root or forked branch, the latter was inherently and antecedently engaged in plowing. The connection is there, but it is the other way around.

Excuse for dwelling upon the fact that life goes on between and among things of which the organism is but one is because this fact is so much ignored and virtually denied by traditional theories. Consider for example, the definitions of life and mind given by Herbert Spencer: correspondence of an inner order with an outer order. It implies there is an inner order and an outer order, and that the correspondence consists in the fact that the terms in one order are related to one another as the terms or members of the other order are connected within themselves. The correspondence is like that of various phonographic records to one another; but the genuine correspondence of life and mind with nature is like the correspondence of two persons who "correspond" in order to learn each one of the acts, ideas and intents of the other one, in such ways as to modify one's own intents, ideas and acts, and to substitute partaking in a common and inclusive situation for separate and independent performances. If the organism merely repeats in the series of its own self-enclosed acts the order already given without, death speedily closes its career. Fire for instance consumes tissue; that is the sequence in the external order. Being burned to death is the order of "inner" events which corresponds with this "outer" order. What the organism actually does is to act so as to change its relationship to the environment; and as organisms get more complex and human this change of relationship involves more extensive and more enduring changes in the environmental order. The aim is not to protract a line of organic events parallel to external events, but to form a new scheme of affairs to which both organic and environmental relations contribute, and in which they both partake. Yet all schemes of psycho-physical parallelism, traditional theories of truth as correspondence, etc., are really elaborations of the same sort of assumptions as those made by Spencer: assumptions which first make a division where none exists, and then resort to an artifice to restore the connection which has been willfully destroyed.

If organic life denotes a phase of history in which natural affairs have reached a point in which characteristic new properties appear, and new ways of acting are released because of integration of fields hitherto unlinked, there does not seem to be anything extraordinary in the fact that what is known about the earlier "physical" series is applied to interpret and direct vital phenomena; nor in the fact that this application does not exhaust their character nor suffice wholly for their description. We cannot direct a course of interactions without counting and measuring, but the interactions are more than numbers, spaces and velocities. To explain is to employ one thing to elucidate, clear, shed light upon, put in better order, because in a wider context, another thing. It is thus subordinate to more adequate discourse, which, applied to space-time affairs, assumes the style of narration and description. Speaking in terms of captions familiar in rhetoric, exposition and argument are always subordinate to a descriptive narration, and exist for the sake of making the latter clearer, more coherent and more significant.

Body-mind designates an affair with its own properties. A large part of the difficulty in its discussion—perhaps the whole of the difficulty in general apart from detailed questions—is due to vocabulary. Our language is so permeated with consequences of theories which have divided the body and mind from each other, making separate existential realms out of them, that we lack words to designate the actual existential fact. The circumlocutions we are compelled to resort to—exemplified in the previous discussion—thus induce us to think that analogous separations exist in nature, which can also only be got around by elaborate circuitous arrangements. But body-mind simply designates what actually takes place when a living body is implicated in situations of discourse, communication and participation. In the hyphenated phrase body-mind, "body" designates the continued and conserved, the registered and cumulative operation of factors continuous with the rest of nature, inanimate as well as animate; while "mind" designates the characters and consequences which are differential, indicative of features which emerge when "body" is engaged in a wider, more complex and interdependent situation.

Just as when men start to talk they must use sounds and gestures antecedent to speech, and as when they begin to hunt animals, catch fish or make baskets, they must employ materials and processes that exist antecedently to these operations, so when men begin to observe and think they must use the nervous system and other organic structures which existed independently and antecedently. That the use reshapes the prior materials so as to adapt them more efficiently and freely to the uses to which they are put, is not a problem to be solved: it is an expression of the common fact that anything changes according to the interacting field it enters. Sounds do not cease to be sounds when they become articulate speech; but they do take on new distinctions and arrangements, just as do materials used in tools and machines, without ceasing to be the materials they formerly were. Thus the external or environmental affairs, primarily implicated in living processes and later implicated in discourse, undergo modifications in acquiring meanings and becoming objects of mind, and yet are as "physical" as ever they were.

Unless vital organizations were organizations *of* antecedent natural events, the living creature would have no natural connections; it would not be pertinent to its environment nor its environment relevant to it; the latter would not be usable, material of nutrition and defence. In similar fashion, unless "mind" was, in its existential occurrence, an organization *of* physiological or vital affairs and unless its functions developed out of the patterns of organic behavior, it would have no pertinency to nature, and nature would not be the appropriate scene of its inventions and plans, nor the subject-matter of its knowledge. If we suppose, per impossible or by a miracle, that a separate mind is inserted abruptly in nature, its operation would be wholly dialectical, and in a sense of dialectic which is non-existential not only for the time being, but forever; that is dialectic would be without any *possible* reference to existence. We are so used by tradition both to separating mind from the world and noting that its acts and consequences are relevant to the world-error—aberration and insanity can exist only with respect to relevancy—that we find it easier to make a problem out of the conjunction of two inconsistent premises than to rethink our premises.

Of pure dialectic it is a truism that it is neither materially true nor false, but only self-consistent or else self-contradictory. Were it not for the distorting influence of material bias, of preference that *existence* be thus and so rather than otherwise, and of desire that other creatures should believe as we do or should accept our conclusions, dialectic and calculation would however not be subject even to inconsistency. Some purely logical operations are better than others, even as purely logical, for they have greater scope and fertility, but none are truer or more correct than others. Purely formal errors are impossible, so-called formal fallacies to the contrary notwithstanding. No one ever actually reasoned that since horses are quadrupeds and cows are quadrupeds, horses are cows. If in some cases, it is made to appear that formal reasoning falls into such fallacies, the reason is that material causes are brought in and their operation is overlooked. Dialectical relations are dialectical, not existential and therefore have no causative power; there is nothing in them to generate misconception. The principle of dialectic is identity; its opposite is not inconsistency to say nothing of falsity; it is nonsense. To say that dialectic as such is infallible is only to say it is truistic.

Nevertheless logic or the *use* of meanings in a dialectic manner *is* actually exposed to all sorts of mistakes. For every instance of dialectic is itself existential. Meanings are taken; they are employed for a purpose, just as other materials are; they are combined and disjoined. It is the act of *taking* which enables dialectic to exist or occur, and taking is fallible, it is often mis-taking. Using meanings is a particular act; into this act enter causative factors, physiological, social, moral. The most perfect structure may be employed for purposes to which it is not apt; wrongly employed for the right purpose, it will buckle or default. Thus in dialectic, reasoning may flag because of fatigue; it may take one meaning for another because of perverse sensory appreciations, due to organic maladjustments; haste, due to absence of inhibition, may lead one to take a meaning to be clear when it is cloudy or ambiguous with respect to the purpose for which it is used, although in itself it is neither clear nor obscure; a desire to show off or to confute an opponent may lead to inconsistency and extraneous irrelevancies. Thousands of things may cause fallacies, when meanings truistically infallible because just what they are, are *used* to reach an end or make a conclusion. Self-contradiction assuredly occurs but it is material and active, not formal and non-existential. We contradict ourselves precisely as we contradict another person and for much the same reasons.

The ownership of meanings or mind thus vests in nature; meanings are meanings *of*. The existence of error is proof, not disproof, of the fact that all meanings intrinsically have reference to natural events. The idealist who employs the existence of error and of detection and possible correction of error as evidence of the existence of a pre-existent truth in which errors are contained in their total relationship, and hence are not errors but constituents of truth, is right in the insistence that error involves objective reference. But in the same way digestion involves food-stuffs; and yet does not prove that there pre-exists a model digestion in which food is perfectly assimilated. Error involves a possibility of detection and corrections because it refers to things, but the possibility has an eventual, not a backward reference. It denotes the possibility of acts yet to be undertaken. Like the criterion of perfect efficiency in respect to machines, the notion of a complete judgment in which errors exist only as a rectified constituent of a perfect truth, is part of the art of examination and invention. Action and reaction are equal, to a hundred per cent of equality; but this formal "law" does not guarantee that in any particular system of action-reaction there is contained perfect efficiency. Similarly the objective reference of meanings is complete; it is a hundred per cent affair; but it takes errors as well as truth to make up the hundred per cent, as it takes waste as well as efficiency to make up the perfect equality of action and reaction.

We mark off certain uses of meanings as reveries in order to control better the cognitive reference of other meanings. So we mark off certain meanings as purely rational or ideal, as dialectical or non-existential, in order to control better an eventual existential reference. Meaning may *become* purely esthetic; it may be appropriated and enjoyed for what it is in the having. This also involves control; it is *such* a way of taking and using them as to suspend cognitive reference.[1] This suspension is an acquired art. It required long discipline to recognize poetry instead of taking it as history, instruction and prediction. The idea that meanings are originally floating and esthetic and become intellectual, or practical and cognitive, by a conjunction of happy accidents, puts the cart before the horse. Its element of truth is that there is genuine distinction between having a meaning and using it; the element of falsity is in supposing that meanings, ideas, are first had and afterwards used. It required long experience to enforce recognition of the distinction; for originally any meaning had, is had in and for use. To hold an idea contemplatively and esthetically is a late achievement in civilization.

Organic and psycho-physical activities with their qualities are conditions which have to come into existence before mind, the presence and operation of meanings, ideas, is possible. They supply mind with its footing and connection in nature; they provide meanings with their existential stuff. But meanings,

---

1. This statement does not rest upon a confusion between objects as causal conditions of meanings and objects as cognitively meant. The distinction is a genuine one, not to be slighted. The former connection is antecedent, the latter is subsequential. But meanings or mind have both kinds of connection. Greek myths for example were adequately conditioned in existence; but they also have a diagnostic status. When not taken as meanings of the behavior of gods, they are taken as meanings of Greek life, just as a hallucinatory ghost when not taken as a spiritual apparition is taken as meaning another event, say, a nervous shock. *Having* a meaning is not a reference, but every meaning had is taken or used as well as had. "Dialectic" means to take it a certain way.

ideas, are also, when they occur, characters of a new interaction of events; they are characters which in their incorporation with sentiency transform organic action, furnishing it with new properties. Every thought and meaning has its substratum in some organic act of absorption or elimination of seeking, or turning away from, of destroying or caring for, of signaling or responding. It roots in some definite act of biological behavior; our physical names for mental acts like seeing, grasping, searching, affirming, acquiescing, spurning, comprehending, affection, emotion are not just "metaphors." But while a burnt child may shrink from flame just as the dog cowers at the sight of a stick, a child may in addition, when the conditions involved have become a matter of discourse and are ideas, respond to the burn-giving flame in playful, inventive, curious and investigative ways. He pokes a stick or piece of paper into it; he uses flame and the fact of its painful and burning consequence not just to keep away from it, but to do things with it in ways which will satisfy his want to have to do with fire but without getting burned. Biological acts persist, but have sense, meaning, as well as feeling, tone. Abrupt withdrawal having only negative, protective consequences is turned into significant and fruitful exploration and manipulation. Man combines meanings, like fire, nearness, remoteness, warmth, comfort, nice, pain, expansion, softening, so that fire enters into new interactions and effects new consequences. By an intra-organic re-enactment of partial animal reactions to natural events, and of accompanying reactions to and from others acquired in intercourse and communication, means-consequences are tried out in advance without the organism getting irretrievably involved in physical consequences. Thought, deliberation, objectively directed imagination, in other words, is an added efficacious function of natural events and hence brings into being new consequences. For images are not made of psychical stuff; they are qualities of *partial* organic behaviors, which are their "stuff." They are partial because not fully geared to extero-ceptor and muscular activities, and hence not complete and overt.

Domination by spatial considerations leads some thinkers to ask *where* mind is. Reserving the discussion of *conscious* behavior for the next chapter, and accepting for the moment the standpoint of the questioner (which ignores the locus of discourse, institutions and social arts), limiting the question to the organic individual, we may say that the "seat" or locus of mind—its static phase—is the qualities of organic action, as far as these qualities have been conditioned by language and its consequences. It is usual for those who are posed by the question of "where" and who are reluctant to answer that mind is "where" there is a spaceless separate realm of existence, to fall back in general on the nervous system, and specifically upon the brain or its cortex as the "seat" of mind. But the organism is not just a structure; it is a characteristic way of interactivity which is not simultaneous, all at once, but serial. It is a way impossible without structures for its mechanism, but it differs from structure as walking differs from legs or breathing from lungs. Prior to communication, the qualities of this action are what we have termed psycho-physical; they are not "mental." The consequences of partaking in communication modify organic ways of acting; the latter attain new qualities.

When I think such meanings as "friend" and "enemy," I refer to external and eventual consequences. But this naming does not involve miraculous "action at a distance." There is something present in organic action which acts as a surrogate for the remote things signified. The words make immediate sense as well as have signification. This something now present is not just the activity of the laryngeal and vocal apparatus. When shortcircuiting through language is carried as far as limitation to this apparatus, words are mere counters automatically used, and language disappears. The ideas are qualities of events in all the parts of organic structure which have ever been implicated in actual situations of concern with extra-organic friends and enemies:—presumably in proprioreceptors and organ-receptors with *all* their connected glandular and muscular mechanisms. These qualities give body and stuff to the activity of the linguistic apparatus. The integration of the qualities of vocal apparatus allied through the nervous mechanism with the qualities of these other events, constitutes the immediate sense of friendliness and animosity. The more intimate the alliance of vocal activity with the total organic disposition toward friends and enemies, the greater is the immediate sense of the words. The nervous system is in no sense the "seat" of the idea. It is the mechanism of the connection or integration of acts.

"Socrates is mortal" is hardly more than a counter of logical text-books; S is M will do just as well—or better. But not so to the disciples of Socrates who had just heard of his condemnation to death. The connection of the auditory act with the totality of organic responses was then complete. In some linguistic situations, such emphatic immediate presence of sense occurs; language is then poetical. For other purposes, action is served by elimination of immediate sense as far as possible. The attitude is prosaic; it is best subserved by mathematical symbolism; mathematical not signifying something ready-made, but being simply the devices by which mind is rigidly occupied with instrumental objects, by means of artificial inhibition of immediate and consummatory qualities, the latter being distracting for the activity in hand. The consummatory phase cannot be suppressed or eliminated however; nature pitched through the door returns through the window. And the common form of its return today is falling down in worship or in fear before the resulting mathematico-mechanical object.

In conclusion, it may be asserted that "soul" when freed from all traces of traditional materialistic animism denotes the qualities of psycho-physical activities as far as these are organized into unity. Some bodies have souls preeminently as some conspicuously have fragrance, color, and solidity. To make this statement is to call attention to properties that characterize these bodies, not to import a mysterious non-natural entity or force. Were there not in actual existence properties of sensitivity and of marvelously comprehensive and delicate participative response characterizing living bodies, mythical notions about the nature of the soul would never have risen. The myths have lost whatever poetic quality they once had; when offered as science they are superstitious encumbrances. But the idiomatic non-doctrinal use of the word soul retains a sense of the realities concerned. To say emphatically of a particular person that he has soul or a great soul is not to utter a platitude, applicable equally to all human beings. It expresses the conviction that the man or woman in question has in marked degree qualities of sensitive, rich and coordinated participation in all the situations of life. Thus works of art, music, poetry, painting, architecture, have soul, while others are dead, mechanical.

When the organization called soul is free, moving and operative, initial as well as terminal, it is spirit. Qualities are both static, substantial, and transitive. Spirit quickens; it is not only alive, but spirit gives life. Animals are spirited, but man is a living spirit. He lives in his works and his works do follow him. Soul is form, spirit informs. It is the moving function of that of which soul is the substance. Perhaps the words soul and spirit are so heavily laden with traditional mythology and sophisticated doctrine that they must be surrendered; it may be impossible to recover for them in science and philosophy the realities designated in idiomatic speech. But the realities are there, by whatever names they be called.

Old ideas do not die when the beliefs which have been explicitly associated with them disappear; they usually only change their clothes. Present notions about the organism are largely a survival, with changed vocabulary, of old ideas about soul and body. The soul was conceived as inhabiting the body in an external way. Now the nervous system is conceived as a substitute, mysteriously within the body. But as the soul was "simple" and therefore not diffused through the body, so the nervous system as the seat of mental events is narrowed down to the brain, and then to the cortex of the brain; while many physiological inquirers would doubtless feel enormously relieved if a specific portion of the cortex could be ascertained to be the seat of consciousness. Those who talk most of the organism, physiologists and psychologists, are often just those who display least sense of the intimate, delicate and subtle interdependence of all organic structures and processes with one another. The world seems mad in preoccupation with what is specific, particular, disconnected in medicine, politics, science, industry, education. In terms of a conscious control of inclusive wholes, search for those links which occupy key positions and which effect critical connections is indispensable. But recovery of sanity depends upon seeing and using these specifiable things as links functionally significant in a process. To see the organism in nature, the nervous system in the organism, the brain in the nervous system, the cortex in the brain is the answer to the problems which haunt philosophy. And when thus seen they will be seen to be in, not as marbles are in a box but as events are in history, in a moving, growing never finished process. Until we have a procedure in actual practice which demonstrates this continuity, we shall continue to engage in appealing to some other specific thing, some other broken off affair, to restore connectedness and unity—calling the specific religion or reform or whatever specific is the fashionable cure of the period. Thus we increase the disease in the means used to cure it.[2]

In matters predominantly physical we know that all control depends upon conscious perception of relations obtaining between things, otherwise one cannot be used to affect the other. We have been marvellously successful in inventing and constructing external machines, because with respect to such things we take for granted that success occurs only upon the conscious plane—that of conscious perception of the relations which things sustain to one another. We know that locomotives and aeroplanes and telephones and power-plants do not arise from instinct or the subconscious but from deliberately ascertained perception of connections and orders of connections. Now after a period in which advance in these respects was complacently treated as proof and measure of progress, we have been forced to adopt pessimistic attitudes, and to wonder if this "progress" is to end in the deterioration of man and the possible destruction of civilization.

Clearly we have not carried the plane of conscious control, the direction of action by perception of connections, far enough. We cannot separate organic life and mind from physical nature without also separating nature from life and mind. The separation has reached a point where intelligent persons are asking whether the end is to be catastrophe, the subjection of man to the industrial and military machines he has created. This situation confers peculiar poignancy upon the fact that just where connections and interdependences are most numerous, intimate and pervasive, in living, psycho-physical activity, we most ignore unity and connection, and trust most unreservedly in our deliberate beliefs to the isolated and specific—which signifies that in action we commit ourselves to the unconscious and subconscious, to blind instinct and impulse and routine, disguised and rationalized by all sorts of honorific titles. Thus we are brought to the topic of consciousness.

2. See F. Matthias Alexander's *Man's Supreme Inheritance*, and *Constructive Conscious Control of the Individual*.

8. Existence, Ideas and Consciousness

In the discussions of the last chapter the word "consciousness" was avoided. It is a word of unsettled signification. Even apart from ambiguities in interpretation, there is no consensus as to what things the word denotes. Two quite different affairs are usually designated by it. On the one hand, it is employed to point out certain qualities in their immediate apparency, qualities of things of sentiency, such as are, from the psychological standpoint, usually termed feelings. The sum total of these immediate qualities present as literal ends or closures of natural processes constitute "consciousness" as an anoetic occurrence. This is consciousness wherever meanings do not exist; that is to say, apart from the existence and employment of signs, or independently of communication. On the other hand, consciousness is used to denote meanings actually perceived, *awareness* of objects: being wide-awake, alert, attentive to the significance of events, present, past, future. It is a lexicographic matter, which will not be discussed, whether the word should be employed to denote two such different affairs. What is important is that the difference in the nature of the things denoted should be registered, and that false ingenuity should not be expended in reducing one to the other.

Our previous discussion enables us, it will appear, to place the two denotations. The existential starting point is immediate qualities. Even meanings taken not as meanings but as existential are grounded in immediate qualities, in sentiencies or "feelings," of organic activities and receptivities. Meanings do not come into being without language, and language implies two selves involved in a conjoint or shared undertaking. Thus while its direct mechanism is found in the vocalizing and auditory apparatuses, this mechanism is in alliance with general organic behavior. Otherwise it becomes a mechanical routine not differing from the "speech" of parrot or a phonographic record. This alliance supplies language with the immediate qualitative "feel" that marks off signs immediately from one another in existence.

The same considerations define the "subconscious" of human thinking. Apart from language, from imputed and inferred meaning, we continually engage in an immense multitude of immediate organic selections, rejections, welcomings, expulsions, appropriations, withdrawals, shrinkings, expansions, elations and dejections, attacks, wardings off, of the most minute, vibratingly delicate nature. We are not aware of the qualities of many or most of these acts; we do not objectively distinguish and identify them. Yet they exist as feeling qualities, and have an enormous directive effect on our behavior. If for example, certain sensory qualities of which we are not cognitively aware cease to exist, we cannot stand or control our posture and movements. In a thoroughly normal organism, these "feelings" have an efficiency of operation which it is impossible for thought to match. Even our most highly intellectualized operations depend upon them as a "fringe" by which to guide our inferential movements. They give us our *sense* of rightness and wrongness, of what to select and emphasize and follow up, and what to drop, slur over and ignore, among the multitude of inchoate meanings that are presenting themselves. They give us premonitions of approach to acceptable meanings, and warnings of getting off the track. Formulated discourse is mainly but a selected statement of what we wish to retain among all these incipient starts, following ups and breakings off. Except as a reader, a hearer repeats something of these organic movements, and thus "gets" their qualities, he does not get the *sense* of what is said; he does not really assent, even though he give cold approbation. These qualities are the stuff of "intuitions" and in actuality the difference between an "intuitive" and an analytic person is at most a matter of degree, of relative emphasis. The "reasoning" person is one who makes his "intuitions" more articulate, more deliverable in speech, as explicit sequence of initial premises, jointures, and conclusions.

Meanings acquired in connection with the use of tools and of language exercise a profound influence upon organic feelings. In the reckoning of this account, are included the changes effected by all the consequences of attitude and habit due to *all* the consequences of tools and language—in short, civilization. Evil communications corrupt (native) good manners of action, and hence pervert feeling and subconsciousness. The deification of the subconscious is legitimate only for those who never indulge in it—animals and thoroughly healthy naïve children—if there be any such. The subconscious of a civilized adult reflects all the habits he has acquired; that is to say, all the organic modifications he has undergone. And in so far as these involve mal-coordinations, fixations and segregations (as they assuredly come to do in a very short time for those living in complex "artificial" conditions), sensory appreciation is confused, perverted and falsified. It is most reliable in just those activities with respect to which it is least spoken of, and least reliable with respect to those things where it is fashionable most to laud it. That is, it operates most successfully in meanings associated with language that is highly technical, affairs remote from fundamental and exigent needs, as in mathematics, or philosophizing far away from concrete situations, or in a highly cultivated fine art. It is surest to be wrong in connection with intimate matters of self-regulation in health, morals, social affairs—in matters most closely connected with basic needs and relationships. Where its use is popularly recommended it is most dangerous. To use feelings which are not the expression of a rectitude of organic action, rectitude that in civilized or artificial conditions is acquired only by taking thought (*taking* thought is radically different to just "thinking"), is to act like an animal without having the structural facilities of animal life. It has the fascination of all easy surrender to fatality and may be eulogized as a return to nature, spontaneity, or to the quasi-divine. It has the charm of lazy and comfortable escape from responsibility; we die, but we die, like animals, upon the field, defeated and mayhap disheartened, but without knowing it.

In a practical sense, here is the heart of the mind-body problem. Activities which develop, appropriate and enjoy meanings bear the same actualizing relation to psycho-physical affairs that the latter bear to physical characters. They present the consequences of a wider range of interactions, that in which needs, efforts and satisfactions conditioned by association are operative. In this widened and deepened activity, there are both added resources and values, and added liabilities and defaults. The actualization of meanings furnishes psycho-physical qualities with their ulterior significance and worth. But it also confuses and perverts them. The effects of this corruption are themselves embodied through habits in the psycho-physical, forming one-sided degraded and excessive susceptibilities; creating both disassociations and rigid fixations in the sensory register. These habitual effects become in turn spontaneous, natural, "instinctive"; they form the platform of development and apprehension of further meanings, affecting every subsequent phase of personal and social life.[1]

Thus while the psycho-physical in man, apart from conscious meaning achieves nothing distinguished, the casual growth and incorporation of meanings cause the native need, adjustment and satisfaction to lose their immediate certainty and efficiency, and become subject to all kinds of aberrations. There then occur systematized withdrawals from intercourse and interaction, from what common sense calls "reality": carefully cultivated and artificially protected fantasies of consolation and compensation; rigidly stereotyped beliefs not submitted to objective tests; habits of learned ignorance or systematized ignorings of concrete relationships; organized fanaticisms; dogmatic traditions which socially are harshly intolerant and which intellectually are institutionalized paranoic systems; idealizations which instead of being immediate enjoyments of meanings, cut man off from nature and his fellows.

In short, there is constituted what Walter Lippmann has well termed a secondary pseudo-environment, which affects every item of traffic and dealing with the primary environment. Thus the concrete problems of mind-body have their locus and import in the educational procedures by which a normal integration of meanings in organic functions shall be secured and perversions prevented; in the remedial operations of psychiatry, and in social arts and appliances that render intercourse substantial, balanced and flexible.

While on the psycho-physical level, consciousness denotes the totality of actualized immediate qualitative differences, or "feelings," it denotes, upon the plane of mind, actualized apprehensions of meanings, that is, ideas. There is thus an obvious

1. See the books of Mr. Alexander already referred to, p. 225.

difference between mind and consciousness; meaning and an idea. Mind denotes the whole system of meanings as they are embodied in the workings of organic life; consciousness in a being with language denotes awareness or perception of meanings; it is the perception of actual events, whether past, contemporary or future, *in* their meanings, the having of actual ideas. The greater part of mind is only implicit in any conscious act or state; the field of mind—of operative meanings—is enormously wider than that of consciousness. Mind is contextual and persistent; consciousness is focal and transitive. Mind is, so to speak, structural, substantial; a constant background and foreground; perceptive consciousness is process, a series of heres and nows. Mind is a constant luminosity; consciousness intermittent, a series of flashes of varying intensities. Consciousness is, as it were, the occasional interception of messages continually transmitted, as a mechanical receiving device selects a few of the vibrations with which the air is filled and renders them audible.

The nature of awareness of meanings cannot be conveyed in speech. As with other immediate qualitative existences, words can only hint, point; the indication succeeding when it evokes an actual experience of the thing in question. Such words as apparency, conspicuousness, outstandingness, vividness, clearness, including of course their opposites vague, dim, confused, may assist the evocation. To denote the characteristics of mind a thoroughly different set of names must be used: organization, order, coherence. The relation of mind to consciousness may be partially suggested by saying that while mind as a system of meanings is subject to disorganization, disequilibration, perturbation, there is no sense in referring to a particular state of awareness *in its immediacy* as either organized or disturbed. An idea is just what it is when it occurs. To call it composed or perturbed is to compare one state with another, a comparison which by nature of the case can be made only indirectly on the basis of respective conditions and consequences. Emotional conditions do not *occur* as emotions, intrinsically defined as such; they occur as "tertiary" qualities of objects. Some cases of awareness or perception are designated "emotions" in retrospect or from without, as a child is instructed to term certain perceptual situations anger, or fear, or love, by way of informing him as to their consequences. Immediately, every perceptual awareness may be

termed indifferently emotion, sensation, thought, desire: not that
it *is* immediately any one of these things, or all of them combined, but that when it is taken in some *reference*, to conditions
or to consequences or to both, it has, in that contextual reference, the distinctive properties of emotion, sensation, thought
or desire.

The relation between mind and consciousness may be indicated by a familiar happening. When we read a book, we are
immediately conscious of meanings that present themselves, and
vanish. These meanings existentially occurring are *ideas*. But we
are capable of getting ideas from what is read because of an
organized system of meanings of which we are not at any one
time completely aware. Our mathematical or political "mind" is
the system of such meanings as possess and determine our particular apprehensions or ideas. There is however, a continuum or
spectrum between this containing system and the meanings
which, being focal and urgent, are the ideas of the moment.
There is a contextual field between the latter and those meanings
which determine the habitual direction of our conscious
thoughts and supply the organs for their formation. One great
mistake in the orthodox psychological tradition is its exclusive
preoccupation with sharp focalization to the neglect of the vague
shading off from the foci into a field of increasing dimness.

Discrimination in favor of the clearly distinguished has a
certain practical justification, for the vague and extensive background is present in every conscious experience and therefore
does not define the character of any one in particular. It represents that which is being used and taken for granted, while the
focal phase is that which is imminent and critical. But this fact
affords no justification for neglect and denial in theory of the
dim and total background consciousness of every distinct
thought. If there were a sharp division between the ideas that are
focal as we read a certain section of a book and what we have
already read, if there were not carried along a sense of the latter,
what we now read could not take the form of an idea. Indeed,
the use of such words as context and background, fringe, etc.,
suggests something too external to meet the facts of the case. The
larger system of meaning suffuses, interpenetrates, colors what is
now and here uppermost; it gives them sense, feeling, as distinct
from signification.

Change the illustration from reading a book to seeing and hearing a drama. The emotional as well as intellectual meaning of each presented phase of a play depends upon the operative presence of a continuum of meanings. If we have to remember what has been said and done at any particular point, we are not aware of what is now said and done; while without its suffusive presence in what is now said and done we lack clew to its meaning. Thus the purport of past affairs is present in the momentary cross-sectional idea in a way which is more intimate, direct and pervasive than the way of recall. It is positively and integrally carried in and by the incidents now happening; these incidents are, in the degree of genuine dramatic quality, fulfillment of the meanings constituted by past events; they also give this system of meanings an unexpected turn, and constitute a suspended and still indeterminate meaning, which induces alertness, expectancy. It is this double relationship of continuation, promotion, carrying forward, and of arrest, deviation, need of supplementation, which defines that focalization of meanings which is consciousness, awareness, perception. Every case of consciousness is dramatic; drama is an enhancement of the conditions of consciousness.

It is impossible to tell what immediate consciousness is—not because there is some mystery in or behind it, but for the same reason that we cannot tell just what sweet or red immediately is: it is something had, not communicated and known. But words, as means of directing action, may evoke a situation in which the thing in question is had in some particularly illuminating way. It seems to me that anyone who installs himself in the midst of the unfolding of drama *has* the experience of consciousness in just this sort of way; in a way which enables him to give significance to descriptive and analytic terms otherwise meaningless. There must be a story, some whole, an integrated series of episodes. This connected whole is mind, as it extends beyond a particular process of consciousness and conditions it. There must also be now-occurring events, to which meanings are assigned in terms of a story taking place. Episodes do not mean what they would mean if occurring in some different story. They have to be perceived in terms of the story, as its forwardings and fulfillings. At the same time, until the play or story is ended, meanings given to events are of a sort which constantly evoke a meaning which was not absolutely anticipated or totally predicted: there is expectancy, but also surprise, novelty. As far as complete and assured prediction is possible, interest in the play lags; it ceases to be an observed drama, it is not subsequently in consciousness.

An oft-told tale repeated without change fails to engage perception; it liberates us for attention to another story where development of meanings is as yet incomplete and indeterminate, possessed of suspense and uncertainty. Thus while perceptions are existentially intermittent and discrete, like a series of signal flashes, or telegraphic clicks, yet they involve a continuum of *meaning* in process of formation. If we became convinced that a succession of flashes or clicks were not a *series* of terms with respect to one and the same unfolding meaning, we should not attend to them or be aware of them. If on the other hand, there are no variations to compel suspense, no unforeseen movement in a new direction; if there is one unbroken luminosity, or one unbroken monotony of sound, there is no perception, no consciousness.

These considerations enable us to give a formal definition of consciousness in relation to mind or meanings. Consciousness, an idea, is that phase of a system of meanings which at a given time is undergoing re-direction, transitive transformation. The current idealistic conception of consciousness as a power which modifies events, is an inverted statement of this fact. To treat consciousness as a power accomplishing the change, is but another instance of the common philosophic fallacy of converting an eventual function into an antecedent force or cause. Consciousness *is* the meaning of events in course of remaking; its "cause" is only the fact that this is one of the ways in which nature goes on. In a proximate sense of causality, namely as place in a series history, its causation is the need and demand for filling out what is indeterminate.

There is a counterpart realist doctrine, according to which consciousness is like the eye running over a field of ready-made objects, or a light which illuminates now this and now that portion of a given field. These analogies ignore the indeterminateness of meaning when there is awareness; they fail to consider a basic consideration, namely, that while there exists an antecedent stock of meanings, these are just the ones which we take for granted and use: the ones of which we are not and do not need to be conscious. The theory takes as the normal case óf consciousness the case where there is a minimum of doubt and inquiry; the case where objects are most familiar and current, and so to speak vouch directly for themselves. It finds consciousness exemplified in being aware of old and often used things (the articles of furniture which figure in most discussions of consciousness) rather than in the case of thinking where reflective inquiry is needed in order to arrive at a meaning. It postulates, even though only implicitly, a pre-established harmony of the knower and things known, passing over the fact that such harmony is always an attained outcome of prior inferences and investigations. It assumes a knowing mind wholly guileless, and extraordinarily competent, whose sole business is to behold and register objects just as what they are, and which is unswervingly devoted to its business.

It is hard to believe that such an amiable and optimistic view of the nature of mind could have obtained currency, had it not been for a theology according to which God is perfect mind and man is created in the image of his maker. Even so, however, it could hardly have persisted when science displaced theology, had not science provided a number of cases which satisfy the requirement of the theory, and thereby given it a kind of empirical content and basis. That is, the development of science does present (a) the rise of cognitional interest to a point of prestige, and (b) it supplies eventually many cases of valid cognitive perceptions. Those who concern themselves with inquiry into the nature of consciousness have a strongly developed intellectual interest; this makes it easy for them to postulate a universal concern in knowing objects as the very essence of mind. These persons have rectitude of cognitive bent, acquired through scientific training; and they with ready benevolence, confer similar rectitude upon perception universally. Then when the existence of error, mistake, dreams, hallucinations, etc. is recognized, these things are treated as deviations and exceptions from the normal, to be accounted for by the introduction of complicating factors.

The problem and its solution thus become essentially dialectical. For empirical facts indicate that not error but truth is the exception, the thing to be accounted for, and that the attainment of truth is the outcome of the development of complex and elaborate methods of searching, methods that while congenial to some men in some respects, in many respects go against the human grain, so that they are adopted only after long discipline in a school of hard knocks. Even to put the matter in terms of proportion of erroneous and true perceptions, is to fail to see the chief objection to the theory. For it postulates the primarily cognitive character of awareness or perception. Empirically, however, the characteristic thing about perceptions in their natural estate, apart from subjection to an art of knowing, is their irrelevance to both truth and error; they exist for the most part in another dimension, whose nature may be suggested by reference to imagination, fancy, reverie, affection, love and hate, desire, happiness and misery. This fact, more than the error-problem, proves the artificial character of the spectator, search-light, notion of consciousness.

Empirical evidence in support of the proposition that consciousness of meanings denotes redirection of meanings (which are always ultimately meanings of events) is supplied by obvious facts of attention and interest on one side, and the working of established and assured habits on the other. The familiar does not consciously appear, save in an unexpected, novel, situation, where the familiar presents itself in a new light and is therefore not wholly familiar. Our deepest-seated habits are precisely those of which we have least awareness. When they operate in a situation to which they are not accustomed, in an unusual situation, a new adjustment is required. Hence there is shock, and an accompanying perception of dissolving and reforming meaning. Attention is most alert and stretched, when, because of unusual situations, there is great concern about the issue, together with suspense as to what it will be. We are engaged at once in taking in what *is* happening and looking ahead to what has not yet happened. As far as we can count upon the contemporary conditions *and* upon their outcome, focalization of meaning is absent. That which is taken to be involved *in any event*, in every issue, *no matter what*, we are not aware of. If we consider the entire field from bright focus through the fore-conscious, the "fringe," to what is dim, sub-conscious "feeling," the focus corresponds to the point of imminent need, of urgency; the "fringe" corresponds to things that just have been reacted to or that will soon require to be looked after, while the remote outlying field corresponds to what does not have to be modified, and which may be dependably counted upon in dealing with imminent need.

Hence the proverbial disparity between things in the scale of consciousness and in the scale of consequences is the most conclusive refutation of subjective idealism. The power of a momentary annoyance or flitting amusement to distract a personage from an enduringly serious question is a familiar theme of comedy; a glass of wine or the whine of a mosquito may exclude issues of life and death. Any trivial thing may swell and swell, if it bothers us. To like effect are the standing complaints of moralists that men sacrifice the great good to the lesser, if the latter be close at hand; and their proclamation that reason and freedom are only found when the near-by and the remote good are weighed with equal balance. Tragedy gives the same testimony. While doom impends the tragic hero fatally pursues his way, unheeding of the web closing in upon him, obvious to all others, and oblivious of what should be done to avert destructive destiny.

The *immediately* precarious, the point of greatest immediate need, defines the apex of consciousness, its intense or focal mode. And this is the point of re-direction, of re-adaptation, re-organization. Hence the aptness of James's comparison of the course of consciousness to a stream, in spite of its intermittent character—a fact empirically recognized in his intimation of its rhythmic waxings and wanings—; of his insistence that only an object, not a concrete consciousness which is had twice, or which remains the same; of his analogy of focus and fringe; of his statement of its movements as a series of perchings and flights, of substantial and transitive phases; for meanings are condensed at the focus of imminent re-direction only to disappear as organization is effected, and yield place to another point of stress and weakness.

Empirical confirmation of this conception of consciousness is found in the extreme instability of every perceived object; in the impossibility of excluding rapid and subtle change, except at the cost of inducing hypnotic sleep; in the passage from being wide awake, awake, drowsy, dreaming and fast asleep, according as an organism is actively partaking, or abstaining from partaking, in the course of events. All that goes by the name of "relativity" of consciousness is to precisely the same effect, including the Weberian principle; perceived changes are those which require a redirection of adaptive behavior. A prior adaptation constitutes a threshold (better called a platform or plateau); what is consciously noted is alteration of one plateau; re-adjustment to another. Similar events may mean cold at one time or place and warmth at another, depending upon the *direction* of organic re-adaptation. Even a tooth-ache is unstable in consciousness for it is notoriously a matter of throbs, pulsations, palpitations, waxings and wanings of intensity, of organic protests and temporary deviations, and of enforced returns—of flights and perchings. The "tooth-ache" which does not change is not the perceived tooth-ache, but the cognitive *object*, the unperceived tooth to which the sequence of all changes is referred.

Confirmation of the hypothesis is found in the fact that wherever perceptual awareness occurs, there is a "moment" of hesitation; there are scruples, reservations, in complete overt action. It seems quite probable that men of the executive type are those of the least subtle and variegated perceptual field; of the lowest degree of consciousness, having the steepest threshold to be crossed in order to induce a state of awareness. We have to "stop and think," and we do not stop unless there is interference. The flood of action at high tide overrides all but the most considerable obstructions. It flows too forcibly and rapidly in one direction to be checked; without inhibition there are no hesitations, crises, alternatives, need of re-direction. Overt action is an enstatement of established organic-environmental integrations. As long as these *can* maintain themselves, they do so; there is then no opportunity for transforming meaning into idea. In completely integrated function there is no room for distinction between things signifying and things signified. Only when behavior is divided within itself, do some of its factors have a subject-matter which stands for present tendencies and for their requirements or indications and implications, while other factors stand for absent and remote objects which, in unifying and organizing activity, complete the meaning of what is given at hand. The readier a response, the less consciousness, meaning, thinking it permits; division introduces mental confusion, but also, in need for redirection, opportunity for observation, recollection, anticipation.

There is then an empirical truth in the common opposition between theory and practice, between the contemplative, reflective type and the executive type, the "go-getter," the kind that "gets things done." It is, however, a contrast between two modes of practice. One is the pushing, slam-bang, act-first and think-afterwards mode, to which events may yield as they give way to any strong force. The other mode is wary, observant, sensitive to slight hints and intimations; perhaps intriguing, timid in public and ruthless in concealed action; perhaps over-cautious and in-hibited, unduly subject to scruples, hesitancies, an ineffective Hamlet in performance; or perhaps achieving a balance between immediately urgent demands and remoter consequences, consis-tent and cumulative in action. In the latter case, there develops a field of perception, rich in hues and subtle in shades of meaning. In the degree in which this occurs, overt action is subordinated to the contribution it renders to sustaining and developing the scope of the conscious field. One lives on a conscious plane; thought guides activity, and perception is its reward. Action is not suppressed but is moderated. Like the scientific experi-menter, one acts not just to act, nor rashly, nor automatically, but with a consciousness of purpose and for the sake of learning. Intellectual hesitations and reservations are used to expand and enrich the field of perception, by means of rendering activity more delicate, and discriminatingly adapted.

The notion that highly thoughtful persons are incompetent in action has its proper corrective in another attitude of belief which is expressed in such words as these: "No one can *make* you see this point; but unless you do see it, you won't change your conduct; if you do get the point you will act differently." The first notion, that thought paralyzes, refers to action in gross, the second relates to change in quality of action. Carry to an extreme the experiences indicated by the first proposition, and the result is the so-called automaton or epiphenomenal theory of consciousness; perception is an idle and superficial attachment to a mechanical play of energies. Carry the experiences involved in the other saying to an extreme, and you have the doctrine of the original creativeness of consciousness; it makes objects what they are.

Empirically the situation stands about like this: The use or intent of instruction, advice, admonition, and honest dialectic is to bring to awareness meanings hitherto unperceived, thereby constituting their ideas. The entanglements, misunderstandings and compromised understandings of life are a sufficient commentary on the difficulties in the way of realizing this intent. But experience demonstrates that as far as it is accomplished, conduct is actually changed; to get a new meaning *is* perforce to be in a new attitude. This does not indicate that consciousness or perception is an entity which *makes* the difference. What follows is that perception or consciousness *is*, literally, the difference in process of *making*. Instruction and reproof that are not an idle flogging of the air involve an art of re-directing activity; given this redirection and there is emergence of change in meanings, or perception. There is here no question of priority or causal sequence; intentional change in direction of events *is* transforming change in the *meaning* of those events. We have at present little or next to no controlled art of securing that redirection of behavior which constitutes adequate perception or consciousness. That is, we have little or no art of education in the fundamentals, namely in the management of the organic attitudes which color the qualities of our conscious objects and acts.

As long as our chief psycho-physical coordinations are formed blindly and in the dark during infancy and early childhood, they are accidental adjustments to the pressure of other persons and of circumstances which act upon us. They do not then take into account the consequence of these activities upon formation of habits and habituations. Hence the connection between consciousness and action is precarious, and its possession a doubtful boon as compared with the efficacy of instinct—or structure—in lower animals. Energy is wasteful and misdirected; in the outcome we effect the opposite of what we intended. Consciousness is desultory and casual. Only when organic activity achieves a conscious plane shall we be adequately aware of what we are about. As long as our own fundamental psycho-physical attitudes in dealing with external things are subconscious, our conscious attention going only to the relations of external things, so long will our perception of the external situations be subject at its root to perversion and vitiation. This state of affairs is the source of that apparent disconnection between consciousness and action which strikes us when we begin to reflect. The connecting links between the two are in our own attitudes; while they remain unperceived, consciousness and behavior must appear to be independent of each other. Hence there will be empirical reason for isolating consciousness from natural events. When so isolated, some persons will assert that consciousness is a slavish and capricious shadow of things and others will proclaim that it is their rightful creator and master. Assertions, like those of this discussion, that consciousness is their recognized meaning when they are undergoing purposeful re-direction by means of organic activity will seem to lack full empirical evidence.

It remains to note and deal with two difficulties that have quite probably troubled the reader. In the first place, the discussion has explicitly gone on the basis that *what* is perceived are meanings, rather than just events or existences. In this respect, the view presented agrees with classic teaching, according to which perception, apprehension, lays hold of form, not of matter. I believe this view properly understood is inherently sound; the error in the classic theory lies in its accompanying assumption that all perceptions are intrinsically cognitive. In the second place, the identification of consciousness with perceptive awareness runs counter to the verbal usage of recent psychology and philosophy which limits perception to apprehension (usually valid) of contemporaneously occurring events in "real" space. The latter issue however is not just a matter of propriety of language—about which it would be absurd to argue. It involves the conviction that perception of real things now existing differs *inherently* from other modes of consciousness, such as emotion, thinking, remembering, fancy and imagination. For this conviction, it must be explicitly noted, is contradicted by the conception which has been stated. According to the latter every mode of awareness—as distinct from "feeling"—in its immediate existence is exactly the same sort of thing, namely a remaking of meanings of events. The difference, it is implied, between awareness of present and "real" things and of absent and unreal is extrinsic, not intrinsic to a consciousness. The sequel will reveal that these two points are intimately connected with each other.

When it is denied that we are conscious of *events* as such it is not meant that we are not aware of *objects*. Objects are precisely what we are aware of. For objects are events *with* meanings; tables, the milky way, chairs, stars, cats, dogs, electrons, ghosts, centaurs, historic epochs and all the infinitely multifarious subject-matter of discourse designable by common nouns, verbs and their qualifiers. So intimate is the connection of meanings with consciousness that there is no great difficulty in resolving "consciousness," as a recent original and ingenious thinker has done, into knots, intersections or complexes of universals.[2]

Serious difficulty sets in however when *events* are resolved into such combinations. The matter is referred to here not to be argued; but to indicate that a "realist" has gone even further than the theory now presented goes in identifying the subject-matter of which there is awareness with meanings, or at least with universals which, as simple subject-matter, colors, sounds, etc., and complex, plants, animals, atoms, etc., are precisely the same as meanings. To cause existences in their particularity to disappear into combinations of universals is at least an extreme measure. And the present thesis sticks to the common-sense belief that universals, relations, meanings, are of and about existences, not their exhaustive ingredients. The same existential events are capable of an infinite number of meanings. Thus an existence identified as "paper," because the meaning uppermost at the moment is "something to be written upon," has as many other explicit meanings as it has important consequences recognized in the various connective interactions into which it enters. Since possibilities of conjunction are endless, and since the consequences of any of them may at some time be significant, its potential meanings are endless. It signifies something to start a fire with; something like snow; made of wood-pulp; manufactured for profit; property in the legal sense; a definite combination illustrative of certain principles of chemical science; an article the invention of which has made a tremendous difference in human history, and so on indefinitely. There is no conceivable universe of discourse in which the thing may not figure, having in each its own characteristic meaning. And if we say that after all it is "paper" which has all these different meanings, we are at bottom but asserting that all the different meanings have a common existential reference, converging to the same event. We are virtually asserting that the *existence* whose usual, standardized meaning in discourse is paper, also has a multitude of other meanings; we are saying in effect that its existence is not exhausted in its being paper, although paper is its ordinary meaning for human intercourse.

2. Holt, *The Concept of Consciousness.*

Ghosts, centaurs, tribal gods, Helen of Troy and Ophelia of
Denmark are as much the meanings of events as are flesh and
blood, horses, Florence Nightingale and Madam Curie. This
statement does not mark a discovery; it enunciates a tautology. It
seems questionable only when its significance is altered; when it
is taken to denote that, because they are all meanings of events,
they all are the same kind of meaning with respect to validity of
reference. Because perception of a ghost does not signify a subtle,
intangible form, filling space as it moves about, it does not follow that it may not signify some other existential happening like
disordered nerves; a religious animistic tradition; or, as in the
play of Hamlet, that it may not signify an enhancement of the
meaning of a moving state of affairs. The existential events that
form a drama have their own characteristic meanings, which are
not the less meanings of those events because their import is
dramatic, not authentically cognitive. So when men gather in
secret to plot a conspiracy, their plans are not the less meanings
of certain events because they have not been already carried out;
and they remain meanings of events even if the conspiracy comes
to naught.

The proposition that the perception of a horse is objectively
valid and that of a centaur fanciful and mythical does not denote
that one is a meaning of natural events and the other is not. It
denotes that they are meanings referable to *different* natural
events, and that confused and harmful consequences result from
attributing them to the same events. The idea that the consciousness of a horse as now present and of a centaur differ *as* perceptions, or states of awareness, is an illustration of the harm
wrought by introspective psychology, which, here as elsewhere,
treats *relationships of objects* as if they were inherent qualities of
an immediate subject-matter, ignoring the fact that causal relationships to unperceived things are involved. The matter of the
cognitive validity of the horse-perception and the cognitive inva-
lidity of the centaur-perception is not an affair of intrinsic difference in the two perceptions, which inspection of the two states
of awareness as such can ever bring to light; it is a causal matter,
brought to light as we investigate the causal antecedents and
consequents of the events having the meanings.

In other words, the difference between assertion of a perception, belief in it, and merely having it is an extrinsic difference;

the belief, assertion, cognitive reference is something additive, never merely immediate. Genuinely to believe the centaur-meaning is to assert that events characterized by it interact in certain ways with other now unperceived events. Since belief that centaur has the same kind of objective meaning as has horse denotes expectation of like efficacies and consequences, the difference of validity between them is extrinsic. It is capable of being revealed only by the results of acting upon them. The awareness of centaur meaning is fanciful not simply because part of its conditions lie within the organism; part of the conditions of *any* perception, valid as well as invalid, scientific as well as esthetic, lie within the organism. Nor is it fanciful, simply because it is supposed not to have adequate existential antecedents. Natural conditions, physiological, physical and social, may be specified in one case as in the other. But since the conditions in the two cases are different, consequences are bound to be different. Knowing, believing, involves something additive and extrinsic to having a meaning.

No knowledge is ever merely immediate. The proposition that the perception of a horse is valid and that a centaur is fanciful or hallucinatory, does not denote that there are two modes of awareness, differing intrinsically from each other. It denotes something with respect to causation, namely, that while both have their adequate antecedent conditions, the specific causal conditions are ascertained to be different in the two cases. Hence it denotes something with respect to consequences, namely, that action upon the respective meanings will bring to light (to apparency or awareness) such different kinds of consequences that we should use the two meanings in very different ways. Both acts and consequences lie outside the primary perceptions; both have to be diligently sought for and tested. Since conditions in the two cases *are* different, they operate differently. That is, they belong to different histories, and the matter of the history to which a given thing belongs is just the matter with which knowledge is concerned. The conscious or perceived affair is itself a consequence of antecedent conditions. But were this conscious or apparent (evident, focal) consequence the *only* consequence of the conditions, if there were not other as yet unapparent consequences, we should have absolutely no way to tell in what sequence of events a perception belongs, and hence absolutely no way of determining its validity or cognitive standing. It is because conditions which generate the perception of a horse have other and different consequences than the perception (and similarly of those which generate the idea of the centaur), that it is possible to make a distinction between the value in knowledge of the two ideas. By discovering the different sequential affairs to which they respectively belong we can differentiate their import for knowledge. Failure to recognize this fact is the ultimate condemnation, it may be remarked in passing, of idealistic theories of knowledge, which identify it with immediate consciousness. If an all-inclusive consciousness were to exist, it would be a piece of esthetic scenery, interesting or tedious as the case might be, but having no conceivable cognitive standing.

That a perception is cognitive means, accordingly, that it is used; it is treated as a sign of conditions that implicate other as yet unperceived consequences in addition to the perception itself. That a perception is *truly* cognitive means that its active use or treatment is followed by consequences which fit appropriately into the other consequences which follow independently of its being perceived. To discover that a perception or an idea is cognitively invalid is to find that the consequences which follow from acting upon it entangle and confuse the other consequences which follow from the causes of the perception, instead of integrating or coordinating harmoniously with them. The special technique of scientific inquiry may be defined as consisting of procedures which make it possible to perceive the eventual agreement or disagreement of the two sets of consequences. For experience proves that it is possible for great disparity between them to exist, and yet the conflict not be perceived or else be explained away as of no importance.

Common sense has no great occasion to distinguish between bare events and objects; objects being events-with-meanings. Events are present and operative *anyway*; what concerns us is their meanings expressed in expectations, beliefs, inferences, regarding their potentialities. The nearest approach that occurs in ordinary life to making the distinction is when there occurs some brute, dumb shock, which we are constrained to interpret, to assign meaning to, that is, to convert into an object. Such situations supply direct empirical evidence of the difference between events and objects; but common sense does not need to formulate the difference as a distinction. Events have effects or consequences anyway; and since meaning is awareness of these consequences before they actually occur, reflective inquiry which converts an event into an object is the same thing as finding out a meaning which the event already possesses by imputation. It is the essence of common sense, one might say, to treat potentialities as given actualities; since its interest is universally practical, bent upon fruitage, there is no need to note its bent in any particular case. The eventual outcome is for it the "reality" of the present situation.

But not so with philosophic discourse. Philosophy must explicitly note that the business of reflection is to take events which brutely occur and brutely affect us, to convert them into objects by means of inference as to their probable consequences. These are the meanings imputed to the events under consideration. Otherwise philosophy finds itself in a hopeless impasse. For, apart from making a distinction between events and objects, it has no way of differentiating cognitive from esthetic and literary meanings, and within cognitive meanings it has no way of distinguishing the valid from the invalid. The outcome of failure in this respect is exemplified in those discussions which find an inherent and generic cognitive problem in the occurrence of dreams, reveries and hallucinations, a problem other than the scientific one of ascertaining their antecedents and effects. For if intrinsic cognitive intent is ascribed to all perceptions, or forms of awareness, which are alleged to pick out a "reality" to which they refer as an image or sign, dreams, etc., have to be squared to this assumption. Draw the distinction between events and objects, and dream-objects are just what they are, events with one kind of meaning, while scientific-objects are just what they are, events with another kind of meaning, a kind that involves an extrinsic and additive function not contained in dream-objects.

In formulating the distinction between existences and objects of reference, whether cognitive, esthetic or moral, philosophy does not exact that violent break with common sense which is found in the assertion of idealism that events themselves are composed of meanings. Nor does it involve that break with common sense found in epistemological realism, with its assertion of a direct dealing of mind with naked existences unclothed by the intervention of meanings. Philosophy has only to state, to make explicit, the difference between events which are challenges to thought and events which have met the challenge and hence possess meaning. It has only to note that bare occurrence in the way of having, being, or undergoing is the provocation and invitation to thought—seeking and finding unapparent connections, so that thinking terminates when an object is present: namely, when a challenging event is endowed with stable meanings through relationship to something extrinsic but connected.

There is nothing new in the facts contained in this statement. It was an axiom of the classic theory that form, not matter, is the object of knowledge. And many other theories, in spite of the violence with which they nominally protest against the statement that existences as such are not the objects of knowledge, contain the essential facts, though in an incredible form. It is straining at a gnat and swallowing a camel to balk at the proposition that we mentally are concerned with events in their meanings and not in themselves, and at the same time to welcome the proposition that the immediate objects of all consciousness are sensations and complexes of sensations, termed images or ideas. For if by sensations (or by sensa) is meant not mere shocks in feeling, but something qualitative and capable of objective reference, then sensations are but one class of meanings. They are a class of meanings which embody the mature results of elaborate experimental inquiry in tracing out causal dependencies and relationships. This inquiry depends upon prior possession of a system of meanings, physical theories of light, sound, etc., and of knowledge of nervous structures and functions.

The alleged primacy of sensory meanings is mythical. They are primary only in logical status; they are primary as tests and confirmation of inferences concerning matters of fact, not as historic originals. For, while it is not usually needful to carry the check or test of theoretical calculations to the point of irreducible sensa, colors, sounds, etc., these sensa form a limit approached in careful analytic certifications, and upon critical occasions it is necessary to touch the limit. The transformation of these ulterior checking meanings into existential primary data is but another example of domination by interest in results and fruits, plus the fallacy which converts a functional office into an antecedent existence. Sensa are the class of irreducible meanings which are employed in verifying and correcting other meanings.

We actually set out with much coarser and more inclusive meanings and not till we have met with failure from their use do we even set out to discover those ultimate and harder meanings which are sensory in character.

The theory that awareness is intrinsically possessed of cognitive reference and intent is Protean in the forms it has assumed in the history of thought. One of these forms, that knowledge is recognition, is worth special attention. The idea that the act of knowing is always one of recognizing or noting is certain to lead the mind astray; dialectically, it breaks upon the impossibility entailed of instituting an initial act of knowing; it commits its holder to a Platonic prior intuition in the realm of eternity. It is easy to see, however, how the idea suggested itself and gained credence. Recognition, identified and distinguished meaning, is an indispensable condition of effective experience. It is a prerequisite of successful practice; except in so far as the situation in which we are to act is distinguished as having a notable character, behavior is hopelessly at a loss. It is a prerequisite to an act of knowing; for without possession of a recognized meaning, there is nothing to know with; there is no indication of the direction inquiry has to take, or of the universe within which inquiry falls. But, recognition is not cognition. It is what the word implicitly conveys; re-cognition; not in the sense that an act of cognizing is repeated, but in the sense that there is a reminder of the meaning in which a former experience terminated, and which may be used as an acceptable tool in further activities.

Most theories of knowing which define a knowledge as an immediate noting seem at bottom to rest upon a confusion of widely differing acts: one that of taking cognizance, which means to pay heed to the apparent in terms of non-apparent consequences; and the other that of being re-minded of something previously known, which is then used in the act of true, inferential, cognition. Recognition is re-instatement of a meaning vouched for in some other situation, plus a sense of familiarity, of immediate greeting of welcome or aversion. It is exemplified in the experience of revisiting the scenes of childhood, with the emotional responses which familiar scenes evoke; it is found in the acknowledgements of the thoroughly practical man, who deferentially notes a character of existence as something which, as a practical man, he must take into account in planning his conduct. Recognition is a nod, either of voluntary piety or of coerced respect, not a knowing.

There is another theory which makes "acquaintance" the primary mode of knowledge, and which treats acquaintance-knowledge as wholly immediate. Acquaintance is empirically distinguished from knowing *about* a thing, and from knowing *that* a thing is thus and so. It is genuinely cognitive. But it has its distinctive features because it involves something more than bare presence of an identified meaning; it involves expectancy which is an extrinsic reference; it involves a judgment as to what the object of acquaintance will do in connection with other events. To be acquainted with a man is at least to "know him by sight" as we truly say; it is to use a meaning conditioned by present vision to form a supposition about something not seen: how the man will behave under other circumstances than those of just being seen. To be *acquainted* with a man is to forecast his general line of conduct; it is to have insight into *character*. And insight, as distinct from sight, means that sight is employed to form inferences regarding what is not seen. It passes beyond apparition of meaning. The difference between acquaintance and "knowing about" or "knowing that" is genuine, but it is not a difference between two kinds of knowledge, one immediate and the other mediate. The difference is an affair of accompaniments, contexts and modes of response. The greater intimacy and directness that marks acquaintance is practical and emotional not logical. To be acquainted with anything is to have the kind of expectancy of its consequences which constitutes an immediate readiness to act, an adequate preparatory adjustment to whatever the thing in question may do. To know *about* it is to have a kind of knowledge which does not pass into direct response until some further term has been supplied. Direct readiness to act involves a sense of community; postponed readiness a sense of aloofness. Where there is acquaintance, there is an immediate emotion of participation in the situations in which the object of acquaintance engages, sympathetic or antipathetic according as readiness takes the form of a disposition to favor or to hinder. Knowledge about a historic or literary figure passes into acquaintance when one arrives at a point of imaginative foresight of his prospective conduct and dramatically shares in it. Knowledge that the earth is round becomes acquaintance when, in some juncture of experience, the meaning comes home to us, as we say, or we get a "realizing sense" of it. Acquaintance, then, instead of being a mode of knowledge prior to knowledge about and knowledge that, marks a later stage in which the latter attain full sense and efficacy.

It follows that theories which identify knowledge with acquaintance, recognition, definition and classification give evidence, all the better for being wholly unintended, that we know not just events but events-with-meanings. To assert that knowledge is classification is to assert in effect that kind, character, has overlaid and overridden bare occurrence and existence. To say that to know is to define is to recognize that wherever there is knowledge there is explicitly present a universal. To hold that cognition is recognition is to concede that likeness, a relation, rather than existence, is central. And to be acquainted with anything is to be aware what it is *like*, in what *sort* of ways it is likely to behave. These features, character, kind, sort, universal, likeness, fall within the universe of meaning. Hence the theories which make them constitutive of knowledge acknowledge that *having* meanings is a prerequisite for knowing. This prerequisite, being universally required, has loomed so large that thinkers have been led to slur over the concrete differential quality of knowledge—a particular act of *taking*, using, responding to, the meanings involved. That curious piece of traditional "analytic" psychology in accordance with which all knowing is a fusion or association of sensation with images is more testimony in the same direction; "associated imagery" being a roundabout equivalent of events with meaning.

Finally, the notion that knowledge is contemplation is likewise accounted for. To contemplate is consciously to possess meanings; to behold them with relish; to view them so absorbingly as to revel in them. It is a name for the perception of significant characters, plus an emphatic allusion to an accompanying esthetic emotion. Hypotheses which, like the one advanced in this book and chapter, hold that no knowing takes place without an overt act of taking and employing things on the basis of their meanings, have been attacked as over-devoted to keeping busy; as ignoring the place and charm of contemplation. Well, contemplation assuredly has a place. But when it is ultimate, and is a fruition, knowing has stepped out of the picture; the vision is esthetic. This may be better than knowing; but its being better is no reason for mixing different things and attributing to knowledge characters belonging to an esthetic object. Omit the esthetic phase, the absorbing charm of contemplation, and what remains for a theory of knowledge is that meanings must be had before they can be used as means of bringing to apparition meanings now obscure and hidden. If I were allowed to call to the witness stand but one historic theory to give testimony to prove that while there is no knowing without perception of meaning, yet that having meanings and rolling them over as sweet morsels under the tongue are not knowing, I should summon the venerable doctrine that knowledge is contemplation.

Another difficulty involved in the theory was mentioned; a difficulty contained in the fact that recent theories have limited the signification of perception. In its older usage, it designated any awareness, any "seeing" whether of objects, ideas, principles, conclusions or whatever. In recent literature it is usually restricted to "sense-perception." There can be no quarrel about the meaning of words except a lexicographical quarrel. The issue at stake concerns then not the appropriate use of a word; it concerns certain matters of fact which are implied or usually associated with the present restricted usage. These implications are two: First, there exists a mode of consciousness or awareness which is original, primitive, simple, and which refers immediately and intrinsically to things in space external to the organism at the time of perception. Secondly, this reference is originally, and *ex proprio motu*, cognitive. Now as against these implications, the theory which has been advanced asserts that awareness in the form of auditory and visual perception is, whenever it is cognitive, just as much a matter of inferential judgment, an instance of a way of taking and using meanings, as is any proposition found in the science of physics.

In its general features, argument as to this point is to the same effect as that of the point just discussed. But we may avoid repetition and introduce greater specification by confining ourselves to the factual traits characteristic of perceptions of present objects in space; showing that these, when they are cognitive, are highly selected and artful instances of awareness, not primitive and innocent. The current theory begins with a distinction between peripherally initiated and centrally initiated awareness.

Peripheral initiation is the defining mark of such operations as are designated "perceptions." But awarenesses do not come to us labelled "I am caused by an event initiated on the surface of the body by other bodies"; and "I on the contrary originate in an intra-organic event only indirectly connected with surface-changes." The distinction is one made by analytic and classifying thought. This fact is enough to place in doubt the notion that some modes of consciousness are originally and intrinsically "sense-perception."

Moreover, there is no absolute separation between the skin and the interior of the body. No sooner is the distinction drawn than it has to be qualified. As a matter of fact there is no such *thing* as an *exclusively* peripherally initiated nervous event. Internal conditions, those of hunger, blood-circulation, endocrine functions, persistences of prior activities, pre-existent opened and blocked neuronic connections, together with a multitude of other intra-organic factors enter into the determination of a peripheral occurrence. And after the peripheral excitation has taken place, its subsequent career is not self-determined, but is affected by literally everything going on within the organism. It is pure fiction that a "sensation," or peripheral excitation, or stimulus, travels undisturbed in solitary state in its own coach-and-four to enter the brain or consciousness in its purity. A particular excitation is but one of an avalanche of contemporaneously occurring excitations, peripheral and from proprioceptors; each has to compete with others, to make terms with them; what happens is an integration of complex forces.

It requires therefore a highly technical apparatus of science to discriminate the exact place and nature of a peripheral stimulation, and to trace its normal course to just the junction point where it becomes effective for redirection of activity and thus capable of perception. "Peripheral origin" marks an interpretation of events, a discrimination scientifically valid and important, but no more an original datum than is the spectrum of Betelgeuse. The same thesis holds good, of course, of the "consciousness" corresponding to the centrally initiated processes. To suppose that there are inherently marked off different forms of awareness corresponding to the distinction arrived at by technical analysis is as flagrant a case of hypostatizing as can be found. The theory that certain kinds or forms of consciousness intrinsically have an intellectual or cognitive reference to things present in space is merely the traditional theory that knowledge is an immediate grasp of Being, clothed in the terminology of recent physiology. While it is offered as if it were established by physiological and psychological research, in reality it presents an intellectual hold-over, a notion picked up from early teachings which have not been subjected to any critical examination; physiology and psychology merely afford a vocabulary with which to deck out an unconscionable survival.

Reference to peripheral stimulation of eye or ear or skin or nose is, whether of the simpler and popular kind or of the more complex neurological kind, part of the technique of checking up the particular sort of extrinsic reference which should be given to an idea; discovery whether it is to be referred to a past, contemporary or future thing, or treated as due to wish and emotion. Even so, ascertainment of mode of stimulation and origin is always secondary and derived. We do not believe a thing to be "there" because we are directly cognizant of an external origin for our perception; we infer some external stimulation of our sensory apparatus because we are successfully engaged in motor response. Only when the latter fails, do we turn back and examine the matter of sensory stimulation. To say that I am now conscious of a typewriter as the source of sensory stimuli is to make a back-handed and sophisticated statement of the fact that I am engaged in active employment of the typewriter to produce certain consequences, so that what I am aware of is these consequences and the relation to them of parts of the typewriter as means of producing them. As matter of fact, we *never* perceive the peripheral stimuli to which we are at that given time responding.

The notion that these stimuli are the appropriate and normal objects of simple original perceptions represents, as we have just said, an uncritical acceptance by psychologists of an old logical and metaphysical dogma, one having neither origin nor justification within scientific psychology. We are aware only of stimuli to other responses than those which we are now making; we become aware of them when we analyze some performed total act to discover the mechanism of its occurrence. To become aware of an optical or auditory stimulation involved in an act signifies that we now apprehend that an organic change is part of the means used in the act, so that soundness of its structure and working is requisite to efficient performance of the act. I do not usually, for example, hear the sounds made by the striking of the keys; hence I therefore bang at them or strike them unevenly. If I were better trained or more intelligent in the performance of this action, I should hear the sounds, for they would have ceased to be just stimuli and become means of direction of my behavior in securing consequences. Not having learned by the "touch-method," my awareness of contact-qualities as I hit the keys is intermittent and defective. Physiological stimulation of fingers is involved as a condition of my motor response; yet there is no consciousness of contact "sensations" or sensa. But if I used my sensory touch appreciation as means to the proper execution of the act of writing, I should be aware of these qualities. The wider and freer the employment of means, the larger the field of sensory perceptions.

It is usual in current psychology to assert or assume that qualities observed are those of the stimulus. This assumption puts the cart before the horse; qualities which are observed are those attendant upon response to stimuli. We are *observantly* aware (in distinction from inferentially aware) only of what *has* been done; we can perceive what is already there, what *has* happened. By description, a stimulus is not an object of perception, for stimulus is correlative to response, and is undetermined except as response occurs. I am not questioning as a fact of *knowledge* that certain things *are* the stimuli of visual and auditory perception. I am pointing out that we are aware of the stimuli only in terms of our response to them and of the consequences of this response. Argument as to the impossibility of stimuli being the object of perception is of course dialectical; like all dialectic arguments it is. not convincing if confronted with facts to the contrary. But facts agree. The whiteness of the paper upon which words are being written and the blackness of the letters have been constantly operative stimuli in what I have been doing. It is equally certain that they have not been constantly perceived objects. If I have perceived them from time to time, it is in virtue of prior responses of which they were consequences, and because of the need of employing these attained consequences as means in further action. In the laboratory, as in the painter's studio, colors are specific objects of perception. But as perceived, they are "stimuli" only proleptically and by a shift in the universe of discourse.[3] The color now and here perceived, in consequence of an organic adjustment to other stimuli than color, is in subsequent situations a stimulus to other modes of behavior, unconscious in so far as just a stimulus; conscious as far as a deliberately utilized means.

When color is perceived, it is in order to paint, or for matching colors in selection of dress goods, or in an estimate of the harmonious value of the hue of a wall-paper, or for determining from a spectral line the nature of a chemical substance. It signifies that we are responding in such a way as to form or bring into being a stimulus adequate to operate without being perceived. But in the meantime in consciousness it is means to an act which will effect desired consequences. Shall this color be used? Will this particular piece of goods or pattern of wall-paper serve the purpose in view? When such questions are determined, a final stimulus is achieved. What is then perceived is either some further consequence, or this consequence as a means in a new predicament, such as wearing the goods, hanging the wall-paper. The consciousness of stimuli marks the conclusion of an investigation, not an original datum; and what is discovered is not the stimuli to *that* act, the inquiry, but to some other act, past or prospective, and it marks the conversion of *de facto* stimulus into potential means. The question of stimuli is a question of existential causation; and if Hume's lesson had been learned as well as we flatter ourselves it is learned, we should be aware that any matter of causation refers to something extrinsic, to be reached by inquiry and inference.

We conclude, therefore, that while the word "perception" may be limited to designate awareness of objects contemporaneously affecting the bodily organs, there is no ground whatever for the assumption which has usually attended this narrowing of the older meaning of the word: namely, that sense-perception has *intrinsic* properties or qualities marking it off from other forms of consciousness. Much less is there justification for the assumption that such perceptions are the original form of

---

3. The shift is evident in the fact that stimuli are stated as vibrations or electromagnetic disturbance or in similar fashion; now vibrations are not observed while color, the consequence, the effected coordination, is in direct consciousness.

elementary awareness from which other forms of cognitive consciousness develop. On the contrary sensory-perceptual meanings are specifically discriminated objects of awareness; the discrimination takes place in the course of inquiry into causative conditions and consequences; the ultimate need for the inquiry is found in the necessity of discovering what is to be done, or of developing a response suitably adapted to the requirements of a situation. When inquiry reveals that an object external to the organism is now operative and affecting the organism, the pertinency of overt action is established and the kind of overt adjustment that should be made is in evidence. Perceptual meanings (sensory-perceptual) contrast with other meanings in that either (a) the latter cannot be overtly acted upon *now* or immediately, but only at a deferred time, when specified conditions now absent have been brought into being—conceptual meanings—; or (b) that the latter are such that action upon them at *any* time must be of a dramatic or literary or playful sort—non-cognitive meanings. The necessities of behavior enforce very early in life the difference between acts demanded at once, and those pertinent only at a later time; yet making and refining the distinction is a matter of constant search and discovery, not, as the traditional theory presumes, an original and ready-made affair.

Thus we returned to the statement that apart from considerations of use and history there are no original and inherent differences between valid meanings and meanings occurring in revery, desiring, fearing, remembering, all being *intrinsically* the same in relation to events. This fact contains in gist the condemnation of introspection.[4] It makes no difference in principle whether the introspective doctrine takes a dialectical form, as in the Cartesian-Spinozistic logical realism in which intrinsic self-evidency, clearness, adequacy, or truth, are imputed to some conceptual meanings or ideas; or whether it takes the more usual form of assigning to things appearing in the field of consciousness intrinsic properties which may be read off by direct inspection and thereby used to denominate them as sensory, perceptual, conceptual, imaginative, fantastic, memory, emo-

4. It is not asserted that observations *called* introspection have never given results. It *is* claimed that in such cases, the procedure does not conform to the theoretical definition of immediate inspection but involves the results of inquiries into relationships with things not directly present.

tional, volitional, etc. It is asserted that in every case, the basis of classification is extrinsic, an affair dependent upon a study, often hard to make, of generating conditions and of subsequent careers. The denominations are interpretations, and like all interpretations are adequate only when controlled by wide and accurate information as to bodies of fact that are remote and extraneous. It is not too much to say that the introspective doctrine—much wider in logical scope than so-called introspective psychology—is the last desperate stand and fortress of the classic doctrine that knowledge is immediate grasp, intuition, envisagement, possession. It is this fact which constitutes the importance of the views that have been criticized. Until they have been criticized, until the assumption of immediate intrinsic differences in the meaning-objects of sensory perceptions, reveries, dreams, desires, emotions, has been expelled, the actual relation of ideas to existences must remain an obscure and confused matter.

If one looks at the net results of physiological inquiry upon psychological insight, one seems bound to conclude that while potentially they are enormous, actually they consist largely in making more emphatic and conspicuous the old metaphysical problem of the relation of mind and body, and in strengthening a leaning to the parallelistic hypothesis. The explanation is that they have not been used for what they really are: an important part of our scientific resources with respect to the intelligent conduct of behavior in general, and the discrimination in particular of various kinds of meanings from one another. It is one thing to employ, for example, the distinction between central and peripheral origin of the existence of this and that idea as part of the technique of determining their respective cognitive validities, and quite another to assume that ideas and conscious contents are already intrinsically marked off in themselves (and therefore for direct observation or introspection), and that the problem is simply to find physiological equivalents for their distinction. As far as it is assumed that modes of consciousness are in themselves already differentiated into sensory, perceptual, conceptual, imaginative, retentive, emotional, conative (or may be so discriminated by direct inspection), physiological study will consist simply of search for the different bodily and neural processes that underlie these differences. The outcome is an exacerbation of the traditional mind-body problem; the doctrine of parallelism, instead of being either a scientific discovery or a scientific postulate, is merely a formulation of the original psychological ready-made distinctions plus a more detailed knowledge of physical existential conditions of their occurrence.

If the problem is put as one of a more adequate control of behavior through knowledge of its mechanism, the situation becomes very different. How should we treat a particular meaning: as sound datum for inference, as an effect of habit irrespective of present condition, as an instance of desire, or a consequence of hope or fear, a token of some past psycho-physical maladjustment, or how? Such questions as these are urgent questions in the conduct of life. They are typical of questions which we must find a way of answering if we are to achieve any method of mastering our own behavior similar to that which we have achieved in respect to heat and electricity, coal and iron. And knowledge of the conditions under which our meanings and our modes of taking and using them organically occur is an indispensable portion of the technique of dealing with such questions. In principle, there is no difference between the neurological inquiry and those astronomical inquiries which enable an astronomer to determine the standing and import of some idea in his universe of discourse. The physiological inquiries no more involve a peculiar problem of mind-body than do the astronomical inquiries. Their subject-matter is part of the objective matter-of-fact considerations which extend and buttress inferential conclusions. In concrete subject-matter, they differ, being concerned with organic structures and processes; but this is *only* a difference in concrete subject-matter, like that between astronomical and botanical. The peculiar importance of the physiological material is that in some form it enters as a factor into the occurrence of every meaning and every act, including the astronomical and botanical.

We return, accordingly, from this excursion to the assertion that the objects of revery-consciousness are just as much cases of perceived meanings or ideas of events as are those of sensory perceptual consciousness. *Only*—they are not as *good* objects with respect to direction of subsequent conduct, including the conduct of knowledge. Revery-consciousness, and the influence upon beliefs of affective wishes of which we are not aware, are facts crucial for any theory of consciousness. If they support the hypothesis that all consciousness is awareness of meanings, they also seem at first sight to contradict the supposition that the meanings perceived are those of natural events. Since their objects are notoriously "unreal," they seem to support the notion that consciousness is disconnected from physical events, and that any valid connection which may be set up, either in practical conduct or in knowing, is adventitious.

There is indeed much to be said for the view that consciousness is originally a dream-like, irresponsible efflorescence, and that it gains reference to actual events in nature only under stern compulsion, and by way of accidental coincidence. There are elements of truth in this view, as against the orthodox tradition which makes consciousness architectonic, having righteous and rational conformity as the corner stone of its structure. Ideas, objects of immediate awareness, are too desultory, fantastic, and impertinent to be consistent with the classic tradition, whether of the sensationalistic or the rationalistic schools. But the view of complete separation of existential consciousness from connection with physical things cannot be maintained in view of what is known of its specifiable connections with organic conditions, and of the intimate, unbroken connection of organic with extra-organic events. It can be maintained only by holding that the connection of consciousness in its varied forms with bodily action is non-natural. The only reason for asserting this position lies in the dialectic compulsion of denial of quality to natural events, and arrogation of superior existence to causal antecedents.

Given the connection of meanings with environmental-organic integrations (including those of social intercourse) and there is nothing surprising that consciousness should often be of the revery and wish type. We find no great occasion for wonder in the fact that a person who has been taught that the sun moves around the earth, rising above it at sunrise and going under it at sunset, should himself hold that belief. Well, past consummatory experiences have taught the individual many things; they have taught him what conjunctions are agreeable and what disagreeable. Just as past teaching regarding sun and earth have conditioned subsequent behavior, have produced organic modifications in the way of habit which influence subsequent reactions, including interpretations, so with what was taught by having been implicated in a consummatory union of environment and organism. Here too a bias in organic modification is set up; it acts to perpetuate, wherever possible, awareness of fruitions, and to avert perception of frustrations and inconvenient interruptions.

A consciousness which is set on the outside over against the course of nature, which is not a partaker in its moving changes, would have to conform to one or other of two schemes. In one alternative, the consciousness of such a being would be gifted with an infallible spectatorship conjoined with perfect innocency of impartial recordership; it would see and report the world exactly as if it were itself knowingly engaged in producing what it saw and reported. Or, in the other alternative, all consciousness would be so completely irrelevant to the world of which it is outside and beyond, that there would be no common denominator or common multiple. Obviously facts do not agree with either of these suppositions. We dream, but the material of our dream life is the stuff of our waking life. Revery is not first wholly detached from objects of purposeful action and belief, coming later by discipline to acquire reference to them. Its objects consist of the objects of daily concern subjected to a strange perspective, perverted in behalf of a bias. Such empirical facts as these, or the fact that the world of fancy is the ordinary world as we like it to be, as we find it agreeable, is fatal to any theory which seriously asserts the wholesale irrelevance of the material of consciousness to the things of the actual world. Irrelevance exists, but it is relative and specifiable. An idea or emotion is irrelevant not as such, through and through, but because it is a version of the meaning of events which if it were differently edited would be relevant to actions *in* the world to which it belongs.

To par-take and to per-ceive are allied performances. To perceive is a mode of partaking which occurs only under complex conditions and with its own defining traits. Everything of importance hangs upon what particular one of the many possible ways of partaking is employed in a given situation. The organism, wherever possible, participates *à son gré*; its taste and bias are conditioned, in the degree of its susceptibility and retentiveness, upon prior *satisfactions*. If a man has experienced a world which

is good, why should not he act to remake a bad world till it
agrees with the good world which he has once possessed? And if
the task of overt transformation is too great for his powers, why
should he not at least act so as to get the renewed *sense* of a good
world? These questions express the working logic of human action; the first, the way of objective transformation, is the method
of action in the arts and sciences; the second, of action that is
fanciful, "wish-fulfilling," romantic, myth-making.

The immense difference between the two modes of action has
had to be learned. There is no original and intrinsic difference in
the respective modes of consciousness accompanying the two
kinds of acts. In some matters, the lesson is readily and quickly
learned. Such matters constitute the objects of usual every-day
sense-perception, the objects of common sense. Certain organic-
integrations have to occur if life is to continue. Sustenance must
be had; destructive enemies must be kept away; the help of
others must be availed of. Meanings and ideas connected with
these organic-environmental adjustments are substantially sound
as far as adjustments are successfully made—and within limits
they are ordinarily so made, or life ceases. Such gross ideas as a
world of things and persons external to our personal wishes and
fancies, and as the continuance of energies once set in motion,
are so recurrently and emphatically taught that they are never
sincerely doubted. Ideas of specific features of this external
world (external to *us*, since it exacts so much of us in effort
before it conforms to the needs that are most deeply ourselves),
ideas of fire, food, furniture, weather and crops, of our friends
and enemies, and of our own past and probable future, are so
repeatedly presented in the connections of actions and so confirmed by consequences that they become matters of course,
substantially valid. They thus form a kind of privileged domain,
which, although an island in a sea of ideas where ground is not
readily touched, has been by too hasty and impatient theories
taken to form the original and inherent constitution of consciousness. In consequence, there is added to genuine natural
realism which accepts the causal connection of ideas with events
and their potential reference to subsequent events, a specious
realistic theory which takes the island for a solid and complete
continent. Characteristic traits of the whole continent of mind
are then looked upon as if they were only incidental faults and

dislocations, to be explained away by dialectic ingenuity; or when the strata of fancy, illusion, error and misinterpretation are realized, wholesale scepticism is indulged in.

Gradually the technique involved in making ordinary organic-environmental adjustments is discovered, and becomes capable of extension to cases where fancy had previously reigned. A larger and larger field of ideas becomes susceptible of analytic objective reference, with the promise of approximate validity. The secret of this technique lies in control of the *ways* in which the organism participates in the course of events. In the case of simple needs and simple environments, existing organic structures practically enforce correct participation; the result is so-called instinctive action. Within this range, modifications undergone by the organism form in the main effective habits. But organic preparation for varied situations having many factors and wide-reaching consequences is not so easily attained. Effective participation here depends upon the use of extra-organic conditions, which supplement structural agencies; namely, tools and other persons, by means of language spoken and recorded. Thus the ultimate buttress of the soundness of all but the simplest ideas consists in the cumulative objective appliances and arts of the community, not in anything found in "consciousness" itself or within the organism.

If any evidence be needed of the artificial character of strictly epistemological discussion it may be found in the fact that it goes on exclusively in terms of an alleged direct contact of "subject" and "object," with total neglect of all the indispensable tools of checking spontaneous beliefs and developing sound ones in their place. Pendulums, lenses, prisms, yard sticks, and pound weights and multiplication and logarithmic tables have a great deal more to do with valid knowing, since they enable the organism to partake with other things in the effecting of consequences, than have bare consciousness or brain and nerves. Without such objective resources to direct the manner of engaging in responsive adaptations, ideas, outside a simple range of constantly tested actions, are at the mercy of any peculiarity of organic constitution and of circumstance; myths are rife and the world is peopled with fabulous personages and is the home of occult forces. Since organic modifications due to past consummatory objects are dominant, since they lead an individual to find or make a world congenial to them; and since man is most at home with his fellows, whether friends or enemies, the world is then taken animistically for the most part. Too many of the traditional ideas of life, soul, mind, spirit, and consciousness, and of the cosmos itself, even in philosophy, are only attenuated versions of this animism, spontaneous, and often gracious even though fantastic, when men lacked instrumentalities by which to direct their active partakings in nature, but which are now graceless and obstructive.

In conclusion, the fact that consciousness of meanings, or having ideas, denotes an exigent re-making of meanings has an import for the theory of nature. Perceptibility is an exponent of contingency as it intersects the regular. The impossibility of "deducing" consciousness from physical laws, the "impassable gulf" between the physical and mental, are in reality but conspicuous cases of the general impossibility of deriving the contingent from the necessary, the uncertain from the regular. The anomaly apparent in the occurrence of consciousness is evidence of an anomalous phase in nature itself. Unless there were something problematic, undecided, still going-on and as yet unfinished and indeterminate, in nature, there could be no such events as perceptions. The point of maximum apparency is the point of greatest stress and undetermined potentiality; the point of maximum of restless shift, while also the point of greatest brightness; it is vivid, but not clear; imminent, urgently expressive of the impending, but not defined, till it has been disposed of and has ceased to be immediately focal. When philosophers have insisted upon the certainty of the immediately and focally present or "given" and have sought indubitable immediate existential data upon which to build, they have always unwittingly passed from the existential to the dialectical; they have substituted a general character for an immediate this. For the immediately given is always the dubious; it is always a matter for subsequent events to determine, or assign character to. It is a cry for something not given, a request addressed to fortune, with the pathos of a plea or the imperiousness of a command. It were, conceivably, "better" that nature should be finished through and through, a closed mechanical or closed teleological structure, such as philosophic schools have fancied. But in that case the flickering candle of consciousness would go out.

The immediate perceptibility of meanings, the very existence of ideas, testifies to insertion of the problematic and hazardous in the settled and uniform, and to the meeting, crossing and parting of the substantial, static, and the transitive and particular. Meanings, characters as such have that solidity, coherence, endurance, and persistent availability, which our idiom calls substance. Yet were this the whole story, meanings not only would not be perceived, but they would not be meanings. They would be tough operative habits, having their own way not to be denied. Organic movements exist to which there occurred in early life meanings so indurated that now they are habits of an overriding power; meaning has disappeared in bare behavior. It is possible to understand the regret with which some persons contemplate the passage of thought into act; to them it seems the obsequies of an idea; thought has been dissipated in an outward mechanical sequence. Similarly, one may feel that the important and interesting thing in human history is not what men have done, their successes, but what they failed in doing—the desires and imaginings, forbidden execution by the force of events. Ideas are largely the obverse side of action; a perception of what might be, but is not, the promise of things hoped for, the symbol of things not seen. A fixed idea is no idea at all, but a routine compulsion of overt action, perfunctorily and mechanically named idea.

"Pure reason" would thus not be rational at all, but an automatic habit; a substance so stable and pervading as to have no limits and vicissitudes, and hence no perceptibility. "Pure" reasoning is best carried on by fixed symbols, automatically manipulated; its ideal is something approaching the well-devised mechanically operative calculating machine. Unless nature had regular habits, persistent ways, so compacted that they time, measure and give rhythm and recurrence to transitive flux, meanings, recognizable characters, could not be. But also without an interplay of these patient, slow-moving, not easily stirred systems of action with swift-moving, unstable, unsubstantial events, nature would be a routine unmarked by ideas. Adjustment of the slow-moving changes of nature to its sudden starts and trepidations, such as gives some degree of order to the latter and as re-adapts the motions of the sluggish and inert core to the volatile surface of hasty movements, makes necessary a conversion of static orders into stable meanings, while it also renders them perceptible, or ideas, as they answer to the flux of things.

Finally, as psycho-physical qualities testify to the presence in nature of needs and satisfactions, of uneasy efforts and their arrest in some limiting termination, so conscious or conspicuously apparent meanings, ideas, are exponents of the deliberate use of the efficacious in behalf of the fulfilling and consummatory, and of the efficient or instrumental nature of the final. This situation is empirically present to us in the arts, and will be discussed in the immediate sequel. For our immediate purpose, it is enough to point out the difference between the explicit natural teleology of classic metaphysics and the implicit teleology of modern science. In the former, the bare *de facto* arrests of nature, which often mark merely exhaustion or else limits imposed by competing energies, were by a *tour de force* assigned eulogistic properties. They were identified with the objects that should be the objects of choice by persons of mature and reflective experience. Thus physics was unwittingly infected by importation of an uncriticized ethic of customary and fixed ends, and of a dialectically ordered hierarchy of fixed means. The identification in modern thought of ends with ends-in-view, with deliberate purpose and planning, of means with deliberately selected and arranged inventions and artifices, is in effect a recognition that the teleology of nature is achieved and exhibited by nature in thinking, not apart from it. If modern theories have often failed to note this implication and have instead contented themselves with a denial of all teleology, the reason is adventitious; it is found in the gratuitous breach of continuity between nature, life, and man.

"This," whatever *this* may be, always implies a system of meanings focussed at a point of stress, uncertainty, and need of regulation. It sums up history, and at the same time opens a new page; it is record and promise in one; a fulfillment and an opportunity. It is a fruition of what has happened and a transitive agency of what is to happen. It is a comment written by natural events on their own direction and tendency, and a surmise of whither they are leading. Every perception, or awareness, marks a "this," and every "this" being a consummation involves retention, and hence contains the capacity of remembering. Every "this" is transitive, momentarily becoming a "that." In its movement it is, therefore, conditioning of what is to come; it presents the potentiality of foresight and prediction. The union of past and future with the present manifest in every awareness of meanings is a mystery only when consciousness is gratuitously divided from nature, and when nature is denied temporal and historic quality. When consciousness is connected with nature, the mystery becomes a luminous revelation of the operative interpenetration in nature of the efficient and the fulfilling.

9. Experience, Nature and Art

Experience, with the Greeks, signified a store of practical wisdom, a fund of insights useful in conducting the affairs of life. Sensation and perception were its occasion and supplied it with pertinent materials, but did not of themselves constitute it. They generated experience when retention was added and when a common factor in the multitude of felt and perceived cases detached itself so as to become available in judgment and exertion. Thus understood, experience is exemplified in the discrimination and skill of the good carpenter, pilot, physician, captain-at-arms; experience is equivalent to art. Modern theory has quite properly extended the application of the term to cover many things that the Greeks would hardly have called "experience," the bare having of aches and pains, or a play of colors before the eyes. But even those who hold this larger signification would admit, I suppose, that such "experiences" count only when they result in insight, or in an enjoyed perception, and that only thus do they define experience in its honorific sense.

Greek thinkers nevertheless disparaged experience in comparison with something called reason and science. The ground for depreciation was not that usually assigned in modern philosophy; it was not that experience is "subjective." On the contrary, experience was considered to be a genuine expression of cosmic forces, not an exclusive attribute or possession of animal or of human nature. It was taken to be a realization of inferior portions of nature, those infected with chance and change, the less *Being* part of the cosmos. Thus while experience meant art, art reflected the contingencies and partialities of nature, while science—theory—exhibited its necessities and universalities. Art was born of need, lack, deprivation, incompleteness, while science—theory—manifested fullness and totality of Being. Thus the depreciatory view of experience was identical with a concep-

tion that placed practical activity below theoretical activity, finding the former dependent, impelled from outside, marked by
deficiency of real being, while the latter was independent and
free because complete and self-sufficing: that is, perfect.

In contrast with this self-consistent position we find a curious
mixture in modern thinking. The latter feels under no obligation
to present a theory of natural existence that links art with nature; on the contrary, it usually holds that science or knowledge
is the only *authentic* expression of nature, in which case art must
be an arbitrary addition to nature. But modern thought also
combines exaltation of science with eulogistic appreciation of
art, especially of fine or creative art. At the same time it retains
the substance of the classic disparagement of the practical in
contrast with the theoretical, although formulating it in somewhat different language: to the effect that knowledge deals with
objective reality as it is in itself, while in what is "practical,"
objective reality is altered and cognitively distorted by subjective
factors of want, emotion and striving. And yet in its encomium
of art, it fails to note the commonplace of Greek observation—
that the fine arts as well as the industrial technologies are affairs
of practice.

This confused plight is partly cause and partly effect of an
almost universal confusion of the artistic and the esthetic. On
one hand, there is action that deals with materials and energies
outside the body, assembling, refining, combining, manipulating
them until their new state yields a satisfaction not afforded by
their crude condition—a formula that applies to fine and useful
art alike. On the other hand, there is the delight that attends
vision and hearing, an enhancement of the receptive appreciation
and assimilation of objects irrespective of participation in the
operations of production. Provided the difference of the two
things is recognized, it is no matter whether the words "esthetic"
and "artistic" or other terms be used to designate the distinction,
for the difference is not one of words but of objects. But in some
form the difference must be acknowledged.

The community in which Greek art was produced was small;
numerous and complicated intermediaries between production
and consumption were lacking; producers had a virtually servile
status. Because of the close connection between production and
enjoyable fruition, the Greeks in their perceptive uses and en-

joyments were never wholly unconscious of the artisan and his work, not even when they personally were exclusively concerned with delightful contemplation. But since the artist was an artisan (the term artist having none of the eulogistic connotations of present usage), and since the artisan occupied an inferior position, the enjoyment of works of any art did not stand upon the same level as enjoyment of those objects for the realization of which manual activity was not needed. Objects of rational thought, of contemplative insight were the only things that met the specification of freedom from need, labor, and matter. They alone were self-sufficient, self-existent, and self-explanatory, and hence enjoyment of *them* was on a higher plane than enjoyment of works of art.

These conceptions were consistent with one another and with the conditions of social life at the time. Nowadays we have a messy conjunction of notions that are consistent neither with one another nor with the tenor of our actual life. Knowledge is still regarded by most thinkers as direct grasp of ultimate reality, although the practice of knowing has been assimilated to the procedure of the useful arts;—involving, that is to say, doing that manipulates and arranges natural energies. Again while science is said to lay hold of reality, yet "art" instead of being assigned a lower rank is equally esteemed and honored. And when within art a distinction is drawn between production and appreciation, the chief honor usually goes to the former on the ground that it is "creative," while taste is relatively possessive and passive, dependent for its material upon the activities of the creative artist.

If Greek philosophy was correct in thinking of knowledge as contemplation rather than as a productive art, and if modern philosophy accepts this conclusion, then the only logical course is relative disparagement of all forms of production, since they are modes of practice which is by conception inferior to contemplation. The artistic is then secondary to the esthetic: "creation," to "taste," and the scientific *worker*—as we significantly say—is subordinate in rank and worth to the dilettante who enjoys the results of his labors. But if modern tendencies are justified in putting art and creation first, then the implications of this position should be avowed and carried through. It would then be seen that science is an art, that art is practice, and that the only distinction worth drawing is not between practice and theory, but between those modes of practice that are not intelligent, not inherently and immediately enjoyable, and those which are full of enjoyed meanings. When this perception dawns, it will be a commonplace that art—the mode of activity that is charged with meanings capable of immediately enjoyed possession—is the complete culmination of nature, and that "science" is properly a handmaiden that conducts natural events to this happy issue. Thus would disappear the separations that trouble present thinking: division of everything into nature *and* experience, of experience into practice *and* theory, art *and* science, of art into useful *and* fine, menial *and* free.

Thus the issue involved in experience as art in its pregnant sense and in art as processes and materials of nature continued by direction into achieved and enjoyed meanings, sums up in itself all the issues which have been previously considered. Thought, intelligence, science is the intentional direction of natural events to meanings capable of immediate possession and enjoyment; this direction—which is operative art—is itself a natural event in which nature otherwise partial and incomplete comes fully to itself; so that objects of conscious experience when reflectively chosen, form the "end" of nature. The doings and sufferings that form experience are, in the degree in which experience is intelligent or charged with meanings, a union of the precarious, novel, irregular with the settled, assured and uniform—a union which also defines the artistic and the esthetic. For wherever there is art the contingent and ongoing no longer work at cross purposes with the formal and recurrent but commingle in harmony. And the distinguishing feature of conscious experience, of what for short is often called "consciousness," is that in it the instrumental and the final, meanings that are signs and clews and meanings that are immediately possessed, suffered and enjoyed, come together in one. And all of these things are preeminently true of art.

First, then, art is solvent union of the generic, recurrent, ordered, established phase of nature with its phase that is incomplete, going on, and hence still uncertain, contingent, novel, particular; or as certain systems of esthetic theory have truly declared, though without empirical basis and import in their words, a union of necessity and freedom, a harmony of the many and one, a reconciliation of sensuous and ideal. Of any artistic act and product it may be said both that it is inevitable in its rightness, that nothing in it can be altered without altering all, and that its occurrence is spontaneous, unexpected, fresh, unpredictable. The presence in art, whether as an act or a product, of proportion, economy, order, symmetry, composition, is such a commonplace that it does not need to be dwelt upon. But equally necessary is unexpected combination, and the consequent revelation of possibilities hitherto unrealized. "Repose in stimulation" characterizes art. Order and proportion when they are the whole story are soon exhausted; economy in itself is a tiresome and restrictive taskmaster. It is artistic when it releases.

The more extensive and repeated are the basic uniformities of nature that give form to art, the "greater" is the art, provided—and it is this proviso that distinguishes art—they are indistinguishably fused with the wonder of the new and the grace of the gratuitous. "Creation" may be asserted vaguely and mystically; but it denotes something genuine and indispensable in art. The merely finished is not fine but ended, done with, and the merely "fresh" is that bumptious impertinence indicated by the slang use of the word. The "magic" of poetry—and pregnant experience has poetical quality—is precisely the revelation of meaning in the old effected by its presentation through the new. It radiates the light that never was on land and sea but that is henceforth an abiding illumination of objects. Music in its immediate occurrence is the most varied and etherial of the arts, but is in its conditions and structure the most mechanical. These things are commonplaces; but until they are commonly employed in their evidential significance for a theory of nature's nature, there is no cause to apologize for their citation.

The limiting terms that define art are routine at one extreme and capricious impulse at the other. It is hardly worth while to oppose science and art sharply to one another, when the deficiencies and troubles of life are so evidently due to separation between art and blind routine and blind impulse. Routine exemplifies the uniformities and recurrences of nature, caprice expresses its inchoate initiations and deviations. Each in isolation is unnatural as well as inartistic, for nature is an intersection of spontaneity and necessity, the regular and the novel, the finished and the beginning. It is right to object to much of current practice on the ground that it is routine, just as it is right to object to much of our current enjoyments on the ground that they are spasms of excited escape from the thraldom of enforced work. But to transform a just objection against the quality of much of our practical life into a description and definition of practice is on the same plane as to convert legitimate objection to trivial distraction, senseless amusement, and sensual absorption, into a Puritanical aversion to happiness. The idea that work, productive activity, signifies action carried on for merely extraneous ends, and the idea that happiness signifies surrender of mind to the thrills and excitations of the body are one and the same idea. The first notion marks the separation of activity from meaning, and the second marks the separation of receptivity from meaning. Both separations are inevitable as far as experience fails to be art:—when the regular, repetitious, and the novel, contingent in nature fail to sustain and inform each other in a productive activity possessed of immanent and directly enjoyed meaning.

Thus the theme has insensibly passed over into that of the relation of means and consequence, process and product, the instrumental and consummatory. Any activity that is simultaneously both, rather than in alternation and displacement, is art. Disunion of production and consumption is a common enough occurrence. But emphasis upon this separation in order to exalt the consummatory does not define or interpret either art or experience. It obscures their meaning, resulting in a division of art into useful and fine, adjectives which, when they are prefixed to "art," corrupt and destroy its intrinsic significance. For arts that are merely useful are not arts but routines; and arts that are merely final are not arts but passive amusements and distractions, different from other indulgent dissipations only in dependence upon a certain acquired refinement or "cultivation."

The existence of activities that have no immediate enjoyed intrinsic meaning is undeniable. They include much of our labors in home, factory, laboratory and study. By no stretch of language can they be termed either artistic or esthetic. Yet they exist, and are so coercive that they require some attentive recognition. So we optimistically call them "useful" and let it go at that, thinking that by calling them useful we have somehow justified and explained their occurrence. If we were to ask useful for what? we should be obliged to examine their actual consequences, and when we once honestly and fully faced these consequences we should probably find ground for calling such activities detrimental rather than useful.

We call them useful because we arbitrarily cut short our consideration of consequences. We bring into view simply their efficacy in bringing into existence certain commodities; we do not ask for their effect upon the quality of human life and experience. They are useful to make shoes, houses, motor cars, money, and other things which *may* then be put to use; here inquiry and imagination stop. What they also *make* by way of narrowed, embittered, and crippled life, of congested, hurried, confused and extravagant life, is left in oblivion. But to be useful is to fulfill need. The characteristic human need is for possession and appreciation of the meaning of things, and this need is ignored and unsatisfied in the traditional notion of the useful. We identify utility with the external relationship that some events and acts bear to other things that are their products, and thus leave out the only thing that is essential to the idea of utility, inherent place and bearing in experience. Our classificatory use of the conception of some arts as merely instrumental so as to dispose of a large part of human activity is no solving definition; it rather conveys an immense and urgent problem.

The same statement applies to the conception of merely fine or final arts and works of art. In point of fact, the things designated by the phrase fall under three captions. There are activities and receptivities to which the name of "self-expression" is often applied as a eulogistic qualification, in which one indulges himself by giving free outward exhibition to his own states without reference to the conditions upon which intelligible communication depends—an act also sometimes known as "expression of emotion," which is then set up for definition of all fine art. It is easy to dispose of this art by calling it a product of egotism due to balked activity in other occupations. But this treatment misses a more significant point. For all art is a process of making the world a different place in which to live, and involves a phase of protest and of compensatory response. Such art as there is in these manifestations lies in this factor. It is owing to frustration in communication of meanings that the protest becomes arbitrary and the compensatory response wilfully eccentric.

In addition to this type—and frequently mingled with it—there is experimentation in new modes of craftsmanship, cases where the seemingly bizarre and over-individualistic character of the products is due to discontent with existing technique, and is associated with an attempt to find new modes of language. It is aside from the point either to greet these manifestations as if they constituted art for the first time in human history, or to condemn them as not art because of their violent departures from received canons and methods. Some movement in this direction has always been a condition of growth of new forms, a condition of salvation from that moral arrest and decay called academic art.

Then there is that which in quantity bulks most largely as fine art: the production of buildings in the name of the art of architecture; of pictures in the name of the art of painting; of novels, dramas, etc., in the name of literary art; a production which in reality is largely a form of commercialized industry in production of a class of commodities that find their sale among well-to-do persons desirous of maintaining a conventionally approved status. As the first two modes carry to disproportionate excess that factor of particularity, contingency and difference which is indispensable in all art, deliberately flaunting avoidance of the repetitions and order of nature; so this mode celebrates the regular and finished. It is reminiscent rather than commemorative of the meanings of experienced things. Its products remind their owner of things pleasant in memory though hard in direct-undergoing, and remind others that their owner has achieved an economic standard which makes possible cultivation and decoration of leisure.

Obviously no one of these classes of activity and product or all of them put together, mark off anything that can be called distinctively fine art. They share their qualities and defects with many other acts and objects. But, fortunately, there may be mixed with any one of them, and, still more fortunately, there may occur without mixture, process and product that are characteristically excellent. This occurs when activity is productive of an object that affords continuously renewed delight. This condition requires that the object be, with its successive consequences, indefinitely instrumental to *new* satisfying events. For otherwise the object is quickly exhausted and satiety sets in. Anyone who reflects upon the commonplace that a measure of artistic products is their capacity to attract and retain observation with satisfaction under whatever conditions they are approached, while things of less quality soon lose capacity to hold attention becoming indifferent or repellent upon subsequent approach, has a sure demonstration that a genuinely esthetic object is not exclusively consummatory but is causally productive as well. A consummatory object that is not also instrumental turns in time to the dust and ashes of boredom. The "eternal" quality of great art is its renewed instrumentality for further consummatory experiences.

When this fact is noted, it is also seen that limitation of fineness of art to paintings, statues, poems, songs and symphonies is conventional, or even verbal. Any activity that is productive of objects whose perception is an immediate good, and whose operation is a continual source of enjoyable perception of other events exhibits fineness of art. There are acts of all kinds that directly refresh and enlarge the spirit and that are instrumental to the production of new objects and dispositions which are in turn productive of further refinements and replenishments. Frequently moralists make the acts *they* find excellent or virtuous wholly final, and treat art and affection as mere means. Estheticians reverse the performance, and see in good *acts* means to an ulterior external happiness, while esthetic appreciation is called a good in itself, or that strange thing an end in itself. But on both sides it is true that in being preeminently fructifying the things designated means are immediate satisfactions. They are their own excuses for being just because they are charged with an office in quickening apprehension, enlarging the horizon of vision, refining discrimination, creating standards of appreciation which are confirmed and deepened by further experiences. It would almost seem when their non-instrumental character is insisted upon as if what was meant were an indefinitely expansive and radiating instrumental efficacy.

The source of the error lies in the habit of calling by the name of means things that are not means at all; things that are only external and accidental antecedents of the happening of something else. Similarly things are called ends that are not ends save accidentally, since they are not fulfillments, consummatory, of means, but merely last terms closing a process. Thus it is often said that a laborer's toil is the means of his livelihood, although except in the most tenuous and arbitrary way it bears no relationship to his real living. Even his wage is hardly an end or consequence of his labor. He might—and frequently does—equally well or ill—perform any one of a hundred other tasks as a condition of receiving payment. The prevailing conception of instrumentality is profoundly vitiated by the habit of applying it to cases like the above, where, instead of an operation of means, there is an enforced necessity of doing one thing as a coerced antecedent of the occurrence of another thing which is wanted.

Means are always at least causal conditions; but causal conditions are means only when they possess an added qualification; that, namely, of being freely used, because of perceived connection with chosen consequences. To entertain, choose and accomplish anything as an end or consequence is to be committed to a like love and care for whatever events and acts are its means. Similarly, consequences, ends, are at least effects; but effects are not ends unless thought has perceived and freely chosen the conditions and processes that are their conditions. The notion that means are menial, instrumentalities servile, is more than a degradation of means to the rank of coercive and external necessities. It renders all things upon which the name of end is bestowed accompaniments of privilege, while the name of utility becomes an apologetic justification for things that are not portions of a good and reasonable life. Livelihood is at present not so much the consequence of a wage-earner's labor as it is the effect of other causes forming the economic régime, labor being merely an accidental appendage of these other causes.

Paints and skill in manipulative arrangement are means of a picture as end, because the picture is *their* assemblage and organization. Tones and susceptibility of the ear when properly interacting are the means of music, because they constitute, make, are, music. A disposition of virtue is a means to a certain quality of happiness because it is a constituent of that good, while such happiness is means in turn to virtue, as the sustaining of good in being. Flour, water, yeast are means of bread because they are ingredients of bread; while bread is a factor *in* life, not just *to* it. A good political constitution, honest police-system, and competent judiciary, are means of the prosperous life of the community because they are integrated portions of that life. Science is an instrumentality of and for art because it is the intelligent factor *in* art. The trite saying that a hand is not a hand except as an organ of the living body—except as a working coordinated part of a balanced system of activities—applies untritely to all things that are means. The connection of means-consequences is never one of bare succession in time, such that the element that is means is past and gone when the end is instituted. An active process is strung out temporally, but there is a deposit at each stage and point entering cumulatively and constitutively into the outcome. A genuine instrumentality *for* is always an organ *of* an end. It confers continued efficacy upon the object in which it is embodied.

The traditional separation between some things as mere means and others as mere ends is a reflection of the insulated existence of working and leisure classes, of production that is not also consummatory, and consummation that is not productive. This division is not a *merely* social phenomenon. It embodies a perpetuation upon the human plane of a division between need and satisfaction belonging to brute life. And this separation expresses in turn the mechanically external relationship that exists in nature between situations of disturbed equilibrium, of stress, and strain, and achieved equilibrium. For in nature, outside of man, except when events eventuate in "development" or "evolution" (in which a cumulative carrying forward of consequences of past histories in new efficiencies occurs) antecedent events are external transitive conditions of the occurrence of an event having immediate and static qualities. To animals to whom acts have no meaning, the change in the environment required to satisfy needs has no significance on its own account; such change is a mere incident of ego-centric satisfactions. This physically external relationship of antecedents and consequents is perpetuated; it continues to hold true of human industry wherever labor and its materials and products are externally enforced necessities for securing a living. Because Greek industry was so largely upon this plane of servile labor, all industrial activity was regarded by Greek thought as a *mere* means, an extraneous necessity. Hence satisfactions due to it were conceived to be the ends or goods of purely animal nature in isolation. With respect to a truly human and rational life, they were not ends or goods at all, but merely "means," that is to say, external conditions that were antecedently enforced requisites of the life conducted and enjoyed by free men, especially by those devoted to the acme of freedom, pure thinking. As Aristotle asserted, drawing a just conclusion from the assumed premises, there are classes of men who are necessary materials of society but who are not integral parts of it. And he summed up the whole theory of the external and coerced relationship of means and ends when he said in this very connection that: "When there is one thing that is means and another thing that is end, there is *nothing common* between them, except in so far as the one, the means, produces, and the other, the end, receives the product."

It would thus seem almost self-evident that the distinction between the instrumental and the final adopted in philosophic tradition as a solving word presents in truth a problem, a problem so deep-seated and far-reaching that it may be said to be *the* problem of experience. For all the intelligent activities of men, no matter whether expressed in science, fine arts, or social relationships, have for their task the conversion of causal bonds, relations of succession, into a connection of means-consequence, into meanings. When the task is achieved the result is art: and in art everything is common between means and ends. Whenever so-called means remain external and servile, and so-called ends are enjoyed objects whose further causative status is unperceived, ignored or denied, the situation is proof positive of limitations of art. Such a situation consists of affairs in which the problem has *not* been solved; namely that of converting physical and brute relationships into connections of meanings characteristic of the possibilities of nature.

It goes without saying that man begins as a part of physical and animal nature. In as far as he reacts to physical things on a strictly physical level, he is pulled and pushed about, overwhelmed, broken to pieces, lifted on the crest of the wave of things, like anything else. His contacts, his sufferings and doings, are matters of direct interaction only. He is in a "state of nature." As an animal, even upon the brute level, he manages to subordinate some physical things to his needs, converting them into materials sustaining life and growth. But in so far things that serve as material of satisfaction and the acts that procure and utilize them are not objects, or things-with-meanings. That appetite as such is blind, is notorious; it may push us into a comfortable result instead of into disaster; but we are pushed just the same. When appetite is perceived in its meanings, in the consequences it induces, and these consequences are experimented with in reflective imagination, some being seen to be consistent with one another, and hence capable of coexistence and of serially ordered achievement, others being incompatible, forbidding conjunction at one time, and getting in one another's way serially—when this estate is attained, we live on the human plane, responding to things in their meanings. A relationship of cause-effect has been transformed into one of means-consequence. Then consequences belong *integrally* to the conditions which may produce them, and the latter possess character and distinction. The meaning of causal conditions is carried over also into the consequence, so that the latter is no longer a mere end, a last and closing term of arrest. It is marked out in perception, distinguished by the efficacy of the conditions which have entered into it. Its value as fulfilling and consummatory is measurable by subsequent fulfillments and frustrations to which it is contributory in virtue of the causal means which compose it.

Thus to be conscious of meanings or to have an idea, marks a fruition, an enjoyed or suffered arrest of the flux of events. But there are all kinds of ways of perceiving meanings, all kinds of ideas. Meaning may be determined in terms of consequences hastily snatched at and torn loose from their connections; then is prevented the formation of wider and more enduring ideas. Or, we may be aware of meanings, may achieve ideas, that unite wide and enduring scope with richness of distinctions. The latter sort of consciousness is more than a passing and superficial consummation or end: it takes up into itself meanings covering stretches of existence wrought into consistency. It marks the conclusion of long continued endeavor; of patient and indefatigable search and test. The idea is, in short, art and a work of art. As a work of art, it directly liberates subsequent action and makes it more fruitful in a creation of more meanings and more perceptions.

It is the part of wisdom to recognize how sparse and insecure are such accomplishments in comparison with experience in which physical and animal nature largely have their way. Our liberal and rich ideas, our adequate appreciations, due to productive art are hemmed in by an unconquered domain in which we are everywhere exposed to the incidence of unknown forces and hurried fatally to unforeseen consequences. Here indeed we live servilely, menially, mechanically; and we so live as much when forces blindly lead us to ends that are liked as when we are caught in conditions and ends against which we blindly rebel. To call satisfactions which happen in this blind way "ends" in a eulogistic sense, as did classic thought, is to proclaim in effect our servile submission to accident. We may indeed enjoy the goods the gods of fortune send us, but we should recognize them for what they are, not asserting them to be good and righteous *altogether*. For, since they have not been achieved by any art involving deliberate selection and arrangement of forces, we do not know with what they are charged. It is an old true tale that the god of fortune is capricious, and delights to destroy his darlings after having made them drunk with prosperity. The goods of art are not the less good in their goodness than the gifts of nature; while in addition they are such as to bring with themselves open-eyed confidence. They are fruits of means consciously employed; fulfillments whose further consequences are secured by conscious control of the causal conditions which enter into them. Art is the sole alternative to luck; and divorce from each other of the meaning and value of instrumentalities and ends is the essence of luck. The esoteric character of culture and the supernatural quality of religion are both expressions of the divorce.

The modern mind has formally abjured belief in natural teleology because it found Greek and medieval teleology juvenile and superstitious. Yet facts have a way of compelling recognition of themselves. There is little scientific writing which does not introduce at some point or other the idea of tendency. The idea of tendency unites in itself exclusion of prior design and inclusion of movement in a particular direction, a direction that may be either furthered or counteracted and frustrated, but which is intrinsic. Direction involves a limiting position, a point or goal of culminating stoppage, as well as an initial starting point. To assert a tendency and to be fore-conscious of a possible terminus of movement are two names of the same fact. Such a consciousness may be fatalistic; a sense of inevitable march toward impending doom. But it may also contain a perception of meanings such as flexibly directs a forward movement. The end is then an end-in-view and is in constant and cumulative reenactment at each stage of forward movement. It is no longer a terminal point, external to the conditions that have led up to it; it is the continually developing meaning of present tendencies—the very things which as directed we call "means." The process is art and its product, no matter at what stage it be taken, is a work of art.

To a person building a house, the end-in-view is not just a remote and final goal to be hit upon after a sufficiently great number of coerced motions have been duly performed. The end-in-view is a plan which is *contemporaneously* operative in selecting and arranging materials. The latter, brick, stone, wood and mortar, are means only as the end-in-view is actually incarnate in them, in forming them. Literally, they *are* the end in its present stage of realization. The end-in-view is present at each stage of the process; it is present as the *meaning* of the materials used and acts done; without its informing presence, the latter are in no sense "means"; they are merely extrinsic causal conditions. The statement is generic; it applies equally at every stage. The house itself, when building is complete, is "end" in no exclusive sense. It marks the conclusion of the organization of certain materials and events into effective means; but these materials and events still exist in causal interaction with other things. New consequences are foreseen; new purposes, ends-in-view, are entertained; they are embodied in the coordination of the thing built, now reduced to material, although significant material, along with other materials, and thus transmuted into means. The case is still clearer, when instead of considering a process subject to as many rigid external conditions as is the building of a house, we take for illustration a flexibly and freely moving process, such as painting a picture or thinking out a scientific process, when these operations are carried on artistically. Every process of free art proves that the difference between means and end is analytic, formal, not material and chronologic.

What has been said enables us to re-define the distinction drawn between the artistic, as objectively productive, and the esthetic. Both involve a perception of meanings in which the instrumental and the consummatory peculiarly intersect. In esthetic perceptions an object interpenetrated with meanings is given; it may be taken for granted; it invites and awaits the act of appropriative enjoyment. In the esthetic object tendencies are sensed as brought to fruition; in it is embodied a means-consequence relationship, as the past work of his hands was surveyed by the Lord and pronounced good. This good differs from those gratifications to which the name sensual rather than sensuous is given, since the former are pleasing endings that occur in ways not informed with the meaning of materials and acts integrated into them. In appreciative possession, perception goes out to tendencies which *have* been brought to happy fruition in such a way as to release and arouse.

Artistic sense on the other hand grasps tendencies as possibilities; the invitation of these possibilities to perception is more urgent and compelling than that of the given already achieved. While the means-consequence relationship is directly sensed, felt, in both appreciation and artistic production, in the former the scale descends upon the side of the attained; in the latter there predominates the invitation of an existent consummation to bring into existence further perceptions. Art in being, the active productive process, may thus be defined as an esthetic perception together with an *operative* perception of the efficiencies of the esthetic object. In many persons with respect to most kinds of enjoyed perceptions, the sense of possibilities, the arousal or excitation attendant upon appreciation of poetry, music, painting, architecture or landscape remains diffuse and inchoate; it takes effect only in direct and undefined channels. The enjoyed perception of a visual scene is in any case a function of that scene in its total connections, but it does not link up adequately. In some happily constituted persons, this effect is adequately coordinated with other endowments and habits; it becomes an integral part of craft, taking effect in the creation of a new object of appreciation. The integration is, however, progressive and experimental, not momentarily accomplished. Thus every creative effort is temporal, subject to risk and deflection. In that sense the difference between the diffuse and postponed change of action due in an ordinary person to release of energies by an esthetic object, and the special and axial direction of subsequent action in a gifted person is, after all, a matter of degree.

Without a sense of moving tendencies which are operative in conjunction with a state of fruition, there is appetitive gratification, but nothing that may be termed appreciation. Sense of moving tendencies supplies thrill, stimulation, excitation; sense of completion, consummation, affords composure, form, measure, composition. Emphasize the latter, and appreciation is of the classic type. This type fits conditions where production is professionalized among technical craftsmen, as among the Greeks; it is adapted to a contemplative enjoyment of the achievements of past ages or remote places, where conditions forbid urge to emulation or productive activity of a similar kind. Any work of art that persistently retains its power to generate enjoyed perception or appreciation becomes in time classic.

In so-called romantic art, the sense of tendencies operative beyond the limits of consummation is in excess; a lively sense of unrealized potentialities attaches to the object; but it is employed to enhance immediate appreciation, not to promote further productive achievement. Whatever is peculiarly romantic excites a feeling that the possibilities suggested go beyond not merely actual present realization, but are beyond effective attainment in any experience. In so far intentionally romantic art is wilful, and in so far not art. Excited and uneasy perceptual enjoyment is made ultimate, and the work of art is accommodated to production of these feelings. The sense of unachieved possibilities is employed as a compensatory equivalent for endeavor in achievement. Thus when the romantic spirit invades philosophy the possibilities present in imaginative sentiment are declared to be the real, although "transcendental," substance of Being itself. In complete art, appreciation follows the object and moves with it to its completion; romanticism reverses the process and degrades the object to an occasion for arousing a predetermined type of appreciation. In classicism, objective achievement is primary, and appreciation not only conforms to the object, but the object is employed to compose sentiment and give it distinction. Its vice, as an "ism," is that it turns the mind to what is given; the given is taken as if it were eternal and wholly separate from generation and movement. Art free from subjection to any "ism" has movement, creation, as well as order, finality.

To institute a difference of *kind* between useful and fine arts is, therefore, absurd, since art involves a peculiar interpenetration of means and ends. Many things are termed useful for reasons of social status, implying deprecation and contempt. Things are sometimes said to belong to the menial arts merely because they are cheap and used familiarly by common people. These things of daily use for ordinary ends may survive in later periods, or be transported to another culture, as from Japan and China to America, and being rare and sought by connoisseurs, rank forthwith as works of fine art. Other things may be called fine because their manner of use is decorative or socially ostentatious. It is tempting to make a distinction of degree and say that a thing belongs to the sphere of use when perception of its meaning is incidental to something else; and that a thing belongs to fine art when its other uses are subordinate to its use in perception. The distinction has a rough practical value, but cannot be pressed too far. For in production of a painting or a poem, as well as in making a vase or a temple, a perception is also employed as means for something beyond itself. Moreover, the perception of urns, pots and pans as commodities may be intrinsically enjoyable, although these things are primarily perceived with reference to some use to which they are put. The only *basic* distinction is that between bad art and good art, and this distinction, between things that meet the requirements of art and those that do not, applies equally to things of use and of beauty. Capacity to offer to perception meaning in which fruition and efficacy interpenetrate is met by different products in various degrees of fullness; it may be missed altogether by pans and poems alike. The difference between the ugliness of a mechanically conceived and executed utensil and of a meretricious and pretentious painting is one only of content or material; in form, both are articles, and bad articles.

Thinking is preeminently an art; knowledge and propositions which are the products of thinking, are works of art, as much so as statuary and symphonies. Every successive stage of thinking is a conclusion in which the meaning of what has produced it is condensed; and it is no sooner stated than it is a light radiating to other things—unless it be a fog which obscures them. The antecedents of a conclusion are as causal and existential as those of a building. They are not logical or dialectical, or an affair of ideas. While a conclusion follows from antecedents, it does not follow from "premises," in the strict, formal sense. Premises are the analysis of a conclusion into its logically justifying grounds; there are no premises till there is a conclusion. Conclusion and premise are reached by a procedure comparable to the use óf boards and nails in making a box; or of paint and canvas in making a picture. If defective materials are employed or if théy are put together carelessly and awkwardly, the result is defective. In some cases the result is called unworthy, in others, ugly; in others, inept; in others, wasteful, inefficient, and in still others untrue, false. But in each case, the condemnatory adjective refers to the resulting work judged in the light of its method of production. Scientific method or the art of constructing true perceptions is ascertained in the course of experience to occupy a privileged position in undertaking other arts. But this unique position only places it the more securely as an art; it does not set its product, knowledge, apart from other works of art.

The existential origin of valid cognitive perceptions is sometimes recognized in form and denied in substance; the name "psychological" is given to the events which generate valid beliefs. Then a sharp distinction is made between genesis as psychological and validity as logical. Of course lexicographic names are of no special moment; if any one wishes to call the efficient causes of knowledge and truth psychological, he is entitled to do so—provided the actual traits of these causative events are recognized. Such a recognition will note however that psychological does not mean psychic, or refer to events going on exclusively within the head or "subcutaneously." To become aware of an object cognitively as distinct from esthetically, involves external physical movements and external physical appliances physically manipulated. Some of these active changes result in unsound and defective perceptions; some have been ascertained to result usually in valid perceptions. The difference is precisely that which takes place when the art of architecture or sculpture is skilfully conducted or is carried on carelessly, and without adequate appliances. Sometimes the operations productive of tested beliefs are called "inductive"; with an implication in the naming, of discrediting them, as compared with deductive functions, which are assigned a superior exclusive status. Of deduction, when thus defined, the following assertions may be made. First, it has nothing to do with truth about any matter of existence. Secondly, it is not even concerned with consistency or correctness, save in a formal sense whose opposite (as has been previously pointed out) is not inconsistency but nonsense. Thirdly, the meanings which figure in it are the conclusions of prior inquiries which are "inductive," that is, are products of an experimental art of changing external things by appropriate external movements and appliances.

Deduction as it actually occurs in science is *not* deduction as deduction should be according to a common definition. Deduction deals directly with meanings in their relations to one another, rather than with meanings directly referred to existence. But these meanings are what they are in themselves and are related to one another by means of acts of taking and manipulating—an art of discourse. They possess intellectual import and enter fruitfully into scientific method only because they are selected, employed, separated and combined by acts extraneous to them, acts which are as existential and causative as those concerned in the experimental use of apparatus and other physical things. The *act* of knowing, whether solicitous about inference or about demonstration, is always inductive. There is only one mode of thinking, the inductive, when thinking denotes anything that actually happens. The notion that there is another kind called deduction is another evidence of the prevalent tendency in philosophy to treat functions as antecedent operations, and to take essential meanings *of* existence as if they were a kind of Being. As a concrete operation, deduction is generative, not sterile; but as a concrete operation, it contains an extraneous act of taking and using which is selective, experimental and checked constantly by consequences.

Knowledge or science, as a work of art, like any other work of art, confers upon things traits and potentialities which did not *previously* belong to them. Objection from the side of alleged realism to this statement springs from a confusion of tenses. Knowledge is not a distortion or perversion which confers upon *its* subject-matter traits which *do* not belong to it, but is an act which confers upon non-cognitive material traits which *did* not belong to it. It marks a change by which physical events exhibiting properties of mechanical energy, connected by relations of push and pull, hitting, rebounding, splitting and consolidating, realize characters, meanings and relations of meanings *hitherto* not possessed by them. Architecture does not add to stone and wood something which does not belong to them, but it does add to them properties and efficacies which they did not possess in their earlier state. It adds them by means of engaging them in new modes of interaction, having a new order of consequences. Neither engineering nor fine art limits itself to imitative reproduction or copying of antecedent conditions. Their products may nevertheless be more effectively natural, more "life like," than were antecedent states of natural existence. So it is with the art of knowing and its works.

The failure to recognize that knowledge is a product of art accounts for an otherwise inexplicable fact: that science lies today like an incubus upon such a wide area of beliefs and aspirations. To remove the deadweight, however, recognition that it is an art will have to be more than a theoretical avowal that science is made by man for man, although such recognition is probably an initial preliminary step. But the real source of the difficulty is that the art of knowing is limited to such a narrow area. Like everything precious and scarce, it has been artificially protected; and through this very protection it has been dehumanized and appropriated by a class. As costly jewels of jade and pearl belong only to a few, so with the jewels of science. The philosophic theories which have set science on an altar in a temple remote from the arts of life, to be approached only with peculiar rites, are a part of the technique of retaining a secluded monopoly of belief and intellectual authority. Till the art of achieving adequate and liberal perceptions of the meanings of events is incarnate in education, morals and industry, science will remain a special luxury for a few; for the mass, it will consist of a remote and abstruse body of curious propositions having little to do with life, except where it lays the heavy hand of law upon spontaneity, and invokes necessity and mechanism to witness against generous and free aspiration.

Every error is attended with a contrary and compensatory error, for otherwise it would soon be self-revealing. The conception that causes are metaphysically superior to effects is compensated for by the conception that ends are superior esthetically and morally to means. The two beliefs can be maintained together only by removing "ends" out of the region of the causal and efficacious. This is accomplished nowadays by first calling ends intrinsic values, and then by making a gulf between value and existence. The consequence is that science, dealing as it must, with existence, becomes brutal and mechanical, while criticism of values, whether moral or esthetic, becomes pedantic or effeminate, expressing either personal likes and dislikes, or building up a cumbrous array of rules and authorities. The thing that is needful, discriminating judgment by methods whose consequences improve the art, easily slips through such coarse meshes, and by far the greater part of life goes on in a darkness unillumined by thoughtful inquiry. As long as such a state of things persists, the argument of this chapter that science is art—like many other propositions of this book—is largely prophetic, or more or less dialectical. When an art of thinking as appropriate to human and social affairs has grown up as that used in dealing with distant stars, it will not be necessary to argue that science is one among the arts and among the works of art. It will be enough to point to observable situations. The separation of science from art, and the division of arts into those concerned with mere means and those concerned with ends in themselves, is a mask for lack of conjunction between power and the goods of life. It will lose plausibility in the degree in which foresight of good informs the display of power.

Evidence of the interpenetration of the efficacious with the final in art is found in the slow emancipation of art from magical rite and cult, and the emergence of science from superstition. For magic and superstition could never have dominated human culture, nor poetry have been treated as insight into natural causes, if means and ends were empirically marked off from each other. The intimacy of their union in one and the same object is that which makes it easy to impute to whatever is consummatory a kind of efficacy which it does not possess. Whatever is final is important; to say this is to enunciate a truism. Lack of instrumentalities and of skill by which to analyze and follow the particular efficacies of the immediately enjoyed object lead to imputation to it of wholesale efficacy in the degree of its importance. To the short-cut pragmatism congenial to natural man, importance measures "reality" and reality in turn defines efficacious power. Loyalties evoked in the passionate citizen by sight of the flag or in the devout Christian by the cross are attributed directly to the intrinsic nature of these objects. Their share in a consummatory experience is translated into a mysterious inner sacred power, an indwelling efficacy. Thus a souvenir of the beloved one, arousing in the lover enjoyment similar to that awakened by the precious one to whom it belonged, possesses delightful, exciting, and consoling efficacies. No matter what things are directly implicated in a consummatory situation, they gain potencies for weal or woe similar to the good or evil which directly marks the situation. Obviously error here resides in the gross and undiscriminating way in which power is attributed; inquiry to reveal the specified elements which form the sequential order is lacking.

It is a commonplace of anthropologists that for the most part clothing originated in situations of unusual awe or prestigious display, rather than as a utility or protection. It was part of a consummatory object, rather than a means to specified consequences. Like the robes of priests, clothes were vestments, and investiture was believed to convey directly to the one ceremonially garbed dread potency or fascinating charm. Clothes were worn to confer authority; a man did not lend his significance to them. Similarly, a victorious hunter and warrior celebrated a triumphant return to camp by affixing to his person in conspicuous fashion claws and teeth of the wild beast or enemy that his prowess had subjugated. These signal proofs of power were integral portions of the object of admiration, loyalty and reverence. Thus the trophy became an emblem, and the emblem was endowed with mystic force. From a sign of glory it became a cause of glorification, and even when worn by another aroused the acclaim due to a hero. In time such trophies became the documented seal of prestigious authority. They had an intrinsic causal potency of their own. Legal history is full of like instances. Acts originally performed in connection with, say, the exchange of property, performed as part of the dramatic ceremony of taking possession of land, were not treated as mere evidences of title, but as having a mystic power to confer title.

Later, when such things lose their original power and become "mere matters of form," they may still be essential to the legal force of a transaction, as seals have had to be affixed to a contract to give it force, even though there was no longer sense or reason in their use. Things which have an efficacy imputed to them simply because they have shared in some eminent consummatory experience are symbols. They are called symbols, however, only afterwards and from without. To the devout in politics and religion they are other than symbols; they are articles possessed of occult potency. To one man, two crossed lines are an indication of an arithmetical operation to be performed; to another, they are evidence of the existence of Christianity as a historic fact, as a crescent is a reminder of the existence of Islam. But to another, a cross is more than a poignant reminder of a tragically significant death; it has intrinsic sacred power to protect and to bless. Since a flag stirs passionate loyalty to sudden and pervasive ebullition, the flag must have properties and potencies not possessed by other and differently configured pieces of cloth; it must be handled with reverence; it is the natural object of ceremonial adoration.

Phenomena like these when manifested in primitive culture are often interpreted as if they were attempts at a causal explanation of natural occurrences; magic is said to be science gone wrong. In reality, they are facts of direct emotional and practical response; beliefs, ideas, interpretations, only come later when responses not being direct and inevitably appropriate seem to demand explanation. As immediate responses they exemplify the fact that anything involved, no matter how incidentally, in a consummatory situation has the power of arousing the awe, excitement, relief, admiration belonging to the situation as a whole. Industry displaces magic, and science reduces myth, when the elements that enter into the constitution of the consummatory whole are discriminated, and each one has its own particular place in sequential order assigned it. Thus materials and efficacies characteristic of different kinds of arts are distinguished. But because the ceremonial, literary and poetic arts have quite other ways of working and other consequences than industrial and scientific arts, it is far from following, as current theories assume, that they have no instrumental power at all, or that a sense of their instrumental agency is not involved in their appreciative perception. The pervasive operation of symbolism in human culture is all the proof that is needed to show that an intimate and direct sense of place and connection in a prolonged history enters into the enjoyed and suffered constituents of the history, and especially into the final or terminal members.

Further confirmation of this proposition is found in classic philosophy itself, in its theory that essential forms "make" things *what* they are, even though not causing them to occur. "Essence," as it figures in Greek theory, represents the mysterious potency of earlier "symbols" emancipated from their superstitious context and envisaged in a dialectic and reflective context. The essences of Greek-medieval science were in short poetic objects, treated as objects of demonstrative science, used to explain and understand the inner and ultimate constitution of things. While Greek thought was sufficiently emancipated from magic to deny "efficient" causality to formal and final essences, yet the latter were conceived of as making particular things to be *what* they are, members of natural kinds. Moreover, by a reversal of causal residence, intrinsic seeking for such forms was imputed to changing events. Thus the ground was prepared for the later frank return of patristic and scholastic thought to a frank animistic supernaturalism. The philosophic theory erred, as did magic and myth, regarding the nature of the efficacy involved in ends; and the error was due to the same causes, namely, failure of analysis into elements. It could not have occurred, were there that sharp division between means and ends, fruitions and instrumentalities, assumed by current thought.

In short, the history of human experience is a history of the development of arts. The history of science in its distinct emergence from religious, ceremonial and poetic arts is the record of a differentiation of arts, not a record of separation from art. The chief significance of the account just given, lies, for our present purpose, in its bearing upon the theory of experience and nature. It is not, however, without import for a theory of criticism. The present confusion, deemed chaos by some, in the fine arts and esthetic criticism seems to be an inevitable consequence of the underlying, even if unavowed, separation of the instrumental and the consummatory. The further men go in the concrete the more they are forced to recognize the logical consequence of their controlling assumptions. We owe it to theories of art prevalent to-day in one school of critics that certain implications, long obscured, of the traditional theory of art and nature have been brought to light. Gratitude for this debt should not be stinted because the adherents of the traditional theory regard the newer views as capricious heresies, wild aberrations. For these critics, in proclaiming that esthetic qualities in works of fine art are unique, in asserting their separation from not only every thing that is existential in nature but also from all other forms of good, in proclaiming that such arts as music, poetry, painting have characters unshared with any natural things whatsoever:— in asserting such things the critics carry to its conclusion the isolation of fine art from the useful, of the final from efficacious. They thus prove that the separation of the consummatory from the instrumental makes art wholly esoteric.

There are substantially but two alternatives. Either art is a continuation, by means of intelligent selection and arrangement, of natural tendencies of natural events; or art is a peculiar addition to nature springing from something dwelling exclusively within the breast of man, whatever name be given the latter. In the former case, delightfully enhanced perception or esthetic appreciation is of the same nature as enjoyment of any object that is consummatory. It is the outcome of a skilled and intelligent art of dealing with natural things for the sake of intensifying, purifying, prolonging and deepening the satisfactions which they spontaneously afford. That, in this process, new meanings develop, and that these afford uniquely new traits and modes of enjoyment is but what happens everywhere in emergent growths.

But if fine art has nothing to do with other activities and products, then of course it has nothing inherently to do with the objects, physical and social, experienced in other situations. It has an occult source and an esoteric character. It makes little difference what the source and the character be called. By strict logic it makes literally no difference. For if the quality of the esthetic experience is by conception unique, then the words employed to describe it have no significance derived from or comparable to the qualities of other experiences; their signification is hidden and specialized to a degree. Consider some of the terms which are in more or less current use among the critics who carry the isolation of art and the esthetic to its limit. It is sometimes said that art is the expression of the emotions; with the implication that, because of this fact, subject-matter is of no significance except as material through which emotion is expressed. Hence art becomes unique. For in works of science, utility and morals the character of the objects forming this subject-matter is all-important. But by this definition, subject-matter is stripped of all its own inherent characters in art in the degree in which it is genuine art; since a truly artistic work is manifest in the reduction of subject-matter to a mere medium of expression of emotion.

In such a statement emotion either has no significance at all, and it is mere accident that this particular combination of letters is employed; or else, if by emotion is meant the same sort of thing that is called emotion in daily life, the statement is demonstrably false. For emotion in its ordinary sense is something called out *by* objects, physical and personal; it is response *to* an objective situation. It is not something existing somewhere by itself which then employs material through which to express itself. Emotion is an indication of intimate participation, in a more or less excited way in some scene of nature or life; it is, so to speak, an attitude or disposition which is a function of objective things. It is intelligible that art should select and assemble objective things in such ways as to evoke emotional response of a refined, sensitive and enduring kind; it is intelligible that the artist himself is one capable of sustaining these emotions, under whose temper and spirit he performs his compositions of objective materials. This procedure may indeed be carried to a point such that the use of objective materials is economized to the minimum, and the evocation of the emotional response carried to its relative maximum. But it still remains true that the origin of the art-process lay in emotional responses spontaneously called out by a situation occurring without any reference to art, and without "esthetic" quality save in the sense in which all immediate enjoyment and suffering is esthetic. Economy in use of objective subject-matter may with experienced and trained minds go so far that what is ordinarily called "representation" is much reduced. But what happens is a highly funded and generalized representation of the formal sources of ordinary emotional experience.

The same sort of remark is to be made concerning "significant form" as a definition of an esthetic object. Unless the meaning of the term is so isolated as to be wholly occult, it denotes a selection, for sake of emphasis, purity, subtlety, of those forms which give consummatory significance to every-day subject-matters of experience. "Forms" are not the peculiar property or creation of the esthetic and artistic; they are characters in virtue of which anything meets the requirements of an enjoyable perception. "Art" does not create the forms; it is their selection and organization in such ways as to enhance, prolong and purify the perceptual experience. It is not by accident that some objects and situations afford marked perceptual satisfactions; they do so because of their structural properties and relations. An artist may work with a minimum of analytic recognition of these structures or "forms"; he may select them chiefly by a kind of sympathetic vibration. But they may also be discriminatively ascertained; and an artist may utilize his deliberate awareness of them to create works of art that are more formal and abstract than those to which the public is accustomed. Tendency to composition in terms of the formal characters marks much contemporary art, in poetry, painting, music, even sculpture and architecture. At their worst, these products are "scientific" rather than artistic; technical exercises, sterile and of a new kind of pedantry. At their best, they assist in ushering in new modes of art and by education of the organs of perception in new modes of consummatory objects; they enlarge and enrich the world of human vision.

Thus, by only a slight forcing of the argument, we reach a conclusion regarding the relations of instrumental and fine art which is precisely the opposite of that intended by seclusive estheticians; namely, that fine art *consciously* undertaken as such is peculiarly instrumental in quality. It is a device in experimentation carried on for the sake of education. It exists for the sake of a specialized use, use being a new training of modes of perception. The creators of such works of art are entitled, when successful, to the gratitude that we give to inventors of microscopes and microphones; in the end, they open new objects to be observed and enjoyed. This is a genuine service; but only an age of combined confusion and conceit will arrogate to works that perform this special utility the exclusive name of fine art.

Experience in the form of art, when reflected upon, we conclude by saying, solves more problems which have troubled philosophers and resolves more hard and fast dualisms than any other theme of thought. As the previous discussion has indicated, it demonstrates the intersection in nature of individual and generic; of chance and law, transforming one into opportunity and the other into liberation; of instrumental and final. More evidently still, it demonstrates the gratuitous falsity of notions that divide overt and executive activity from thought and feeling and thus separate mind and matter. In creative production, the external and physical world is more than a mere means or external condition of perceptions, ideas and emotions; it is subject-matter and sustainer of conscious activity; and thereby exhibits, so that he who runs may read, the fact that consciousness is not a separate realm of being, but is the manifest quality of existence when nature is most free and most active.

10. Existence, Value and Criticism

Recent philosophy has witnessed the rise of a theory of value. Value as it usually figures in this discussion marks a desperate attempt to combine the obvious empirical fact that objects are qualified with good and bad, with philosophic deliverances which, in isolating man from nature, qualitative individualities from the world, render this fact anomalous. The philosopher erects a "realm of values" in which to place all the precious things which are extruded from natural existence because of isolations artificially introduced. Poignancy, humor, zest, tragedy, beauty, prosperity and bafflement, although rejected from a nature which is identified with mechanical structure, remain just what they empirically are, and demand recognition. Hence they are gathered up into the realm of values, contradistinguished from the realm of existence. Then the philosopher has a new problem with which to wrestle: What is the relationship of these two "worlds"? Is the world of value that of ultimate and transcendent Being from which the world of existence is a derivation or a fall? Or is it but a manifestation of human subjectivity, a factor somehow miraculously supervening upon an order complete and closed in physical structure? Or are there scattered at random through objective being, detached subsistences as "real" as are physical events, but having no temporal dates and spatial locations, and yet at times and places miraculously united with existences?

Choice among such notions of value is arbitrary, because the problem is arbitrary. When we return to the conceptions of potentiality and actuality, contingency and regularity, qualitatively diverse individuality, with which Greek thought operated, we find no room for a theory of values separate from a theory of nature. Yet if we are to recur to the Greek conceptions, the return must be a return with a difference. It must surrender the identification of natural ends with good and perfection; recognizing that a natural end, apart from endeavor expressing choice, has no intrinsic eulogistic quality, but is the boundary which writes "Finis" to a chapter of history inscribed by a moving system of energies. Failure by exhaustion as well as by triumph may constitute an end; death, ignorance, as well as life, are finalities.

Again, the return must abandon the notion of a predetermined limited number of ends inherently arranged in an order of increasing comprehensiveness and finality. It will have to recognize that natural termini are as infinitely numerous and varied as are the individual systems of action they delimit; and that since there is only relative, not absolute, impermeability and fixity of structure, new individuals with novel ends emerge in irregular procession. It must recognize that limits, closures, ends are experimentally or dynamically determined, presenting, like the boundaries of political individuals or states, a moving adjustment of various energy-systems in their cooperative and competitive interactions, not something belonging to them of their own right. Consequently, it will surrender the separation in nature from each other of contingency and regularity, the hazardous and the assured; it will avoid that relegation of them to distinct orders of Being which is characteristic of the classic tradition. It will note that they intersect everywhere; that it is uncertainty and indeterminateness that create the need for and the sense of order and security; that whatever is most complete and liberal in being and possession is for that very reason most exposed to vicissitude, and most needful of watchful safeguarding art.

The connotation of "value" in recent thought contains some hint of the changes which experience has compelled in the classic notion of natural ends. For by implication at least values are recognized to be fugitive and precarious, to be negative and positive, and indefinitely diversified in quality. Even that metaphysical theory of super-idealism which finds them to be eternal, and the eternal foundation and source of shifting temporal events, bases its argument upon the undeniable insecurity, the interminable elusiveness, the appearance and disappearance, of values in actual experience. Because of this sense of the evanescence and uncertainty of what used to be called ends but are now called values, the important consideration and concern is not a theory of values but a theory of criticism; a method of discriminating among goods on the basis of the conditions of their appearance, and of their consequences.

Values are values, things immediately having certain intrinsic qualities. Of them as values there is accordingly nothing to be said; they are what they are. All that can be said of them concerns their generative conditions and the consequences to which they give rise. The notion that things as direct values lend themselves to thought and discourse rests upon a confusion of causal categories with immediate qualities. Objects, for example, may be distinguished as contributory or as fulfilling, but this is distinction of place with respect to causal relationship; it is not a distinction of values. We may be interested in a thing, be concerned with it or like it, for a reason. The reason for appreciation, for an enjoyed appropriation, is often that the object in question serves as a means to something; or the reason is that it stands as the culmination of an antecedent process. But to take into account the reason for liking and enjoyment concerns the cause of the existence of a value, and has nothing to do with the intrinsicalness or nature of the value-quality, which either does or does not exist. Things that are means and things that are fulfillments have different qualities; but so do symphonies, operas and oratorios among themselves. The difference is not one that has anything to do with the immediacy or intrinsicalness of value-quality; it is a difference between one affair and quality and another.

It is self-contradictory to suppose that when a fulfillment possesses immediate value, its means of attainment do not. The person to whom the cessation of a tooth-ache has value, by that very fact finds value in going to a dentist, or in whatever else is means of fulfillment. For fulfillment is as relative to means as means are to realization. Means-consequences constitute a single undivided situation. Consequently when thought and discussion enter, when theorizing sets in, when there is anything beyond bare immediate enjoyment and suffering, it is the means-consequence relationship that is considered. Thought goes beyond immediate existence to its relationships, the conditions which mediate it and the things to which it is in turn mediatory. And such a procedure is criticism. The all but universal confusion in theories of value of determined position in causative or sequential relationship with value proper is indirect testimony to the fact that every intelligent appreciation is also criticism, judgment, of the thing having immediate value. Any *theory* of values is perforce entrance into the field of criticism. Value as such, even things having value, cannot in their immediate existence be reflected upon; they either are or are not; are or are not enjoyed. To pass beyond direct occurrence, even though the passage be restricted to an attempt to define value, is to begin a process of discrimination which implies a reflective criterion. In themselves, values may be just pointed at; to attempt a definition by complete pointing is however bootless. Sooner or later, with respect to positive or negative value, designation will have to include everything.

These remarks are preparatory to presenting a conception of philosophy; namely, that philosophy is inherently criticism, having its distinctive position among various modes of criticism in its generality; a criticism of criticisms, as it were. Criticism is discriminating judgment, careful appraisal, and judgment is appropriately termed criticism wherever the subject-matter of discrimination concerns goods or values. Possession and enjoyment of goods passes insensibly and inevitably into appraisal. First and immature experience is content simply to enjoy. But a brief course in experience enforces reflection; it requires but brief time to teach that some things sweet in the having are bitter in aftertaste and in what they lead to. Primitive innocence does not last. Enjoyment ceases to be a datum and becomes a problem. As a problem, it implies intelligent inquiry into the conditions and consequences of a value-object; that is, criticism. If values were as plentiful as huckleberries, and if the huckleberry-patch were always at hand, the passage of appreciation into criticism would be a senseless procedure. If one thing tired or bored us, we should have only to turn to another. But values are as unstable as the forms of clouds. The things that possess them are exposed to all the contingencies of existence, and they are indifferent to our likings and tastes.

Good things change and vanish not only with changes in the environing medium but with changes in ourselves. Continued perception, except when it has been cultivated through prior criticism, dulls itself; it is soon satiated, exhausted, blasé. The infinite flippancy of the natural man is a standing theme for discourse by shrewd observers of human nature. Cultivated taste alone is capable of prolonged appreciation of the same object; and it is capable of it because it has been trained to a discriminating procedure which constantly uncovers in the object new meanings to be perceived and enjoyed. Add to exhaustion of the organs of perception and enjoyment, all the other organic causes which render enjoyed objects unstable, and then add the external vicissitudes to which they are subjected, and there is no cause to wonder at the evanescence of immediate goods; nor at the so-called paradoxes of pleasure and virtue, according to which they are not secured by aiming at them but by attention to other things;—a fact however, which is not a paradox in a world where nothing is attained in any other way than by attention to its causal conditions.

When criticism and the critical attitude are legitimately distinguished from appreciation and taste, we are in the presence of one case of the constant rhythm of "perchings and flights" (to borrow James's terms), characteristic of alternate emphasis upon the immediate and mediate, the consummatory and instrumental, phases of all conscious experience. If we are misled into ignoring the omnipresence in all observations and ideas of this rhythm, it is largely because, under the influence of formal theories, we attach too elaborate and too remote a signification to "appreciation" and "criticism." Values of some sort or other are not traits of rare and festal occasions; they occur whenever any object is welcomed and lingered over; whenever it arouses aversion and protest; even though the lingering be but momentary and the aversion a passing glance toward something else.

Similarly, criticism is not a matter of formal treatises, published articles, or taking up important matters for consideration in a serious way. It occurs whenever a moment is devoted to looking to see what sort of value is present; whenever instead of accepting a value-object wholeheartedly, being rapt by it, we raise even a shadow of a question about its worth, or modify our sense of it by even a passing estimate of its probable future. It is well upon the whole that we use the terms "appreciation" and "criticism" honorifically, to designate conspicuous instances. But it is fatal to any understanding of them to fail to note that formally emphatic instances are of exactly the same nature as the

rhythmic alternation between slight agreeable acceptances, an-
noyed rejections and passing questionings and estimates, which
make up the entire course of our waking experience, whether in
revery, in controlled inquiry or in deliberate management of
affairs.

The rhythmic succession of the two modes of perception
suggests that the difference is one of emphasis, or degree. Critical
appreciation, and appreciative, warmly emotionalized criticism
occur in every matured sane experience. After the first dumb,
formless experience of a thing as a good, subsequent perception
of the good contains at least a germ of critical reflection. For this
reason, and only for this reason, elaborate and formulated criticism is subsequently possible. The latter, if just and pertinent,
can but develop the reflective implications found within appreciation itself. Criticism would be the most wilful of undertakings if
the possession and enjoyment of good objects had no element of
memory and foresight in it; if it lacked all circumspection and
judgment. Criticism is reasonable and to the point, in the degree
in which it extends and deepens these factors of intelligence
found in immediate taste and enjoyment.

Conscience in morals, taste in fine arts and conviction in beliefs pass insensibly into critical judgments; the latter pass also
into a more and more generalized form of criticism called philosophy. How is the assertion of "canons" of taste and criticism
compatible with the declaration that there is no discussing
tastes? What is meant by a distinction between apparent good
and real good? How can the distinction between seeming and
being be capable of application to what is good? Is critical appraisal possible without a standard measure of values? Is the
standard of values itself a value? Is it derived from the value-
objects to which it is applied? If so, what authority does it possess over and beyond that of particular cases? What right has it
to pass judgment upon its own source and authors? Does a
standard exist transcendentally in independence of concrete
cases judged? If so, what is its source, and what is the ground
and guarantee of its applicability to alien material? Is taste,
immediate appreciation, sense and moral sense, ultimate, its own
final judge in every case as it arises? What, in that event, saves us
from chaotic anarchy? Is there among men a common measure

of value? If so, is it grounded outside of man, in an independent objective form of Being?

Such questions as these, which may be multiplied as one pleases, indicate that no great difficulty would attend an effort to derive all the stock issues of philosophy from the problems of value and their relationship to critical judgment. Whether it be a question of the good and bad in conviction and opinion, or in matters of conduct, or in appreciated scenes of nature and art, there occurs in every instance a conflict between the immediate value-object and the ulterior value-object: the given good, and that reached and justified by reflection; the now apparent and the eventual. In knowledge, for example there are beliefs *de facto* and beliefs *de jure*. In morals, there are immediate goods, the desired, and reasonable goods, the desirable. In esthetics, there are the goods of an undeveloped or perverted taste and there are the goods of cultivated taste. With respect to any of these distinctions, the true, real, final, or objective good is no *more* good as an immediate existence than is the contrasting good, called false, specious, illusory, showy, meretricious, *le faux bon*. The difference in adjectives designates a difference instituted in critical judgment; the validity of the difference between good which is approved and that which is good (immediately) but is *judged bad*, depends therefore upon the value of reflection in general, and of a particular reflective operation in especial. Even if good of the reflective object is different from that of the good of the non-reflective object, it does not follow that it is a better good, much less that it is such a difference in goodness as makes the non-reflective good *bad*:—except upon one proviso, namely, that there is something unique in the value or goodness of reflection.

Either, then, the difference between genuine, valid, good and a counterfeit, specious good is unreal, or it is a difference consequent upon reflection, or criticism, and the significant point is that this difference is equivalent to that made by discovery of relationships, of conditions and consequences. With this conclusion are bound up two other propositions: Of immediate values as such, values which occur and which are possessed and enjoyed, there is no theory at all; they just occur, are enjoyed, possessed; and that is all. The moment we begin to discourse

about these values, to define and generalize, to make distinctions
in kinds, we are passing beyond value-objects themselves; we are
entering, even if only blindly, upon an inquiry into causal antecedents and causative consequents, with a view to appraising
the "real," that is the eventual, goodness of the thing in question.
We are criticizing, not for its own sake, but for the sake of
instituting and perpetuating more enduring and extensive values.

The other proposition is that philosophy is and can be nothing
but this critical operation and function become aware of itself
and its implications, pursued deliberately and systematically. It
starts from actual situations of belief, conduct and appreciative
perception which are characterized by immediate qualities of
good and bad, and from the modes of critical judgment current
at any given time in all the regions of value; these are its data, its
subject-matter. These values, criticisms, and critical methods, it
subjects to further criticism as comprehensive and consistent as
possible. The function is to regulate the further appreciation of
goods and bads; to give greater freedom and security in those
acts of direct selection, appropriation, identification and of rejection, elimination, destruction which enstate and which exclude
objects of belief, conduct and contemplation.

Such a conclusion wears an air of strangeness. It may appear
to indicate an attempt by a dialectic trick to make the category of
good-and-bad supreme in its jurisdiction over intellectual life
and over all objects. This impression will, I think, be readily
dissipated by consideration of the actual meaning of what is said.
Objects of belief and of refusals to believe are value-objects; for
each object is some thing acquiesced in, accepted, adopted, appropriated. This is the same as saying it is found good or satisfactory to believe or disbelieve; truistically, whatever is accepted is
as such and in so far good. There is no occult significance in this
statement; it is not preliminary to an argument which shall
sweep away the properties which objects possess independent of
their being objects of belief, or of their being values. It does not
annihilate the difference among beliefs; it does not set up the *fact*
that an object believed in is perforce found good as if it were a
reason for belief. On the contrary: the statement is preliminary.
The all-important matter is what lies back of and causes acceptance and rejection; whether or no there is method of discrimination and assessment which makes a difference in what is assented

to and denied. Properties and relations that *entitle* an object to be found good in belief are extraneous to the qualities that are its immediate good; they are causal, and hence found only by search into the antecedent and the eventual. The conception that there are some objects or some properties of objects which carry their own adequate credentials upon their face is the snare and delusion of the whole historic tradition regarding knowledge, infecting alike sensational and rational schools, objective realisms and introspective idealisms.

Concerning beliefs and their objects taken in their immediacy *"non-disputandum"* holds, as truly as it does concerning tastes and their objects. If a man believes in ghosts, devils, miracles, fortune-tellers, the immutable certainty of the existing economic régime, and the supreme merits of his political party and its leaders, he does so believe; these are immediate goods to him, precisely as some color and tone combinations are lovely, or the mistress of his heart is charming. When the question is raised as to the "real" value of the object for belief, the appeal is to criticism, intelligence. And the court of appeal decides by the law of conditions and consequences. Inquiry duly pursued leads to the enstatement of an object which is directly accepted, good in belief, but an object whose character now depends upon the reflective operations whose conclusion it is. Like the object of dogmatic and uncritical belief, it marks an "end," a static arrest; but unlike it, the "end" is a *conclusion*; hence it carries credentials.

Were not objects of belief immediate goods, false beliefs would not be the dangerous things which they are. For it is because these objects are good to believe, to admit and assert, that they are cherished so intolerantly and unremittingly. Beliefs about God, Nature, society and man are precisely the things that men most cling to and most ardently fight for. It is easier to wean a miser from his hoard, than a man from his deeper opinions. And the tragedy is that in so many cases the *causes* which lead to the thing in question being a value are not *reasons* for its being a good, while the fact that it is an immediate good tends to preclude that search for causes, that dispassionate judgment, which is prerequisite to the conversion of goods *de facto* into goods *de jure*. Here, again and preeminently, since reflection is the instrumentality of securing freer and more enduring goods, reflection is a unique intrinsic good. Its instrumental efficacy determines it to be a candidate for a distinctive position as an immediate good, since beyond other goods it has power of replenishment and fructification. In it, apparent good and real good enormously coincide.

In traditional discussion the fact is overlooked that the subject-matter of belief is a good, since belief means assimilation and assertion. It is overlooked that its immediate goodness is both the obstacle to reflective examination and the source of its necessity. The "true" is indeed set up along with the good and the beautiful as a transcendent good, but the role of empirical good, of value, in the sweep of ordinary beliefs is passed by. The counterpart of this error, which isolates the subject-matter of intellect from the scope of values and valuations, is a corresponding isolation of the subject-matter of esthetic contemplation and immediate enjoyment from judgment. Between these two realms, one of intellectual objects without value and the other of value-objects without intellect, there is an equivocal mid-country in which moral objects are placed, with rival claimants striving to annex them either to the region of purely immediate goods (in this case termed pleasures) or to that of purely rational objects. Hence the primary function of philosophy at present is to make it clear that there is no such difference as this division assumes between science, morals, and esthetic appreciation. All alike exhibit the difference between immediate goods casually occurring and immediate goods which have been reflectively determined by means of critical inquiry. If bare liking is an adequate determinant of values in one case, it is in the others. If intelligence, criticism, is required in one, it is in the others. If the end to be attained in any case is an enhanced and purified immediate appreciative, experienced object, so it is in the others. All cases manifest the same duality and present the same problem; that of embodying intelligence in action which shall convert casual natural goods, whose causes and effects are unknown, into goods valid for thought, right for conduct and cultivated for appreciation.

Philosophic discourse partakes both of scientific and literary discourse. Like literature, it is a comment on nature and life in the interest of a more intense and just appreciation of the meanings present in experience. Its business is reportorial and transcriptive only in the sense in which the drama and poetry have that office. Its primary concern is to clarify, liberate and extend the goods which inhere in the naturally generated functions of experience. It has no call to create a world of "reality" *de novo*, nor to delve into secrets of Being hidden from common sense and science. It has no stock of information or body of knowledge peculiarly its own; if it does not always become ridiculous when it sets up as a rival of science, it is only because a particular philosopher happens to be also, as a human being, a prophetic man of science. Its business is to accept and to utilize for a purpose the best available knowledge of its own time and place. And this purpose is criticism of beliefs, institutions, customs, policies with respect to their bearing upon good. This does not mean their bearing upon *the* good, as something itself attained and formulated in philosophy. For as philosophy has no private store of knowledge or of methods for attaining truth, so it has no private access to good. As it accepts knowledge of facts and principles from those competent in inquiry and discovery, so it accepts the goods that are diffused in human experience. It has no Mosaic nor Pauline authority of revelation entrusted to it. But it has the authority of intelligence, of criticism of these common and natural goods.

At this point, it departs from the arts of literary discourse. They have a freer office to perform—to perpetuate, enhance and vivify in imagination the natural goods; all things are forgiven to him who succeeds. But philosophic criticism has a stricter task, with a greater measure of responsibility to what lies outside its own products. It has to appraise values by taking cognizance of their causes and consequences; only by this straight and narrow path may it contribute to expansion and emancipation of values. For this reason the conclusions of science about matter-of-fact efficiencies of nature are its indispensable instruments. If its eventual concern is to render goods more coherent, more secure and more significant in appreciation, its road is the subject-matter of natural existence as science discovers and depicts it.

Only in verbal form is there anything novel in this conception of philosophy. It is a version of the old saying that philosophy is love of wisdom, of wisdom which is not knowledge and which nevertheless cannot be without knowledge. The need of an organon of criticism which uses knowledge of relations among events to appraise the casual, immediate goods that obtain among men is not a fact of philosophy, but of nature and life. We can conceive a happier nature and experience than flourishes among us wherein the office of critical reflection would be carried on so continuously and in such detail that no particular apparatus would be needed. But actual experience is such a jumble that a degree of distance and detachment are a prerequisite of vision in perspective. Thinkers often withdraw too far. But a withdrawal is necessary, unless they are to be deafened by the immediate clamor and blinded by the immediate glare of the scene. What especially makes necessary a generalized instrument of criticism, is the tendency of objects to seek rigid non-communicating compartments. It is natural that nature, variegatedly qualified, should exhibit various trends when it achieves experience of itself, so that there is a distribution of emphases such as are designated by the adjectives scientific, industrial, political, religious, artistic, educational, moral and so on.

But however natural from the standpoint of causation may be the institutionalizing of these trends, their separation effects an isolation which is unnatural. Narrowness, superficiality, stagnation follow from lack of the nourishment which can be supplied only by generous and wide interactions. Goods isolated as professionalism and institutionalization isolate them, petrify; and in a moving world solidification is always dangerous. Resistant force is gained by precipitation, but no one thing gets strong enough to defy everything. Over-specialization and division of interests, occupations and goods create the need for a generalized medium of intercommunication, of mutual criticism through all-around translation from one separated region of experience into another. Thus philosophy as a critical organ becomes in effect a messenger, a liaison officer, making reciprocally intelligible voices speaking provincial tongues, and thereby enlarging as well as rectifying the meanings with which they are charged.

The difficulty is that philosophy, even when professing catholicity, has often been suborned. Instead of being a free messenger of communication it has been a diplomatic agent of some special and partial interest; insincere, because in the name of peace it has fostered divisions that lead to strife, and in the name of loyalty has promoted unholy alliances and secret understandings. One might say that the profuseness of attestations to supreme devotion to truth on the part of philosophy is matter to arouse suspicion. For it has usually been a preliminary to the claim of being a peculiar organ of access to highest and ultimate truth. Such it is not; and it will not lose its esoteric and insincere air until the profession is disclaimed. Truth is a collection of truths; and these constituent truths are in the keeping of the best available methods of inquiry and testing as to matters-of-fact; methods, which are, when collected under a single name, science. As to truth, then, philosophy has no preeminent status; it is a recipient, not a donor. But the realm of meanings is wider than that of true-and-false meanings; it is more urgent and more fertile. When the claim of meanings to truth enters in, then truth is indeed preeminent. But this fact is often confused with the idea that truth has a claim to enter everywhere; that it has monopolistic jurisdiction. Poetic meanings, moral meanings, a large part of the goods of life are matters of richness and freedom of meanings, rather than of truth; a large part of our life is carried on in a realm of meanings to which truth and falsity as such are irrelevant. And the claim of philosophy to rival or displace science as a purveyor of truth seems to be mostly a compensatory gesture for failure to perform its proper task of liberating and clarifying meanings, including those scientifically authenticated. For, assuredly, a student prizes historic systems rather for the meanings and shades of meanings they have brought to light than for the store of ultimate truths they have ascertained. If accomplishment of the former office were made the avowed business of philosophy, instead of an incidental by-product, its position would be clearer, more intelligent and more respected.

It is sometimes suggested, however, that such a view of philosophy derogates from its dignity, degrading it into an instrument of social reforms, and that it is a view congenial only to those who are insensitive to the positive achievements of culture and over-sensitive to its evils. Such a conception overlooks outstanding facts. "Social reform" is conceived in a Philistine spirit, if it is taken to mean anything less than precisely the liberation and expansion of the meanings of which experience is capable. No doubt many schemes of social reform are guilty of precisely this narrowing. But for that very reason they are futile; they do not succeed in even the special reforms at which they aim, except at the expense of intensifying other defects and creating new ones. Nothing but the best, the richest and fullest experience possible, is good enough for man. The attainment of such an experience is not to be conceived as the specific problem of "reformers" but as the common purpose of men. The contribution which philosophy can make to this common aim is criticism. Criticism certainly includes a heightened consciousness of deficiencies and corruptions in the scheme and distribution of values that obtains at any period.

No just or pertinent criticism in its negative phase can possibly be made, however, except upon the basis of a heightened appreciation of the positive goods which human experience has achieved and offers. Positive concrete goods of science, art and social companionship are the basic subject-matter of philosophy as criticism; and only because such positive goods already exist is their emancipation and secured extension the defining aim of intelligence. The more aware one is of the richness of meanings which experience possesses, the more will a generous and catholic thinker be conscious of the limits which prevent sharing in them; the more aware will he be of their accidental and arbitrary distribution. If instrumental efficacies need to be emphasized, it is not for the sake of instruments but for the sake of that full and more secure distribution of values which is impossible without instrumentalities.

If philosophy be criticism, what is to be said of the relation of philosophy to metaphysics? For metaphysics, as a statement of the generic traits manifested by existences of all kinds without regard to their differentiation into physical and mental, seems to have nothing to do with criticism and choice, with an effective love of wisdom. It begins and ends with analysis and definition. When it has revealed the traits and characters that are sure to turn up in every universe of discourse, its work is done. So at least an argument may run. But the very nature of the traits discovered in every theme of discourse, since they are ineluctable traits of natural existence, forbids such a conclusion. Qualitative individuality and constant relations, contingency and need, movement and arrest are common traits of all existence. This fact is source both of values and of their precariousness; both of immediate possession which is casual and of reflection which is a precondition of secure attainment and appropriation. Any theory that detects and defines these traits is therefore but a ground-map of the province of criticism, establishing base lines to be employed in more intricate triangulations.

If the general traits of nature existed in water-tight compartments, it might be enough to sort out the objects and interests of experience among them. But they are actually so intimately intermixed that all important issues are concerned with their degrees and the ratios they sustain to one another. Barely to note and register that contingency is a trait of natural events has nothing to do with wisdom. To note, however, contingency in connection with a concrete situation of life is that fear of the Lord which is at least the beginning of wisdom. The detection and definition of nature's end is in itself barren. But the undergoing that actually goes on in the light of this discovery brings one close to supreme issues: life and death.

The more sure one is that the world which encompasses human life is of such and such a character (no matter what his definition), the more one is committed to try to direct the conduct of life, that of others as well as of himself, upon the basis of the character assigned to the world. And if he finds that he cannot succeed, that the attempt lands him in confusion, inconsistency and darkness, plunging others into discord and shutting them out from participation, rudimentary precepts instruct him to surrender his assurance as a delusion; and to revise his notions of the nature of nature till he makes them more adequate to the concrete facts in which nature is embodied. Man needs the earth in order to walk, the sea to swim or sail, the air to fly. Of necessity he acts within the world, and in order to be, he must in some measure adapt himself as one part of nature to other parts.

In mind, thought, this situation, this predicament becomes aware of itself. Instead of the coerced adaptation of part to part with coerced failure or success as consequence, there is search for the meaning of things with respect to acts to be performed, plans and policies to be formed; there is search for the meaning of proposed acts with respect to objects they induce and preclude. The one cord that is never broken is that between the energies and acts which compose nature. Knowledge modifies the tie. But the idea that knowledge breaks the tie, that it inserts something opaque between the interactions of things, is hardly less than infantile. Knowledge as science modifies the particular interactions that come within its reach, because it *is* itself a modification of interactions, due to taking into account their past and future. The generic insight into existence which alone can define metaphysics in any empirically intelligible sense is itself an added fact of interaction, and is therefore subject to the same requirement of intelligence as any other natural occurrence: namely, inquiry into the bearings, leadings and consequences of what it discovers. The universe is no infinite self-representative series, if only because the addition within it of a representation makes it a different universe.

By an indirect path we are brought to a consideration of the most far-reaching question of all criticism: the relationship between existence and value, or as the problem is often put, between the real and ideal.

Philosophies have usually insisted upon a wholesale relationship. Either the goods which we most prize and which are therefore termed ideal are identified completely and throughout with real Being; or the realms of existence and of the ideal are wholly severed from each other. In the European tradition in its orthodox form the former alternative has prevailed. *Ens* and *verum, bonum* are the same. Being, in the full sense, is perfection of power to be; the measure of degrees of perfection and of degrees of reality is extent of power. Evil and error are impotences; futile gestures against omnipotence—against Being. Spinoza restated to this effect medieval theology in terms of the new outlook of science. Modern professed idealisms have taught the same doctrine. After magnifying thought and the objects of thought, after magnifying the ideals of human aspiration, they have then sought to prove that after all these things are not ideal but are real—real not *as* meanings and ideals, but as existential being. Thus the assertion of faith in the ideal belies itself in the making; these "idealists" cannot trust their ideal till they have converted it into existence—that is, into the physical or the psychical, which, since it lacks the properties of the empirically physical and psycho-physical becomes a peculiar kind of existence, called metaphysical.

There are also philosophies, rarer in occurrence, which allege that the ideal is too sacredly ideal to have any point of contact whatever with existence; they think that contact is contagion and contagion infection. At first sight such a view seems to display a certain nobility of faith and fineness of abnegation. But an ideal realm that has no roots in existence has no efficacy nor relevancy. It is a light which is darkness, for shining in the void it illumines nothing and cannot reveal even itself. It gives no instruction, for it cannot be translated into the meaning and import of what actually happens, and hence it is barren; it cannot mitigate the bleakness of existence nor modify its brutalities. It thus abnegates itself in abjuring footing in natural events, and ceases to be ideal, to become whimsical fantasy or linguistic sophistication.

These remarks are made not so much by way of hostile animadversion as by way of indicating the sterility of wholesale conceptions of the relation of existence and value. By negative implication, they reveal the only kind of doctrine that can be effectively critical, taking effect in discriminations which emancipate, extend, and clarify. Such a theory will realize that the meanings which are termed ideal as truly as those which are termed sensuous are generated by existences; that as far as they continue in being they are sustained by events; that they are indications of the possibilities of existences, and are, therefore, to be used as well as enjoyed; used to inspire action to procure and buttress their causal conditions. Such a doctrine criticizes particular occurrences by the particular meanings to which they give rise; it criticizes also particular meanings and goods as their conditions are found to be sparse, accidental, incapable of conservation, or frequent, pliant, congruous, enduring; and as their consequences are found to afford enlightenment and direction in conduct, or to darken counsel, narrow the horizon of vision, befog judgment and distort perspective. A good is a good anyhow, but to reflection those goods approve themselves, whether labelled beauty or truth or righteousness, which steady, vitalize and expand judgments in creation of new goods and conservation of old goods. To common sense this statement is a truism. If to philosophy it is a stumbling-block, it is because tradition in philosophy has set itself in stiff-necked fashion against discriminations within the realm of existences, on account of the pluralistic implications of discrimination. It insists upon having all or none; it cannot choose in favor of some existences and against others because of prior commitment to a dogma of perfect unity. Such distinctions as it makes are therefore always hierarchical; degrees of greater and less, superior and inferior, in one homogeneous order.

I gladly borrow the glowing words of one of our greatest American philosophers; with their poetry they may succeed in conveying where dry prose fails. Justice Holmes has written: "The mode in which the inevitable comes to pass is through effort. Consciously or unconsciously we all strive to make the kind of world that we like. And although with Spinoza we may regard criticism of the past as futile, there is every reason for doing all that we can to make a future such as we desire." He then goes on to say, "there is every reason also for trying to make our desires intelligent. The trouble is that our ideals for the most part are inarticulate, and that even if we have made them definite we have very little experimental knowledge of the way to bring them about." And this effort to make our desires, our strivings and our ideals (which are as natural to man as his aches and his clothes) articulate, to define them (not in themselves which is impossible) in terms of inquiry into conditions and consequences is what I have called criticism; and when carried on in the grand manner, philosophy. In a further essay, Justice Holmes touches upon the relation of philosophy (thus conceived) to our scientific and metaphysical insight into the kind of a world in which we live.

"When we come to our attitude toward the universe I do not see any rational ground for demanding the superlative—for being dissatisfied unless we are assured that our truth is cosmic truth, if there is such a thing. . . . If a man sees no reason for believing that significance, consciousness and ideals are more than marks of the human, that does not justify what has been familiar in French sceptics; getting upon a pedestal and professing to look with haughty scorn upon a world in ruins. The real conclusion is that the part can not swallow the whole. . . . If we believe that we came out of the universe, not it out of us, we must admit that we do not know what we are talking about when we speak of brute matter. We do know that a certain complex of energies can wag its tail and another can make syllogisms. These are among the powers of the unknown, and if, as may be, it has still greater powers that we cannot understand . . . why should we not be content? Why should we employ the energy that is furnished to us by the cosmos to defy it and to shake our fist at the sky? It seems to me silly."

"That the universe has in it more than we understand, that the private soldiers have not been told the plan of campaign, or even that there is one . . . has no bearing on our conduct. We still shall fight—all of us because we want to live, some, at least, because we want to realize our spontaneity and prove our powers, for the joy of it, and we may leave to the unknown the supposed final valuation of that which in any event has value to us. It is enough for us that the universe has produced us and has within it, as less than it, all that we believe and love. If we think of our existence not as that of a little god outside, but as that of a ganglion within, we have the infinite behind us. It gives us our only but our adequate significance. If our imagination is strong enough to accept the vision of ourselves as parts inseparable from the rest, and to extend our final interest beyond the boundary of our skins, it justifies even the sacrifice of our lives for ends outside of ourselves. The motive to be sure is the common wants and ideals that we find in man. Philosophy does not furnish motives, but it shows men that they are not fools for doing what they already want to do. It opens to the forlorn hopes on which we throw ourselves away, the vista of the farthest stretch of human thought, the chords of a harmony that breathes from the unknown."

Men move between extremes. They conceive of themselves as gods, or feign a powerful and cunning god as an ally who bends the world to do their bidding and meet their wishes. Disillusionized, they disown the world that disappoints them; and hugging ideals to themselves as their own possession, stand in haughty aloofness apart from the hard course of events that pays so little heed to our hopes and aspirations. But a mind that has opened itself to experience and that has ripened through its discipline knows its own littleness and impotencies; it knows that its wishes and acknowledgments are not final measures of the universe whether in knowledge or in conduct, and hence are, in the end, transient. But it also knows that its juvenile assumption of power and achievement is not a dream to be wholly forgotten. It implies a unity with the universe that is to be preserved. The belief, and the effort of thought and struggle which it inspires are also the doing of the universe, and they in some way, however slight, carry the universe forward. A chastened sense of our importance, apprehension that it is not a yard-stick by which to measure the whole, is consistent with the belief that we and our endeavors are significant not only for themselves but in the whole.

Fidelity to the nature to which we belong, as parts however weak, demands that we cherish our desires and ideals till we have converted them into intelligence, revised them in terms of the ways and means which nature makes possible. When we have used our thought to its utmost and have thrown into the moving unbalanced balance of things our puny strength, we know that though the universe slay us still we may trust, for our lot is one with whatever is good in existence. We know that such thought and effort is one condition of the coming into existence of the better. As far as we are concerned it is the only condition, for it alone is in our power. To ask more than this is childish; but to ask less is a recreance no less egotistic, involving no less a cutting of ourselves from the universe than does the expectation that it meet and satisfy our every wish. To ask in good faith as much as this from ourselves is to stir into motion every capacity of imagination, and to exact from action every skill and bravery.

While, therefore, philosophy has its source not in any special impulse or staked-off section of experience, but in the entire human predicament, this human situation falls wholly within nature. It reflects the traits of nature; it gives indisputable evidence that in nature itself qualities and relations, individualities and uniformities, finalities and efficacies, contingencies and necessities are inextricably bound together. The harsh conflicts and the happy coincidences of this interpenetration make experience what it consciously is; their manifest apparition creates doubt, forces inquiry, exacts choice, and imposes liability for the choice which is made. Were there complete harmony in nature, life would be spontaneous efflorescence. If disharmony were not in both man and nature, if it were only between them, man would be the ruthless overlord of nature, or its querulous oppressed subject. It is precisely the peculiar intermixture of support and frustration of man by nature which constitutes experience. The standing antitheses of philosophic thought, purpose and mechanism, subject and object, necessity and freedom, mind and body, individual and general, are all of them attempts to formulate the fact that nature induces and partially sustains meanings and goods, and at critical junctures withdraws assistance and flouts its own creatures.

The striving of man for objects of imagination is a continuation of natural processes; it is something man has learned from the world in which he occurs, not something which he arbitrarily injects into that world. When he adds perception and ideas to these endeavors, it is not after all he who adds; the addition is again the doing of nature and a further complication of its own domain. To act, to enjoy and suffer in consequence of action, to reflect, to discriminate and make differences in what had been but gross and homogeneous good and evil, according to what inquiry reveals of causes and effects; to act upon what has been learned, thereby to plunge into new and unconsidered predicaments, to test and revise what has been learned, to engage in new goods and evils is human, the course which manifests the course of nature. They are the manifest destiny of contingency, fulfillment, qualitative individualization and generic uniformities in nature. To note, register and define the constituent structure of nature is not then an affair neutral to the office of criticism. It is a preliminary outline of the field of criticism, whose chief import is to afford understanding of the necessity and nature of the office of intelligence.

If I mistake not, the actual animus of subjectivity in modern philosophy is not where its antagonists have placed it. Its actual animus and its obnoxious burden are exemplified in the doctrine of its hostile critics. For they assign to knowledge alone valid reference to existence. Desires, beliefs, "practical" activity, values are attributed exclusively to the human subject; this division is what makes subjectivity a snare and peril. The case of belief is crucial. For it is admitted that belief involves a phase of acquiescence or assertion; it presents qualities which involve *personal* factors, and (whatever definition of value be employed) value. A sharp line of demarcation has therefore to be drawn between belief and knowledge, for the latter has been defined in terms of pure objectivity. The need to control belief is admitted; knowledge figures, even though according to these theories only *per accidens*, as the organon of such control. Practically then, in effect, knowledge, science, truth, is the method of criticizing beliefs. It is the method of determining right participation in beliefs on the part of personal factors. Why then keep up any other distinction between knowledge and beliefs, save that between methodical agencies, efficacious instrumentalities, and the accepted objects which being conclusions, are hence marked by characters due to the method of their production, in contrast with objects of belief blindly and accidentally generated? Why perturbation at the intimation that science is inherently an instrument of critically determining what is good and bad in the way of acceptance and rejection?

I can see but one answer. The realm of desire, belief, search, choice is thought of as "subjective" in a sense which isolates it from natural existence and which makes it an inexplicable irruption. This is the reason for sharp separation of belief and knowledge. Aversion to making science a means of determining the right operation of personal factors, just as the technical and material apparatus of a painter determines his product, is well grounded if the personal is outside of nature. Made a means to something personal conceived in this sense, science loses its objectivity, and becomes infected with the traits which characterize the merely private and arbitrary.

There is involved, however, in the conclusion an unexamined and uncriticized assumption. The reason for isolating doubt, striving, purpose, the variegated colored play of goods and bads, rejections and acceptances, is they do not belong in the block universe which forms the object of generalized knowledge, whether the block be conceived as mechanical or as rational in structure. The argument thus moves in a vicious circle; the question is begged at the outset. If individualized qualities, status arrests, limiting "ends," and contingent changes characterize nature, then they manifest themselves in the uses, enjoyments and sufferings, the searchings and strivings which form conscious experience. These are as realistic, as "objectively" natural, as are the constituents of the object of cognitional experience. There is then no ground for denying or evading the full import of the fact that the latter are the means and the only means of regulative appraisals of values, of their revision, rectification, of their regulated generation and fortification.

The habitual avoidance in theories of knowledge of any reference to the fact that knowledge is a case of belief, operates as a device for ignoring the monstrous consequences of regarding the latter as existentially subjective, personal and private. No such device is available in dealing with esthetic and moral goods. Here the obnoxious one-sided conception operates in full force. The usual current procedure is to link values with likings as merely personal affairs, ignoring the inconvenient fact that the theory logically thereby makes all *beliefs* also matters of arbitrary, undiscussable preference. It is no cause for wonder therefore that there is next to no consensus in esthetic and moral theories. Since their subject-matter is totally segregated from that of science, since they are assigned to independent non-participating realms of existence, the only possible method of achieving agreement has been exiled in advance.

Practically this consequence is intolerable; accordingly it is rarely faced. "Standards" of value suddenly make their appearance to serve as criteria of taste and conscience. The distinction between likings and that which is worth liking, between the desired and the desirable, between the is and the ought, descends out of the blue. There are, it seems, immediate values, but there also are standard values, and the latter may be used to judge and measure immediate goods and bads. Thus the reflective distinction between the true and the false, the genuine and the spurious is brought upon the scene. In strict logic, however, it enters only to disappear. For if the standard is itself a value, then it is by definition only another name for the object of a particular liking, on the part of some particular subjective creature. If the liking for it conflicts with some other liking, the strongest wins. There is no question of false and true, of real and seeming, but only of stronger and weaker. The question of which one *should* be stronger is as meaningless as it would be in a cock-fight.

Such a conclusion puts an end to all attempt at consistency and organization and calls out in reaction an opposite theory. The "standard" is not, it is decided, for us at least, a good. It is rather a principle rationally apprehended. It is that which is "right" rather than that which is good; and since it is the right, it is the standard for judging all goods. If right is also good, the identification subsists in some transcendental realm; in some eternal, non-empirical realm of Being which is also a realm of values. The standard of good thus conceived as a principle of reason and as a form of supreme Being, is set over against the outside of actual desires, striving, satisfactions and frustrations. It ought to enter into their determination but for the most part it does not. The distinction between is and ought is one of kind, and a separation. It is not surprising that the wheel completes a full circle, and that the finale is a retort that the alleged standard is itself but another dignified disguise for some one's arbitrary liking—the *ipse dixit* of some one accidentally clothed with extraneous authority.

It is as irritating to have experience of beauty and moral goodness reduced to groundless whims as to have that of truth. Common sense has an inexpugnable conviction that there are immediate goods of enjoyment and conduct, and that there are principles by which they may be appraised and rectified. Common sense entertains this firm conviction because it is innocent of any rigid demarcation between knowledge on one side and belief, conduct and esthetic appreciation on the other. It is guiltless of the division between objective reality and subjective events. It takes striving, purposing, inquiring, wanting, the life of "practice," to be as much facts of nature as are the themes of scientific discourse; to it, indeed, the former has a more direct and urgent reality. Hence it has no difficulty with the idea of rational or objective criticism and rectification of immediate goods. If it were articulate, it would say that the same natural processes which generate goods and evils generate also the striving to secure the one and avoid the other, and generate judgments to regulate the strivings. Its weakness is that it fails to recognize that deliberate and systematized science is a precondition of adequate judgments and hence of adequate striving and adequate choice. Its organs of criticism are for the most part half-judgments, uncriticized products of custom, chance circumstance and vested interests. Hence common sense when it begins to reflect upon its own convictions easily falls a victim to traditional theories; and the vicious circle begins over again. It is sound as to the need and possibility of objective criticism of values, it is weak as to the method of accomplishing.

Yet all this time there is an example of the way out in the case of beliefs. There was a time when beliefs about external events were largely matters of what it was found immediately good to accept or reject; as far as there was a distinction made between the immediately good in belief and the real or true, it lay chiefly in the fact that the latter was the object sanctioned by authorities of church and state. Yet it is now all but commonplace that every belief-value must be subjected to criticism; in scientific undertakings, it is a commonplace that criticism does not depend upon reference to a transcendent standard truth. The distinction between an immediate belief-value, which is but a challenge to inquiry, and an eventual object of belief that concludes critical inquiry, and has the value of fulfilling the causal relationships discovered, is made in the course of intelligent experiment. The result is a distinction between the apparent and the real good. Gradually a reluctant world is persuaded that meanings so determined define what is good for acceptance and assertion. Meantime beliefs determined by passion, class-interest, routine and authority remain sufficiently prevalent to enforce the perception that it makes all the difference in the world in the value of a belief how its object is formed and arrived at. Thus the lesson is enforced that critical valuations of immediate goods proceed in terms of the generation and consequences of objects qualified with good.

In outward forms, experimental science is infinitely varied. In principle, it is simple. We know an object when we know how it is made, and we know how it is made in the degree in which we ourselves make it. Old tradition compels us to call thinking "mental." But "mental" thought is but partial experimentation, terminating in preliminary readjustments, confined within the organism. As long as thinking remained at this stage, it protected itself by regarding this introverted truncation as evidence of an immaterial reason superior to and independent of body. As long as thought was thus cooped up, overt action in the "outer" natural scene was inevitably shorn of its full meed of meaning; it was to that extent arbitrary and routine. When "outer" and "inner" activity came together in a single experimental operation, used as the only adequate method of discovery and proof, effective criticism, consistent and ordered valuation, emerged. Thought aligned itself with other arts that shape objects by informing things with meanings.

Psychology, which reflects the old dualistic separation of mind from nature, has made current the notion that the processes which terminate in knowledge fare forth from innocent sensory data, or from pure logical principles, or from both together, as original starting points and material. As a natural history of mind this notion is wholly mythological. All knowing and effort to know starts from some belief, some received and asserted meaning which is a deposit of prior experience, personal and communal. In every instance, from passing query to elaborate scientific undertaking, the art of knowing criticizes a belief which has passed current as genuine coin, with a view to its revision. It terminates when freer, richer and more secure objects of belief are instituted as goods of immediate acceptance. The operation is one of doing and making in the literal sense. Starting from one good, treated as apparent and questionable, and ending in another which is tested and substantiated, the final act of knowing is acceptance and intellectual appreciation of what is significantly conclusive.

Is there any reason for supposing that the situation is any different in the case of other values and valuations? Is there any intrinsic difference between the relation of scientific inquiry to belief-values, of esthetic criticism to esthetic values, and of moral judgments to moral goods? Is there any difference in logical method? If we adopt a current theory, and say that immediate values occur wherever there is liking, interest, bias, it is clear that this liking is an act, if not an overt one, at least a dispositional tendency and direction. But most likings, all likings in their first appearance, are blind and gross. They do not know what they are about nor why they attach themselves to this or that object. Moreover, every such act takes a risk and assumes a liability, and does so ignorantly. For there are always in existence rival claimants for liking. To prefer *this* is to exclude *that*. Any liking is choice, unwittingly performed. There is no selection without rejection; interest and bias are selective, preferential. To take this for a good is to declare in act, though not at first in thought, that it is better than something else. This decision is arbitrary, capricious, unreasoned because made without thought of the other object, and without comparison. To say that an object is a good may seem to be an absolute and intrinsic declaration particularly when the assertion is made in direct act rather than in thought. But when we recognize that in effect the assertion is that one thing is better than another thing, the issues shift to something comparative, relational, causal, intellectual and objective. *Immediately* nothing is better or worse than anything else; it is just what it is. Comparison is comparison of things, things in their efficacies, their promotions and hindrances. The better is that which will do more in the way of security, liberation and fecundity for other likings and values.

To make a valuation, to judge appraisingly, is then to bring to conscious perception relations of productivity and resistance and thus to make value significant, intelligent and intelligible. In becoming discriminately aware of the causal conditions of the object liked and preferred, we become aware of its eventual operations. If in the case of esthetic and moral goods, the causal conditions which reflection reveals as determinants of the good object are found to lie within organic constitution in greater degree than is the case with objects of belief, this finding is of enormous importance for the technique of critical judgment. But it does not modify the logic which obtains in knowledge of the relationship of values and valuations to each other. It indicates the particular subject-matter which has to be controlled and used in the conscious art of re-making goods. As inquiries which aim at knowledge start from pre-existent beliefs, so esthetic and moral criticism start from antecedent natural goods of contemplative enjoyment and social intercourse. Its purpose is to make it possible to like and choose knowingly and with meaning, instead of blindly. All criticism worthy of the title is but another name for that revealing discovery of conditions and consequences which enables liking, bias, interest to express themselves in responsible and informed ways instead of ignorantly and fatalistically.

The meaning of the theory advanced concerning the relationship of goods and criticism may be illustrated by ethical theory. Few I suppose would deny that in spite of the attention devoted to this subject by many minds of a high order of intention and intellectual equipment, the outcome, judged from the standpoint of scientific consensus, is rather dismaying. The outcome is due in part to the importance of the subject, its intimate connection with man's deepest concerns, with his most cherished traditions and with the most acutely perplexing problems of his contemporary social life. Objective detachment and development of adequate intellectual instruments are necessarily difficult under such conditions. But I think that we find, amid all the diversity, one common intellectual preconception which inevitably defers the possibility of attainment of scientific method. This is the assumption, implicit or overt, that moral theory is concerned with ends, values rather than with criticism of ends and values; the latter being in fact not only independent of moral theory but not themselves having even moral quality. To discover and define once for all the *bonum* and the *summum bonum* in a way which rationally subserves all virtues and duties, is the traditional task of morals; to deny that moral theory has any such office will seem to many equivalent to denial of the possibility of moral philosophy. Yet in other things repeated failure of achievement is regarded as evidence that we are going at the affair in a wrong way. And to a mind willing to surrender the traditional preconception, failure to achieve consensus in method and even in generic conclusions in morals as a branch of philosophy may be similarly explained.

It is not meant of course that the tradition assumes that the good and the highest good are created by moral theory. The assumption is not so bad as that; it is to the effect that it is the province of moral theory to reveal moral goods; to bring them to consciousness and to enforce their character in perception. As empirical fact, however, the arts, those of converse and the literary arts which are the enhanced continuations of social converse, have been the means by which goods are brought home to human perception. The writings of moralists have been efficacious in this direction upon the whole not in their professed intent as theoretical doctrines, but in as far as they have genially participated in the arts of poetry, fiction, parable and drama. Conversion into doctrinal teachings of the imaginative relations of life with which great moral artists have dowered humanity has been the great cause of their ossification into harsh dogmas; illuminating insight into the relations and goods of life has been lost, and an arbitrary code of precepts and rules substituted. Direct appeal of experience concentrated, vivified and intensified by the insight of an artist and embodied in literary creations similar in kind to the revelation of meanings which is the work of any artist, has been treated as a discovery and definition of things true to scientific or philosophic reason.

Meantime the work which theoretical criticism might do has not been done; namely, discovery of the conditions and consequences, the existential relations, of goods which are accepted as goods not because of theory but because they are such in experience. The cause in large measure is doubtless because the prerequisite tools of physics, physiology and economics were not at hand. But now when these potential instrumentalities are more adequately prepared they will not be employed until it is recognized that the business of moral theory is not at all with consummations and goods as such, but with discovery of the conditions and consequences of their appearance, a work which is factual and analytic, not dialectic, hortatory, nor prescriptive. The argument does not forget that there have been would-be naturalistic and empirical ethics which have asserted that goods are such prior to moral conduct as well as to moral theory, and that they become moral only when employed in conduct as objects of reflective choice and endeavor. But the apparent exception proves the rule. For these forms of moral theory while releasing morals from the obligation of telling man what goods are, leaving that office to life itself, have failed to note that the office of moral philosophy is criticism; and that the performance of this office by discovery of existential conditions and consequences involves a qualitative transformation, a re-making in subsequent action which experimentally tests the conclusions of theory.

Therefore like the Aristotelian ethics, they have been dialectic, defining and classifying in hierarchical order antecedent goods and terminating in a notion of *the* good, the *summum bonum*; or, like hedonistic ethics, they have made a dialectic abstraction of a feature of concrete goods, their pleasantness; and instead of providing a method of analysis of concrete situations have laid down rules of calculation and prescribed policies to be pursued as fixed, not intellectually experimental, results of prior calculations. When they were, like Jeremy Bentham, persons of human sensitiveness to evils from which men suffer in virtue of institutions which may be altered; or, like John Stuart Mill, of genial insight into the constituents of a liberal and humane happiness, they have stirred their generation to beneficent action. But the connection between their theories and the practical outcome was adventitious; their ideas operated when all is said and done as literary rather than as scientific apparatus, as much so as in the case of reforms to which Charles Dickens not meanly contributed.

The implications of the position which has been taken import a "practical" element into philosophy as effective and verifiable criticism, obnoxious to the traditional view. Yet if man is within nature, not a little god outside, and is within as a mode of energy inseparably connected with other modes, interaction is the one unescapable trait of every human concern; thinking, even philosophic thinking, is not exempt. This interaction is subject to partiality because the human factor has bent and bias. But partiality is not obnoxious just because it is partial. A world characterized by qualitative histories with their own beginnings, directions and terminations is of necessity a world in which any interaction is intensive change—a world of partialities, particulars. What is obnoxious in partiality is due to the illusion that there are states and acts which are not also interactions. Immature and undisciplined mind believes in actions which have their seat and source in a particular and separate being, from which they issue. This is the very belief which the advance of intelligent criticism destroys. The latter transforms the notion of isolated one-sided acts into acknowledged interactions. The view which isolates knowledge, contemplation, liking, interest, value, or whatever from action is itself a survival of the notion that there are things which can exist and be known apart from active connection with other things.

When man finds he is not a little god in his active powers and accomplishments, he retains his former conceit by hugging to his bosom the notion that nevertheless in some realm, be it knowledge or esthetic contemplation, he is still outside of and detached from the ongoing sweep of inter-acting and changing events; and being there alone and irresponsible save to himself, is as a god. When he perceives clearly and adequately that he is within nature, a part of its interactions, he sees that the line to be drawn is not between action and thought, or action and appreciation, but between blind, slavish, meaningless action and action that is free, significant, directed and responsible. Knowledge, like the growth of a plant and the movement of the earth, is a mode of interaction; but it is a mode which renders other modes luminous, important, valuable, capable of direction, causes being translated into means and effects into consequences.

All reason which is itself reasoned, is thus method, not substance; operative, not "end in itself." To imagine it the latter is to transport it outside the natural world, to convert it into a god, whether a big and original one or a little and derived one, outside of the contingencies of existence and untouched by its vicissitudes. This is the meaning of the "reason" which is alleged to envisage reality *sub specie aeternitatis*. It is indeed true that all relations, all universals and laws as such are timeless. Even an order of time as an order is timeless, for it is relational. But to give irrelevancy to time the name of eternal in an eulogistic sense, is but to proclaim that irrelevancy to any existence forms a higher kind of existence. Orders, relations, universals are significant and invaluable as objects of knowledge. They are so because they apply to intensive and extensive, individualized, existences; to things of spacious and temporal qualities. Application is not for the sake of something extraneous, for the sake of something designated an utility. It is for the sake of the laws, principles, ideals. Had they not been detached for the purpose of application, they would not have meaning; intent and potentiality of application in the course of events lends them all their significance. Without *actuality* of application, without effort to realize their intent, they are meanings, but they possess neither truth nor falsity, since without application they have no bearing and test. Thus they cease to be objects of knowledge, or even reflection; and become detached objects of contemplation. They may then have the esthetic value possessed by the objects of a dream. But after all we have not left temporal experience, human desire, liking, and passion behind or below us. We have merely painted nature with the colors of an all too local and transitory flight from the hardships of life. These eternal objects abstracted from the course of events, although labeled Reality, in opposition to Appearance, are in truth but the idlest and most evanescent of appearances, born of personal craving and shaped by private fantasy.

Because intelligence is critical method applied to goods of belief, appreciation and conduct, so as to construct freer and more secure goods, turning assent and assertion into free communication of shareable meanings, turning feeling into ordered and liberal sense, turning reaction into response, it is the reasonable object of our deepest faith and loyalty, the stay and support of all reasonable hopes. To utter such a statement is not to indulge in romantic idealization. It is not to assert that intelligence will ever dominate the course of events; it is not even to imply that it will save from ruin and destruction. The issue is one of choice, and choice is always a question of alternatives. What the method of intelligence, thoughtful valuation will accomplish, if once it be tried, is for the result of trial to determine. Since it is relative to the intersection in existence of hazard and rule, of contingency and order, faith in a wholesale and final triumph is fantastic. But some procedure has to be tried; for life is itself a sequence of trials. Carelessness and routine, Olympian aloofness, secluded contemplation are themselves choices. To claim that intelligence is a better method than its alternatives, authority, imitation, caprice and ignorance, prejudice and passion, is hardly an excessive claim. These procedures have been tried and have worked their will. The result is not such as to make it clear that the method of intelligence, the use of science in criticizing and re-creating the casual goods of nature into intentional and conclusive goods of art, the union of knowledge and values in production, is not worth trying. There may be those to whom it is treason to think of philosophy as the critical method of developing methods of criticism. But this conception of philosophy also waits to be tried, and the trial which shall approve or condemn lies in the eventual issue. The import of such knowledge as we have acquired and such experience as has been quickened by thought is to evoke and justify the trial.

Appendixes

Appendix 1
The Unfinished Introduction

Editor's Note

In October 1948 Dewey finished his extensive Introduction to a reissue of *Reconstruction in Philosophy*. Shortly thereafter he turned to the task of writing a similar Introduction to a reissue of *Experience and Nature*. Early in July 1949, I received the first installment of Dewey's manuscript, densely corrected by hand and typewriter. Within a day or two I returned a clean copy. By the end of July, I received two revisions of parts of the first installment and two additional installments. The revisions were more than editorial; they were reworkings resulting in new versions, even the repetitions significantly modified by contextual changes. By the end of August, the manuscript totaled over one hundred pages of clean double-spaced copy.

The Introduction was unfinished in three respects; it had a beginning but no ending, and the material, besides having divergent repetitions, was fragmented and necessarily deficiently coordinated; secondly, there were promises to deal more extensively with this and that topic that remained promises; and finally, there were notices and outlines of new topics which Dewey never got around to at all. The unfinished Introduction projected a grand design—a philosophical interpretation of the history of Western man. Dewey's original intention was to write such a book after he finished the Introduction. But the idea of the book was too compelling to be effectively postponed: it forced its way into the writing of the Introduction.

In editing the manuscript I have concentrated on Dewey's ideas, including only a minimum of the historical material. The ideas are organized, as far as possible, to reveal their interrelationships in Dewey's thought but I have not tried to fill in or obscure whatever gaps there are in Dewey's unfinished work.

While keeping Dewey's meaning intact, I have been obliged to transpose, rearrange, prune, cut up and splice Dewey's text. I have not felt obliged to call attention to my editorial effort by the conventional devices.

JOSEPH RATNER

Experience and Nature: A Re-Introduction

Twenty-five years of crucially important history have elapsed since the lectures that became the basis of this volume were delivered. The impact of history is particularly crucial upon the philosophical problem which is pointed to in the title of the volume and upon the themes discussed in the text. It is obvious that the views entertained in philosophy about Nature must be profoundly affected by developments in natural science. Virtually within the short period of a quarter of a century, the change in natural science is the greatest that has occurred since the appearance of Newton's *Principia*. Upon the side of human affairs, concerns, values and outlook (designated "experience" in the title and text) disturbances are taking place which are sufficiently extensive and profound as to threaten what, in the hopes of some and in the fears of others, is an overturn in the entire structure of the old and supposedly firmly established order. How do the positions set forth in the text stand, especially how do they stand *up*, when they are re-viewed in the light of the present situation in the science of nature and the human estate?

The fact that the second edition of *Experience and Nature* is reprinted unchanged may be taken as evidence that its author does not find anything in the text which is seriously incompatible with what he would find it necessary to say were it written today. But he also finds that the direction taken by intervening events places the positions taken a quarter of a century ago in a larger context than it was possible to envisage at that time. This Introduction will be devoted to an exposition of that larger context.

II.

When the text was written one of the features that distinguished it was its use of "experience"; "experience" was asserted to be *of* the natural world in the most pregnant sense; it was employed to stand for every actual and every possible way in which man, himself a part of nature, has dealings with all other aspects and phases of nature, including man's delusions, errors and daydreams, as well as his useful and fine arts; his discoveries and inventions; his tested and approved knowings. "Experience" is a word used to designate, in a summary fashion, the complex of all which is distinctively human.

The events in science and in the ordering and disordering of human life that have occurred in the intervening years have indicated that while "experience" is a fitting name for the special way in which man, at least in the Western world, has shaped his participations in and dealings with nature, its peculiarly distinctive application may be said to lie within the cultures that have followed from, and mark the break with, the medieval period. This limitation of the expression "experience and nature" is overcome by the more generalized statement that the *standing problem* of Western philosophy throughout its entire history has been the connection-and-distinction of what on one side is regarded as *human* and on the other side as *natural.*

Something will be said later as to the appropriateness of "experience" in denoting what is distinctive of the spirit of the post-medieval period. The indefiniteness of the word as a name is part of that fitness. The reference of experience is not to be pinned down to any narrow and limited meaning; and, as we shall see in the course of later discussion, the attempt in philosophy to hold it down to an aspect that at its very best is but a highly specialized cross-section of experience is a main reason why the philosophy of the period finally got out of touch with the moving spirit of the very events it supposedly was concerned with.

Before expanding upon this point it is proper to note that to regard "experience" as a name that is especially suited to apply to the human phase of philosophic subject-matter in its relation to the natural phase in a particular cultural period and age entails the recognition of philosophy's variability in different cultural eras and areas. This point of view stands in sharp opposition to an assumption about philosophy which is often made.

To hold that the scope of philosophy is comprehensive, inclusive, in the sense that philosophy, whatever the time and place, is always concerned with the connection-and-distinction of the human and the natural, is in effect to deny that it is comprehensive in the sense that it is identical in content at all times and places. It is to deny that the scope of philosophy can be stated in terms once for all as it could be if philosophy were independent of time and place; if, in words made familiar in traditional philosophy, its subject-matter were eternal, immutable and universal, and hence entirely unaffected by the changes in human events, including those that occur in the science of nature as well as in other cultural activities and conditions, esthetic, industrial, political, etc.

The assumption that "experience" has an inherent meaning which provides a sure standard of judgment by which to determine the status of everything else is, as we shall see in later discussion, one of the things that rendered the philosophies purporting to be philosophies of experience so unable to deal effectively with experience that they eventually lost both intrinsic vitality and extrinsic popular esteem.

It is also appropriate at this point to call attention to the fact that although the Nineteenth Century was par excellence the period in which definitive discovery was made of the comprehensive scope of history, culminating in the inclusion in history of plant and animal *species* (which had been considered immutable), nevertheless philosophers failed, to a very large extent, to learn the lesson the discovery taught.

Before leaving the theme of the necessary historical variation of the *content* of the problems comprehensive enough to be those of philosophy, I would call attention to the common tendency of philosophers, who nominally believe that the concern of philosophy is with the comprehensive in the sense of the eternal and the universally identical or uniform, to dodge the inconvenient fact that variation has extended so far that the controversial and polemic nature of philosophy and the failure of representatives of opposed doctrinal schools to reach agreement are among the great causes of the general loss of esteem that philosophy is progressively undergoing. Furthermore there is something intrinsically pretentious in philosophy's claim to deal with what transcends time and space while progress is continuously made in natural science in dealing with temporal and spatial subjects. Those who are sympathetically concerned with philosophy have every reason for anxiety.

The position here taken does not of course make the controversial state of philosophical schools a highly creditable matter but it makes the course of philosophy more significant and instructive for it discloses that philosophy is a highly generalized handling of human problems in connection with their setting in nature as nature is understood at a given time. Consequently, diversity of proposed solutions of issues of such range and depth is not only to be expected but when interpreted in historical-cultural context provides an increase in the resources at our disposal. It is surely instructive to note that as a rule problems once central in philosophy fade in importance, that they are *dissolved* with respect to actuality rather than *solved* with respect to validity in the universal and eternal scheme of things. What we validly know seems to indicate that process, if anything, is what is "universal."

III.

I am fortunate in being able to locate the cultural historic period and geographical area in which my use of "experience" is warranted by means of a quotation from a historian whose insight is as penetrating as his learning is comprehensive. I refer to Lord Acton who, in his inaugural address on assuming the professorship of history at the University of Cambridge, used the following words: "I describe as modern history that which begins four hundred years ago, which is marked off by an evident and intelligible line from the time immediately preceding, and displays in its course specific and distinctive characteristics of its own. The modern age did not proceed from mediaeval by normal succession, with outward tokens of legitimate descent. Unheralded, it founded a new order of things, under a law of innovation, sapping the ancient reign of continuity. In those days Columbus subverted the notions of the world, and reversed the conditions of production, wealth, and power; in those days Machiavelli released government from the restraint of law; Erasmus diverted the current of ancient learning from profane into Christian channels; Luther broke the chain of authority and tradition at the strongest link; and Copernicus erected an invincible power that set forever the mark of progress upon the time that was to come. There is the same unbound originality and disregard for inherited sanctions in the rare philosophers as in the discovery of Divine Right, and the intruding Imperialism of Rome. The like effects are visible everywhere, and one generation beheld them all. It was an awakening of new life; the world revolved in a different orbit, determined by influences unknown before. . . . The sixteenth century went forth *armed for untried experience,* and ready to watch with hopefulness a *prospect of incalculable change.*"[1]

It is gilding refined gold to comment upon special portions of the marvellous survey that is condensed into the brief statement just cited. But I cannot refrain from calling attention away from the conventionally recognized geographical feat accomplished by Columbus to the revolution thereby effected in commerce and consequently in political and economic orders. Nor is the grouping together of the rise of Divine Right of Kings with the new Imperialistic policies of Rome as two aspects of the same tendency the conventionally current idea, while what is said about the work of Erasmus throws more light upon what the Renaissance did in preparing for the Reformation than does many a historical treatise. If the statement about the work of Copernicus in invincibly setting "the mark of progress" upon the time to come seems to date the statement as an expression of the optimism prevailing before the advent of two world wars, that impression is corrected by proper attention to the phrase "incalculable change" that I have taken the liberty of italicizing; for the heart of the new era initiated by the events Lord Acton mentioned is precisely the movement away from the fixities that were taken to be the necessary conditions of stability and order towards the release of processes of change tending to the unforeseen and the unpredictable.

1. *Essays on Freedom and Power,* selected and with an introduction by Gertrude Himmelfarb (Boston: Beacon Press, 1948), pages 5–6. Italics mine. The lecture from which the quoted passages are extracted was entitled "The Study of History" and was delivered in 1895.

The other phrase that I have made emphatic by use of italics, "armed for untried experience," may be taken without violence or distortion of its import as the text of what follows. In the centuries before the time dealt with by Lord Acton *"untried experience"* would have been absurd, a contradiction in terms. For the method and subject-matter named by the word "experience" had been identified during at least fifteen centuries of European history with the *empirical* in a sense indicated in the following quotation from the Oxford Dictionary: "Of a remedy or rule of treatment, etc., that is adopted because found (or believed) to have been successful in practice, the reason for its efficacy being unknown." While the definition quoted refers specifically to medical practice, it reveals in a highly instructive way the entire view taken of experience up to the time of the revolution in natural science. For "experience" as empirical had to do only with "practical" matters in a sense in which *practice* was held to be completely isolated from *theory* and could be at its very best (as expressly stated by Aristotle) an unintended and rationally unguided outcome of an accumulation of *ad hoc* activities which were so frequently repeated that it formed a practically useful habit. Furthermore, in accordance with Aristotle's idea of the formal cause, the way in which the habit was produced determined its status and function in "knowledge." It was produced without any aid or direction that was rational or reasonable and consequently could not be or promote any rational understanding, which is what knowledge or science is.

With the change of which Galileo's experiments with falling bodies are typically representative, "experience" was completely transformed in character and function. The empirical became the experimental. The *source* of knowledge is found (i) in the consequences *to be* brought into existence; (ii) in the activities which are deliberately shaped and constituted, neither on the basis of habits formed in the past nor by power of "pure thought" but by reflection upon materials and their possibilities as constituents in a plan of action which when carried out will be useful in discovering new[2] materials and/or methods that will enlarge or correct what had been previously regarded as knowledge; (iii) the plan of action is tentative and hypothetical; its validity is *not*

---

2. Rhetorically the word "new" is pleonastic, but it may serve to draw attention to what is involved in "discovery."

known; its outcome is *not* known; and for these very reasons the hypothesis or hypothetical construction is useful in evoking and directing overt activities of making and doing which bring to light—that is, disclose to observation—new materials and processes which are in turn used in initiating and directing further undertakings of inquiry. To get a vivid sense of the difference between "empirical" as it was understood before Galileo and "experimental" as it has become known since Galileo, one need only compare the state of knowledge four hundred years ago when the "modern age" began with the state of knowledge today. The difference is not merely quantitative, but qualitative. Knowing-inquiring is a going concern of indefinitely expanding range and depth.

IV.

Revolutions in the formal organization of human relationships are much easier to effect than revolutions in the hearts and minds of men. Those who have from infancy drawn their intellectual and moral sustenance from the institutional conditions into which they were born and by the necessities of the case have not known any other do not change their desires and convictions when governments topple and new laws are enacted. Habituations to the old persist long after the old has changed its form. Ways of observing, of communicating, of prizing and disapproving are engrained in character and are neither thrown off nor greatly modified by what are deemed revolutions by those who record the course of history. Only when revolutionary changes are the consummation of actual moral and intellectual changes are their consequences free from internal divisions; but it is not often if ever that more than a minority of those affected by a revolution will have already undergone changes in personal outlook and deep-seated conviction that are consonant with the aims and interests of the revolution. Habits of belief are even tougher than habits of overt action. The changes that constitute the passage of the institutional organization of the medieval period into that of the modern are so extensive in range and so intense in quality that they would have plunged the peoples into chaos if they had not carried their old habitudes over into their dealings with the new. But salvation from chaos is not salvation from inner division, from the confusion and conflict that inevitably attend attraction and attempted movement in opposite directions.

The obvious manifestation of the incompatibility that penetrated to the depths of the transition that constitutes the period called modern is what is known as The Warfare of Science and Religion. But the events which are recorded in the history of this particular division and conflict in the struggle of the old to give birth to the new is in fact incidental, almost episodic, in the deeper civil or internal war that has continued for centuries; to name a few outstanding events of that war: the conflict of church and state, of rulers and subjects, of aristocracy and bourgeoisie, of bourgeoisie and proletariat, of employers and employed. And in multitudes of human beings the conflict took the form of an uneasy half-recognized and half-concealed confusion that the standards and principles which were taught to be ideal and spiritual pointed one way while everyday interests and occupations that were considered worldly and secular pulled vigorously in the opposite direction. Ambivalence of this sort in personal life is subtle and Protean. In the social arena, it is quite easily identified, "spotted" one may say with verbal propriety, in the large-scale compromises that are rife between success in business and adherence to acknowledged moral obligations, between private and public integrity. There are also the other accommodations and adaptations which are dilutions of the older out-and-out warfare of the sacred and the secular—the compromises and reciprocal accommodations which it now sometimes seems to be the chief office of current institutions to maintain.

Our concern here is with the ambivalence as it is reflected in the philosophies that reflect the doubleness, the unintended but inevitable intellectual duplicity, that marks the unanticipated and unprepared-for change from an order that had prevailed till a few short centuries ago in every variety of life that ranked as civilized to one of which now the most that can be said is that it is in process of change but no one knows toward just what.

V.

In classic philosophy, both the cosmos and knowledge were linked in two radically different grades or ranks. Cosmologically, the low kind was of things and affairs which sometimes are and sometimes are not; they are shown thereby not to have Being on their own account, to be dependent on that which is external to them; in sum their occurrence is inherently contingent instead of necessary. It follows, on the assumption of complete correspondence between grade of Being and grade of knowing, that the organ and operation of apprehension is low with respect to low things; the very lowest of organs and operations of the lowest is sensation. Knowledge of things which usually, upon the whole, but not always, are such and such is empirical knowledge. At the other end of the scale of the cosmos is Being which is perfect, complete in itself, having no dependence on anything outside its own self-sustaining existence; hence it is immutable, changeless in time and universal, everywhere the same, and in that sense without location. With respect to knowing, science is in one-to-one correspondence with Being in this supreme and final sense.

If there were a word completely antithetical to "one-to-one correspondence," a word that expressed difference carried to the extreme of outright opposition, that word would apply to science as now conducted and understood. In classic Greek-medieval theory science is of that, and *only* of that, which so transcends space and time as to be unaffected by differences of place and date. In modern practice, natural science has to do inclusively and exclusively with events, existences having specifiable space-time connections with one another; particulars are scientifically known when they are *specifically* located and dated in a system of interconnected events. Again science in the classic scheme was of fixed *natures* in a sense in which the nature of a thing is the essence by virtue of which it is always and everywhere *what* it is. Because of the connection of science with essence and with essence alone or exclusively, all classic scientific knowledge was taxonomic—it classified things into fixed, static kinds or species according to the unchangeable Being of each kind. To cap the climax of anti-correspondence, scientific knowing today substitutes for the isolation between species or kinds demanded in the classic scheme a continuity which so intimately binds together all the members of scientific subject-matter that reflection or inference can travel freely from any one to any other without being balked.

In the Greek theory "a sensation" was the medium and organ of knowing that the sensible and sensations are proverbially fleeting. Greek scientific knowing was of the universal; sensation or sense-perception was of the particular—a stone, a bug or whatever—in its particularity. In the present conduct of natural science, sense-perception is doubly involved in scientific knowing of nature, although not of itself constituting such knowing. Sense-perception is indispensable in the occurrence of a problem as the occasion of scientific knowing. Sense-perception is also indispensable in the testing of the proposed solution of the problem.

The revolutionary change-over from the Greek to the modern method of scientific knowing was effected by the modern use of experiment. Experiment—the indispensable instrument of modern scientific knowing—is the art of conducting a sequence of observations in which natural conditions are intentionally altered and controlled in ways which will disclose, discover, natural subject-matters which would not otherwise have been noted. Noting the latter is a *sine qua non* of determining the problem to be investigated and of testing any general principles or theory entertained concerning the state of facts. Theory thereby lost, once and forever as far as concerns the conduct of scientific knowing, the Greek status of finality and acquired the modern status and office of a working hypothesis. The Greek view of theory had stood obstinately and obstructively in the way of the development of systematic understanding of the events of the natural world.

The experimental method of scientific inquiry broke down the wall that had been erected between theory and practice. Knowing was not Theoria, the contemplation of pure and complete Being, free from even the slightest trace of "practical" activity. Knowing involved some kind of doing and making. It turned away from immutability toward process, change. It turned from the past toward the future, from precedents to consequences; from isolation to continuity; from laws imposed upon particulars to connections through which particulars became interchangeable parts of a whole ever-extending its spatio-temporal range.

Human beings cannot transfer their point of view over from the immutable to an orbit of innovating change of which neither the scope nor the direction could be figured in advance without involving themselves in all sorts of deviations, backslidings and movements in opposite directions. Hence the incompatibilities and the distractions, the confusions and conflicts, the uncertain tackings to and fro, of the past few centuries, and hence the ambivalent character of the philosophies sympathetic to the new but for that very reason caught in the relatively undirected ebb and flow of its tides.

VI.

What has been said about sensation, sense-perception and theory raises the question: what is the nature of the kind of thinking designated as reflective?

The implication of the traditional view is rarely explicitly stated. The basic implication or underlying assumption is that there is a unique organ, faculty, agency, kind of activity which engages in reflection. In the case of everyday activities, in the area of commonsense knowings, it will probably be generally admitted that what is called reflective thinking is concerned with issues and problems that have to do with determining ends to be pursued on the one hand, and on the other hand with selecting the means and arranging the sequence of means for attaining the ends with maximum ease and minimum waste. If this is not admitted, it, at any rate, sets forth the postulate of the present discussion.

In the everyday cases of going over matters reflectively, in deliberating about alternative means-consequences (or consequences-means), reflection has to do with *practical* issues in the sense of being concerned with things to be done, *facienda*, in the ongoing course of one's life-activity. The office reflection is called upon to perform demands looking-into-the-probable-future-in-connection-with-surveying-the-actual-past. During this reflection every shift in an end proposed requires an adaptive shift in that aspect of reflective behavior which surveys past experiences of doing and suffering.

If in the reflective survey one happens to think of something that was conspicuously successful under somewhat similar conditions in the past, its presence in reflection may bring about a very great change in the end entertained and tentatively proposed.

The word "happens" is used intentionally. One who is expert or practiced in reflection is usually able to set his mind firmly on the practical issue that calls out reflection, and the accompanying emotive quality of the issues urges going over future possibilities and past actualities in their means-consequence connections. But he cannot by an act of "will" decide just what conditions or ends-in-view to summon. That is a matter of his already formed mechanisms or disposition—usually termed in psychological literature "associations" but also often placed in opposition to reflection instead of being recognized as the mechanism or apparatus by which reflection goes on. And while I am on the topic I add with no attempt at development that language, namings already in use supply the apparatus or mechanism by which elements of *past-future* present themselves in reflections which are, in respect to time, affairs of the *present*.

The conclusion in behalf of which the immediately foregoing considerations are advanced is two-fold. Negatively it shows the gratuitous futility of appealing to some special "mental" organ or capacity to account for reflective activity. It is literally reflective in that it *turns back* to go over (sometimes over *and* over) one's past experiences, whether obtained directly or through the media of conversation and reading, so as to find facts that are relevant to the specific *faciendum* that is the occasion of reflection: therefore (so the present writer holds) it is hardly possible to exaggerate the applicability of the expression "going over" or the semi-slang expression "*giving* it a good going-over." The subject-matter is there for whatever it is worth; what is *not* there is its *bearing* upon the specific means-consequence, consequence-means relation that has to be determined if the behavior is to be intelligent.

VII.

How are scientific knowings and knowns related to those of common sense?

The bringing-up, the rearing, the out-of-school education of every normally equipped human being consists, from infancy through life, in learning what to do and how to do it in situations of doing and enjoying. Compared to scientific knowing, the distinguishing feature of common sense, everyday kind of knowing, is that it is specific.

The kind of specificity involved is linguistically expressed by delimiting terms. The activities are pinned down to *this, that* and *the other*; they are further pinned down by specific references to date (*now, then, not yet*) and to place (*here, there, yonder*). These delimiting linguistic specificities reduce to their bare bones or, if one prefers, to their fighting weight, the chronological and geographical information necessary to establish the spatio-temporal location and connections of the commonsense activities involved.

In contrast, scientific language is completely neutral. It is intended to apply to events whenever and wherever they occur. It is as exempt from references to B.C. and A.D. as historical and biographical statements are attentive to them. What happened in some remote geological aeon is as if it happened five minutes ago. What takes place in some remote astronomical galaxy is as if it were taking place next door. To state the matter summarily, scientific language is a code by means of which that which happens at any specified place and time is capable of translation into what happens at other places and times. Science transcends local events and existences *as far as* it is able to treat space-time as one locale.

Theoretically, the "as far as" of the last sentence admits no exception. Actually, or as a matter of fact, it is limited by the range and/or scope of the practical means developed and at command. The import of this statement may be gathered from a consideration of the relationship that the practical or doing-making aspects and the intellectual or theoretical aspects of knowing sustain to each other in the case of commonsense and scientific knowings.

In commonsense knowing the knowing is for the sake of the *faciendum*; in scientific knowing the reverse is the case. Not that it does not entail plenty of doing and making. The scientific laboratory is not a rhetorical flourish; it is a working place devised and used for the sake of knowing. But just as the doing-making in commonsense knowing is limited by the amount and kind of knowns at disposal, so the extent to which interchange

- and transmutation can be achieved in scientific knowing is limited by the extent and refinement of the practical operations of laboratory instruments and other apparatus and techniques at command. In industry, there is no *a priori* limit set to conversion of raw material into finished goods for consumption and enjoyment; limits are not set by anything inherent and immutable in the "nature" of the materials involved; the limits are the limitations of technological equipment and operations, which are to be overcome by invention and advance in technological procedures and processes. Correspondingly, difficulties and obstructions encountered in natural science are "practical" and are tackled and overcome by experimentation with and upon experimental techniques and materials.

Commonsense knowing is enmeshed in the individual situation. Scientific knowing liberates itself from the individual situation and its pressing practicality. This liberation does not destroy the practical possibilities of scientific knowing; it is the very source of its practical power. Aloofness from immediate practical use provides the occasion and opportunity for employment of experimental operations for knowing as knowing which terminate in an extension of practically useful commonsense, everyday activities, once literally incredible.

As I have said, everyday knowings are concerned with *facienda*, with things to be done and/or made; with things necessary for making a livelihood; with meeting emergencies as they arise and taking advantage of opportunities as they offer themselves; fulfilling all manner of obligations; evading and surmounting obstacles; helping and being helped by one's friends; getting ahead of or making terms with one's rivals; ways of adding to the conveniences and delectations of life, and so on and so on, indefinitely in situations which supply an inexhaustible fund of material for dramas, novels, histories, biographies, day-dreaming.

The liberation of scientific knowing has been facilitated by and deepened and broadened because of the creation of a special language, indeed, to speak more exactly, of many special languages. On the other hand, for all everyday doing-enjoying, everyday language suffices. Compare, for example, the water of everyday use and language with that of H_2O. Our everyday use of water is limited by our commonsense knowledge that solid, liquid and gaseous conditions constitute its range of possible transformations.

Extensive as are the uses-enjoyments thereby ensured they are very limited as compared with the fact that H_2O and every other compound have common denominators and, accordingly, are in theory indefinitely transformable into one another, the hindrances to transformability being (as has been indicated) of a practical nature. This view is perhaps most clearly warranted by recent scientific progress. It has now been shown that what holds of compounds holds also of "elements." They were for such a long time held to be ultimate and hence immutable, but now in theoretical-experimental promise they also are reciprocally inter-convertible. What is intellectually a most highly instructive aspect of the whole matter is that the discovery of indefinitely extensive translatability was arrived at not by set intention but as a consequence of experimental inquiries in pursuit of other hypotheses. Similarly, recent experimental scientific inquiry has transformed what were previously independent, isolated "special" sciences into an interconnected series constituting an increasingly fluid, traversable continuum.

The radical unlikeness of scientific and commonsense knowledge is held to be a great "problem" of philosophy. Philosophers seriously maintain that solution of the "problem" compels making a thoroughgoing cosmic distinction between a world of mere "appearance" and a world of "reality" even though to arrive at "reality" we must start from, and move along and ahead by, indications received from the world of mere "appearance."

How can we account for the extraordinary doctrine that to reach reality we must first give full faith and credit to what is condemned as illusory? I do not know what the accounting can be if it is not the assumption that only the immutable, universal and eternal can be truly known. For unless that assumption is indulged in, the explanation of the difference between scientific and commonsense knowing is so simple as to stare us in the face. Commonsense knowing has to do with the concerns of living; and nowadays living in an environment pervaded by the activities and consequences of scientific knowing involves a wide-ranging, diversified network of communications. Articulate speech, written and printed words, indeed everything that happens may become a sign speaking to us as evidence of something else where scientific inquiry has taken it out of its specific, com-monsense spatial-temporal setting. The remoteness of the for-mulae of physical science from the subject-matters that are known in one kind or another of use-enjoyment—the charac-teristic of all commonsense knowing—does not remain in iso-lated remoteness. For centuries rather directly and today actually as a matter of course they are followed by inventions providing various levels, degrees and kinds of use-enjoyment. It is a com-monplace that the age of machinery is now passing into the age of power.

In the classic tradition, the difference between science and everyday experience is not one of degree but of absolute kind. Ironically enough, modern scientific knowing establishes its superiority to commonsense knowing in the very respect for which the latter is disparaged by classic traditionalists. It is pre-cisely in respect to practicality, to utility, that scientific knowings and knowns are superior to those of everyday common sense. By subordinating theory to experimental practice, by liberating knowing from immediate concern with practical gain, what needed to be done for maintaining and enriching human life was widely accomplished. Since it is human life that is sustained and enhanced by this modern scientific mode of knowing, the lives of the most highly civilized men, artists as well as artisans, of the wisest statesmen as well as of ditch diggers, are the beneficiaries. Only the age-old snobbishness of a professionally leisure class puts the practical and useful in bondage to the servile and me-nial.

VIII.

Since the theme of this Re-Introduction is particularly concerned with the philosophical mirroring of the cultural tran-sition from Greek-medieval to modern, we must consider how philosophic systems carried over into their generalized accounts of the new the very assumption which was formulated in the older systems. What I have in mind is the fact that devotion to the immutable and hence to that which could not be affected by the tooth of time nor be hemmed in by any spatial location led the philosophers in sympathy with the new to feel that they could strengthen it by providing an underpinning of the eternal and universal.

I select for special discussion an instance which is intimately and pervasively bound up with the early history of the new physical science. I refer to the incompatible mixture of old and new in the scientific status and role given to matter, motion and quantitative measurement. With regard to their position and office in the scientific knowing of nature the new is profoundly revolutionary. From a strictly historical point of view the mixture of the revolutionary new with the old may have been inevitable; from the vantage point of the present development of physical science it appears so curiously out of the way as to be almost incredible.

In the Greek-medieval cosmological-ontological scheme, matter, motion and quantitative measurement held the lowest, literally the basest, place in the hierarchical gradation of both natural existence and ways of knowing. Matter was totally without character; it had no nature of its own—the *sine qua non* of any kind of knowledge. Matter itself was incapable of being known not only in a scientific way but even by means of "sensation" until it had received by contingent concurrence of external circumstances some form of particular perishable existence or particular transitory event. Since science was of Being, self-active and self-sustaining, independent of contingencies, self-identical or universal eternally and immutably, nothing in terms of the classic scheme could be more self-contradictory, intellectually more absurd, than a science of matter.

Only a few short centuries ago, the revolution in physical science established matter as a "substance" in its own right. It became a "substance" in the old cosmological-ontological sense—self-sustaining in its solidity and self-identical through all its incessant "sensible" changes. The new physical science measured the direction and extent of motion quantitatively; the measurements implicitly had the status of the immutable by assumption of necessary recurrence of identical conditions of motion. The revolution in treatment of motion was as total as in the case of matter because in the Greek-medieval scheme motion was a mode of change, change was by its very nature infected with lack of Being and hence incapable of scientific knowing. Furthermore, in the old scheme, quantity was merely an "accident" of substance (in the ancient meaning of "accident"); quantities were contingent variations that did not affect the form and essence of a substance. Measurement in its modern sense and "measure" in its ancient sense are fundamentally different in kind. Measure was the well-proportioned, structural ordering which, when projected to embrace the natural world, endowed it with esthetic-artistic properties, justifying the name Cosmos.

It is instructive to pursue the preceding analysis a little further.

Time and space were, in the new physical science, immutably self-subsistent and self-sustaining, each a cosmological-ontological substance. Time and space were independent of each other and also independent, as wholly external containers or envelopes, of the atomic bodies moving about within them. The atomic bodies of which matter consisted were immutable as well as indivisible; the infinite number of collisions they endured did not even infinitesimally affect their ultimate, essential nature, their cosmological-ontological material substance.

Without going into further detail, it is evident that wherever we look into the fundamentals of the new physical science we find inherited conceptions of immutability and universality retained as necessary support for revolutionary innovations which, if carried through, would utterly destroy the classic scheme. It does not demand any extraordinary keenness of vision to realize that precisely what did not happen has now happened. Recent developments in astronomy and physics have destroyed the separate independence of space and time and their immutable self-identical universality; they are no longer containers or envelopes. The terms "space-time" and "relativity" broadly summarize the recent achievement. The transformability of the immutable atoms we have already noted. The Greek-medieval cosmological-ontological structure of thought has, in astronomy and physics, been utterly destroyed. The new has in these areas been liberated from the old.

IX.

By a complicated historical route we need not follow, the typical problems of "modern" philosophical systems were generated as a result of the new astronomy and physics converting the *physical* into the *material*. The words "natural" and "physical" are derived from Latin and Greek expressions which designate the same subject-matter. The Latin *natura* is, with respect to philosophy, a translation of the Greek *phusis*, whence the English noun "physics" and the adjective "physical." From the standpoint of Greek cosmological-ontological science and that science affected by supernaturalism in medieval philosophy, the identification of the physical and the material is totally unimaginable, totally incomprehensible. In Greek-medieval philosophy, physical and material were radically different in kind—as different as is the formed from the formless. The physical *(phusis)* determined the growth of seed to mature form; the movement of growth is movement towards ends, terminal goals; consequently, the physical is involved with meanings akin to what is highest in human purpose and value. Although the physical *(phusis)* lacked the necessary self-activity of ideal and rational Being and therefore was not subject to science in its supreme form, it was subject to a lower mode of knowing. Furthermore its performance was sufficiently regular to serve all man's lowly, common needs and the higher purposes of the political and moral life of free men.

When the physical became identified with the material, the status and understanding of the human estate—first and foremost of the human mind—underwent a great change. Greek theory envisioned the human mind and its operations as the culminating actualization of vital activities. In the accepted ontological cosmology there existed hierarchical grades of life and a corresponding hierarchy of culminating actualizations or grades of "mind." The lowest human grade was sensation, the highest nous; the lowest had to do with the most imperfect, the most subject to change; the highest had to do with the most perfect, with Being, eternal and immutable.

Although the cosmological-ontological hierarchy of Greek philosophy was a hierarchy of fixed species it nevertheless constituted a Cosmos. All constituents, from the lowest grades to the highest grades, from physical aspects to ideal, spiritual aspects, were harmoniously, indeed one may say beautifully, unified systemically.

The physics and astronomy of Galileo and Newton shattered the foundations of the Greek cosmic structure. The identification

of the physical as material substance eventuated in the establishment of mind as a separate and independent substance. The
unity of the Greek system was thus destroyed. Nature was split
into two parts—if the word "parts" can be applied to two substances having nothing in common with each other. Matter and
mind were out-and-out opposites: matter was external, mind
internal; matter was objective, mind subjective; matter was impersonal, mind personal. The study of Matter, of Physical Nature, was the domain of the new sciences. The study of Mind, of
Human Nature, was the domain of philosophy. From Locke on-
wards, treatises on Human Nature were devoted not so much to
Psychology as to Epistemology—to explaining how the inner
and personal could know the outer and impersonal. In classic
philosophy, theory of knowledge was a concern of Logic; Logic's
displacement by Epistemology in "modern" philosophy is profoundly symptomatic.

With Human Nature disconnected from Physical Nature, epistemological solutions produced a bewildering variety of insoluble puzzles. But the enterprise was not abandoned. The pinnacle
was reached when the epistemological problem became: How is
Knowledge possible anyway, *überhaupt*? And this at the very
time when Natural Knowledge was in fact advancing more securely and more rapidly than at any previous time in human
history!

X.

The dualism of matter and mind may no longer overtly
supply currently dominant philosophical problems with their
raison d'être. The assumptions underlying the cosmic dichotomy
have, however, not been eliminated; on the contrary, they are the
abiding source of issues which command today the attention of
the very philosophers who pride themselves upon having replaced the philosophical "thinking" of a bygone period with a
mode of treatment as exact as the former discussions were
sloppy. One striking example is found in the efforts now put
forth to provide "foundations" for science in both its physical
and mathematical aspects. In formulated statement, this concern
differs from that of how knowledge is possible anyway; no ex-

plicit reference is made to the chasm between knowing subject as mental and "object to be known" as physical as the source of the problem. But what is not explicit is, in principle, implicit. It is assumed that science as a total enterprise is inherently non-self-supportive, that it is necessarily incapable of supplying itself with whatever "foundations" it may need and hence it is the task of the new type of rigoristic philosophers and their Logic to do for science what science cannot do for itself.

In view of the fly-blown condition of most of what passes as "logic" today there is something outright comical, rather than merely ironical, in the assumption that Logic is the author of and authority for the required foundations. This claim of competence is supposedly based on the fact that the new Logic is formulated in esoteric symbols which simulate, at least in form, the symbolism of mathematics. But the "foundations" of mathematics have undergone a radical, indeed, a revolutionary change. The old view that mathematical subject-matter is deduced from an ultimate set of self-evident or axiomatic truths has been supplanted by the view that the ultimates, the "foundations" of the mathematical enterprise are deliberately designed postulates. The method of postulation puts mathematical subject-matter beyond the need of any "foundation" supplied from without. The old view produced Kant. The ultra-moderns are, unwittingly, neo-Kantians of a very special and very peculiar sort. Roughly to place their efforts in historical context, they attempt to free the *a priori* conditions of Kantian philosophy from hampering psychological properties and to present them as a rigorous logical structure arrayed in quasi-mathematical symbols.

I pointed out earlier that the creation of the new physics involved the integrative use of experiments, hypotheses and mathematics. This new way of knowing has, in the intervening centuries, become the most thoroughly tried and tested method of knowing that exists and the conclusions attained by its use are, of all that is humanly known, the most securely established. To be "most securely established" is of course a far cry from being "infallibly established." Only the immutable and eternal can be known infallibly. Underlying the search for "foundations" outside of natural science to justify the scientific character of natural science is the ancient, unavowed, principle that the necessary requirements of scientific knowing are the immutable and eternal and that only philosophy has access to the transcendently supra-natural realm which is their abode.

The history of scientific knowing is a history of experimentally developing methods of experimenting, testing, checking, controlling both inquiry and conclusions. The unremitting self-discipline of scientific knowing is infinitely more severe than the discipline of theory of knowledge. The most elementary lesson to be learned from observation of scientific inquiry is the primary and prime importance of making sure of factually observable data as the needed "foundation" for a theoretical view. But philosophers who are determined to supply physics with "foundations" that are not subject to spatial-temporal contingencies have nothing observable to observe. They are unaware of the absurdity of seeking foundations outside the methods of knowing which have been tested and retested in the course of the very operations of inquiry in which they are put to use.

Another striking example of the persistence of the assumptions underlying the cosmic dichotomy is the (literally) painful effort by up-to-date philosophers to find a justification for "induction" outside and independent of the operations constituting the ongoing continuum of scientific inquiry. It is an old cosmological view that some things are inherently of and by their own nature merely *particular* and therefore are by nature or essence incapable of validating generalizations. It is an obvious consequence that "the problem of induction" is insoluble when the old assumptions are introduced into the new science; whence the laborious attempts to solve the problem outside the domain of natural science.

In actual scientific practice, the ground of inference, a much less ambiguous word than "induction," is not numbers of particulars but the outcome of experimentally controlled analysis which is treated, on the basis of what has been scientifically verified in the past, as a *typical* case. If it be not fully typical it will have its a-typicality and degree of variant error disclosed and determined not by ultimate speculative principles invoking essential Being but by operational demonstrations and evaluations of experimental consequences in continuing scientific inquiry.

A third striking example of the persistence of ancient assumptions in ultra-modern philosophy is provided by its treatment of scientific "law." The dualistic anthropomorphism of laws that "govern" particulars and of particulars that "obey" laws is nowhere professed by sophisticated philosophers. But in some form or other, the distinction between existences as *particular* (inherently and by nature) and laws as *universal* (inherently and by nature) persists. Indeed the view that a law is a recurrent uniformity is often regarded as marking the triumph of positivism over metaphysics when in fact it represents an ontologizing of a distinction of functions, of services performed, in the conduct of inquiry.

The commonest of all philosophical fallacies is the fallacy of converting eventual outcomes into antecedent conditions thereby escaping the need (and salutary effect) of taking into account the operations and processes that condition the eventual subject-matter. When we avoid this fallacy and consult the facts of scientific inquiry we find that the discovery of "law" is not the end-in-view of mature physical science.

The facts of science enforced recognition on the part of those who kept in actual touch with developments in physical science that its subject-matter consists of spatial-temporal connections in which the spatial-temporal component is the determined conclusion of inquiry quite as much as are the methods that are used. This is fatal to the notion that laws as uniformities are the objectives of science. It shows philosophers who observe—heeding as well as noting—that whatever else the objectives of recent developments in scientific inquiry are or are not they are of the order of *events*.

When viewed in contemporary light, the objective sought by scientific inquiry is seen to be an order of fact that is indefinitely inclusive with respect to its temporal-spatial range, and that so-called "laws" are useful instruments in bringing particulars previously unplaced in an existential space-time continuum within the order that is under construction or reconstruction.

To sum up: A scientific law is a formulation which *per se* is neither universal nor particular; it is a means by which factual or spatial-temporal connections are instituted that introduce continuity where there had been spatial-temporal interruptions and isolations.

In the course of its continuing operations of inquiry and reinquiry, physical science discovered that its best, most securely verified conclusions, are of some order of probability. Philosophers wittingly or unwittingly motivated by ancient cosmological-ontological assumptions responded negatively to this development. Committed to the view that necessity (not probability) is of the essence of true science and that necessity demands the immutable and eternal, they redoubled their efforts to shore up natural science with transcendent, supra-natural principles mere science inherently lacked and desperately needed.

XI.

Abstractly considered, one might reasonably expect that the cosmic status "matter" attained at the very outset of modern science would result in a thoroughgoing materialistic philosophy of nature. But the efforts in this direction were rare and of no great moment in determining the dominant course of philosophy. Why? The origins of the "warfare of science and religion" provide the answer. The warfare early received open and important acknowledgement because what was at stake was not just religion as a personal predilection nor just theological-ontological theory; warfare broke out and persisted because personal religion and theology were organized in powerful institutions, deeply rooted in the culture of the period.

When the physical was identified with material substance, the Greek-medieval doctrine of the mind was fixed by sacred and erudite tradition in moral-religious beliefs and institutions; its sudden abandonment (supposing the impossible) would have created intolerable intellectual as well as moral-religious chaos. Concretely considered, thoroughgoing materialism was then only a metaphysical theory, without institutional-cultural support. Dualism, on the other hand, was responsive to and supported by the historical-cultural situation.

The short-run effects of dualism must be distinguished from its long-run effects.

When mind acquired the status of an independent and separate order of existence, philosophers, as a matter of course, cultivated a method of knowing independent and separate from the physicists' method of knowing physical nature. The short-run effect of severance from "the external world" existentially and methodologically was to enhance the importance of human nature. For the first time in history, the study of human nature had opening before it a career in its own right. Philosophers gave priority, even primacy, to the study of mind, the inner and mental. They proclaimed that mind was concerned with Nature, not as it presented itself externally, but as it presented itself to man as he internally and really is, intimately, immediately.

In the short-run the "subjective" note in modern philosophy caused little concern; in the long-run it became a major source of insoluble philosophical problems.

Another long-run effect of the "subjective" bias was the building up and solidifying of distorted interpretations of the most important phases of human life—interpersonal relations and their connection with the origin, status and dynamics of institutions.

XII.

It may safely be doubted whether classic Greek philosophy has any reality for a modern philosophical lecturer outside the history of philosophical doctrines. Yet in its own day those to whom it gave a high order of intellectual and emotional satisfaction were among the best informed and ablest of men. Today, for men neither stupid nor unlearned it is intellectually and emotionally satisfying to solve all basic problems by the unclassical "modern" dualism of matter and mind; of the actual and the ideal; of the merely empirical and the supremely rational; of physical things which are mere means, never ends, and spiritual things that are inherently, essentially, necessarily ends-in-themselves and must be treated reverently even though it is admitted that the means at our disposal are of such an inferior order that there is no possibility of realizing the ends-in-themselves. Indeed, to many persons this very impossibility is only added proof that the ends-in-themselves are Ideals which *ought* to be realized. We have here another case of changing the words in which an old doctrinal view is stated while the old doctrinal assumptions are retained.

Popular language does not employ the technical phraseology used in philosophy to formulate the dichotomy, but it is celebrated in familiar speech. There is the realm of the other-worldly, of ultimate and eternal values, necessarily exempt from the contingencies to which mundane things and human existence are subject. Whatever may be the function of the ultimate and eternal in this life it is not to increase security here and now by reducing the number and/or intensity of the contingencies we encounter and the chances we run. Diderot, the great spokesman for the Enlightenment in France, saw how mathematics could be made the instrumentality of insurance against the evils wrought by accidents when it was not possible to prevent accidents from occurring. His teachings find wide application today with regard to accidents that are considered physical or material. When, however, insurance against "accidents" due to maladjustments in the social order is urged and sought for, we hear that such a course weakens self-respect, slackens manly resolution and destroys the motive for providing for the future that is the ground of man's willingness to engage in onerous work. The current two-faced attitude toward insurance against mishaps is a simple and clear example of the consequences of a morality which removes the link joining means-ends and substitutes an unbridgeable chasm. It typifies how we face one way when the subject involved is located in the profane territory of the material and face the other way when the subject involved is located in the sacred realm of the moral, spiritual and ideal.

The doctrine of ideal, separate and independent ends-in-themselves is one of the prime means whereby in modern philosophy morals, as a subject of knowledge, maintained its fixed devotion to the eternal and immutable. The more everyday commonsense and scientific knowings were clearly shown to be relational, concerned with spatial-temporal events and existences, the more did moral knowledge and moral theory become concerned with espousing eternal and immutable absolutes. The doctrine was advanced that moral knowledge is *a priori*, that its organ and seat are unique and isolated in the most sacred element of the psychic constitution of man. This doctrine may be dismissed as a matter of technical philosophy, of interest only to those occupied with the scholastic aspects of abstract theory. It is, however, anything but an abstract technicality that a denigrating discrimination was made between the truly moral and the mundane and secular when mundane and secular activities were absorbing a continually increasing share of human interest and commanding an ever-increasing amount of the attention and energy of mankind.

Absolutistic supra-rational moralists made common cause with traditional supernaturalists (of various theological persuasions) in denouncing "secularism" as the major, if not the sole, *fons et origo* of the evils that beset mankind. A denunciation of "secularism" could be immensely valuable if (a mighty if) its purpose and method were to focus attention on the actual pervasive uncertainties, confusions, deep divisions, tensions and conflicts that are the inevitable consequences of failure to develop means-ends relevant and equal to the problems created by vast, ongoing transformations in the modern world. The dualisms of philosophic theory are but a pale reflection of these problems— the complex of difficult moral problems constituting "secularism." But instead of helping to clarify our moral problems and giving guidance in solving them, the supra-rational moralists and traditional, institutionally supported supernaturalists do just the opposite. All the better to glorify the absolute, eternal and immutable, they incessantly disparage, denounce and bemoan mundane, secular life; they pronounce it to be inherently low, "fallen," or a trivial order of existence.

It was natural (in one of the many senses of that word) for man prior to the rise of scientific knowing as it is now practiced to have recourse to that which was taken to be so inherently fixed, so forever settled, that it and it alone could be depended upon. But now that the dependability of spatial-temporal subject-matter for warranted knowings and knowns has been massively demonstrated by science, there is really no longer any need to search for the treasure and guidance of wisdom in the unnatural kingdom of eternal and immutable absolutes.

XIII.

The identification of the distinctively human with the inner and private made psychology or whatever was taken to be the science of the inner and private a prime factor in originating and propagating the creed of economic laissez-faire liberalism or individualism. The legal and political inheritance from feudalism

obstructed, deflected and distorted the movements that constituted "the orbit of innovation"—the liberation of the activities
of individuals from the heavy hand of precedent, tradition and
government.

Because the innovative movements had organized embodiment only in voluntary associations of persons having no official
status, the conflict of the new with the inherited institutional
order was conceived to be a conflict between irreconcilable
antagonists—the individual and the state. The state was, by inherent nature, oppressive; the freedom of the individual was, by
inherent nature, the freedom of a self-contained complete individual. The proper function of the state was tangential and
negative, namely, to provide sanctions for the infringement by
individuals of the freedom of individuals. The state could not act
to fulfill a positive social purpose, no matter how urgent and
obvious, without necessarily violating the sanctity of natural law
and the inalienable rights of its citizens.

The appeal to natural law and natural right undeniably played
a part in promoting greater freedom in the conduct of economic
affairs. It also undeniably had anti-social consequences. It degraded political law and rights to the level of sheer artificiality,
totally devoid of moral authority. Any attempt to regulate or
control economic enterprise in the public interest was denounced
as interference by merely man-made legislation with the beneficent operations of "natural law" and hence necessarily destructive of "freedom."

Laissez-faire individualistic liberalism outlived its original
liberating function; it became hardened and fixed in regressive
social attitudes and institutional forms. Among the opponents of
the increasingly anarchic tendencies of laissez-faire liberalism
were those who, early in the 19th century, identified restoration
of social stability and order with return to the moral-political
absolutism of medieval authoritarian organization. The neo-
medievalists, besides romanticizing the earlier epoch, ignored the
fact that the industrial revolution had already effectively destroyed the pre-scientific, pre-technological, pre-democratic
foundations of feudalism.

Scientific economists do not make the mistakes of the neo-
medievalists. But in their own peculiar "scientific" ways, they
also fly in the face of facts.

The subject-matter of full-fledged "scientific" economics has been identified with aspects of life economists designate as *material*. The consequence of this identification or definition is to separate and isolate the economic from the moral and political.

I doubt if it is possible to overstate the importance of the dualism thus set up, as if on basic ontological ground, between the sphere of economic activity and the sphere of moral-political interests and values. If any construction of a theoretical nature could be more disastrous to human welfare (in the broadest sense of the term) I confess ignorance as to what it could be. Nothing could more effectively make moral philosophy irrelevant and more completely reduce political philosophy to futility.

It is a fact that modern means of production and distribution of commodities are the consequences of technologies made possible by physical (or material) science. But it is also a fact that the sphere of economic activity—the economic enterprise in all its vast and intricate complications—is inextricably enmeshed in social life, that it serves human needs, personal and institutional, and is to be judged by how well or ill it serves them.

It can be confidently affirmed that every aspect, content, structure and phase of human life has been radically changed, directly or indirectly, for weal or woe, by proliferating and accelerating industrial-technological revolutions. For example: they have changed the structure of family life, the status of women, the relations of the sexes, of parents and children; education has been changed in every respect, quantitatively and qualitatively; vast populations have been urbanized, imposing new occupations and new ways of life; transportation and communication have been revolutionized, with incalculable human consequences; intra-national and international relations, friendly and hostile, cooperative and competitive have been multiplied and intensified; local and world-wide class and race problems have been generated or exacerbated. And overshadowing all, the industrial-technological revolutions are largely, if not wholly, responsible for two world wars in one generation and the threat of another of ultimate destructiveness. The cumulative, ramifying consequences of wars past and in preparation constitute the heart and lifeblood of all our problems, from personal affairs of daily life to world-wide affairs of social and political order, industry, trade and finance.

Scientific economists are inspired by a dehumanized conception of the nature of science, still widely prevalent. The great majority of those who now attribute the scientific backwardness of social subjects to absence of proper methods of inquiry advocate, as the remedy for this grievous state of affairs, the outright adoption of the techniques of inquiry that have proved themselves in dealing with physical subject-matter. They are unmindful of the fact that these techniques have worked successfully just because they were designed for experimental operations with subject-matters from which human (value) considerations were explicitly ruled out.

Economists are only one class of "scientific" inquirers into human subjects who cannot professionally admit the part played by need, purpose and an unceasing valuing (as distinct from evaluating judgments) in the generation and management of human affairs.

But whatever reasons scientific economists may use to justify excluding from their professional concern the human consequences of economic enterprise, philosophy cannot agree that economics is a domain having its own independent subject-matter and career without denying its claim to be comprehensive in scope. Philosophy which does not take into account the economic enterprise and its human consequences is an escapist intellectual gymnastic.

The full bearing of this discussion of economic activity in its relations to the problems which are dominant in life and which therefore should be dominant in philosophy will be postponed till certain other philosophic questions have been considered. As we shall see, the challenge offered to philosophy can be met only by resolute willingness to reformulate its problems with the systematic thoroughness demanded by the conditions of the present crisis.

XIV.

It can hardly have escaped the attention of the reader that as the discussion has proceeded a change of emotional tone has occurred; it may even have aroused querying whether a shift in intellectual substance, amounting to an internal conflict, may not have occurred. Whatever may have been the attitude of Lord Acton in the passage I quoted there is no doubt that the comments of the present writer hailed the facts Lord Acton recorded as the initiation of an era in which man's relations with nature offered the promise of a change from conformity to invention and thereby from subjection to command. Yet no sooner had the reader been asked to consider that exhilarating prospect than he found himself confronted with a world literally torn more deeply and sharply apart than ever before since man appeared on earth.

The contrast is surely there and not as a rhetorical or dramatic device. The contrast is there because it is found in the course of events, especially the events of cultural history as reflected in the accounts given of them in the story of philosophy. If no attempt had been made to report in generalized terms what was going on it might have escaped notice that it takes time for events to disclose in which direction they are moving, that in the very degree in which a new movement is felt to be in a new orbit, to be revolutionary, it will of necessity be reported in terms which inject into the report habitudes and dispositions which are residues of bygone history. It may even be said that the more acute and more assured is the sense of revolutionary break, the more will it be necessary to make the intellectual reckoning under conditions that are going to be gradually, more or less insensibly, replaced. Not till a new movement is mature in development, until it is a fact, something done, can it be perceived in its own perspective.

The persuasion that actuates the following section of this Re-Introduction is, then, that events of the present century, including positive and negative alike, taking accomplishments and the breakdowns together, indicate the path to be followed in order to arrive at an awareness of the orbit of change-in-process during the past four centuries or so. This path will enable us to observe with some effective degree of intellectual clarity the clogging, deflecting and distorting factors inherited from pre-scientific, pre-technological and pre-democratic conditions of living and knowing. In consequence, it will enable us to pursue with reasonable degree of confidence and resolution the orbit of change; having the advantage of sense of direction, the orbit will become clearer as it becomes increasingly unified.

I know of no more promising place from which to attempt to

foreshadow the direction to be pursued by philosophy than to go back to the concern of the age (now drawing to a close) with *experience*. We must here view experience not from the side of the stammering account given of it in philosophy but must see the new faith which found expression in our common tongue, our idiomatic speech as well as in the various disjointed because independent movements undertaken in pursuit of experience. Thus to see and grasp experience it is necessary to overcome the cultivated inability to see what is to be seen in the continuities displayed by what is in process and only by what is in process.

Editor's Note

A crowd of burdensome events in September-October 1949 interrupted Dewey's work on the Introduction. The interruption was temporarily renewed several times by refreshing changes in work and by an enervating bout with a virus. In March 1950 and again in July Dewey considered getting back to work on the Introduction but on both occasions the lure of other projects was too enticing. When Dewey at long last returned in January 1951 to where he left off in August 1949, he transformed the task of finishing the Introduction into a formidable new problem.

J.R.

Were I to write (or rewrite) *Experience and Nature* today I would entitle the book *Culture and Nature* and the treatment of specific subject-matters would be correspondingly modified. I would abandon the term "experience" because of my growing realization that the historical obstacles which prevented understanding of my use of "experience" are, for all practical purposes, insurmountable. I would substitute the term "culture" because with its meanings as now firmly established it can fully and freely carry my philosophy of experience.

I am not convinced that the task I undertook was totally misguided. I still believe that on theoretical, as distinct from historical, grounds there is much to be said in favor of using "experience" to designate the inclusive subject-matter which characteristically "modern" (post-medieval) philosophy breaks up into the dualisms of subject and object, mind and the world, psychological and physical. If "experience" is to designate the inclusive subject-matter it must designate both what is experienced and the ways of experiencing it.

There is, assuredly, nothing novel in holding that philosophy is distinguished from other intellectual or cognitive undertakings by the comparative comprehensiveness of its subject-matter; nor is it innovative to maintain that a linguistic expression is needed to name philosophy's singular distinction. But by an ironical twist of events which I failed to comprehend, the *theoretical* grounds that can be cited for using "experience" as the needed name are *historically* identical with the obstacles that effectively stand in the way of the name being understood in the senses I intended.

The historical obstacles are now so conspicuous that I can at times but wonder how they came to be overlooked. There was a period in modern philosophy when the appeal to "experience" was a thoroughly wholesome appeal to liberate philosophy from desiccated abstractions. But I failed to appreciate the fact that subsequent developments inside and outside of philosophy had corrupted and destroyed the wholesomeness of the appeal—that "experience" had become effectively identified with experiencing in the sense of the psychological, and the psychological had become established as that which is intrinsically psychical, mental, private. My insistence that "experience" also designates *what* is experienced was a mere ideological thundering in the Index for it ignored the ironical twist which made this use of "experience" strange and incomprehensible.

The name "culture" in its anthropological (not its Matthew Arnold) sense designates the vast range of things experienced in an indefinite variety of ways. It possesses as a name just that body of substantial references which "experience" as a name has lost. It names artifacts which rank as "material" and operations upon and with material things. The facts named by "culture" also include the whole body of beliefs, attitudes, dispositions which are scientific and "moral" and which as a matter of cultural fact decide the specific uses to which the "material" constituents of culture are put and which accordingly deserve, philosophically speaking, the name "ideal" (even the name "spiritual," if intelligibly used).

It is a prime philosophical consideration that "culture" includes the material and the ideal in their reciprocal interrelationships and (in marked contrast with the prevailing use of "experience") "culture" designates, also in their reciprocal interconnections, that immense diversity of human affairs, interests, concerns, values which compartmentalists pigeonhole under "religion" "morals" "aesthetics" "politics" "economics" etc., etc. Instead of separating, isolating and insulating the many aspects of a common life, "culture" holds them together in their human and humanistic unity—a service which "experience" has ceased to render. What "experience" now fails to do and "culture" can successfully do for philosophy is of utmost importance if philosophy is to be comprehensive without becoming stagnant.[3]

Culture "comprises inherited artifacts, goods, technical processes, ideas, habits, values. Social organization cannot be really understood except as a part of culture." Even this brief quotation indicates the inclusive or comprehensive summarizing of the conditions and aspects of human life designated by the word. Artifacts include habitations, temples and their rituals, weapons, paraphernalia, tools, implements, means of transportation, roads, clothing, decorations and ornamentations, etc., etc. They, together with the technical processes involved in their use, constitute the "material aspect of culture." But then follows the significant statement: "The material equipment of culture is not, however, a force in itself. Knowledge is necessary in the production, management and use of artifacts . . . and is essentially connected with mental and moral discipline, of which religion, laws and ethical rules are the ultimate source. The handling and possession of goods imply also the appreciation of their value." The kind of cooperation involved in *production* of goods and the common modes of *enjoyment* of the products "are always based on a definite type of social organization." In short, "material culture requires a complement . . . consisting of the body of intellectual knowledge, of the system of moral, spiritual, and economic values, of social organization and of language."

The intimate connection of philosophical systems with culture is further clarified by the fact that "the formation of sentiments

3. See Malinowski's article "Culture" in the *Encyclopaedia of the Social Sciences*, edited by Alvin Johnson.

and thus of values is always based on the cultural apparatus in a society," the sentiments and values defining man's attitudes "toward the realities of his magical, religious or metaphysical *Weltanschauung*." And while I cannot dwell upon its implications here, I cannot refrain from quoting the statement that "Culture is *at the same time* psychological and collective."[4]

4. The quotations are from Vol. 4, pp. 621–23. The italics in the last quotation are mine.

Appendix 2
1. Experience and Philosophic Method

As Mr. Ralph Perry has said, experience is a weasel word. Its slipperiness is evident in an inconsistency characteristic of many thinkers. On the one hand they eagerly claim an empirical method; they forswear the *a priori* and transcendent; they are sensitive to the charge that they employ data unwarranted by experience. On the other hand, they are given to deprecating the conception of experience; experience, it is said, is purely subjective, and whoever takes experience for his subject-matter is logically bound to land in the most secluded of idealisms.

Interesting as the theme is, it is aside from our purpose to account for this contradictory attitude. It may be surmised, however, that those guilty of the contradiction think in two insulated universes of discourse. In adherence to empirical method, they think of experience in terms of the modern development of scientific method; but their idea of experience as a distinctive subject matter is derived from another source—introspective psychology as it was elaborated in the nineteenth century.[1] But we must make a choice. If the identification of experience with purely mental states is correct, then the last thing one should profess is acceptance of empirical method as the scientific road to the understanding of the natural and social world in which we live. And if scientific method is intrinsically empirical, then the subject-matter of experience cannot be what introspective psychologists have told us it is.

Whether or no this suggestion is correct, recognition of the inconsistency is of use in enabling us, writer and reader alike, to trap and hold the slippery idea of experience, whenever it is

---

1. "Psychological: Consciousness as a process taking place in time." This is the primary definition given in Baldwin's *Dictionary of Philosophy and Psychology*.

proposed to set forth the implications of experience for philosophy; especially when, as in this discussion, its implications for a theory of nature, of the world, of the universe, form the issue. And I know of no better way of warning the reader against misconception of this purpose than to remind him that, as he reads the statement, he should interpret "experience" in the sense in which he himself uses the term when he professes to be faithful to the empirical method, not in the sense in which he uses it when he implies that experience is momentary, private and psychical.

There are two avenues of approach to the goal of philosophy. We may begin with experience in gross, experience in its primary and crude forms, and by means of its distinguishing features and its distinctive trends, note something of the constitution of the world which generates and maintains it. Or, we may begin with refined selective products, the most authentic statements of commended methods of science, and work from them back to the primary facts of life. The two methods differ in starting point and direction, but not in objective or eventual content. Those who start with coarse, everyday experience must bear in mind the findings of the most competent knowledge, and those who start from the latter must somehow journey back to the homely facts of daily existence.

Each way of approach has its advantages and its dangers. Those who are able to pursue the road of that technical and refined knowledge called science are fortunate. But the history of thought shows how easy it is for them to forget that science is after all an art, a matter of perfected skill in conducting inquiry; while it reveals that those who are not directly engaged in the use of this art readily take science to be something finished, absolute in itself, instead of the result of a certain technique. Consequently "scientific" philosophies have over and over again made the science of their own day the premises of philosophy only to have them undermined by later science. And even when reasonably sure foundations are provided by the science of a period, a philosopher has no guarantee save his own acumen and honesty that he will not employ them in such a way as to get lost on a bypath. Professed scientific philosophers have been wont to employ the remoter and refinished products of science in ways which deny, discount or pervert the obvious and immediate facts of gross experience, unmindful that thereby philosophy itself commits suicide.

On the other hand, the method which sets out with macroscopic experience requires unusual candor and patience. The subject-matter of science, for better or worse, is at least "there"; it is a definite body of facts and principles summed up in books and having a kind of independent external existence. But coarse and vital experience is Protean; a thing of moods and tenses. To seize and report it is the task of an artist as well as of an informed technician. As the history of thought shows, the usual thing, a thing so usual as probably to be in some measure inevitable, is for the philosopher to mix with his reports of direct experience interpretations of it made by previous thinkers. Too often, indeed, the professed empiricist only substitutes a dialectical development of some notion about experience for an analysis of experience as it is humanly lived.

The philosophy which since the seventeenth century has almost achieved a monopoly of the title "empiricism" strikingly illustrates this danger. Not safely can an "ism" be made out of experience. For any interpretation of experience must perforce simplify; simplifications tend in a particular direction; and the direction may be set by custom which one assumes to be natural simply because it is traditionally congenial. For at least two hundred years many interests, religious, industrial, political, have centered about the status of the individual. Hence the drift in all systems save the classic traditional school, has been to think in ways that make individuality something isolated as well as central. When the notion of experiences is introduced, who is not familiar with the query, uttered with a crushingly triumphant tone, "Whose experience?" The implication is that experience is not only always somebody's, but that the peculiar nature of "somebody" infects experience so pervasively that experience is merely somebody's and hence of nobody and nothing else.

The dialectical situation which results may be illustrated by a quotation which is selected because it is typical of much contemporary philosophizing. "When I look at a chair, I say I experience it. But what I actually experience is only a very few of the elements that go to make up a chair, namely, that color that belongs to the chair under these particular conditions of light, the shape which the chair displays when viewed from this angle, etc." The man who has the experience, as distinct from a philosopher theorizing about it, would probably say that he experienced the chair most fully not when looking at it but when meaning to sit down in it, and that he can mean to sit down in it precisely because his experience is *not* limited to color under specific conditions of light, and angular shape. He would probably say that when he looks at it, instead of experiencing something less than a chair he experiences a good deal more than a chair: that he lays hold of a wide spatial context, such as the room where the chair is, and a spread of its history, including the chair's period, price paid for it, consequences, public as well as personal, which flow from its use as household furniture, and so on.

Such remarks as these prove nothing. But they suggest how far away from the everyday sense of experience a certain kind of philosophic discourse, although nominally experiential, has wandered. Interesting results can be had by developing dialectically such a notion of experience as is contained in the quotation; problems can be made to emerge which exercise the ingenuity of the theorizer, and which convince many a student that he gets nearer to the reality of experience the further away he gets from all the experience he has ever had. The exercise would be harmless, were it not finally forgotten that the conclusions reached have but a dialectical status, being an elaboration of premises arrived at by technical analysis from a specialized physiological point of view. Consequently, I would rather take the behavior of the dog of Odysseus upon his master's return as an example of the sort of thing experience is for the philosopher than trust to such statements. A physiologist may for his special purpose reduce Othello's perception of a handkerchief to simple elements of color under certain conditions of light and shapes seen under certain angular conditions of vision. But the actual experience was charged with history and prophecy; full of love, jealousy and villainy, fulfilling past human relationships and moving fatally to tragic destiny.

The excuse for saying obvious things is that much that now passes for empiricism is but a dialectical elaboration of data taken from physiology, so that it is necessary for any one, who seriously sets out to philosophize empirically, to recall to attention that he is talking about the sort of thing that the unsophisticated man calls experience, the life he has led and undergone in the world of persons and things. Otherwise we get a stencilled stereotype in two dimensions and in black and white instead of the solid and many colored play of activities and sufferings which is the philosopher's real datum.

The way of approach that sets out from that which is closest at hand, instead of from refined products of science no more signifies beginning with the results of psychological science than it does with those of physical science. Indeed the former material is further away from direct experience than that of physics. It signifies beginning back of any science, with experience in its gross and macroscopic traits. Science will then be of interest as one of the phases of human experience, but intrinsically no more so than magic, myth, politics, painting, poetry and penitentiaries. The domination of men by reverie and desire is as pertinent for the philosophic theory of nature as is mathematical physics; imagination as much to be noted as refined observation. It is a fact of *experience* that some men, as Santayana has pointed out concerning Shelley, are immune to "experience," retaining intact the attitude of childhood. And for a thoroughgoing empiricist the most transcendental of philosophies is an empirical phenomenon. It may not prove intellectually what its originator supposed it to demonstrate, but it shows something about experience, something possibly of immense value for a subsequent interpretation of nature in the light of experience.

Hence it is that experience is something quite other than "consciousness," that is, that which appears qualitatively and focally at a particular moment. The common man does not need to be told that ignorance is one of the chief features of experience; so are habits skilled and certain in operation so that we abandon ourselves to them without consciousness. Yet ignorance, habit, fatal implication in the remote, are just the things which professed empiricism, with its reduction of experience to states of consciousness, denies to experience. It is important for a theory of experience to know that under certain circumstances men prize the distinct and clearly evident. But it is no more important than it is to know that under other circumstances twilight, the vague, dark and mysterious flourish. Because intellectual crimes have been committed in the name of the subconscious is no reason for refusing to admit that what is not explicitly present makes up a vastly greater part of experience than does the conscious field to which thinkers have so devoted themselves.

When disease or religion or love, or knowledge itself is experienced, forces and potential consequences are implicated that are neither directly present nor logically implied. They are "in" experience quite as truly as are present discomforts and exaltations. Considering the rôle which anticipation and memory of death have played in human life, from religion to insurance companies, what can be said of a theory which defines experience in such a way that it logically follows that death is never a matter of experience? Experience is no stream, even though the stream of feelings and ideas that flows upon its surface is the part which philosophers love to traverse. Experience includes the enduring banks of natural constitution and acquired habit as well as the stream. The flying moment is sustained by an atmosphere that does not fly, even when it most vibrates.

When we say that experience is one point of approach to an account of the world in which we live, we mean then by experience something at least as wide and deep and full as all history on this earth, a history which, since history does not occur in the void, includes the earth and the physical relatives of man. When we assimilate experience to history rather than to the physiology of sensations, we note that history denotes both objective conditions, forces, events and also the human record and estimate of these events. Similarly experience denotes whatever is experienced, whatever is undergone and tried, and also processes of experiencing. As it is the essence of "history" to have meanings termed both subjective and objective, so with "experience." As William James has said, it is a "double-barrelled" fact.[2] Without sun, moon and stars, mountains and rivers, forests and mines, soil, rain and wind, history would not be. These things are not just external conditions of history and experience; they are integral with them. But also without the human attitude and interest, without record and interpretation, these things would not be historical.

There is an obvious retort to this plea to take the conception of experience with the utmost of naïveté and catholicity, as the common man takes it when he experiences illness and pros-

2. Lloyd Morgan, *Instinct and Experience*, pp. 126–28.

perity, love, marriage, and death. The objection is that experience is then made so inclusive and varied as to be useless for philosophic purposes. Experience, as we are here told to conceive it, includes just everything and anything, actual or potential, that we think of and talk about. So we might just as well start with everything and anything and drop out the idea and word, "experience." The traditional notion of experience, which has been disowned, may be erroneous. But at least it denotes something specific, differential; something which may be set in contrast with other things and may thus serve as a principle of criticism and estimate. But the whole wide universe of fact and dream, of event, act, desire, fancy and meanings, valid or invalid, can be set in contrast to nothing. And if what has been said is taken literally, "experience" denotes just this wide universe.

Here is indeed a vulnerable spot in experience as a guiding method for philosophy. It is presented to us as a catholic and innocent neutral, free from guile and partisanship. But then unwittingly there is substituted for this free, full, unbiased and pliable companion of us all, a simplified and selected character, which is already pointed in a special direction and loaded with preferred conclusions. So often does this occur, that one does well to exercise a wary scepticism whenever an inquirer insistently professes that *he* keeps to an empirical method. And when this biased course, (easy to fall into as the history of thought testifies), is avoided, the alternative seems to be everything without discrimination, so that experience ceases to have a meaning.

The objection uncovers the exact meaning of a truly empirical method. For it reveals the fact that experience for philosophy is method, not distinctive subject-matter. And it also reveals the sort of method that philosophy needs. Experience includes dreams, insanity, illness, death, labor, war, confusion, ambiguity, lies and error; it includes transcendental systems as well as empirical ones; magic and superstition as well as science. It includes that bent which keeps one from learning from experience as well as that skill which fastens upon its faint hints. This fact convicts upon sight every philosophy that professes to be empirical and yet assures us that some especial subject-matter is experience and some other not.

The value of experience as method in philosophy is that it compels us to note that *denotation* comes first and last, so that to settle any discussion, to still any doubt, to answer any question, we must go to some thing pointed to, denoted, and find our answer in that thing. As method it has a contrast which it does not possess as subject matter, that with "rationalism," understanding by rationalism method which assumes the primacy and ultimacy of purely logical thought and its findings. There are two kinds of demonstration: that of logical reasoning from premises assumed to possess logical completeness, and that of showing, pointing, coming upon a thing. The latter method is that which the word experience sums up, generalizes, makes universal and ulterior. To say that the right method is one of pointing and showing, not of meeting intellectual requirements or logical derivation from rational ideas, does not, although it is non-rational, imply a preference for irrationality. For one of the things that is pointed out, found and shown, is deduction, and the logic that governs it. But these things have also to be found and shown, and their authority rests upon the perceived outcome of this empirical denotation. The utmost in rationality has a sanction and a position that, according to taste, may be called sub-rational or supra-rational.

The value, I say, of the notion of experience for philosophy is that it asserts the finality and comprehensiveness of the method of pointing, finding, showing, and the necessity of seeing what is pointed to and accepting what is found in good faith and without discount. Were the denotative method universally followed by philosophers, then the word and the notion of experience might be discarded; it would be superfluous, for we should be in possession of everything it stands for. But as long as men prefer in philosophy, (as they so long preferred in science) to define and envisage "reality" according to esthetic, moral or logical canons, we need the notion of experience to remind us that "reality" includes whatever is denotatively found.

When the varied constituents of the wide universe, the unfavorable, the precarious, uncertain, irrational, hateful, receive the same attention that is accorded the noble, honorable and true, then philosophy may conceivably dispense with the conception of experience. But till that day arrives, we need a cautionary and directive word, like experience, to remind us that the world which is lived, suffered and enjoyed as well as logically thought of, has the last word in all human inquiries and surmises. This is a doctrine of humility; but it is also a doctrine of direction. For it tells us to open the eyes and ears of the mind, to be sensitive to all the varied phases of life and history. Nothing is more ironical than that philosophers who have so professed universality have so often been one-sided specialists, confined to that which is authentically and surely *known*, ignoring ignorance, error, folly and the common enjoyments and adornments of life; disposing of these by regarding them as due to our "finite" natures—a blest word that does for moderns what "non-being" was made to do for the Greeks.

The history of thought sufficiently manifests the need for a method of procedure that sets pointing, finding and showing, ahead of methods that substitute ratiocination and its conclusions for things that are done, suffered and imagined. Philosophers are wont to start with highly simplified premises. They do this not inadvertently, but with pride, as evidence that they really understand philosophic business. Absolute certainty in knowledge of things and absolute security in the ordering of life have often been assumed to be the goal of philosophic search; consequently philosophers have set out with data and principles sufficiently simple to yield what is sought. When some historic religion is ceasing to confer upon men a sense of certainty and security men especially resort to philosophy for a substitute. So they did in Greece; in Europe in the seventeenth century, and so we do today. Forms and essences, inner introspective facts, mathematical truths may be resorted to. This is a varying matter of the temporal scene. The constant is demand for assurance and order, and the demand is met only by ignoring a vast number of the things that nature presents to us.

When we look for instances of a simplifying procedure exercised in this bias, we think perhaps most readily of Descartes with his certainty of thinking, of Spinoza with his conviction that a true idea carries truth intrinsically in itself so whatever must be thought, must—and alone must—*be*. But thinkers who profess empiricism also afford examples: there is Locke with his "simple idea," Hume with his "impression." And I do not see that contemporary hankering after ultimate "sense-data," or conviction that mathematical logistic is at last to open to philosophy the arcana of ultimate truth, differ in principle.

Now the notion of experience, however devoid of differential subject-matter—since it includes all subject-matters—, at least tells us that we must not start with arbitrarily selected simples, and from them deduce the complex and varied, assigning what cannot be thus deduced to an inferior realm of being. It warns us that the tangled and complex is what we primarily find; that we work from and within it to discriminate, reduce, analyze; and that we must keep track of these activities, pointing to *them*, as well as to the things upon which they are exercised, and to their refined conclusions. When we contemplate their fruits we are not to ignore the art by which they are produced. There is a place for polishers of stones and for those who put the stones together to make temples and palaces. But "experience" reminds us that a stone was once part of some stratum of the earth, and that a quarryman pried it loose and another workman blew the massive rock to smaller pieces, before it could be smooth-hewn and fitted into an ordered and regular structure. Empirical method warns us that systems which set out from things said to be ultimate and simple have always worked with loaded dice; their premises have been framed to yield desired conclusions.

Professed sceptics rarely fare better, whether they consistently maintain the attitude, or whether they employ doubt in order to discover a triumphant exit into certitude. Man is naturally a credulous animal. It is well to be warned against too easy and inflexible acceptance of beliefs which, before they command acceptance, should exhibit credentials. But some things, things of action and suffering, are not matters of belief at all; they just are. No one ever doubted birth, death, love or hate, no matter how much theories about them justly provoke doubts. Philosophers have exhibited proper ingenuity in pointing out holes in the beliefs of common sense, but they have also displayed improper ingenuity in ignoring the empirical things that every one has; the things that so denote themselves that they *have* to be dealt with. No wonder Hume's doubts vanished when he played backgammon and made merry with his friends. Not that many of his doubts of doctrines were not suitable, but that in his companionships he was involved in another world from that to which he confined his philosophizing. Merriment and sorrow are not of the same order as beliefs, impressions and ideas. The advice of Epictetus to a fellow-slave whose master adhered to the school of sceptics, to rub his master with a curry-comb and anoint him with pepper-sauce is irrelevant to doubt about systematized beliefs, but it is a pertinent reminder that whatever things we are compelled to pay heed to, things of joy and suffering, cannot have their *existence* honestly called in question.

When a thinker ventures to begin with things which are too crude and coarse to come within the ken of intellectualists, he finds, moreover, that as an empiricist he is not obliged to face the miscellaneous world *en masse*. Things are pointed to in kinds, possessed of order and arrangement. Pre-philosophic selections and arrangings may not be final for reflective thought, but they are significant for it. The bias they manifest is not that of the closet or library, but of men who have responded to the one-sided pressures of natural events. The key to the trends of nature is found in the adjectives that are commonly prefixed to experience. Experience is political, religious, esthetic, industrial, intellectual, mine, yours.

The adjectives denote that things present themselves in characteristic contexts, with different savors, colors, weights, tempos and directions. Experience as method warns us to give impartial attention to all of these diversifications. Non-empirical method sets out with the assumption that some one of these groupings of things is privileged; that it is supreme of its own right, that it furnishes a standard by which to measure the significance and real quality of everything else. The sequel is then but a dialectic. Philosophers deduce results in accordance with what is logically implied in their own choice of standard and measure.

Philosophy is a branch of that phase of things which is qualified by the adjective "intellectual." Since it is the express and proper business of the philosopher to subject things to reflection with a view to knowledge (to justifiable belief), he is prone to take the outcome of reflection for something antecedent. That is to say, instead of seeing that the product of knowing is *statement* of things, he is given to taking it as an *existential equivalent* of what things really are "in themselves," so that the subject-matter of other modes of experience are deviations, shortcomings, or trespasses—or as the dialectical philosopher puts it, mere "phenomena." The experiential or denotative method tells us that we must go behind the refinements and elaborations of reflective experience to the gross and compulsory things of our doings, enjoyments and sufferings—to the things that force us to labor, that satisfy needs, that surprise us with beauty, that compel obedience under penalty. A common divisor is a convenience, and a greatest common divisor has the greatest degree of convenience. But there is no reason for supposing that its intrinsic "reality" or truth is greater than that of the numbers it divides. The objects of intellectual experience are the greatest common divisor of the things of other modes; they have that remarkable value, but to convert them into exclusive reality is the sure road to arbitrary divisions and insoluble problems.

Not all philosophies have assumed that reflective experience, with logic as its norm, is the standard for experiential, religious, esthetic, industrial, social objects. Many thinkers have concluded that dialectic ends in an impasse; that it involves us in contradictory statements. Then they have appealed to something which they assert is higher than thought. But it is significant that they think of this higher recourse as a higher kind of *knowledge*, as intuition, or immediate insight, mystical certainty of the truly real. Thus the thinker still shows his inability to take things as he has to take them as a human being, as things to pay heed to under penalty of death and defeat, things to use and enjoy, to master and submit to. The notion still lurks that in their intrinsic being they are things of knowledge.

Then there are philosophers who, like Kant, finding themselves in intellectual difficulties, assert that moral experience reveals things-in-themselves at a deeper level than does science. There are a larger number who look askance upon science, and who claim that religious experience penetrates behind the screen that limits the vision of intellect. These apparent exceptions prove the rule. For the claim implies that moral or religious experience takes the place of knowledge, doing sufficiently, absolutely, what natural knowledge does only partially and relatively. The implication is that morals and religion have a direct revelatory worth. Now it is one thing to say that the world is such that men approach certain objects with awe, worship, piety, sacrifice and prayer, and that this is a fact which a theory of existence must reckon with as truly as with the facts of science. But it is a different thing to say that religious experience gives *evidence* of the reality of its *own* objects, or that the consciousness of an obligation proves the validity of its special object, or the general fact of duty carries within itself any deliverance as to its source in reality. Helen of Troy, Hamlet of Denmark are instances of things that require as much attention from the philosopher as do molecules and integers: but their presence in experience does not guarantee that they are the same kind of things as the latter.

We must conceive the world in terms which make it possible for devotion, piety, love, beauty, and mystery to be as real as anything else. But whether the loved and devotional objects have all the qualities which the lover and the devout worshipper attribute to them is a matter to be settled by evidence, and evidence is always extrinsic. Injunctions and prohibitions which are empirically unescapable, may be called categorical imperatives, and their existence may be quite as significant for a just theory of nature as is the law of gravitation. But what sort of objects beyond themselves they give evidence of, whether tribal taboos, a Kantian thing-in-itself, God, a political sovereign or a net work of social customs evolved in the effort to satisfy needs, is a question to be settled by the denotative method, by finding and pointing to the things in the concrete contexts in which they present themselves.

Even the classic empiricisms of philosophical history have been concerned almost exclusively with experience as knowledge, and with objects as known or unknowable. But, since objects are found and dealt with in many other ways than those of knowledge, a genuine empiricism will set out with all the adjectival groupings of macroscopic experience, starting from them as all upon the same level of worth; subsequent inquiry can review the starting point when it is found necessary. One can be insane without knowing he is insane and one may know insanity without being crazy; indeed absence of the direct experience is said to be an indispensable condition of study of insanity. Adequate recognition of the implications of such a fact as this might almost be said to be the chief contribution which empirical method has to make to philosophy.

For it indicates that *being* and *having* things in ways other than knowing them, in ways never identical with knowing them, exist, and are preconditions of reflection and knowledge. *Being* angry, stupid, wise, inquiring; *having* sugar, the light of day, money, houses and lands, friends, laws, masters, subjects, pain and joy, occur in dimensions incommensurable to knowing these things which we are and have and use, and which have and use us. Their existence is unique, and, strictly speaking, indescribable; they can *only be* and be *had*, and then be pointed to in reflection. In the proper sense of the word, their existence is absolute, being qualitative. All cognitive experience must start from and must terminate in being and having things in just such unique, irreparable and compelling ways. And until this fact is a commonplace in philosophy, the notion of experience will not be a truism for philosophers.

Inevitably our argument travels in a circle and comes back to where we started. Modern philosophy is openly, ancient philosophy covertly, a theory of knowledge, and of things as known. A theory of knowledge in the sense of how to know most economically, liberally, effectively, a technique of instructive and rewarding inquiry is indispensable. But what has gone by the name of theory of knowledge has not been such an affair. It has been a discussion of whether we can know at all, a matter of validating or refuting wholesale scepticism (instead of how to conduct doubt profitably); of how far knowledge extends, what its limits are, limits not at a specific time and place, but inherent and final. What has been said professes to give the explanation of this fact. It is due to failure to take the various phases of experienced things simply, directly, and impartially. It is due to bias of the intellectualist in favor of his own specialized professional experience.

Bias in favor of things in their capacity of being objects of knowledge, when it is yielded to, renders it impossible to distinguish between being and having things and knowing them. If *having* sweet, red, hard, pain, etc., is of necessity identical with knowing these things, then the classic problems of epistemology, and the necessity of defending science against wholesale sceptical doubts are inevitable. I mention in illustration the two traditional questions. First, there is the dispute between the epistemological idealist and realist. Are sweet, hard, solid, pain, square, etc., psychical or physical? Empirically, the obvious answer is that they are neither. They are the unique qualities which they are, the things pointed to and had. But *knowledge* involves classification. If to have is also to know, then these things cannot "really" be simply the qualities they are; they must be related, subsumed, interpreted. And the two most general terms of classificatory knowing are physical and mental. Hence the dispute.

Another problem which is inevitable is the relation of immediate or "presentative" knowledge, sensory acquaintance or whatever, to reflective and inferential knowledge, to science. How is the reality of the proper objects of the latter to be "reconciled" with the reality of the things—whether defined as physical or psychical—of immediate sensuous or presentative "knowledge"? The problem is dialectically attractive, as is shown by the immense amount of ingenuity that has been expended upon it. But no generally satisfactory answer has ever been found and it is predictable that none ever will be. For the problem, empirically speaking, is unreal. There are not two kinds of knowledge whose objects have to be reconciled. There are two dimensions of experienced things: one that of having them, and the other that of knowing about them so that we can again have them in more meaningful and secure ways. It is no easy matter to know about the things we have and are, whether it be the state, measles, virtue or redness. Hence there *is* a problem of knowledge; namely, the problem of how to find out what it is needful to find out about these things in order to secure, rectify and avoid being and having them.

But a problem of knowledge in general is, to speak brutally, nonsense. For knowledge is itself one of the things that we empirically *have*. While scepticism may be in place at any time about any specific intellectual belief and conclusion, in order to keep us on the alert, to keep us inquiring and curious, scepticism as to the things which we *have* and *are* is impossible. No one ever frankly engaged in it. Its pretentiousness is concealed, however, by the failure to distinguish between objects of knowledge where doubt is legitimate, since they are matters of interpretation and classification, (of theory), and things which are directly had. A man may doubt whether he has the measles, because measles is an intellectual term, a classification, but he cannot doubt what he empirically has—not as has so often been asserted because he has an immediately certain knowledge of it, but because it is not a matter of knowledge, an intellectual affair, at all, not an affair of truth or falsity, certitude, or doubt, but one of existence.

He may not know that he is ailing, much less what his ailment is; but unless there is something immediately and non-cognitively present in experience so that it is capable of being pointed to in subsequent reflection and in action which embodies the fruits of reflection, knowledge has neither subject-matter nor objective. In traditional epistemologies, this fact has been both recognized and perverted; it is said that while we can doubt whether a particular thing is red or sweet, we have an immediate or intuitive cognitive certitude that we are affected by redness or sweetness or have a sensation of sweet and red. But as cognized, red and sweet are data only because they are *taken* in thought. Their givenness is something imputed; they are primary and immediate relatively to more complex processes of inquiry. It required a high degree of intellectual specialization, backed by technical knowledge of the nervous system, before even the concept of sensory data could emerge. It still taxes the resources of investigation to determine just what are "immediate data" in a particular problem. To know a quality *as* sensation is to have performed an act of complicated objective reference; it is not to register an inherently given property. The epistemological sensationalist and the epistemological rationalist share the same error; belief that cognitive property is intrinsic, borne on the face.

Because empirical method is denotative, it is realistic in the unsophisticated sense of the word. Things are first acted toward, suffered; and it is for the things themselves as they are followed up to tell by their own traits whether they are "subjective" or "objective." These terms, like physical and psychical, express classificatory discriminations, and there is no presumption of primacy on the side of the subjective. As a matter of historic fact, the primitive bias of man is all toward objective classifications. Whatever can be denoted is there independent of volition (volition itself occurring without volition), and its thereness, its independence of choice, renders it, for uncritical man, cosmic and fated. Only when vanity, prestige, and property rights are involved does the natural man tend, like Jack Horner with his plum, to employ a subjective or personal interpretation.

Subsequently, reflection attributes occurrences like disease, misfortune, and error to the individual person's own doings, instead of imputing them to gods or enemies or wizardry or fate. There is then an intelligible sense in which these things may be said to have been transferred from an objective to a subjective field. But there is even more sense in saying that they have been given a *different* objective reference, in those cases where they are referred to a personal subject as their seat and source. When we say that a man's illness is due to his own imprudence and not to a foreign substance magically projected into his interior by a subtle enemy, we are still discoursing within the realm of objective events. The case is not otherwise when we attribute error to something in a man's own disposition, instead of to the intent of hostile gods to blind him, or to the inherently illusory nature of things. Practically, the distinction thus drawn between subjective and objective, personal and impersonal, causation and locus is of immense importance. But for theory, it falls within a continuous world of events.

Most of the things that have been called subjective by philosophers have an even more obvious objective status. Political institutions, the household, art, technologies, embodied objective events long before science and philosophy arose. Political experience deals with barriers, mountains, rivers, seas, forests and plains. Men fight for these things; for them they exercise jurisdiction; they obey and rebel. Being and having, exercising and suffering such things as these, exist in the open and public world. As we digest foods derived from the extra-personal world long before we study or are aware of processes occurring in our own bodily tissues, so we live in a world of objective acceptances and compulsions long before we are aware of attitudes of our own, and of the action of say the nervous system, in bringing us into effective relationship with them. The knowledge of our own attitudes and of the operation of the nervous system is no more a substitute for the direct operation of the things than metabolic processes are a substitute for food materials. In one case as in the other we have become acquainted with an added *object*; and by means of this added object further active relationships with the extra-personal world are instituted.

When we speak of esthetic experience we do not mean something private and psychical. The choir of heaven and the consent of the earth are implicated, as are paints, brushes, marbles, chisels, temples, palaces, and theaters. Appreciation is appreciation of some *thing*, not of itself. We are lovingly and excitedly aware of the objects long before we are aware of our own attitude; and the acquisition of ability to distinguish that attitude marks only an increase of distinctions in original subject-matter.

Although contemporary theory emphasizes the psychologic and personal aspect of religion, historic religions have always had their holy places, times, persons and rites. One may believe that these objects did not have in the order of objects of knowledge the qualities ascribed to them in belief, but the testimony in behalf of the natural objective reference of the subject-matter of experience then becomes only the more impressive. Myths would not be taken to be on a level with physical facts were not the bias of experience toward the objective. Recognition of objects of worship and prayer as ideal or as "essences," treatment of them as poetic or esthetic, represents a late achievement of reflection, not an original datum. If research into religious phenomena has proved anything it is that acts, rites, cults, ceremonies, institutions, are primary, emotional beliefs then clustering about them. Even religious experience does not escape the objective compulsions which inhere in the more direct experience where man tills the soil with the sweat of his brow and woman brings forth in labor. The objects that are auxiliary and hostile to success in these acts affect the most refined and spiritualized sentiments and conceptions.

The notion that experience is solely experiencing, a succession of personal sensations, images and feelings is wholly a recent notion. There is a genuine and important discovery implied by it. But it may be asserted that no one ever took it literally; it has been only a starting-point for dialectical developments which are sufficiently interesting to obscure the absurdity of the basic conception. The discovery is important; for it marks the discovery of operation of organic attitudes and dispositions in the beliefs we hold and the necessity of controlling them if beliefs are to be effectively controlled. The literal isolation of processes of experiencing, as if they were actually something solid and integral, is absurd; because dispositions and attitudes are always towards or from things beyond themselves. To love and hate, desire and fear, believe and deny, are not just states of mind in nor states of an animal body; they are *active* performances to and about other things,—acceptances and rejections, assimilations and forthspewings of other things, strugglings to obtain and to escape things.

The fact that the characteristic structure and function of these acts, in complexly organized animal forms, can be detected, shown, and in turn made the subject of new modes of responsive action expresses one of the most valuable philosophic uses of empirical method. It undermines rigid dogmatism, while it also changes scepticism from a wholesale and barren possession of a few aloof thinkers into a common and fertile method of inquiry into specific beliefs. The things which a man experiences come to him clothed with meanings which originate in custom and tradition. From his birth an individual sees persons about him treat things in certain ways, subject them to certain uses, assign to them certain potencies. The things are thereby invested for him with certain properties, and the investiture appears intrinsic and indissoluble. The potency of custom over beliefs never received a fatal wound until physiology and psychology showed how imitation, suggestion, stimulation, prestige, operate to call out certain responses, and how habit confirms and consolidates the responses into apparent matter-of-course unquestioned necessities.

Man lives by expectation, but the content of expectation, *what* is anticipated, depends upon memory; and memories are group affairs before they are personal recalls. The tradition that controls belief, expectation and memory, is limited and usually perverted. Not even wood always burns; seeds do not always grow, nor foodstuffs always nourish; water in quenching thirst may bring a malignant plague. In complex matters the frustration of conduct based upon expectant belief is still more pervasive. The man enmeshed in labor accounts up to a certain point for these unaccountable behaviors of things by noting further qualifying conditions that affect efficacy; soon reaching the end of his tether, he then falls back upon mysterious potencies, concealed personal agencies and magical counteractions. The thinker who enjoys leisure and is removed from the immediate necessity of doing something about these predicaments, seeks certitude in a higher, more metaphysical realm of Being, and defines as mere "appearance" the region of actual and possible frustrations. Or he turns disillusioned sceptic, and will abstain from all intellectual commitment to objects. The first method creates superstitions; the second is sterile, because it affords no solution of the actual problem, that of regulating specific beliefs about objects, so that they take account of what is ulterior and eventual. The finding and pointing out of the roles of personal attitudes and dispositions in inference and belief as well as in all other relationships with things (a discovery that constitutes psychology as it becomes systematic), is an indispensable part of this art of regulating ideas about objects; and this art is an indispensable factor in liberation.

Philosophers however misinterpreted the discovery. The old confusion persisted; the identification of direct having with knowing seemed to be the one sound and permanent part of the classic philosophic tradition. "Having" these personal dispositions being in a sense basic to other "havings," it was translated into the belief that they were the first and primary objects of knowledge, possessed of the attributes of reality attributed by classic philosophy to *its* prior and primary objects of knowledge. Meanwhile men of science and affairs *used* the discovery; it was to them an assurance that by taking better care of the generation and employment of these personal attitudes, mankind could attain to a more secure and meaningful regulation of its ineradicable and coercive concern with things of the environment.

Thus the value of the notion of experience for philosophic reflection is that it denotes both the field, the sun and clouds and rain, seeds, and harvest, and the man who labors, who plans, invents, uses, suffers, and enjoys. Experience denotes what is experienced, the world of events and persons; and it denotes that world caught up into experiencing, the career and destiny of mankind. Nature's place in man is no less significant than man's place in nature. Man in nature is man subjected; nature in man, recognized and used, is intelligence and art. The value of experience for the philosopher is that it serves as a constant reminder of something which is neither exclusive and isolated subject or object, matter or mind, nor yet one plus the other. The fact of integration in life is a basic fact, and until its recognition becomes habitual, unconscious and pervasive, we need a word like experience to remind us of it, and to keep before thought the distortions that occur when the integration is ignored or denied.

The denotations that constitute experience point to history, to temporal process. The technically expert are aware how much ingenuity has been spent upon discovering something which shall be wholly present, so completely present as to exclude movement and change. There are *phases* of things to which this search is pertinent. There are moments of consummation when before and after are legitimately forgotten, and the sole stake of man is in the present. But even such objects are discovered to arise as culminations of processes, and to be in turn transitive and effective, while they may be also predictive or cognitively significant. The legitimacy of timeless absorption is no argument in behalf of the legitimacy of timeless objects. Experience is history; and the *taking* of some objects as final is itself an episode in history. The testimony of an absorbed consciousness that at last it rests upon something superior to the vicissitudes of time is of no more cognitive worth than the testimony of any other purely immediate consciousness. That is, it is not testimony at all, it is a having, not a knowing. And hence when treated as cognition, it is never natural and naïve; it is suborned in the interest of a sophisticated metaphysics. There is no testimony in such moments just because of absorption in the immediate qualities of the object. There is enjoyment and possession, with no need of thought as to how the object came or whither it is going, what evidence it gives. And when it turns evidence, it always testifies to an existence which is partial or particular, and local.

The assumption that the ultimate and the immediate object is timeless is responsible for one of the insoluble problems of certain types of philosophy. The past and future are rendered purely inferential, speculative, something to be reached by pure faith. But in fact anything denoted is found to have temporal quality and reference; it has movement from and towards *within* it; it is marked by waxings and wanings. The translation of temporal quality into an *order* of time is an intellectual arrangement, and is subject to doubt and error. Although pastness and futurity are qualities of everything present, such presence does not guarantee the date at which Columbus discovered America nor when the next eclipse of the moon will occur. For these things are matters that require measurements, comparisons, connection with remote occurrences. But objects of present experience have the actuality of a temporal procession, and accordingly reflection may assign things an order of succession within something which non-reflectively exists and is had.

The import of these remarks is anticipatory. Their full meaning can be had only when some of the denotations summed up in the notion of experience have been followed out and described. A justification of recapitulation of our prefatory considerations is the fact that experience has so often been employed to designate not a method but a stuff or subject-matter. It then gains a discriminatory and selective meaning and is used to justify, apart from actual experience and antecedent to it, some kinds of objects and to disparage and condemn others. "Experience" becomes a theory, and, like all theories as such, dialectic and *a priori*. The objection that the alternative notion of experience is so catholic and universal in application that it no longer has any distinctive meaning is sound in principle. But in the face of historic philosophies and the reigning tradition, the alternative notion is instructive and useful. It serves as a caution against methods that have led to wrong conclusions, and a reminder of a proper procedure to be followed.

In the first place it guards us against accepting as original, primitive and simple, distinctions that have become familiar to us, that are a customary part of our intellectual inheritance—such distinctions for example as that of the physical and mental. It warns us that all intellectual terms are the products of discrimination and classification, and that we must, as philosophers, go back to the primitive situations of life that antecede and generate these reflective interpretations, so that we re-live former processes of interpretation in a wary manner, with eyes constantly upon the things to which they refer. Thus empiricism is the truly critical method; it puts us knowingly and cautiously through steps which were first taken uncritically, and exposed to all kinds of adventitious influence.

In the second place, the notion of experience reminds us that, prior to philosophic reflection, objects have fallen into certain groupings, designated by the adjectives we readily prefix to the word experience:—adjectives like moral, esthetic, intellectual, religious, personal, political. The notion thus warns us against the tradition which makes the objects of a certain kind of experience, the cognitive, the fixed standard for estimating the "reality" and import of all other kinds of things. It cautions us against transferring the qualities characteristic of objects in a certain mode of organization to objects in other modes. Knowledge itself must be experienced; it must be had, possessed, enacted, before it can be known, and the having of it is no more identical with knowing it, or knowing it with having it, than is the case with anger, being ill, or being the possessor by inheritance of an estate. We have to identify cases of knowing by direct denotation before we can have a reflective experience of them, just as we do with good and bad, red and green, sweet and sour.

In the third place, the notion cautions us that we must begin with things in their complex entanglements rather than with simplifications made for the purpose of effective judgment and action; whether the purpose is economy or dialectical esthetic or moral. The simplifications of philosophic data have been largely determined by apologetic methods, that is by interest in dignifying certain kinds and phases of things. So strong is this tendency that if a philosopher points to any particular thing as important enough to demand notation, it is practically certain that some critic will shift the issue from whether the denoted thing is found to be as he has described it to be, to the question of value. For example, I have asserted that all denoted things possess temporal quality. It is reasonably certain that this statement will be taken by some critic to indicate a preference on my part for change over permanence, an implied statement that it is *better* that things should be in flux. It has been stated that objects are primarily denoted in their practical relationships, as things of doing, suffering, contact, possession and use. Instead of being discussed as a question of denotation, the philosophic tradition is such that the statement will be taken as an eulogy; as implying that practice is better than theory. It is then "refuted" by pointing out the superior charm of the contemplative life.

This bias is so strong and so persistent that it testifies, I suppose, to a fact of importance, to the fact that most philosophical simplifications are due to a moral interest which is ignored and denied. Our constant and inalienable concern is with good and bad, prosperity and failure, and hence with choice. We are constructed to think in terms of value, of bearing upon welfare. The ideal of welfare varies, but the influence of interest in it is pervasive and inescapable. In a vital, though not the conventional, sense all men think with a moral bias and concern, the "immoral" man as truly as the righteous man; wicked and just men being characterized by bents toward different kinds of things as good. Now this fact seems to me of great importance for philosophy; it indicates that in some sense all philosophy is a branch of morals. But acknowledgment that the ultimate ground of reflection is to enable men better to make choice of things as good and bad is in truth the opposite attitude from that which immediately converts traits of existence into moral qualities, and which transforms preferred qualities into properties of true and real being. For the former concerns action to be performed, the direction of desire, purpose and endeavor. The latter is an affair of existence as it is found to be; material, it may be, of choice and action, but material, not goal or finished object.

For reflection the eventual is always better or worse than the given. But since it would also be better if the eventual good were now given, the philosopher, belonging by status to a leisure class relieved from the more urgent necessity of dealing with conditions, converts the eventual into some kind of Being, something which *is*, even if it does not *exist*. Permanence, real essence, totality, order, unity, rationality, the *unum, verum, et bonum* of the classic tradition, are obviously eulogistic predicates. When accordingly we find such terms used to describe the foundations and proper conclusions of a philosophic system, there is ground for suspecting that an artificial simplification of existence has been performed. Reflection determining preference for an eventual good has dialectically wrought a miracle of transubstantiation. Here if anywhere it is needful that we return to the mixed and entangled things expressed by the term experience.

The occurrence of the moral fallacy is obscured and disguised in subtle ways. That having the greatest power of self-deception springs from the conventional associations of the word moral. When a thinker has escaped from them he fancies that he has escaped morals. His conclusions are fixed by a preference for a reflective "good," that is to say by preference for things which have a quality of goodness that satisfies the requirements of reasonable examination and judgment. But overtly he may contemn the moral life, on the ground that it involves struggle, effort, disappointment, constantly renewed. Hence he asserts that the true good is non-moral, since it includes none of these things. According to special temperament and to accidents of education, due in turn largely to social and economic status, the true good is then conceived either esthetically, or dialectically, or in terms borrowed from a religious context. Then "reality" as the object of philosophic research is described with the properties required by the choice of good that has occurred. The significant thing, however, is not the thinker's disparaging view of moral life as conflict and practical effort; it is that his *reflective* idea of the good, which after all is the essence of morals, has been converted into a norm and model of Being. His choice of what is good, whether logically conceived or instigated by cultivated taste, is the heart of the matter.

The operation of choice is, I suppose, inevitable in any enterprise into which reflection enters. It is not in itself falsifying. Deception lies in the fact that its presence is concealed, disguised, denied. An empirical method finds and points to the operation of choice as it does to any other event. Thus it protects us from conversion of eventual functions into antecedent existence: a conversion that may be said to be *the* philosophic fallacy, whether it be performed in behalf of mathematical subsistences, esthetic essences, the purely physical order of nature, or God. The present writer does not profess any greater candor of intent than animates fellow philosophers. But the pursuance of an empirical method, is, it is submitted, the way to secure execution of candid intent. Whatever is employed as subject-matter of choice, determining its need and giving it guidance, an empirical method frankly indicates for what it is; and the fact of choice, with its workings and consequences, an empirical method points out with equal openness.

The adoption of an empirical method is no guarantee that all the things relevant to any particular conclusion will actually be found or pointed to, or that when found they will be correctly shown or communicated. But the empirical method points out when and where and how things of a designated description have been arrived at. It places before others a map of the road that has been travelled; they may accordingly, if they will, re-travel the road to inspect the landscape for themselves. Thus the findings of one may be rectified and extended by the findings of others, with as much assurance as is humanly possible of confirmation, extension and rectification. The adoption of empirical, or denotative, method would thus procure for philosophic reflection something of that cooperative tendency toward consensus which marks inquiry in the natural sciences. The scientific investigator convinces others not by the plausibility of his definitions and the cogency of his dialectic, but by placing before them the specified course of experiences of searchings, doings and findings in consequence of which certain things have been found. His appeal is for others to traverse a similar course, so as to see how what they find corresponds with his report.

Dialectic thereby itself receives a designated status and office. As it occurs in philosophic thought its dependence upon an original act of selective choice is often not avowed. Its premises are alleged to be indubitable and self-guaranteeing. Honest empirical method will state when and where and why the act of selection took place, and thus enable others to repeat it and test its worth. Selective choice, denoted as an empirical event will reveal the basis and bearing of intellectual simplifications; they then cease to be of such a self-enclosed nature as to be affairs only of opinion and argument, admitting no alternatives save complete acceptance or rejection. Choice that is disguised or denied is the source of those astounding differences of philosophic belief that startle the beginner and that become the plaything of the expert. Choice that is avowed is an experiment to be tried on its merits and tested by its results. Under all the captions that are called immediate knowledge, or self-sufficient certitude of belief, whether logical, esthetic or epistemological, there is something selected for a purpose, and hence not simple, not self-evident and not intrinsically eulogizable. State the purpose so that it may be re-experienced, and its value and the pertinency of selection made in its behalf may be tested. The purport of thinking, scientific and philosophic, is not to eliminate choice but to render it less arbitrary, and more significant. It loses its arbitrary character when its quality and consequences are such as to commend themselves to the reflection of others after they have betaken themselves to the situations indicated; it becomes significant when reason for the choice is found to be weighty, and its consequences momentous. This statement is not a commendation of the will to believe. It is not a statement that we *should* choose, or that *some* choices are self-justifying. It is a statement that wherever reflection occurs and intelligence operates, a selective discrimination *does* occur. The justification of a choice is wholly another matter; it is extrinsic. It depends upon the extent in which observation, memory and forethought have entered into making the choice, and upon the consequences that flow from it. When choice is avowed, others can repeat the course of the experience; it is an experiment to be tried, not an automatic safety device.

This particular affair is referred to here not so much as matter of doctrine as to afford an illustration of the nature of empirical method. Truth or falsity depends upon what others find when they warily perform the experiment of observing reflective events. An empirical finding is refuted not by denial that one finds things to be thus and so, but by giving directions for a course of experience that results in finding its opposite to be the case. To convince of error as well as to lead to truth is to assist another to see and find something which he hitherto has failed to find and recognize. All of the wit and subtlety of reflection and of dialectic find scope in the elaboration and conveying of directions that intelligibly point out a course to be followed. Every system of philosophy presents the consequences of some such experiment. As experiments, each has contributed something of worth to our observation of the events and qualities of experienceable objects. Some harsh criticisms of traditional philosophy have already been suggested; others will doubtless follow. But the criticism is not directed at the experiments; it is aimed at the denial to them by the philosophic tradition of selective experimental quality, a denial which has isolated them from their actual context and function, and has thereby converted potential illuminations into arbitrary assertions.

All philosophies employ empirical subject-matter, even the most transcendental; there is nothing else for them to go by. But in ignoring the kind of empirical situation to which their themes pertain and in failing to supply directions for experimental pointing and searching they become non-empirical. Hence it may be asserted that the final issue of empirical method is whether the guide and standard of beliefs and conduct lies within or without the *shareable* situations of life. The ultimate accusation levelled against professedly non-empirical philosophies is that in casting aspersion upon the events and objects of experience, they deny the power of common life to develop its own regulative methods and to furnish from within itself adequate goals, ideals, and criteria. Thus in effect they claim a private access to truth and deprive the things of common experience of the enlightenment and guidance that philosophy might otherwise derive from them. The transcendentalist has conspired with his arch-enemy, the sensualist, to narrow the acknowledged subject-matter of experience and to lessen its potencies for a wider and directed reflective choice. Respect for experience is respect for its possibilities in thought and knowledge as well as an enforced attention to its joys and sorrows. Intellectual piety toward experience is a precondition of the direction of life and of tolerant and generous cooperation among men. Respect for the things of experience alone brings with it such a respect for others, the centres of experience, as is free from patronage, domination and the will to impose.

Appendix 3
The Paul Carus Foundation

Dr. Paul Carus was born in Ilsenburg, Germany, in 1852. He was educated at the Universities of Strassburg and Tübingen, from the latter of which he received the doctorate of philosophy in 1876. It was, however, in the United States, to which he shortly after removed, that his life-work was performed. He became editor of the *Open Court* in 1888, and later established *The Monist*, remaining throughout his career, editor of these two periodicals and Director of the editorial policies of the Open Court Company. He died in February, 1919, at La Salle, Illinois.

The primary interests which actuated Dr. Carus's life-work were in the field of philosophy, touching with almost equal weight the two great phases of modern speculative concern represented by the philosophy of science and comparative religion. To each of these he devoted numerous special studies, and to each he gave the influence of the press which he directed. This influence was in no sense narrow or specialistic. Dr. Carus was personally profoundly concerned for the broadening of that understanding in all intellectual fields which he felt must be the foundation of whatever is to be valuable in our future human culture; he saw his philosophy never as a closet pursuit, but always as a quest for the social illumination of mankind, in which his hope of betterment lay. In this interest he combatted prejudice, in religion and science alike, seeking to divest the spirit of truth of all cloaking of formula, and turning with eager and open eyes in every direction in which there was a suggestion of light and leading—to men and to thought of every complexion and to all levels of active human concern with matters of reflection. Dr. Carus was, in fact, strongly Socratic in disposition: he wished to bring philosophy down from the skies of a too studied abstraction and habituate it to the houses of men's souls and to the rich and changing tides of cultural interests. Certainly so far as America is concerned his service is a signal one. During much of his career he stood almost alone as a philosopher outside academic walls, a living exponent of the fact that philosophy is significant as a force as well as useful as an educational discipline. He looked to the cultivation of philosophy as a frame of mind open to all, lay and professional, who should come to see that social liberty is made secure only where there is growth of a sympathetic public intelligence.

It is with the spirit and intention of Dr. Carus's life-work in mind that his family have established in his memory the Paul Carus Lectures. In the United States, foundations devoted to the cultivation of philosophy are so confined to scholastic institutions that the whole field of philosophic concern tends to assume the slant of an immured and scholastic discipline; and the observer is tempted to say that the greatest gift that can befall philosophic liberalism is one that will cause its followers to forget their professional character. Such a gift, certainly, is more than suggested by a lectureship which comes with no institutional atmosphere to further the free play of the mind upon all phases of life. In the stipulations for the Carus lectures, the themes of the lectures are left without definition, for it is recognized that philosophy is a spirit of approach rather than a set of problems or theories; and the choice of the lecturers, while it is properly placed in the hands of those who make the study of philosophy their profession, is in no manner limited. The Foundation is free, and it asks of its beneficiaries no other response than the spirit of liberalism.

The conditions governing the lectures are few. They are established as a memorial and are to be called the "Paul Carus Lectures." The lecturers are to be chosen by committees appointed from the Divisions of the American Philosophical Association. The lecturer is recognized by an honorarium of one thousand dollars, and the lectures are to be published by the Open Court Company in a series of volumes, which, it is hoped, as the years pass, will become representative of the finest phases of our speculative thought. It is expected that series of lectures will be delivered biennially, the time and place being set by the committees to whom is delegated the selection of the lecturers. It is more than happy that the first series of the Paul Carus Lectures should have been delivered by John Dewey, for there is no living American philosopher of whom it can more truly be said that his influence is of the type which represents Dr. Carus's ideal.

HARTLEY BURR ALEXANDER.

First Edition Pagination Key

Scholarly studies have in the past referred only to the pagina-tion of the 1925 Open Court edition or the 1929 W.W. Norton "second edition" of *Experience and Nature*. The list below relates that pagina-tion to the pagination of the present edition. Before the colon appear the 1925 and 1929 edition pages; after the colon are the pages (with corre-sponding text) from the present edition. First chapter numbers refer only to the Norton printing.

1a:10	22:28–29	47:46–47	72:64–65
2a:10–11	23:29–30	48:47–48	73:65
3a:11–12	24:30–31	49:48–49	74:65–66
4a:12–13	25:31	50:49	75:66–67
1:13	26:31–32	51:49–50	76:67–68
2:13–14	27:32–33	52:50–51	77:68
3:14–15	28:33–34	53:51	78:69
4:15–16	29:34	54:51–52	79:69–70
5:16	30:34–35	55:52–53	80:70–71
6:16–17	31:35–36	56:53	81:71
7:17–18	32:36	57:53–54	82:71–72
8:18–19	33:36–37	58:54–55	83:72–73
9:19	34:37–38	59:55	84:73–74
10:19–20	35:38–39	60:56	85:74
11:20–21	36:39–40	61:56–57	86:74–75
12:21–22	37:40	62:57–58	87:75–76
13:22	38:40–41	63:58	88:76–77
14:22–23	39:41	64:58–59	89:77
15:23–24	40:42	65:59–60	90:77–78
16:24–25	41:42–43	66:60	91:78–79
17:25	42:43–44	67:60–61	92:79
18:25–26	43:44	68:61–62	93:79–80
19:26–27	44:44–45	69:62–63	94:80–81
20:27–28	45:45–46	70:63	95:81
21:28	46:46	71:63–64	96:81–82

269:205–6	312:236	355:266–67	398:297–98
270:206–7	313:236–37	356:267–68	399:298–99
271:207	314:237–38	357:268	400:299–300
272:208	315:238	358:268–69	401:300
273:208–9	316:238–39	359:269–70	402:300–301
274:209–10	317:239–40	360:270–71	403:301–2
275:210	318:240	361:271	404:302
276:210–11	319:241	362:271–72	405:303
277:211–12	320:241–42	363:272–73	406:303–4
278:212	321:242–43	364:273	407:304–5
279:212–13	322:243	365:273–74	408:305
280:213–14	323:243–44	366:274–75	409:305–6
281:214–15	324:244–45	367:275–76	410:306–7
282:215	325:245	368:276	411:307
283:215–16	326:245–46	369:276–77	412:308
284:216–17	327:246–47	370:277–78	413:308–9
285:217	328:247–48	371:278	414:309–10
286:217–18	329:248	372:278–79	415:310
287:218–19	330:248–49	373:279–80	416:310–11
288:219–20	331:249–50	374:280–81	417:311–12
289:220	332:250	375:281	418:312–13
290:220–21	333:250–51	376:281–82	419:313
291:221–22	334:251–52	377:282–83	420:313–14
292:222	335:252	378:283	421:314–15
293:222–23	336:252–53	379:283–84	422:315
294:223–24	337:253–54	380:284–85	423:315–16
295:224–25	338:254–55	381:285	424:316–17
296:225	339:255	382:285–86	425:317–18
297:225	340:255–56	383:286–87	426:318
298:226	341:256–57	384:287–88	427:318–19
299:226–27	342:257	385:288	428:319–20
300:227–28	343:258	386:288–89	429:320
301:228	344:258–59	387:289–90	430:320–21
302:228–29	345:259–60	388:290	431:321–22
303:229–30	346:260	389:290–91	432:322–23
304:230–31	347:260–61	390:291–92	433:323
305:231	348:261–62	391:292–93	434:323–24
306:231–32	349:262	392:293	435:324–25
307:232–33	350:263	393:293–94	436:325
308:233	351:263–64	394:295	437:325–26
309:233–34	352:264–65	395:295–96	
310:234–35	353:265	396:296–97	
311:235–36	354:266	397:297	

Textual Apparatus
Index

Textual Commentary

John Dewey was selected in 1922 by what the official announcement called "committees appointed from the Divisions of the American Philosophical Association" to present the first series of lectures on the Paul Carus Foundation. From the time this new foundation's establishment was announced, philosophers proclaimed it "an undertaking of high import for the intellectual life of America."[1] The choice of Dewey to inaugurate such a prestigious series clearly certified him as America's preeminent philosopher: as the chairman of the selection committee wrote, "There is no living American philosopher of whom it can more truly be said that his influence is of the type which represents Dr. Carus's ideal."[2]

Dewey delivered the first Carus Lectures, a series of three, before a joint session of the Eastern and Western Divisions of the American Philosophical Association, held at the Union Theological Seminary in New York City on 27, 28, and 29 December 1922. Whether he read the addresses from completed drafts is not known. Some forty pages of sketchy notes from 1922, handwritten and typewritten, labeled "Carus Lectures," survive for the three lectures, which were entitled "Existence as Stable and Precarious," "Existence, Ends, and Appreciation," and "Existence, Means, and Knowledge."[3] None of these titles appears in the notes, however, and it seems likely that the extant notes were early ones and that Dewey read fairly finished papers that also, in turn, served as working material for the book *Experience and Nature*.

Experience and Nature was published by the Open Court Publishing Company in February 1925, just over two years after Dewey's presentation of the Lectures. Dewey developed the three Lectures into ten chap-

1. Review signed "E. N.," *Boston Evening Transcript*, 9 May 1925, p. 5.
2. Hartley Burr Alexander, "The Paul Carus Foundation," *Experience and Nature* (Chicago, London: Open Court Publishing Co., 1925), p. ix; see this volume, Appendix 3.
3. The titles of the lectures were noted in *Journal of Philosophy* 19 (1922): 720–21; the notes are in the John Dewey Papers, Special Collections, Morris Library, Southern Illinois University at Carbondale.

ters; however, the only original title used as a chapter title (with the order of the adjectives reversed) was "Existence as Precarious and as Stable." Some reviewers, misled by the "Carus Lectures" description in the volume, thought Dewey had actually delivered ten lectures.[4] Rather, he had devoted much time to expanding the original ideas of the lectures into a very full statement of his mature philosophy.

Experience and Nature was widely expected after the presentation of the Carus Lectures. Therefore, when the book appeared, it received more than ordinary critical notice: in 1925, twenty-five reviews appeared and ten more followed in 1926, 1927, and 1928. When the book was reprinted with revisions in 1929, however, only eight reviews were published and several of these, by failing to comment on the revisions, seemed to treat the book as if it were a newly published work.[5]

4. John Laird, Mind, n.s. 34 (1925): 482; E. N., Boston Evening Transcript, 9 May 1925, p. 5.

5. The reviews of Experience and Nature were: C. E. Ayres, New Republic, 25 March 1925, pp. 129–31; George Brown, Springfield Daily Republican, 20 September 1925; Norborne H. Crowell, Quarterly Journal of the University of North Dakota 15 (1925): 363–66; Robert L. Duffus, New York Times Book Review, 3 May 1925, p. 4; Irwin Edman, New York Herald Tribune Books, 3 May 1925, pp. 1–2; C. E. M. Joad, Nation and Athenaeum 37 (1925): 682, 684; Paul Jones, World Tomorrow 8 (1925): 383; John Laird, Mind, n.s. 34 (1925): 476–82; Matthew T. McClure, Nation, 14 October 1925, supp. 430–32; E. N., Boston Evening Transcript, 9 May 1925; Ralph Barton Perry, Saturday Review of Literature, 4 July 1925, pp. 874–75; C. F. Salmond, Australasian Journal of Psychology and Philosophy 3 (1925): 230–31; Hugh W. Sanford, Sewanee Review 33 (1925): 496–99; George Santayana, "Dewey's Naturalistic Metaphysics," Journal of Philosophy 22 (1925): 673–88; F. C. S. Schiller, Spectator 135 (1925): 494, 497; Robert Mark Wenley, Anglican Theological Review 8 (1925–26): 277–78; Henry Nelson Wieman, Journal of Religion 5 (1925): 519–42; A.L.A. Booklist 21 (1925): 356; American Review of Reviews 72 (1925): 560; Dial 78 (1925): 429; Independent 115 (1925): 396; Journal of Religion 5 (1925): 445; Outlook 140 (1925): 267–68; George Plimpton Adams, International Journal of Ethics 36 (1926): 201–5; H. Wildon Carr, Philosophical Review 35 (1926): 64–68; Joseph Kinmont Hart, Survey 54 (1925): 534; 55 (1925–26): 239–40, 377, 509–10, 570, 697; 56 (1926): 103–4, 266, 387, 471, 551, 642; Joseph Jastrow, Forum 76 (1926): 316; C. R. Morris, Hibbert Journal 24 (1926): 370–73; Roy Wood Sellars, Journal of Religion 6 (1926): 89–91; Thomas Dawes Eliot, Welfare Magazine 18 (1927): 1401–2; M. O., Social Forces 5 (1927): 686–87; Everett W. Hall, "Some Meanings of Meaning in Dewey's Experience and Nature," Journal of Philosophy 25 (1928): 169–81; Herbert H. Farmer, Journal of Theological Studies 31 (1929): 82–86; C. Hartley Grattan, New York World, 27 October 1929; C. E. M. Joad, Nation and Athenaeum 45 (1929): 832, 834; E. M. Whetnall, Mind, n.s. 38 (1929): 527–28; Bookman 69 (1929): iv; Expository Times (Edinburgh) 40 (1929): 493; Nature 126 (1930): 680; Times Literary Supplement (London), 23 January 1930, p. 63.

The reviews were of varying lengths, from a simple listing to Joseph Kinmont Hart's eleven-part discussion in eleven issues of *Survey* between November 1925 and September 1926, a discussion that was the basis of his book *Inside Experience: A Naturalistic Philosophy of Life and the Modern World* (New York: Longmans, Green and Co., 1927), for which Dewey wrote an "Introductory Note," pp. xxi–xxvi.

Most of the reviews had one common feature: they identified *Experience and Nature* as a major, important work; indeed, many scholars continue to regard it as Dewey's *magnum opus.*

Reviews that found little ground for agreeing with the book's content were in religious journals—*Journal of Religion, Anglican Theological Review, Journal of Theological Studies* (Edinburgh)—that objected to Dewey's naturalism. Even amid his objections, however, one of these critics went so far as to say,

> I have been critical of this book because it deserves that attitude. I mean this in the way of a compliment. I believe that Dewey is on the right track and that something of the nature of a humanistic naturalism has come upon the modern world to stay. Let those who are working in the field of religion take note.[6]

Most of the reviews had another feature in common: reviewers generally commented—whether favorably or unfavorably—on Dewey's writing style. The following two examples illustrate the extremes of such commentary:

> [*Experience and Nature* is] an exposition of his philosophy which while having experience as its starting point and being concerned with the vital problems of human existence is expressed in such difficult and involved language as to discourage all but the serious student and most patient reader.[7]

One may compare the following:

> While we are not in agreement with the philosophical standpoint of the author, we recognize the ability with which he argues, and are specially grateful for the lucidity and intelligibility of his writing. He has kept in view all through not only the expert, but the reader of ordinary intelligence.[8]

Several reviewers offered explanations for difficulties occasioned by Dewey's style. Thomas Dawes Eliot remarked in *Welfare Magazine,* "Dewey's style is sometimes very clear, sometimes very difficult. Punc-

6. Roy Wood Sellars, *Journal of Religion* 6 (1926): 91.
7. *A.L.A. Booklist* 21 (1925): 356.
8. *Expository Times* (Edinburgh) 40 (1929): 493.

tuation and type-reading are occasionally accountable."[9] Two others agreed that readers too often tried to make Dewey's work unnecessarily complicated. M. T. McClure wrote in Nation, "The readers of Mr. Dewey almost always complain that he is difficult to understand. The reason is that they fail to grasp the profound simplicity, the utter naivete of the man."[10] C. E. Ayres added in New Republic:

> The simplicity of this philosophy [is] a simplicity not of style, but of ideas. As writing its pattern is complicated and irregular, as thinking, compact, symmetrical, and clear as a March morning; clear of fogs that rise from the miasma of unconscious intellectual motives, and clear of the showers of unnecessary terminology that usually come down in a perpetual drizzle in the humid climate of metaphysics.[11]

Ralph Barton Perry provided perhaps the most balanced view of these widely recognized stylistic difficulties in Dewey's work. He wrote:

> While the present volume does not mitigate [the] characteristic difficulties of Professor Dewey's philosophy, it has distinction of style and a certain eloquence and persuasiveness. It has the obscurity of discourse which is both abstract and literary, having neither schematic precision nor concrete vividness; but how the author's peculiar philosophy could be more skilfully and more aptly insinuated into the reader's mind is difficult to conceive.[12]

As the Ayres passage quoted above exemplifies particularly well, many reviewers who praised the book were not content to do so in simple prose; instead, Experience and Nature seems to have inspired them to flights of metaphor, such as the following:

> Irwin Edman: With monumental care, detail and completeness Professor Dewey has in this volume revealed the metaphysical heart that beats its unvarying alert tempo through all his writings, whatever their explicit themes.[13]

> Robert L. Duffus: Professor Dewey . . . does believe . . . that something can be done to make the universe more habitable. He believes in life, in activity, in adventure. When certain clouds of dust, now in the air and not always too pleasant smelling, have blown away it is possible that we shall see the artists and thinkers of America marching

9. Thomas Dawes Eliot, Welfare Magazine 18 (1927): 1401–2.
10. Matthew T. McClure, Nation, 14 October 1925, supp. 430.
11. C. E. Ayres, New Republic, 25 March 1925, p. 130.
12. Ralph Barton Perry, Saturday Review of Literature, 4 July 1925, p. 875.
13. Irwin Edman, New York Herald Tribune Books, 3 May 1925, p. 1.

with resolute gayety along the trail Professor Dewey has marked out.[14]

Joseph Kinmont Hart: [This book] plows up old sod-bound meadows of fact, belief, institution and habitual "mind," and lets new supplies of oxygen in upon the almost dead roots below, to say little of the light it lets in upon the field mice, the bumble bees and the yellow jackets that have too long been nesting there.[15]

Two of the longer reviews evoked responses from Dewey. His "Meaning and Existence," *Journal of Philosophy* 25 (1928): 345–53, was an answer to Everett W. Hall's "Some Meanings of Meaning in Dewey's *Experience and Nature*," which appeared in the same volume of the *Journal of Philosophy*, pp. 169–81. Earlier he had addressed Santayana's "Dewey's Naturalistic Metaphysics," *Journal of Philosophy* 22 (1925): 673–88, along with Frank Thilly's "Contemporary American Philosophy," *Philosophical Review* 35 (1926): 522–38; his response to these two articles was "Half-Hearted Naturalism," *Journal of Philosophy* 24 (1927): 57–64. Both sides of these two exchanges will appear in *The Later Works of John Dewey*.

Twenty-seven months elapsed between December 1922 when Dewey gave the Carus Lectures and February 1925 when Open Court published *Experience and Nature*. Although this may seem over-long to develop a body of well thought-out ideas from addresses into a book, it must be recalled that it took time to produce and publish a book, as well as to expand the three lectures into ten chapters. In fact, the time seems fairly short when we realize that in March 1924, eleven months before publication, Dewey expected to deliver the finished manuscript to Open Court.[16]

Experience and Nature was registered for copyright (A822037) "following publication on February 9, 1925." Inexplicably, a second copyright (A822122) was registered "following publication February 14, 1925." No clues exist in the Copyright Office records as to why two almost simultaneous copyrights were so registered. The 1925 first impression carried the "Chicago : London" notice on the title page; it was distributed in England by Open Court.

14. Robert L. Duffus, *New York Times Book Review*, 3 May 1925, p. 4.
15. Joseph Kinmont Hart, *Survey* 55 (1925): 240.
16. Dewey to A. W. Burnett, 5 March 1924, Henry Holt Publishing Company Archives, Princeton University Library:
   I have no book on the philosophy of education coming out. The book formed by the Carus Lectures will be called, "Experience and Nature". Mrs. Carus wished it to be published by the Open Court Company, and of course I felt bound to accede to her desire. I have not placed the manuscript in their hands yet, but hope to do so during the present month.

Experience and Nature was plated in 1925 for this first impression. With only minor changes, the plates served for a 1926 second impression of the entire book as well as for the 1929 third impression of chapters 2–10.

The 1926 second impression, identified by the title-page date below the Open Court Publishing Company imprint, provided an opportunity for the publisher to make a number of corrections in the plates. Comparison of the 1925 and 1926 impressions on the Hinman Machine reveals, however, that efforts to repair plate damage at various other places in the book led to the introduction of nine new errors, five of which were in a single paragraph on one page.

A third impression of the work was called for in 1929. The word "experience," as Dewey had used it in the 1925 and 1926 impressions of *Experience and Nature,* caused many misunderstandings among his readers and continued to plague him up to 1951, the year before his death.[17] Thus, he seized the opportunity of this new impression to rewrite the first chapter in an effort to clear up some of the misunderstandings. In a letter of early January 1929, he asked Max Otto for specific comments about this chapter:

> I hope very much that you will sometime find the time to develop more fully your criticism regarding method and content. I realized soon after the book was published that the first chapter gave more difficulty to even careful readers than probably any other chapter in the book, in addition to frightening off persons who had no special technical preparation. A year ago, I had some conversation with Miss Cooke, of the Open Court Co., about completely re-writing the chapter for the next edition. They were very generous about consenting to changing plates, etc. I learned a few weeks ago that they expect to print the third edition this spring, and that it would be necessary if anything was to be done about changing, for me to have the manuscript ready by February 1st. I am sorry the time is so soon, because it makes it impossible for me to do what I had decided needs to be done. I expect to undertake it, however, before the next edition is called for, and I hope you can give me any suggestions along the lines you mention, for they will be gratefully received.[18]

Dewey's request for more "suggestions along the lines you mention" referred to a letter that Otto had written to him in December of 1928:

17. See the last draft of Dewey's proposed new introduction to *Experience and Nature,* Appendix 1, this volume.
18. Dewey to Otto, 8 January 1929, Max Otto Papers, Archives Division, The State Historical Society of Wisconsin.

I might as well finish the page by *suggesting* the thing that troubled me in *Experience and Nature,* the thing to which I have several times referred. You make a distinction between method and content and insist upon philosophy as method. I took this lead very seriously. But if one does take it seriously, that is, if one takes you seriously as to method, he will have a content which he would not have if he chose the rationalistic method. It seems to me there is no way to avoid the use of experience as meaning different things, not only for different people, but for the same people. Little more can be done, I think, than to indicate this fact and to keep the different meanings distinct. Moreover, I am persuaded that the adoption of a certain method implies certain things as found and certain things as not found. I mean that there is no philosophic method which even as method leaves its user neutral as to the content of experience. . . . I still hope to present the matter to you in greater detail.[19]

While awaiting Otto's presentation of "greater detail," Dewey seems to have pondered that earlier letter about his definition of "experience." The analysis helped him immensely; Dewey wrote to Otto on 25 January 1929:

I have been rewriting ch. one for the new edition. I can't tell you how illuminating was your passage in which you quoted my sentence about exp. as method not subject-matter. It is ridiculous how that one thing opened up to me what was wrong in the chapter. I mean it is now ridiculous that I shouldn't have seen it before. What I meant—only didn't know it—was that *reflective analysis* & its products form a *method* for leading back to the *subjectmatter* of direct or "gross" experience; so that the *former* designates or denotes a path & projects a goal to be found in the latter—which being illuminated, clarified & directed by reflective findings as method, *also* tests and checks the latter. I don't know whether I have succeeded in stating it, but my own mind has cleared up enormously. Ratner helped me a lot with criticisms & suggestions which while made from a different point of view to yours fitted in wonderfully well.[20]

The preface to the 1929 revised third impression makes concrete acknowledgment of the contributions of Otto and Ratner to Dewey's revisions: "If the original intent is now better fulfilled, it is largely due to the help of kindly critics. I wish to record my especial indebtedness to Professor M. C. Otto of the University of Wisconsin and Mr. Joseph Ratner of Columbia University."[21]

19. Otto to Dewey, 19 December 1928.
20. Dewey to Otto, 25 January 1929.
21. *Experience and Nature* (New York: W. W. Norton and Co., 1929), p. i.

As Dewey had written to Otto, the Open Court Publishing Company had itself planned to undertake the "third edition" of *Experience and Nature*, but before Dewey's revisions were completed, negotiations began between Open Court and W. W. Norton Company and led to Norton's leasing the plates and setting the new material for a preface and a completely new chapter one in type for the third impression, under its own imprint. Norton also added a photograph of Dewey at his desk as a new preliminary page. The 1929 impression carries, in addition to the 1925 Open Court copyright notice, a 1929 Open Court copyright notice, presumably covering the new material. This copyright was, however, apparently never registered, as no record of it now exists in the Copyright Office. The Norton "second edition" (1929 impression) also appeared in London with a "George Allen & Unwin, Ltd." title page, using sheets labeled "Printed in the United States of America."

The eclectic text of the present edition uses the new 1929 material as copy-text for the preface as well as for chapter one. (The 1925, 1926 Chapter One appears as Appendix 2 in this volume.) Copy-text for the remaining chapters, 2–10, is the 1925 first impression.

Of the twenty-seven changes between the 1925 and 1926 impressions of chapters 2–10—all apparently made without Dewey's intervention— only two were necessary substantive corrections, both adopted here: 249.14, "is to" for "is" and 326.15, "in" for "is." In two instances, single quotation marks were changed to double, and eleven desirable alterations were made in accidentals, as for example, substitution of the proper French accents at 259.38 and 298.40, and the correction of a number of spelling and punctuation errors. All these were used in emending the 1925 text for the present edition.

As mentioned, the 1926 impression, in repairing plates without proper proofreading of the reset material, had also introduced nine new errors. Four of these were perpetuated in the 1929 third impression: 44.31, "dire" for "direct"; 72.31, "enchanced" for "enhanced" and on the following line, also reset, "imposition" for "impositions"; and at 145.25, "stablishes" for "establishes." The remaining five 1926 errors, and one continued from 1925, were corrected for the 1929 impression, in which, by resetting only one paragraph on page 194, four 1926 errors and the one continued from 1925 were all corrected: 194.10, "epiphenomenalisn"; 194.11, period dropped after "array" (and 194.11, the 1925 and 1926 "portentious" was corrected); 194.17, "conceptinos"; and 194.19–20, transposition of "the" and semicolon. Finally, the incorrect "a" at 220.14 was changed to "as."

Besides adding the preface and rewriting the first chapter completely, Dewey made some changes in the plates for the remainder of the book for the Norton 1929 impression, as he had planned to do for Open Court. These additions and corrections were completed in a remarkably short time. On 23 January 1929, Dewey wrote to Norton, "I have made a draft of the Preface, new material, although not the to be re-written first chapter."[22] A week later, he wrote: "I have finished the revision of the first chapter and have simplified it decidedly. The mss was so ragged that I have given it to a typist to copy. She says she will mail you two copies Monday."[23] Typesetting of the new first chapter moved along rapidly, so that Dewey was able to write to Norton on 8 February 1929: "I enclose the small corrections for plates. . . . The changes you made in the preface are all right; go ahead on that basis. The proofs haven't come; if they come before noon or three oclock I can do them today."[24]

In the second through the tenth chapters, seventeen changes (in addition to the correction of the 1926 errors described above) were made for the 1929 third printing. One was an error, the introduction of a comma after "Anyone" at 274.3, which occurred in connection with repair of the plate. Another change, the substitution of "is" for "while" at 262.24, has been rejected, as it seems to have been no more than a misguided attempt—whether by Dewey or by an editor—to complete a sentence that upon hasty reading might have appeared incomplete. The other changes have been accepted here as emendations of the copy-text representing Dewey's intentional corrections and improvements in the text, the "small corrections for plates" mentioned in his 8 February 1929 letter to Norton. They can be categorized as follows: four corrections of typographical errors—"contradictions" for "contraditions" at 46.29, "portentous" for "portentious" at 194.11 (mentioned above), "causally" for "casually" at 274.9 and "occurred" for "occured" at 263.10; substantive alterations—at 220.12, the addition of "what"; at 220.13, the deletion of "But"; rewriting at 254.7 to make a complete sentence; deletion of "to" at 272.27; "enters" for "enter" at 307.13; and at 307.21, "truth" for "truths." The accidentals alterations are: deletion of a comma at 101.32 after "philosophy"; addition of a comma after "urgent" at 231.17; changing a semicolon to a comma at 234.39; changing "consciously" to italic type at 293.19; and adding a comma after "made" at 308.11.

On 8 January 1930, Dewey wrote to W. W. Norton that he had sent a letter to "Miss K. Cooke of the Open Court Co., approving the sale of remainders & waiving any royalty payment on same," referring to the remaining copies of the 1925 and 1926 printings still held by Open Court.[25] Neither of the 1925 copyrights was renewed, so that, techni-

---

22. Dewey to Norton, 23 January 1929, W. W. Norton Publishing Company Correspondence, Columbia University.
23. Dewey to Norton, 31 January 1929.
24. Dewey to Norton, 8 February 1929.
25. Dewey to Norton, 8 January 1930.

cally, the entire work entered the public domain in 1953. Open Court published a somewhat corrected edition of *Experience and Nature* in 1958, which has sold widely in paperback; Dover Publications, using the 1929 plates, also issued a paperback in 1958—both companies waiting the full twenty-eight years after the presumably registered second copyright date of 1929.

Although W. W. Norton probably reprinted *Experience and Nature* several times during the 1930s and 1940s,[26] extensive search has failed to reveal any copy with a post-1929 date on the title page. Collation on the Hinman Machine of five 1929 exemplars that appear physically identical revealed no variants and it can reasonably be concluded that any printings after 1929 were not identified as such but instead merely reproduced the 1929 title page and verso without alteration. In addition, the plates of the text seem to have remained invariant, despite Dewey's having written to W. W. Norton on 20 July 1933, "I enclose statement of typographical corrections for Exp. & Nature." The statement to which Dewey referred was not his own, and, in fact, was not one he even checked carefully before forwarding; it was a list of twenty-two presumed errors sent to him gratuitously 18 July 1933 by Harold K. Beers, a St. Louis lawyer, who wrote to Dewey:

> My ability to detect these errors is due to experience in comparing judgments in our City Law Dep't. I really do not know whether it is an asset or liability since the errors for the most part do not detract from a clear understanding, and the fact that I notice them at all distracts my attention.[27]

Although most of the items on Beers's list were errors that have been corrected in the present edition, about a third were misinterpretations of correct readings.[28]

---

26. The Open Court Publishing Company Archives (Special Collections, Morris Library, Southern Illinois University at Carbondale) have no specific information about the dates or sizes of reprintings; they do note continuing payment of royalties by W. W. Norton to Open Court for this title through the 1940s.

27. Beers to Dewey, 18 July 1933, W. W. Norton Co. Correspondence.

28. The Beers list, with Dewey's holograph "Experience & Nature" at the top, and with page and line numbers from the present edition in brackets, was:
P. 57 [54.11] —2nd Paragraph 1st line "spiritualistic" has one "i" omitted.
P. 101 [85.29] 9th line "loosely" should be —loose.
P.102 [86.25] commencing with 18th line: "And when they are attained" to and including the word "perfections" in the 2nd line the sentence is not clear. I inserted the word "but" immediately before the italicized word "only."
P.143 [115.23] -5th l. word -as- should be inserted between "such" and "up".
P.144 [116.37] next to last line "that" is unnecessary.

Unfortunately, Dewey's revisions of the first chapter of *Experience and Nature* for the 1929 impression failed to eliminate the continuing misunderstandings of his meaning. Therefore, when in 1948 Beacon Press proposed to him a new edition of the book with a substantial new introduction, he accepted enthusiastically. Throughout 1948, 1949, and 1950, he worked intermittently, writing and rewriting the many pages of various drafts of the introduction, but finally came to recognize that he could never successfully communicate his conception of "experience" if he used that already-overloaded word. In 1951, putting aside the long, incomplete drafts for the introduction, he wrote six new pages that started, "Were I to write (or rewrite) *Experience and Nature* today, I would entitle the book *Culture and Nature* and the treatment of specific subject-matters would be correspondingly modified." That independent six-page statement appears intact in the present volume as the second part of Appendix 1 with Dewey's title, "Experience and Nature: A Re-Introduction."

Dewey was never able to complete a new introduction to *Experience and Nature*. Joseph Ratner, who worked closely with him on that material in 1948–50—retyping, suggesting directions and changes, editing—has recently conflated the incomplete drafts into a single cohesive document for the present volume, where it appears as the first part of Appendix 1, with the title "The Unfinished Introduction." The content of this "Unfinished Introduction" is all Dewey's own and Ratner

---

P149 [119.24] — 2nd line "to" should be inserted between "ble" and "historic".

P158 [126.18] -18th and 19th L. letter "t" should be omitted from the word phenomenal.

P.185 [145.25] -2nd L. —e— is omitted from word establishes.

P 187 [147.27] — last line "Whenever this" should be -Whenever there-.

P.194 [152.23] — 4th line from bottom I inserted the word -If- as the first word in the sentence commencing "In trying new".

P.199 [155.37] - line 21 ### "case" should be—cases-.

P.229 [177.2] - 1st L. letter -e- omitted from word "seventeenth".

P.230 [177.39] -13th line word "basis" should be "bias".

P. 236- [182.6–7] -be- should be inserted between "to" and "found" in 7 th Li

P.256 [197.18] — last line "as well" should be omitted.

P.272 [208.27] #next to last line "of" after "each" should be omitted.

P.314 [237.32] — 15th line "others" should be - other-.

P.323 [244.14] — 23rd line should be a comma after the word "cognitive".

P.347 [261.15] — 25th line-the first word in this line should be plural.

P.388 [290.35] — 3rd L. from bottom "ing" should be omitted from word "regarding".

P.395 [296.2] — 10th line "a" and "part" should be one word -apart-.

P.436 [325.34] — 2nd last line punctuation should be omitted after the word "construct".

has made few changes in Dewey's prose. Ratner has, however, as he explains in his "Editor's Note," necessarily deleted duplicated material and arranged parts from the several unfinished drafts to make a unified whole. Because it is not Dewey's own finished typescript, this edited material is presented here in an appendix rather than as part of the text. Thus, the reader has access in one volume to the accurate and complete record of Dewey's thoughts—both early and late—about *Experience and Nature*.

Textual Notes

44.31   direct] the last two letters of this word were dropped when corrections were made in the 1925 plates before the 1926 impression, creating a substantive variant that cannot be considered a revision.

72.32–33   impositions] As with "direct" at 59.26, a letter was inadvertently dropped from this word before the 1926 impression. The original reading is the correct one.

262.24   while] The substitution of "is" for "while" in the 1929 impression seems to have been an effort to complete a sentence which, upon hasty reading, might have appeared incomplete but was in fact acceptable in the 1925 and 1926 impressions.

Emendations List

All emendations in both substantives and accidentals introduced into the copy-text (preface and chapter 1, 1929; chapters 2–10, 1925) are recorded in the list that follows, with the exception of certain regularizations described and listed in this introductory explanation. Page-line number at left (all lines of print except running heads are counted) and the reading to the left of the square bracket are from the present edition. The bracket is followed by a symbol identifying the first appearance of the reading. W means Works—the present edition—and is used for emendations made here for the first time. The three impressions of the single edition of *Experience and Nature* are identified by the last two digits of the year of publication—25, 26, 29. When 25, 26, and 29 were invariant, no symbols are used in W emendations. Substantive variants in all texts collated are recorded here; the list thus serves as a historical collation as well as a record of emendations.

For emendations restricted to punctuation, the curved dash ~ means the same word(s) as before the bracket; the inferior caret ‸ indicates the absence of a punctuation mark. *Stet* used with an impression abbreviation indicates a substantive reading retained from an impression subsequently revised; the rejected variant follows the semicolon. The asterisk before an emendation page-line number indicates the reading is discussed in the Textual Notes.

A number of formal, or mechanical changes have been made throughout:

1. Book titles are in italic type; sections of books are in quotation marks. Book titles have been supplied and expanded where necessary.

2. Superior numbers have been assigned consecutively throughout a chapter to Dewey's footnotes.

3. Single quotation marks have been changed to double when not inside quoted material; however, opening or closing quotation marks have been supplied where necessary and recorded.

4. The following spellings have been editorially regularized to the known Dewey usage appearing before the brackets:

all-embracing] all embracing 49.2
coexistence] co-existence 278.7
commonplace (noun)] common-place 319.4
common sense (noun)] common-sense 15.26, 18.19, 95.11, 176.19,
    244.21, 244.40, 260.14, 305.5, 311.33, 318.11, 318.13–14
common sense (noun)] commonsense 318.31
cooperate (all forms)] coöperate 44.22, 104.18, 157.36, 158.38–39
coordinate (all forms)] coördinate 48.37, 108.20, 150.10 (2), 244.24,
    276.6, 280.26, 281.30
enterprise] enterprize 103.21
fulfillments] fulfilments 127.3, 207.18–19, 275.1
fullness] fulness 283.24
matter-of-fact] matter of fact 119.8
naïvely] naively 181.2
near-by] nearby 213.10
overlapping] over lapping 94.9
overridden] over ridden 249.11
overriding] over-riding 263.12
practice] practise 247.16
preeminent (all forms)] preëminent 78.33, 269.34, 274.28
preeminent (all forms)] pre-eminent 202.37, 283.29, 307.10
pre-established] preëstablished 167.4
pre-existing] preëxisting 168.25
premises] premisses 20.2, 38.18
preoccupation] pre-occupation 224.28
prerequisite] pre-requisite 303.38, 306.7
ready-made] ready made 223.10
realize] realise 325.19
re-creating] recreating 326.15
reenactment] reënactment 280.3
régime] regime 303.14
role] rôle 16.7, 72.11, 77.13, 79.8, 135.18, 171.8, 183.2
so-called] socalled 113.9, 113.22, 113.25
starting point] starting-point 13.27
subject-matter] subject matter 60.25, 76.33, 110.26, 126.1
wall-paper] wall paper 254.15
well-recognized] well recognized 45.36
whenever] when ever 196.34
wherever] where ever 320.21

5.18	forgo] W; forego
16.33	led] W; lead 29
17.19	mandatory,] W; ~∧ 29
20.33	with] W; witth 29
23.3	effect] W; affect 29

30n.6	and wider] W; and and wider 29
38.8	Morley] W; Moley 29
41.13	waste] W; Waste 29
*44.31	direct] *stet* 25; dire 26, 29
46.20	apparent$_\wedge$] 26, 29; ~, 25
46.20	actual),] 26, 29; ~)$_\wedge$ 25
46.29	contradictions] 29; contraditions 25, 26
47.29	Lao-tze] W; Laotze
49.28	logic, although] W; ~$_\wedge$ ~
51.15	ongoing] W; ungoing
54.6	again,] W; ~$_\wedge$
54.11	spiritualistic] W; spirtualistic
54.25	powers] W; power
55.2	terminates] W; terminate
60.2	fall] W; full
60.32	forms;] W; ~,
60.32	real,] W; ~;
65.9	Constitution] W; constitution
69.4	enjoyment:] W; ~,
69.4	festivities,] W; ~;
69.5	pantomime] 26, 29; pantomine 25
69.20	preceded] 26, 29; preceeded 25
72.7	customs],] W; ~)$_\wedge$
*72.32–33	impositions] *stet* 25; imposition 26, 29
72.36;73.2	Jespersen] W; Jesperson
73.9	suppose,] W; ~$_\wedge$
75.20	deals$_\wedge$] W; ~,
76.26	proffered] W; proferred
77.25	climactic] W; climatic
78.16–17	hypostatized] W; hypostasized
81.17	Helvétius] W; Helvetius
81.32	architectonic] W; architechtonic
83.21	show] W; shows
85.21	affairs,] W; ~$_\wedge$
85.29	loose] W; loosely
86.26	fulfillments;] W; ~,
88.11	senses] W; sense
89.15	more nor less blue than] W; more or less blue nor than
89.21	tooth-aches] W; toothaches
93.26	race.] 26, 29; ~, 25
95.13	slow,] W; ~;
97.22–23	consciousness] 26, 29; conciousness 25
97.33	things] W; thing
98.28	inquirers] W; inquiries
100.23	effects] W; effect

101.32	philosophy$_\wedge$] 29; ~, 25, 26
104.4	end] W; ends
104.18	short,] W; ~$_\wedge$
104.35	millennia] W; millenia
106.39	sentimental, moral,] W; ~$_\wedge$ ~$_\wedge$
107.2	just so] W; so
107n.1	665–66] W; 605–06
111.33–34	outstanding;] W; ~,
114.5	it is] W; it
114.34	order,] W; ~;
115.23	such as] W; such
116.8	conditions$_\wedge$] W; ~,
117.2,n.1	Adolf] W; Adolph
117.33	variables] 26, 29; varibles 25
119.24	to historic] W; historic
119.28	rival$_\wedge$ materialistic] W; ~, ~
119.28	doctrines;] W; ~,
119.30	matter,] W; ~$_\wedge$
119n.7	$_\wedge$terms$_\wedge$] W; "~,
119n.10	respects] W; respect
120.1	parallelism] W; paralellism
124.33	what] W; which
126.18	phenomenal] W; phenomental
127.14	symmetrical,] W; ~$_\wedge$
128.13	end-in-view] W; ~$_\wedge$~-~
129.27	loses] W; lose
132.25	traversable] W; traversible
133n.1	96] W; 98
134.30	thus$_\wedge$] W; ~,
137.1	makes] W; marks
138.27	affecting] W; effecting
142.15	they are] W; they
146.11	fact that] W; fact is that
147.27	there] W; this
149.31	persons$_\wedge$] W; ~,
152.19	general] W; genial
155.7	crime,] W; ~$_\wedge$
155.37	cases] W; case
158.7	loyalty] W; loyality
161n.1	that is,] W; ~$_\wedge$
161n.13	Crude Substance$_\wedge$ or] W; crude substance, of
163.20	mind] W; kind
164.9	invention$_\wedge$] W; ~,
168.1	Italian] W; Italians

168.2	Protestant] W; protestant
175.11	insanity,] W; ~.
177.2	seventeenth] W; sevententh
177.8	*pensée*] W; *penseé*
178.24–25	are, are exactly] W; are exactly
179.40	desire,"] W; ~,ₐ
180.1	"*it*] W; ₐ~
183.3–4	waysₐ which] W; ~, ~
186.10	impasse] W; impassé
186.36	abruptₐ] W; ~,
192.25	eternal] W; external
194.11	portentous] 29; portentious 25, 26
194.12	renders] W; render
197.18	is] W; is as
197.36	implicitly] W; implicity
198.6	redistribution] W; redistributuion
199.8	reliable] W; relia-/able
200.14	danger,] W; ~.
201.5	accelerationₐ] W; ~,
204.27	psychical] W; physical
207.38	Interactingₐ events] W; ~-/~
208.27	Each one] W; Each of one
211.7	severanceₐ] W; ~,
211.24	worldₐ] W; ~,
215.15–16	because,] W; ~ₐ
215.39	but] 26, 29; But 25
219.27	existenceₐ] W; ~,
219.29	is] W; are
220.1	action-reaction] W; ~—~
220.12	for what it] 29; for it 25, 26
220.13	This] 29; But this 25, 26
222.11	once,] W; ~ₐ
225n.1–2	*Constructive Conscious Control of the Individual*] W; *Conscious Constructive Control*
228.25	thoughtₐ] 26, 29; ~, 25
231.15	ideas.] 26, 29; ~, 25
231.17	urgent,] 29; ~ₐ 25, 26
233.15	unforeseen] W; unforseen
234.7	the case] W; case
234.39	exception,] 29; ~; 25, 26
236.33	in the] W; the
236.35	in the] W; the
237.32	other] W; others
238.1	thatₐ] 26, 29; ~" 25

248.17	line] W; life
249.14	is to] 26, 29; to 25
249.27	roundabout] W; round/about
254.7	perceived . . . paint, or] 29; perceived as it is, say, for painting or 25, 26
254n.3	color,] W; ~ ͏ ‸
256.19	psychological] W; psychologist
259.38	à son gré] 26, 29; a son grè 25
260.36	causal] W; casual
261.15	situations] W; situation
262.14	impassable] W; impassible
*262.24	while] stet 25, 26; is 29
263.10	occurred] 29; occured 25, 26
263.37	slow-moving] W; ~ ‸ ~
265.4	gratuitously] 26, 29; gratuitiously 25
267.4	is,] W; ~ ‸
270.37	exemplifies] W; exemplies
272.27	fall] 29; to fall 25, 26
273.4	modes of] W; modes or
273.13	moral] W; mortal
274.9	causally] 29; casually 25, 26
276.10	temporally] W; temporarily
278.12	cause-effect] 26, 29; cause- effect 25
279.6	us to] W; to us
280.23	materials] W; material
282.33	"ism,"] W; 'ism, ‸
287.8	things] W; thing
289.28	consequences ‸] W; ~,
290.35	regard] W; regarding
291.4	consummatory] W; consummation
293.19	consciously] 29; [rom.] 25, 26
296.2	apart] W; a part
298.40	blasé] 26, 29; blasè 25
305.16	store] W; score
306.15	emphases] W; emphasis
306.31	liaison] W; liason
307.13	enters] 29; enter 25, 26
307.21	truth] 29; truths 25, 26
308.11	made,] 29; ~ ‸ 25, 26
312.16	ideals ‸] W; ~,
312.25	superlative—for] W; ~ ‸ ~
313.23	chords] W; chord

315.33	assertion;] W; ~,
315.34	factors,] W; ~;
322.11	are going] W; going
325.5	*aeternitatis*] W; *eternatatis*
325.34	construct‸] W; ~,
326.15	in] 26, 29; is 25

Emendations List for Appendix 2

Some corrections were made in the plates for this chapter before the book was reprinted in 1926; other corrections and changes have been made for the present edition. All appear in the following list.

365.6	forswear] W; foreswear 25, 26
366.23	existence] 26; existsnce 25
369.19	"experience,"] W; "~ᵥ" 25, 26
370.37	naïveté] 26; naiveté 25
372.21	say,] W; ~ᵥ 25, 26
378.34	solid,] W; ~ᵥ 25, 26
379.40	capable] W; capa-/able 25, 26
380.9	imputed] 26; inputed 25
380.37	wizardry] W; wizardy 25, 26
385.39	prefatory] W; prefactory 25, 26
385.40	is] W; in 25, 26
386.14	familiar] W; familar 25, 26

Line-End Hyphenation

I. Copy-text list.

The following are the editorially established forms of possible compounds which were hyphenated at the ends of lines in the copy-text:

6.22	coordination	212.2	physico-chemical
10.16	superimposed	222.29	extra-organic
16.25	far-reaching	222.30	proprioreceptors
17.35	non-empirical	228.35	psycho-physical
18.25	double-barrelled	233.28	remaking
18.35	downcast	247.18	prerequisite
35.2	self-enclosed	249.37	over-devoted
54.15	pigeon-holes	251.5	intra-organic
78.25	self-enclosed	251.25–26	proprioceptors
102.9	safeguard	252.27	typewriter
127.21	backhanded	260.8	myth-making
153.30	cooperative	280.40	interpenetrated
192.19	framework	296.8	predetermined
204.25	superadded	303.39	preeminently
207.33	psycho-physical	307.14	preeminent

II. Critical-text list.

In transcriptions from the present edition, no line-end hyphens in ambiguously broken possible compounds are to be retained except the following:

17.10	subject-matter	29.20	subject-matters
18.35	double-barrelled	38.26	subject-matter
23.22	de-personalizing	61.15	re-order
25.40–26.1	subject-matter	62.14	radio-activity
26.4	subject-matter	63.33	non-being

72.13	so-called	196.5	Psycho-physical
74.8	type-forms	196.40	root-tips
75.22	subject-matter	211.26	subject-matter
118.29	self-sufficient	219.18	Self-contradiction
129.25	non-existential	221.13	burn-giving
129.33	at-homeness	228.8	mal-coordinations
133.16	non-natural	237.30	subject-matter
134.22	ready-made	241.7	subject-matter
139.3	over-flow	254n.1	electro-magnetic
139.33	food-finding	255.30	self-evidency
147.3	food-plants	261.12	so-called
151.34	by-products	293.40	subject-matter
166.2	semi-divine	298.25	after-taste
185.5	ready-made	299.10	so-called
185.31	re-organizing	305.34	subject-matter

Substantive Variants in Quotations

In general, Dewey represented source material in varying ways, from memorial paraphrase to verbatim copy, in some places citing his source fully, in others mentioning only authors' names, and, in still others, omitting documentation altogether.

Dewey's substantive variations in the quotations themselves have been considered important enough to warrant this special list. To prepare the critical text for *Experience and Nature,* all material inside quotation marks, except that obviously being emphasized or restated, has been searched out; the documentation has been verified and, when necessary, emended.

All quotations have been retained within the text as they were first published, except for required corrections noted in the Emendations List. Substantive or accidentals changes that restore original readings in cases of possible compositorial or typographical errors are similarly noted as *Middle Works* emendations (W). The variable form of quotation suggests that Dewey, like many scholars of the period, was unconcerned about precision in matters of form, but many of the changes in cited materials may have arisen in the printing process. For example, comparing Dewey's quotations with the originals reveals that some journals and editors house-styled the quoted materials as well as Dewey's own. In the present edition, the spelling and capitalization of the source have been reproduced, except for capitalized concept words which Dewey put in lowercase; these are noted in this list or in the Emendations List.

Dewey's most frequent alteration in quoted material was changing or omitting punctuation. No citation of the Dewey material or of the original appears here if the changes were only of this kind. He also often failed to use ellipses or to separate quotations to show that material had been left out. In the case of Dewey's failure to use ellipses, omitted short phrases appear in this list; omissions of more than a line are noted by a bracketed ellipsis [. . .]. If changed or omitted accidentals have substantive implications, as in the capitalization of some concept words, the quotation is noted.

The form used in this section is designed to assist the reader in determining whether Dewey had the book open before him or was relying on his memory. Notations in this section follow the fomula: page-line numbers from the present text, followed by the text condensed to first and last words or such as make for sufficient clarity, then a square bracket; after the bracket comes the necessary correction, whether of one word or a longer passage, as required. Finally, in parentheses, the author's surname and shortened source-title from the Checklist of Dewey's References are followed by a comma and the page-line reference to the source.

42.8	morals, custom] morals, law, custom (Tylor, *Primitive Culture,* 1:1.10)
42.9	capabilities] capabilities and habits (Tylor, *Primitive Culture,* 1:1.10–11)
42.9	a man] man (Tylor, *Primitive Culture,* 1:1.11)
42.17	psychological] psychological (or active-psychological) (Goldenweiser, "History, Psychology and Culture," 604.19–20)
42.17	objective] objective (or potential-psychological) (Goldenweiser, "History, Psychology and Culture," 604.20)
42.20	synthetic unity] unity (Goldenweiser, "History, Psychology and Culture," 604.25)
73.1	sedate citizens] sedate, alderman-like citizens, (Jespersen, *Progress in Language,* 357.1)
73.1	strong interest in] prominent sense for (Jespersen, *Progress in Language,* 357.2)
73.2	aspects] side (Jespersen, *Progress in Language,* 357.3)
73.4	interjections; they] interjections, [. . .]; they (Jespersen, *Progress in Language,* 356.2–4)
73.7	found] not to be sought in the prosaic, but (Jespersen, *Progress in Language,* 357.10–11)
106.32–33	more sentimental] sentimental (James, *Principles of Psychology,* 2:665.29)
106.36	ones] systems (James, *Principles of Psychology,* 2:666.1)
106.38	results. Call] results. [. . .] Call (James, *Principles of Psychology,* 2:666.7–13)
107.4	the consequences] all the *consequences* (James, *Principles of Psychology,* 2:666.25)
117.5	neuronic] neurone (A. Meyer, *Psychiatric Milestone,* 32.22–23)
117.5	standpoints] starting-points (A. Meyer, *Psychiatric Milestone,* 32.23)

117.6	such a] such postulates of (A. Meyer, *Psychiatric Milestone*, 32.24)
117.9	find] find and live (A. Meyer, *Psychiatric Milestone*, 33.4)
117.17	be a] be like a (A. Meyer, *Psychiatric Milestone*, 38.9–10)
118n.4	also has nevertheless] nevertheless has (Windelband, *Introduction to Philosophy*, 299.13)
119n.4	conceive] consider (Brown, *Creative Intelligence*, 159.19–20)
119n.9	*effective*] [*rom.*] (Brown, *Creative Intelligence*, 160.5)
133.33	animals] animal (Boas, *Mind of Primitive Man*, 96.6)
133.35	speech] language (Boas, *Mind of Primitive Man*, 96.8)
139.20	functioning] function (M. Meyer, *Psychology of the Other-One*, 195.15)
139.24	lighting] lighting up (M. Meyer, *Psychology of the Other-One*, 195.23)
139.25	cuttle-fish, the] cuttle-fish, the communication of a shock by an electric eel, the (M. Meyer, *Psychology of the Other-One*, 195.24–25)
139.26	tail] tail feathers (M. Meyer, *Psychology of the Other-One*, 195.26–27)
139.27	activities affect] activities, we said, are to affect (M. Meyer, *Psychology of the Other-One*, 195.27–28)
160n.9	experience] experience of it (Malinowski, "Problem of Meaning," 488.33–34)
160n.18	language. In] language. [. . .] In (Malinowski, "Problem of Meaning," 474.23–25)
160n.27–28	words. In] words. [. . .] In (Malinowski, "Problem of Meaning," 475.20–23)
160n.28	speech is] speech as found in primitive communities is (Malinowski, "Problem of Meaning," 475.24)
160n.31	human nature] man's nature (Malinowski, "Problem of Meaning," 477.5)
160n.34	character. The] character. [. . .] The (Malinowski, "Problem of Meaning," 477.22–24)
161n.4	*Weltanschauung*] [*rom.*] (Malinowski, "Problem of Meaning," 498.23)
161n.5	language] Language (Malinowski, "Problem of Meaning," 498.24–25)
161n.6	man] mankind (Malinowski, "Problem of Meaning," 498.27)
161n.10	its] its own (Malinowski, "Problem of Meaning," 509.17)
161n.10	meaning. The] meaning. [. . .] The (Malinowski, "Problem of Meaning," 509.18–22)

161n.13   *Protousia*] [*rom.*] (Malinowski, "Problem of Meaning,"
            509.27)
161n.15   world] real world (Malinowski, "Problem of Meaning,"
            509.30)
164.36   situations] matter-of-fact situations (Goldenweiser, *Early
            Civilization*, 407.28–29)
164.36   task. In] task. [. . .] In (Goldenweiser, *Early Civilization*,
            407.29–408.2)
165.19–21   When tradition . . . age.] In a society where personal ob-
            servation and the absorption of tradition are the only
            sources of knowledge and wisdom, age is a tremendous
            advantage. (Goldenweiser, *Early Civilization*, 403.19–21)
165.21   elder is] elders are (Goldenweiser, *Early Civilization*,
            404.3)
165.31–33   ratiocination . . . inventions become] ratiocination arise in
            the course of the industrial activity, they are presently
            submerged, the objective results alone being passed on to
            the following generation. [. . .] They become
            (Goldenweiser, *Early Civilization*, 406.28–407.2)
177.1   unfriendliness] friendless (Royce, *Spirit of Modern Phi-
            losophy*, 93.15)
177.1   of] of the (Royce, *Spirit of Modern Philosophy*, 93.15)
277.10–13   When there . . . the product.] when there are two things
            one of which is a means and the other an end, between
            these there is nothing common except in so far as the one
            viz. the means produces and the other *viz. the end* receives
            the product. (Aristotle, *Politics*, 183.1–5)
312.29   human] finite (Holmes, *Collected Legal Papers*, 315.6)
313.14   significance. If] significance. [. . .] If (Holmes, *Collected
            Legal Papers*, 316.13–16)
313.15   inseparable] inseverable (Holmes, *Collected Legal Papers*,
            316.17)

Checklist of Dewey's References

Titles and authors' names in Dewey references have been corrected and expanded to conform accurately and consistently to the original works; all corrections appear in the Emendations List.
This section gives full publication information for each work cited by Dewey. When Dewey gave page numbers for a work, the edition he used was identified exactly by locating the reference. Similarly, the books in Dewey's personal library have been used to verify his citations of a particular edition. For other references, the edition listed here is the one from among the various editions possibly available to him that was his most likely source by reason of place or date of publication, or on the evidence from correspondence and other materials, and its general accessibility during the period.

Acton, John Emerich Edward Dalberg Acton, 1st Baron. "The Study of History." In *Essays on Freedom and Power,* selected and with an introduction by Gertrude Himmelfarb. Boston: Beacon Press, 1948.
Alexander, Frederick Matthias. *Constructive Conscious Control of the Individual.* New York: E. P. Dutton and Co., 1923.
———. *Man's Supreme Inheritance.* New York: E. P. Dutton and Co., 1918.
Aristotle. *Metaphysics.* Translated by W. D. Ross. Oxford: Clarendon Press, 1908.
———. *The Politics of Aristotle.* Translated by J. E. C. Welldon. London: Macmillan and Co., 1883.
Baldwin, James Mark, ed. *Dictionary of Philosophy and Psychology.* Vol. 2. New York: Macmillan Co., 1902.
Boas, Franz. *The Mind of Primitive Man.* New York: Macmillan Co., 1911.
Brown, Harold Chapman. "Intelligence and Mathematics." In *Creative Intelligence: Essays in the Pragmatic Attitude.* New York: Henry Holt and Co., 1917.
Democritus. In *Die Fragmente der Vorsokratiker: Griechisch und Deutsch,* vol. 1, edited by Hermann Diels. Berlin: Weidmannsche Buchhandlung, 1906.

430

Goldenweiser, Alexander. *Early Civilization.* New York: F. S. Crofts and Co., 1822.

———. "History, Psychology and Culture: A Set of Categories for an Introduction to Social Science." *Journal of Philosophy, Psychology and Scientific Methods* 15 (1918): 561–71, 589–607.

Holmes, Oliver Wendell. *Collected Legal Papers.* New York: Harcourt, Brace and Co., 1920.

Holt, Edwin Bissell. *The Concept of Consciousness.* New York: Macmillan Co., 1914.

James, William. *Essays in Radical Empiricism.* New York: Longmans, Green, and Co., 1912.

———. *The Principles of Psychology.* Vol. 2. New York: Henry Holt and Co., 1890.

Jespersen, Otto. *Progress in Language.* London: Swan Sonnenschein and Co., 1909.

Malinowski, Bronislaw. "Culture." In *Encyclopaedia of the Social Sciences,* vol. 4, edited by Edwin R. Seligman and Alvin Johnson. New York: Macmillan Co., 1931.

———. "The Problem of Meaning in Primitive Languages." Supplementary essay in *The Meaning of Meaning* by C. K. Ogden and I. A. Richards. New York: Harcourt, Brace and Co., 1923.

Meyer, Adolf. "The Contributions of Psychiatry to the Understanding of Life Problems." In *A Psychiatric Milestone.* Privately printed by the Society of the New York Bloomingdale Hospital, 1921.

Meyer, Max. *Psychology of the Other-One.* 2d ed. Columbia: Missouri Book Co., 1922.

Morgan, Lloyd. *Instinct and Experience.* New York: Macmillan Co., 1912.

Plato. *Philebus.* In *The Dialogues of Plato,* 3d ed., vol. 3, edited by B. Jowett. New York: Macmillan Co., 1892.

Royce, Josiah. *The Spirit of Modern Philosophy.* Boston: Houghton Mifflin Co., 1892.

Russell, Bertrand. *Mysticism and Logic and Other Essays.* London: George Allen and Unwin, 1918.

Santayana, George. *The Life of Reason.* Vols. 1 and 5. New York: Charles Scribner's Sons, 1906.

Spencer, Herbert. *First Principles.* 3d ed. London: Williams and Norgate, 1905.

Tylor, Edward B. *Primitive Culture.* 3d ed. Vol. 1. London: John Murray, 1891.

Windelband, Wilhelm. *An Introduction to Philosophy.* Translated by Joseph McCabe. London: T. Fisher Unwin, 1921.

Index

The Collected Works of John Dewey, 1882–1953

Index to The Collected Works of John Dewey, 1882–1953

The Early Works, 1882–1898

The Middle Works, 1899–1924

The Later Works, 1925–1953